G
May 7, 2015

CUBA
and Its
NEIGHBOURS

CUBA

and Its

NEIGHBURS

★

Democracy in Motion

ARNOLD AUGUST

FERNWOOD PUBLISHING
HALIFAX WINNIPEG

ZED BOOKS
LONDON NEW YORK

Editing: Veronica Schami Editorial Services
Cover design: John van der Woude
Printed and bound in Canada by Hignell Book Printing

Published in Canada by Fernwood Publishing
32 Oceanvista Lane, Black Point, Nova Scotia B0J 1B0
and 748 Broadway Avenue, Winnipeg, Manitoba R3G 0X3
www.fernwoodpublishing.ca

Published in the rest of the world by Zed Books Ltd.
7 Cynthia Street, London N1 9JF, UK & Room 400, 175 Fifth Avenue, New York, NY 10010, USA
www.zedbooks.co.uk

Distributed in the USA exclusively by Palgrave Macmillan, a division of St. Martin's Press, LLC, 175 Fifth Avenue, New York, NY 10010, USA

Fernwood Publishing Company Limited gratefully acknowledges the financial support of the Government of Canada through the Canada Book Fund and the Canada Council for the Arts, the Nova Scotia Department of Communities, Culture and Heritage, the Manitoba Department of Culture, Heritage and Tourism under the Manitoba Book Publishers Marketing Assistance Program and the Province of Manitoba, through the Book Publishing Tax Credit, for our publishing program.

A catalogue record for this book is available from the British Library
Library of Congress Cataloging in Publication Data available

9781848138674 hb (Zed Books)
9781848138667 pb (Zed Books)

Library and Archives Canada Cataloguing in Publication

August, Arnold
Cuba and its neighbours : democracy
in motion / Arnold August.

Includes bibliographical references and index.

ISBN 978-1-55266-404-9

1. Cuba--Politics and government--1990-.
2. Democracy--Cuba.   I. Title.

F1788.A83 2013   972.9107   C2012-903148-8

To Gerardo Hernández, Ramón Labañino,

Antonio Guerrero, Fernando González, René González

and all the peoples of Cuba, Latin America and the Caribbean,

as well as the peoples of the United States,

especially those academics and writers who dare to defy the status quo

Contents

Acronyms

ALBA   Alianza Bolivariana para los Pueblos de Nuestra América (Bolivarian Alliance for the Peoples of Our America)

ANAP   Asociación Nacional de Agricultores Pequeños (National Association of Small Farmers)

ANPP   Asamblea Nacional del Poder Popular (National Assembly of People's Power, or Parliament)

CCN   Comisión de Candidaturas Nacional (National Candidacies Commission)

CDR   Comités de Defensa de la Revolución (Committees for the Defence of the Revolution)

CEC   Comisiones Electorales de Circunscripciones (*Circunscripción* Electoral Commissions)

CELAC   Comunidad de Estados Latinoamericanos y Caribeños (Community of Latin-American and Caribbean States)

CEM   Comisión Electoral Municipal (Municipal Electoral Commission)

CEN   Comisión Electoral Nacional (National Electoral Commission)

CEP   Comisión Electoral Provincial (Provincial Electoral Commission)

CP   Consejo Popular (People's Council)

CTC   Central de Trabajadores de Cuba (Workers' Central Union of Cuba)

DNC   Democratic National Convention

FEEM   Federación de Estudiantes de la Enseñanza Media (Federation of Pre-University Students)

FEU   Federación de Estudiantes Universitarios (Federation of University Students)

FMC   Federación de Mujeres Cubanas (Federation of Cuban Women)

GPP   Gran Polo Patriótico (Great Patriotic Pole)

MAS   Movimiento al Socialismo (Movement Towards Socialism)

OAS   Organization of American States

OLPP   Órganos Locales del Poder Popular (Local Organs of People's Power)

OPP   Órganos del Poder Popular (Organs of People's Power)

PCC   Partido Comunista de Cuba (Communist Party of Cuba)

PRC   Partido Revolucionario Cubano (Cuban Revolutionary Party)

PSP   Partido Socialista Popular (People's Socialist Party)

PSUV   Partido Socialista Unido de Venezuela (United Socialist Party of Venezuela)

TIPNIS Territorio Indígena y Parque Nacional Isiboro-Secure (Isiboro-Secure National Park and Indigenous Territory)

UJC   Unión de Jóvenes Comunistas (Communist Youth League)

UPEC   Unión de Periodistas de Cuba (Union of Cuban Journalists)

VAP   Voting Age Population

VEP   Voting Eligible Population

Illustrations

Figures

Tables

Preface

Between 2006 and 2012, I carried out extensive research on Latin America, the Caribbean and the U.S., as well as fieldwork and investigative study in Cuba. This book is the fruit of these efforts. It is also the product of my long-time interest in the contrasting approaches of Southern countries to change. This pursuit continued to evolve after I completed my M.A. thesis at McGill University in Montreal in the late 1960s, in which I contrasted revolutionary change with status quo reforms in India. The 1960s were also a defining historical period when many of us in the North were confronted with an official approach based on racism and superiority with regard to the South. This is why, in 1968, I was instrumental in organizing the first Political Science Student Association in Canada and its resulting strike. One of our main demands was to open the curriculum. We wanted to include new approaches to the South that did not encompass only theories and analyses based on the racist assumption of innate superiority that dominated academia in the North at the time. Therefore, in a sense, this work is a culmination of my lifelong concerns.

The goal of this book is to explore the Cuban approach to democracy. To do so, however, the reader must be willing to clear away at least some of the misconceptions surrounding the island's political approach and even to consider that the term "democracy" can indeed be associated with Cuba. These foggy notions are similar to the ones I stood against in the 1960s, even though we have made considerable headway in the last 50 years.

I first travelled to Cuba in 1991, returning several times in the early 1990s. Each visit proved to be a revelation. It was not at all like the former U.S.S.R. and Eastern Europe. My first book on Cuba (1999), based on 1997–98 field research and investigation, concentrated on the electoral process. Since 1997, I have continued to carry out ethnographic research in that country.

This 2013 publication, based primarily on my own lengthy field research in Cuba, expands on the first one by contextualizing Cuban democracy within a framework of democracy as it is unfolding in the U.S., Venezuela, Bolivia and Ecuador. Furthermore, this book deals with an updated, renewed and more critical analysis of the Cuban electoral process. Unlike the first book, I deal here with the functioning of the state between elections.

I was present during each stage of the 2007–08 general elections and carried out some investigation of the 2010 partial elections. The 2012–13 elections follow the same procedures as the ones that I researched. In order to deal with the functioning of the state between elections, I had the opportunity to attend several sessions of the National Assembly (Parliament) in 2008 and 2009. This included some proceedings of its permanent working commissions. During this same period, I also attended a number of sessions pertaining to my two local case studies. One such investigation consisted of the municipal assembly and the second was the grass-roots people's council within this municipal assembly.

I conducted many one-on-one, exclusive interviews in Havana, Cuba, in 2007–08. Twenty-eight such interviews were conducted mainly with elected National Assembly deputies and a close adviser. Some of these interviews also included local municipal delegates. All of the dialogues with deputies and delegates related to the functioning of the Cuban state at all levels between elections. Ten interviews were held with academics, researchers and journalists in Cuba on the electoral procedures, on the functioning of the Cuban state and on Cuban political thought and heritage. In addition, thirteen formal exchanges were held with Cuban professors, researchers and authors holding a wide range of views on the Cuban political system and political culture. Given the large number of personal interviews that form the basis of this work, I provide the details in a separate list at the end of the book, after the Works Cited. These include short descriptions of the people interviewed, along with the city in which each interview took place.

Exploring Cuba in contrast with the U.S. (as well as with the Venezuelan, Bolivian and Ecuadorian cases) necessarily raises the question of objectivity. I believe that any scholar or author approaches a contentious political subject with an outlook already formed. Thus one cannot be "objective." However, an affinity for or tendency toward a particular approach to democracy does not preclude balance or equilibrium. Readers will notice in the text that I refer to "prejudices" and "preconceived notions." These terms seem pejorative; indeed, they are intended thus. For example, a racist "prejudice" is necessarily debasing. This path of prejudgment is not akin to consciously cultivating a perspective to guide oneself in balanced and equilibrated investigation, writing and analysis. This is why, in dealing with Cuba, I strive to look at its positive aspects as well as its weaknesses. Readers can judge for themselves. As some peers have commented to me after reading the manuscript, my experiences as an observer and analyst allow reality to speak for itself, fleshing out the fundamentals of the Cuban political system.

Dealing with the U.S. political system is something else. My outlook, based on accumulated experience and research, prevents me from carrying a favourable attitude toward its system, even though I hold the peoples of the U.S. in high esteem. At the same time, however, my approach to the U.S. rejects a superficial, blanket condemnation in favour of trying to discover how the political system actually works. In the same way, I also reject an idealized view of Cuba that does not expose the weaknesses of its inner workings. Substantial supplemental material on democracy in the U.S. is available on my website www.democracyintheus.com. The book directs the reader through footnotes to specific entries on this website as a source of further information and analysis related to parts of the text. On the website, click on the corresponding chapter tab to find the entry.

There is a need for clarity and healthy discussion on this topic of Cuba's political system among different sectors of society outside of Cuba. This book is written for three audiences: first, and most important, the academic and research milieu at all levels; second, parliamentarians and municipal councillors in the U.S. and other countries, some of whom visit Cuba or receive Cuban parliamentarian and other delegations, thereby creating a desire to know more about its political system; and third, the informed public, such as social, political, trade union and student activists. The goal of this book is to address these three different audiences while promoting mutual respect and understanding among different types of democracy, governance and electoral procedures around the world.

Furthermore, the book comprises three parts. Part I, "Clearing the Cobwebs Around Democracy," sets the parameters by discussing my views on democracy. In this context, it challenges the notion that the U.S. model is superior — indeed, as some would have it, that it is the only one that the world should adopt. This section goes on to examine the foundations of democracy in the U.S. and its inner workings based on a case study of Barack Obama. These findings are contrasted with the very different path that Cuba has taken to democracy. Thus Cuba's course cannot be measured by the standards of the U.S. system. In order to broaden horizons to include a variety of different approaches to democracy, I also examine Venezuela, Bolivia and Ecuador. All of this indicates that there is not just one route toward democracy, as some U.S. pundits would have us believe.

Part II, "Cuba: Constitutions, Elections and New States," is dedicated to placing contemporary Cuba in the historical context from which it has been politically nourished. This includes the relatively unknown role of elections and constitutions in Cuba's grass-roots and revolutionary political culture.

Part III, "Contemporary Cuba: The Test for Democratization," focuses on today's Cuba, starting with the important economic changes that are taking place. I examine the extent to which the Cuban path of democracy is involved in these transformations that are changing the country. This section then moves on to provide readers with an inside view of how elections take place in Cuba, including opinions from Cuban specialists on its weak points and perspectives on improvement. I explore the national and local levels of government from within the assemblies. The study also exposes the work and role of the elected. It encompasses perspectives of Cubans' thoughts on improving the system at this crucial juncture in its history, when Cuba is once again at a crossroads.

Finally, all translations in the book from Spanish to English are my own unless otherwise indicated.

Acknowledgments

This book is necessarily the result of a collective effort and would not have been possible without the support of people from Cuba, Canada, Britain and the United States.

I am grateful for the assistance of Cuba's National Assembly (Parliament) President, at the time, Ricardo Alarcón de Quesada. He made available to me one of his principal advisers, Jorge Lezcano. He and his support staff, including Alfredo Rodríguez and Mirtha Carmenate, responded to all of my requests, many times difficult and no doubt overly demanding. Thanks to Lezcano's efforts, I was permitted to attend National Assembly sessions, including its permanent working commissions, to access important documents and to interview many of the presidents and members of the working commissions. My everlasting gratitude goes to these deputies for taking time out of their busy schedules to talk to me. With the utmost patience, they provided frank and honest answers to all of my probing questions and challenges on even the most sensitive issues. Silvia García, a member of the National Assembly staff, also furnished me with important data and information about this body that is not generally available to researchers.

Additionally, the National Assembly allowed me to conduct detailed interviews with members of the candidacies commissions, which are instrumental in the Cuban national electoral process. These officials patiently explained the complex process. Similarly, interviews with members of the electoral commissions at the national, provincial and municipal levels provided important insights.

Lezcano was also responsible for obtaining permission for me to attend local municipal assembly sessions and to carry out interviews for my case study. Just as for the 1997–98 fieldwork for my first book, the National Assembly did not place any restrictions or conditions on my investigation.

I made the most of my own familiarity, links with and access to the grassroots level dating back to my first book. Within the municipality, I was able to attend sessions of a people's council — one level closer to the people — for my case study. I am bound to the amenable collaboration of its president, Eduardo González Hernández, who made me feel at home during the sessions.

A sincere and sentimental expression of gratitude is in order to the Workers' Central Union of Cuba (CTC), which assisted me in attending local union meetings and interviewing union members. It also coordinated with Lezcano to hold valuable interviews with the candidacies commissions, which are headed by the union. In this regard, special thanks are extended to Raymundo Navarro and Amarilys Pérez Santana of the CTC, and to the trade union's Ernesto Freire Cazanas, who was the head of the candidacies commission in 1997–98, when I first met him.

My own academic contacts over several years enabled me to carry out many interviews in Havana with professors and researchers. While the list is too long to be mentioned here, the names of all those interviewed and their academic positions are recorded in the "Personal Interviews with the Author" section.

This book would not have been possible without the full collaboration and encouragement of Errol Sharpe, my Canadian publisher at Fernwood Publishing. Errol's main preoccupation was the reader, especially the academic community, and he exhibited an indispensable firmness regarding academic standards. From the beginning, he showed his confidence in me, despite the very long road from the initial proposal. He never ceased to astonish me with his political insights into the U.S., Venezuela and Cuba. In fact, his 2011 visit to Venezuela and his resulting increased interest in this country, as well as in the processes in Bolivia and Ecuador, enhanced his valuable input. Beverley Rach, production coordinator, proved to be a *sine qua non* in converting the manuscript into a book. She was always there to answer my questions with regard to the requirements for design and publication. Brenda Conroy was responsible for the text layout and proofreading, converting the manuscript into a book. John van der Woude did an excellent job in designing the jacket by reflecting the political content of the book. Nancy Malek showed her sincere eagerness right from the start in promoting this publication. Her contribution cannot be overstated, because, after all the effort to bring the manuscript to fruition, the goal is to get the book into the hands of academics and other readers.

I am grateful to Zed Books, based in the U.K., for co-publishing the book. Fernwood and Zed are making an inestimable contribution to opening up, on a mass scale, the possibilities for an alternative, critical view of the world.

I am forever indebted to the academic peer reviewers of initial versions of the manuscript. This includes academics specializing in Cuba and Latin America hailing from several countries: from Canada, John Kirk (Dalhousie University, Halifax) and Claude Morin (Université de Montréal); from Britain, Antoni Kapcia (University of Nottingham) and Ken Cole (University of East Anglia); from the U.S., Cliff DuRand (Morgan State University, Baltimore) and Claudia Kaiser-Lenoir (Tufts University, Medford, Massachusetts), who were very helpful in taking the time to write elaborate and constructive comments; and, finally, from Cuba. In the latter case, I am appreciative of the careful attention and invaluable suggestions from the following academics and authors: Jesús García Brigos, researcher and doctoral thesis supervisor at the Instituto de Filosofía; Olga Fernández Ríos, researcher at the Instituto de Filosofía and University of Havana professor; Martha Prieto Valdés, University of Havana professor; and Rafael Alhama Belamaric, researcher at the Instituto de Estudios e Investigaciones del Trabajo, Ministry of Labour and Social Security. In addition, veteran Cuban journalists Carlos Iglesias and Luis Chirino Gamez read and commented on the manuscript from a critical point of view.

While I may not have agreed with all of the suggestions and criticisms from academic peer readers in these countries, they forced me to consider varying views and options and thus deal with all of their perspectives. The final product, of course, is entirely my own responsibility.

Chilean Ricardo Astudillo, specialist on Venezuela, Bolivia and Ecuador, contributed his insights in reviewing the content. He also lent his technical computer skills to help draft the tables.

In Montreal, Odile Dobler undertook the difficult task of overseeing, verifying and classifying the many sources. She also participated in preparing the manuscript. Without Odile's assistance, it would not have been possible for me to concentrate on the content of the book.

There are two websites related to the book, www.democracycuba.com and www.democracyintheus.com. Webmaster William Lurie provided crucial suggestions and is to be commended for making the sites user-friendly. One could not hope for a more professional translator from English to Spanish for the website articles than Alicia Loría. She was devoted to having the Spanish language version reflect the original English while maintaining the integrity of Spanish.

Perhaps one of the most difficult tasks in the latter stages fell on the shoulders of the copy-editor Veronica Schami. This book has the unorthodox goal of appealing to three different audiences, as outlined in the Preface. Keeping in mind the need to make the text academically sound above all, it also had to be reader-friendly to academia as well as to parliamentarians, social/political activists and others. She provided no dearth of suggestions to improve the text and make it increasingly erudite. Veronica, assisted by her colleagues Jo Howard and Florencia Lukuc, put aside personal plans to ensure the copy-editing was completed in time to meet the publisher's schedule. During the editing process, it was gratifying to receive feedback from Veronica about the relevancy of the book. This is promising for other lay readers who may also be exploring some of the book's themes for the first time.

PART I

Clearing the Cobwebs
Around Democracy

Chapter 1

Democracy and U.S.-Centrism

Can democracy exist without full and effective participation of the majority of people? Is it possible for the vast majority of people to participate fully in a political system that is based on the absolute right to unlimited accumulation of private property? To tackle these questions, Part I deals with the concept of "democracy" and looks at different types of democracies, such as those existing in Cuba's neighbours the United States, Venezuela, Bolivia and Ecuador. This section also briefly examines the U.S.-centric view of democracy as an outgrowth — and the current most notable expression — of Eurocentrism. This Western-centrism is the principal source of the misconceptions surrounding the concept of democracy. In this context, the section also touches on the recent upsurge in favour of democracy and the related economic demands in Egypt, Spain and the U.S. itself (the Occupy Movement). To a certain extent (and depending on each context, since these movements are different), the movements in these countries pose a summons to contest U.S.-centrism. The purpose is to juxtapose U.S.-centric notions and related structures of democracy with these historic mass movements. The latter are in favour of another type of democracy and an economic–social system based on justice, even though the demands may not yet be fully articulated.

Cuba represents yet another variety of democracy, which Parts II and III will address. The goal firstly in Part I is to sweep away the strands of the cobwebs that surround the concept and practice of democracy. The attempt to clear this confusion relates to Cuba's neighbours the U.S., Venezuela, Bolivia and Ecuador as systems.

Democracy literally means "power of the people," from the Greek terms δῆμος (dêmos) "people" and κράτος (krátos) "power"). In a capitalist country such as the U.S., however, a small minority has all the economic power, while the overwhelming majority does not possess, or profit from, this economic wealth. Thus where does political "power" of the "people" appear? There is a contradiction between the increasing demands for democracy at the grass-roots level and the political system controlled by the wealthy elites. In this situation, how can the people attain political power?

In some countries — such as Cuba's other neighbours Venezuela, Bolivia and Ecuador — revolutionary or progressive movements have started to reverse the political and economic structures and consciousness. These new trends are to different degrees in favour of the majority and to the detriment of the wealthy elites. The latter, in many cases, have been traditionally controlled and assimilated by mainly U.S. economic and political ruling circles. Despite new social projects in these countries, however, the issue of democracy has yet to be solved.

Cuba's 1959 Revolution overthrew the U.S.-backed, privileged elites and immediately started to transform the economic and political system in favour of the population's majority. Does this mean, though, that ipso facto democracy in this country does not have to be further developed?

Cuba's socialist system is currently undergoing a radical update. The Venezuelan Bolivarian Revolution is taking steps toward deepening socialist transformations. The Bolivian and Ecuadorian governments sympathize with socialism in the course of searching for an alternative to the capitalist system. The Bolivian and Ecuadorian governments, led by Evo Morales and Rafael Correa respectively, have many hurdles to overcome in this direction. However, they stand firm against U.S. domination in their respective countries and in the entire region. They also are proud to fully identify with and support the more advanced Cuban experience, as well as the recent Venezuelan experiments.

What is socialism? There are many books published, including very recently, that focus on this subject alone. Therefore, in this book dedicated to democracy, there is no space to deal with this other concept, socialism. However, since democracy cannot be discussed without taking into account the social and economic system in which it evolves, a brief outline of socialism is in order. There is no single path toward socialism. The countries being examined, that is, Venezuela, Bolivia and Ecuador, consider their own versions and steps as being taken toward varieties of twenty-first-century socialism. Today, Cubans themselves are reinventing socialism in order to extract themselves from old models and mentalities.

Socialism, like democracy, is in motion and is thus a moving target whose varieties are arrived at by many different paths. It is nonetheless possible to highlight some salient features, in order to help orient us in this exploration of democracy. In very general terms, the different approaches have in common a social project that differs from the U.S. strategy. Socialism is a system in which the vast majority of people control the main means of production, either through the state or directly. This does not exclude secondary forms of production and services that remain outside direct state control. For example, non-state sectors include independent farmers and the self-employed as well as cooperatives, both in the cities and in the countryside. These are often linked to market mechanisms. Nevertheless, the main features of these economic and social undertakings are the values of collectivity and social consciousness. This stands in contrast with the unlimited accumulation of private property as the foundation of capitalism. In socialism, state planning of the overall economy, including tax systems, predominates. Therefore, in a socialist project, the majority of the people benefit from the socialized production and services, providing basic human rights in the realms of health, education, housing, food, culture and other fundamental needs. Venezuela is an example whereby, through the Bolivarian Revolution, the wealth generated by the oil industry is directed toward fulfilling these societal needs. Before Hugo Chávez, the country did not employ this natural asset in this manner. Socialism in Cuba, the socialist route undertaken by Venezuela and the aspirations expressed in Bolivia and Ecuador share an important orientation and mentality: the defence of each country's sovereignty and independence in the face of Western powers, especially the U.S. Without opposition to U.S. domination and interference, it is futile to envisage socialism in Latin America and the Caribbean at any stage of its genesis or development. For example, had Cuba not opposed U.S. domination and its allies in 1953 as the very first step toward Cuba's Revolution, socialism would never have got off the ground.

On the surface, the economic and social system in a socialist country seems to be made-to-measure for the political definition of democracy, that is, power of the people. However, being a socialist country does not mean that democracy automatically translates into real and effective power for the vast majority of the people. Only participatory democracy — the people's ongoing, daily involvement in the political and economic affairs of the country — assures democracy.

The common thread running through the movements at the grass-roots level in Egypt, Spain and the U.S. is participatory democracy. Many people see the need to fill the void of people's empowerment. In Cuba, Venezuela, Bolivia and Ecuador, participatory democracy has been on their respective agendas since the inception of their transformations — from 1959 in Cuba to the more recent experiences in Venezuela, Bolivia and Ecuador. This is possible because of the social projects that favour people's participation. This stands in opposition to representative democracy, even though the systems in Venezuela, Bolivia, Ecuador and Cuba do not exclude elected representatives. The concept of "representatives" is not used here in the sense of the representative system found in the U.S. In countries such as Cuba and Venezuela, representatives are part of a revolution. The Bolivarian Revolution in Venezuela, especially taking into account the October 7, 2012, presidential elections, provides us with the first example (Chapter 3) to elaborate on this concept of "representatives" from a revolutionary perspective. Participatory democracy is elusive and thus difficult to define. It is continually developing. For this reason, it is best to take a cautious approach to defining it, as expressed by U.S. Professor Emeritus of Social Philosophy Cliff DuRand: "We do not yet have a theory of participatory democracy" (DuRand 2012: 212). The goal of this book is therefore to accompany the reader though a variety of countries' experiences in order to extrapolate and characterize certain features of participatory democracy. In this manner, the objective is to contribute to the debate that has increasingly captured the interest of people around the world.

The U.S. political system is a genre of democracy, based on capitalism as the socio-economic foundation. Its government is of the representative variety. The competitive multi-party system is the instrument through which people are supposed to govern. It does not help our understanding to uncritically accept the U.S. model of democracy, nor simply to reject it as a "bourgeois democracy" or as a "fraudulent" one. By the same token, it cannot be idealized as the epitome of democracy. Both approaches overlook the need to analyze in detail the inner workings of how this U.S. democracy actually operates. The next chapter addresses this topic.

Within capitalist countries (including Spain and the U.S.) and neo-colonial victims, such as Egypt, the new grass-roots movements are also demanding democracy. One of the main features of these movements is that people are learning about participating democratically in spaces that *they themselves are creating.* These openings lie outside the limitations of the formal political structures. Not only are the new movements accomplishing this, but they are also learning that "this is what democracy looks like" — one of the Wall Street Movement slogans (DuRand 2012: 212) — in the course of practice and setting standards. If the desired approach is participatory democracy, this necessarily raises the need for *constant and ongoing* participation that far surpasses the limited electoral or representative process. Participatory democracy involves daily action, a new way of living. In Venezuela, Bolivia and Ecuador, the structures of elections as such bear some resemblance to those of the U.S. However, as we will see in Chapter 3, participation is a key ingredient that becomes far more important to citizens than being "represented" by others in the political system. In the process, the concept of representation is changed as being part of a revolutionary movement.

In Cuba, even after so much time since the 1959 Revolution, the issue of effective people's participation and control is on the agenda more than ever. This common thread connects the chapters dedicated to Cuba. If democracy means power of the people, then the people have to be constantly in action.

The experiences in Egypt and Spain, as well as the U.S. Wall Street Movement, have taken place in entirely different historical and political settings than that of Cuba. However, these new movements, as well as the experiences of countries such as Venezuela, force us to widen our horizons on democracy. By broadening our perspectives, the need to highlight the essential *ongoing participatory* role of the people at the grass-roots level becomes more apparent. This is why "democratization" is preferred over the term "democracy," as it stresses democracy as a progression, constantly in motion. "Democracy" as an abstraction tends to be fixed in time, restrained by predetermined structures and often without any socio-economic content.

Democracy *without* this content of democratization strips common notions of democracy of any value. The expression "democracy" as employed here takes into account the fact that most of the countries explored in this book contain the formulation "democracy" in their constitutions. The only exception is the U.S., where its Constitution does not mention the term "democracy." This book thus uses "democracy" as a catchall phrase for lack of another term to also include those systems and traditions that do not employ the designation "democracy." This is done to elaborate upon "democratization" as applicable to all systems. Thus "democracy" includes the traditions of the Indigenous peoples from the North and South as well as others outside of the Eurocentric and U.S.-centric ones. It is important to recall that some of the Indigenous peoples' egalitarian values and collective perspective on economy and politics impressed Jean-Jacques Rousseau, considered a founder of a progressive view of democracy. Yet, the term "democracy" was foreign to these peoples. Therefore, the across-the-board or sweeping phrase of "democracy" as employed here includes the traditions of some of these Indigenous equality-based societies. In fact, those Indigenous peoples who were nurtured on equality (many, of course, were not) and on opposition to selfish individual interests point to one of the most important considerations: the necessity to look into the socio-economic bases of a society in evaluating democracy. Is the U.S.-based textbook definition of democracy, as being "representative democracy" and "free-market capitalism," to be adopted by the world as the unique classification of democracy?

While the definition of democracy employed here stems from formal Greek heritage, it does not imply agreement with Eurocentrism, which finds its quintessential expression today in the U.S. political and economic system of representative democracy and capitalism. U.S.-centrism is the notion, emerging originally out of Greco-Roman antiquity, that only in the European and U.S. "civilizations" are legitimate thinking and practices to be found in all realms of activity. "Eurocentrism" is not used here in the general cultural sense of the term, but rather in the context of its main political features. This characteristic consists of Eurocentrism's self-proclaimed superiority over the South through its political and economic system, held up to be the model for the world. For the purposes of this book, therefore, the focus will be on social science, originally characterized as Eurocentric, but later encompassing U.S.-centrism to become the main banner of the "West."

Eurocentrism has developed since the sixteenth century. It reached its zenith after the initial expansion of modern universities in the middle of the eighteenth century. In the course of its evolution, it later incorporated North America, coinciding with the reach exercised by the U.S. itself toward domination in the South.

When Eurocentrism later evolved into U.S.-centrism, it included concepts of "democracy," "human rights" and the superiority of "Western" "civilization" over all others. In addition, U.S.-centrism incorporates the supremacy of capitalism (also referred to as the "free market"), "individual freedom" and its political expression in "electoral politics" and the "competitive multi-party system." It encompasses the assumption of the superiority of "races" originating in the North as opposed to those in the South. It actually translates as the supposition of white Anglo-Saxon Germanic "race" supremacy. With colonialism came the invention of ethnicity and race, and they served as a justification for slavery and the coerced cash-crop labour of Indigenous peoples in the Americas. The Americas, as a geo-social construct of colonialism in that period, were essential to the birth and eventual flourishing of the European- and, thereafter, the U.S.-dominated world economy.

U.S.-centrism became the pinnacle of the West. The post-1945 period ensued, and the global university erupted further, playing an important role in fulfilling the needs of economic and government elites in Europe and North America. After World War II, universities and academia were further compelled to develop social science, which refers to a plurality of fields outside of natural science, such as political science, history, philosophy, sociology, anthropology, economics, linguistics and law. The privileged few required the support of social science in their quest for post-World War II expansion. Social science emerged first in response to European problems, and then to requirements posed by the U.S. Therefore, theories and methods inevitably took shape based on the needs of the geographical areas in which they were born and flourished. The status quo approach is so ingrained, despite resistance by many, that it is not sufficient to aim at "rethinking social science." Rather, "unthinking social science" is more appropriate on a long-term basis as a common effort by many contributors to a new manner of thinking, a new paradigm (Wallerstein 1997, 2001, 2006; Quijano 2000: 215–32; Quijano 2010a: 4–15; Quijano 2010b; Quijano and Wallerstein n.d.: 23–40; Amin 2009: 1–20, 154–85).

Various other valuable works directly question Eurocentrism, and thus U.S.-centrism. For example, in *The Critical Development Studies Handbook*, one of the authors, Alain Gresh, scholar and editor of *Le Monde diplomatique*, asks, "How many of us are aware that the first industrial revolution began in the eleventh century, in Song Dynasty China? … The British industrial revolution would have been impossible without China's contribution" (Gresh 2011: 30–31). This *Handbook* goes on to contest the U.S.-centric and Eurocentric notion that all authoritative thinking, including "democracy" as a "universally" applicable ideal, comes directly from Greece to the West over many centuries and, finally, to the entire contemporary world (Gresh 2011: 29–32). Other books, by their very nature, defy the domination of U.S.-centrism and Eurocentrism while opening up new perspectives unfettered by dogma. One such example is the recent publication edited by Henry Veltmeyer, professor of development studies in Mexico and Canada (Veltmeyer 2011). The issue of Eurocentrism and its offspring, U.S.-centrism, is very complex and ingrained, operating, as Samir Amin warns, "without anyone noticing it. This is why many specialists, historians and intellectuals can reject particular expressions of the Eurocentric construct without being embarrassed by the incoherence of the overall vision that results" (Amin 2009: 186). For example, while certain academics may distance themselves from some of the most grotesque features of Eurocentrism and U.S.-centrism — such as their claims to be the defenders of a superior political and economic model for the world — they may still fall prey to the main ideological and political underpinnings of the U.S-centric model.

U.S. anthropologist Lynn Stephen's frank observation provides a counter to this danger of eclecticism. She states, "Latin American Studies was created as a geographical discipline largely to generate information that could be used in advancing U.S. foreign policy and development interests in Latin America and the Caribbean [that] have been constructed with U.S.-centric priorities and visions" (Stephen 2008: 435).[1] Some anthropologists claim, and rightly so, that in dealing with both a discipline and a subject matter that have been marginalized, these scholars are in fact in a privileged position. They can more easily approach "radical rethinking of the state [government] that a view from the margins requires" (Das and Poole 2004: 4). Furthermore, anthropology is often seen "as a discipline that speaks for (and at times with) those populations that have been marginalized by the political and economic structures of colonial and postcolonial rule" (Das and Poole 2004: 4).

In the same vein, but dealing with twenty-first-century socialism, Canadian academic Errol Sharpe claims that it must "look beyond a Eurocentric view, a view which posits that all human progress will flow out of Europe and the clones, such as the United States, Canada and Australia, of its empire" (Sharpe 2011: 60). Like the anthropologists cited above, Sharpe also points to the importance of learning from the heritage of non-European societies and Indigenous peoples from both the North and South. They have "different paradigms from which to build." Whether taking advantage of the anthropologists' natural vocation of ethnographic studies in the South or studying in the North, the common factor is to break out of being "cloistered in the [university] institution" (Sharpe 2011: 49, 60).

The focus of this book does not allow for a full examination of Eurocentrism and its extension into U.S.-centrism. Many scholars have dedicated a good part of their long academic careers to this problem, such as Samir Amin, Immanuel Wallerstein and Aníbal Quijano. In Cuba, Thalía Fung Riverón, University of Havana professor, president of the Sociedad Cubana de Investigaciones Filosóficas and director of the Grupo de Ciencia Política of the University of Havana, and others have also focused their scholarly efforts on a critical examination of Eurocentrism. The main interest

---

1. Professor Claude Morin, Latin Americanist historian at the Université de Montréal, has brought to my attention (in reviewing an early draft of this book) that the explosion of Latin American Studies is linked to the Cuban Revolution. Soon after 1959, the U.S. government and some of its foundations assisted in creating research institutes and programs.

here is to point out the historical background in order to place the supposed superiority of the Eurocentric and U.S.-centric notions of democracy in its context. The goal is to widen horizons to include other forms and contents of democracy that do not fit into the Western paradigm, such as the Cuban example. A U.S.-centric perspective results in a virtual reflex action with regard to any socio-political, historical, scientific and geographical phenomena, of which democracy is only one. U.S.-centrism is intricate and multifaceted, and thus acts as a fog enshrining serious discussion and debate on democracy. Therefore, this book deals with only some of the most important features of U.S.-centrism linked to the U.S. official view on democracy that are necessary for the focus of this discussion.

Democracy or Democratization?

As this author argued in 1999, to understand Cuba, one must appreciate Cubans' ability to think and act "on their own while adopting the most progressive contemporary ideas available [in the nineteenth century]" (August 1999: 199). In dealing with important tasks facing the contemporary period since 1959, when the Cuban Revolution finally succeeded, "the nation dealt with the conditions in the country while taking advantage of the international progressive thinking available" (August 1999: 221). In this sense, the term *cubanía* (which normally refers to cultural heritage in a broad sense) was also employed in a political way. It was adapted to emphasize the characteristic of Cubans "thinking on their own," as handed down from one generation of revolutionaries and independence fighters to the next. In other words, "*Cubanía* means ... putting things Cuban on the agenda" (August 1999: 69).

Other authors, in striving to come to grips with the unique features of the Cuban Revolution, have given rise to some rich literature. Let us take first some examples of non-Cuban scholars. Antoni Kapcia has developed in a far more mature, multifaceted and profound manner the concepts of *cubanía* and *cubanía revolucionaria* in a book largely dedicated to this (Kapcia 2000). George Lambie, for his part, emphasizes the "marrying [of] European revolutionary theory with specific Cuban conditions" as he traces the evolution of Cuba's revolutionary thinking and actions from the nineteenth and twentieth centuries to date (Lambie 2010: 148). D.L. Raby devotes much of her work to the subject, arguing, "The true originality of the Cuban revolution has yet to be appreciated" (Raby 2006: 7). Isaac Saney coins the expression "revolution in motion" in order to illustrate Cuba's trait, which distinguishes it from static revolutions (Saney 2004). One of many examples from Cuba is Concepción Nieves Ayús, head of the Instituto de Filosofía. She has been leading, along with her colleagues, a long-standing and profound investigation by her institute on the work of Fidel Castro. In an interview, she provided numerous examples of how, in theory and in practice — right from the onset — the Cuban Revolution has been and continues to be a "permanent process" (Interview, Nieves Ayús 2008). In another interview, Olga Fernández Ríos, a researcher at the same institute, explains her view that Cuba is a revolution of *búsqueda*, of searching, of seeking out solutions to problems (Interview, Fernández Ríos 2008).

In order to come to grips with today's Cuba, it is necessary to appreciate the Cuban Revolution's innovative approach, as characterized right from its beginnings. The term "innovative" is employed in the sense of innovating as an *ongoing* feature. The unique, durable aspect of the Cuban Revolution's resilience faces dogmatism from some on the left and outright opposition from those on the right. The buoyancy brings to the fore the capacity of the Cuban experience to *continually* break new ground. This antithesis to being uncreative and unimaginative explains much of what is currently occurring in Cuba. The Cuban Revolution's appropriation of "innovativeness" explains its capacity to defy all odds over such a long period. Cuba is virtually a case unto itself as a revolution. It has been deviceful at every turn of history right from the beginning, in the nineteenth century. In this sense, the Cuban experience is a laboratory.[2] The term "laboratory" conjures up notions of experimentation, going as far as "trial and error" as a manner of acting. This is true to a large extent, but it is not necessarily a pejorative description of a revolution. On the contrary, trial and error is at the essence of being innovative.

This book explores the road that democracy in Cuba is following from this perspective of democratization, or as a democracy in motion. Among those non-Cubans who pioneered the early writing regarding democracy in Cuba, Sheryl Lutjens views the Cuban example as being "a process of democratization." She rejects ready-made "models of democracy," "noting the absence of a perfect democracy of any type.... Perhaps it must be built rather than legislated or decreed from within or without" (Lutjens 1992: 71). Seventeen years later, in reviewing works published on the 50th anniversary of the Cuban Revolution, Lutjens highlights the current "intellectual and political ferment within Cuba" (Lutjens 2009: 1). Therefore, one may better understand Cuba's reality by viewing its political system and brand of socialism in transformation as a process. This optic stands the test of time because Cuba is always in "ferment." Lambie, orienting himself in the study of democracy in Cuba, likewise places emphasis on democracy as a "process." It is "based on an alternative ontological foundation to the one which underpins liberal and structuralist perceptions of democracy" (Lambie 2010: 115–16).

A revolution or movement cannot be innovative if it is limited by *static* structures. No matter how indispensable institutions may be, if accorded absolute pre-eminence as structures fixed in time, they can act as a detriment to the various daily interventions by the people at all levels. By closely observing

---

2. I am indebted to Professor Claude Morin for a conversation in 2011 in which he provided this notion of Cuba being a laboratory.

the ongoing movements in Egypt, Spain and the U.S., one could make the leap toward viewing democracy as a daily way of life, applied to all systems — capitalist and socialist — in different ways. A political institution, such as an electoral system, a state, a political party or even a demonstration, can be viewed as immobile, part of a routine, a bureaucracy. In this context, rather than being an instrument for political and social liberation, the structures become an obstacle. The difference between the two opposite approaches toward structures lies in the active, conscious and ongoing participation of the people. This applies to any system.

Democratization from the Bottom Up: Occupying Public Spaces (2011–12)

In 2011–12, historical events in various parts of the world, such as Egypt, Spain and the U.S., opened up new horizons for reflections and practices regarding participatory democracy.

In 2011, Egypt's Tahrir Square best symbolized the year of rebellions. One of its core demands was democracy, in both its economic and political dimensions, that is, the need to democratize the economy and political system. Egyptians carried out their revolt, which is ongoing, without foreign backing and *in spite of* U.S. support for the Mubarak regime, camouflaged toward the end of his reign.

Tahrir Square is significant because it potentially represents a rejection of U.S.-centric notions of political change and democracy. This is why Hillary Clinton, in addressing the Egyptian people on May 19, 2011, exhorted them "to move from protests to politics" (Clinton 2011b). In other words, as far as the official view is concerned, Tahrir Square is *not politics*, while the goals of Washington *do represent politics:* implementation of a U.S.-centric system of representative democracy based on political parties, representatives and elections. This, however, gives rise to all the resulting negative consequences, such as division and competition among the people. By its very nature, the U.S.-centric, multi-party representative system lies in sharp contrast with the Egyptian rebellion. This revolt and its ironclad unity resulted in the Tahrir movement succeeding in overthrowing the 30-year reign of U.S.-backed dictator Mubarak. Thus, repudiating this rebellion, Hillary Clinton insisted, in the midst of ongoing violent attacks by the "post-Mubarak military" regime against Tahrir, in a September 29, 2011, interview, "We are very impressed and encouraged," "elections are scheduled," "they are moving toward elections, I think, is not only important, but essential" (Clinton 2011a). The U.S. is still fully supporting the Egyptian military regime with "the continued flow of Foreign Military Financing to Egypt" (Voice of America News 2012). This consists of a yearly injection of $1.3 billion in military aid to "Mubarakism," without Mubarak (Nuland 2012).

The organizing of U.S.-style (and often easily manipulated) elections is a *sine qua non* to replace the potential political power of people emerging at the base and creating new forms of democracy, such as Tahrir. U.S.-sponsored representative democracy not only replaces participatory democracy in motion, but also strives to crush it.

Egypt held elections for president in May–June 2012. The U.S.-backed elections managed to place the pro-Western Muslim Brotherhood as the winner.[3] Voter turnout was only 52 percent — garnering the winner with about half of the votes. Morsi is therefore "mandated" by approximately 25 percent of registered voters.

The U.S. model of elections was responsible for maintaining the Egyptian military in power. The Obama administration, in a telephone conversation, congratulated the Armed Forces for its role. In addition, Washington recognized the position of its ally by congratulating Morsi, declaring that he "and the new Egyptian government have both the *legitimacy* and responsibility of representing a diverse and courageous citizenry" (White House 2012, emphasis added). It is important to note that these types of elections — whether in Egypt or other countries — serve only to provide *legitimacy* for the rule of the respective oligarchies, including the military.

However, the Egyptian rebellion is not over. Compare the low participation rate (52 percent) with the eighteen-day revolt in January–February 2011 by the Egyptian people that emanated from decisions made in Tahrir Square. The low voter turnout highlights the lack of interest in the U.S.-imposed elections when one considers that the vast majority of Egyptians participated in the struggle to overthrow the U.S.-backed Mubarak at a cost of 850 lives and 5,500 injuries. There is no comparison. Voting is one thing; putting one's life on the line to overthrow a U.S.-supported dictator is another altogether.

Following the application of the U.S.-model of elections, Samir Amin, an expert academic on, among other subjects, Egypt, where he was born, observes, "The Egyptian people are fully aware that the struggle must continue. Let us see what happens next" (Amin 2012b). Amin's words reflect the ongoing and profound nature of the Egyptian rebellion.

The uprisings in that region first started in Tunisia and then developed in Egypt, becoming the model for the occupation of public spaces. The Egyptian domino effect first took place *in the U.S. itself.* In February 2011, in Madison, Wisconsin, while Egypt was in open revolt, a series of major demonstrations and occupations took place. The Egyptian revolt directly influenced and inspired people in the U.S. to take action against arbitrariness and in favour of democratic control of their economic and political lives.

---

3. I first read Samir Amin's book entitled *Eurocentrism* before the 2011–12 events in Egypt. At that time, I was somewhat skeptical about his analysis of the Muslim Brotherhood being part of the historic Western strategy to maintain Egypt in the grips of the West (now U.S.). However, the unfolding of events in Egypt has proven that Amin is entirely correct.

Noam Chomsky reminds us that the antecedent of the 2011 Egypt revolt was the 2008 workers' strikes in that country supported by some U.S. unions. This solidarity was explicitly reciprocated in Tahrir in February 2011 by a prominent Egyptian union leader (Chomsky 2012a: 259–60). There was a massive occupation of Madison's state government building. This edifice had served as the centre from which the state decreed its policy of drastically limiting the role of trade unions, as a part of sharp cutbacks in social spending. The state government building, containing within it ample space, became Wisconsin's Tahrir Square. In the Wisconsin case, the grass-roots occupying of public space as a potential source for new participatory political power was temporarily hijacked into the "lesser of two evils" two-party system machinations.

The next main ripple effect of the Egyptian rebellion was embodied in Spanish youth who stepped up to confront the "lesser of two evils" trap head-on, as part of U.S.-centric democracy. On May 15, 2011 (three months after the January–February Egyptian rebellion), young people started to revolt against both their precarious socio-economic conditions (over 40 percent unemployment rate) and the de facto disenfranchisement of the people under the current political system. The political process alternates between the right wing and the "socialist" political parties, which exhibit similar policies once in power. Youth and people from all walks of life occupied the main squares under the banner *¡Democracia Real Ya!* (Real Democracy Now!). In addition, there were other movements known together as the *indignados* (the outraged). It started in Madrid's Puerta del Sol Square and then spread to 50 other main squares and cities in the country. Spain's squares, and later its neighbourhoods, served as bases for discussion, formally recorded decisions and planned actions. Many people in Spain had never seen this type of collective action at the grass-roots level outside — and despite — the state structures. As in Egypt, and Madison, people do not lose sight of this exposure.

In the U.S., inspired in principle by Tahrir Square, the Occupy Movement (initiated in September 2011) featured the occupation of squares, strategic parks and other points in more than 50 cities across the country. Right from the beginning, it was designed, even if only implicitly, to be different from the U.S.-centric political system and its "acceptable" forms of protest. Chapter 2 discusses the Occupy Movement in more detail.

This introductory chapter has provided the overall context of the book. It has situated democracy as existing in different genres and explored democratization as a participatory process. In this framework, it has alerted readers to U.S.-centrism as a block to opening horizons. The next two chapters will deal with different approaches to democracy, beginning with the U.S. variety.

Chapter 2

Democracy in the U.S.

Geographically, the U.S. is the closest of the Cuban neighbours being analyzed in this book. Based on its U.S.-centric outlook, the U.S. claims to be the model for democracy in the world. Thus we must investigate how this democracy actually operates and, in the process, come to appreciate other experiences, such as the Cuban one.

Birth of the U.S. and the American Dream

The U.S. notion of democracy — and indeed its very centricity as the basis of U.S. foreign policy toward the South — originates with the birth of the country itself. The original colonizers forming the Thirteen Colonies were from Britain — both in 1620, with the Pilgrims on the *Mayflower,* half of whom were Puritans, and in 1630, with the Puritans on their own led by John Winthrop. What they had in common was a conflict with the Church of England, which they believed had to be cleansed of Catholic ritual and heritage. They also held the mutual notion of a chosen people based on a biblical reference, as illustrated in the words of Winthrop in 1630: "Consider that we shall be as a City upon a Hill, the eyes of all people are upon us" (Winthrop 1630). This statement was in reference to Matthew 5:14, "You are the light of the world. A city [that is] set on a hill cannot be hid." It is on the basis of this "light of the world" and a "city on a hill" for all to see that the Puritans started to build their notion of the chosen people and its inherent superiority. In addition, considering the role of slavery in the economy from the very first days of the settlers (1620) and the drive to the West by massacring the Indigenous peoples, many questions arise. Eurocentrism, one of whose pillars is racism, was applied by the Thirteen Colonies' leaders inside the colonies themselves. It was expressed as U.S.-centrism and expanded from there well beyond the U.S. frontiers.[1]

Along with this biblical "chosen people" vision of the world, the Thirteen Colonies came into conflict with Britain. While France supported the colonies, it was also wary of them, an apprehension that would be corroborated, as, after independence, the colonies soon allied themselves with Britain. Thus the Thirteen Colonies' independence was ultimately part of the growing intercolonial power struggle.[2]

There was an interruption, however, in the alliance with Britain.

---

1. See www.democracyintheus.com, "The American Dream, Indigenous Peoples and Slavery."
2. See www.democracyintheus.com, "The U.S. War of Independence: A Power Struggle Between the Thirteen Colonies, Britain and France?"

Although the Thirteen Colonies immediately allied themselves with Britain after independence, later on, in 1812, the U.S. was at war with Britain once again. Britain invaded Washington; the White House was burned down. Nonetheless, this important development does not contradict the thesis that the Thirteen Colonies' War of Independence bore the seeds of intercolonial rivalry. Britain, "scenting a dangerous rival," tried everything to prevent the expansion of the U.S. in North America. This was one cause of the War of 1812 (Foster 1951: 212). Howard Zinn writes that the War of 1812 "was not (as usually depicted in American textbooks) just a war against England for survival, but a war for the expansion of the new nation, into Florida, into Canada [English territory], into Indian territory" (Zinn 2005: 127).

A clause in the Declaration of Independence claims that the U.S. is "to assume among the powers of the earth" its own position for itself. This takes on its full meaning when one draws conclusions from relatively recent research illustrating that the Thirteen Colonies were complicit participants in the rivalry for world domination between Britain and France. The American Dream evolved, built on slavery and the massacre of the Indigenous peoples.

The Declaration of Independence stipulates, "We hold these truths to be self-evident, that all men are created equal, that they are endowed by their Creator with certain unalienable Rights, that among these are Life, Liberty, and the pursuit of Happiness" (Hardt 2007: 16). According to Jim Cullen, this is the key to the Declaration. It survives in the collective memory because it "underwrites the American Dream" (Cullen 2003: 38). Cullen indicates that it is based on John Locke's invocation of life, liberty and the pursuit of property. However, Cullen hedges this by writing that Thomas Jefferson, as the main drafter of the Declaration of Independence, "tweaked [effecting a minor alteration, small adjustment or fine-tuning] that locution by replacing the last phrase with 'the pursuit of happiness'" (Cullen 2003: 46). To Cullen's credit, he described this modification to the all-important term "private property" as a "tweak." It was a superficial fine-tuning to make it appear more acceptable, yet, at the same time, the phrase maintains the essence of "private property" as the real thrust of one of the components (life, liberty and the pursuit of happiness — the latter tweaked from "property"). The fact that Jefferson considered Locke to be one of "the three greatest men that had ever lived" supports the superficial nature of this alteration (Jefferson 1975: 434–35). From Jefferson to President Barack Obama, the U.S. cannot shake off its historical preservation of private property to the detriment of other far more positive values coming out of the Enlightenment and the French Revolution epoch. For example, during a 2009 visit to France as president, Obama tried to rewrite history. Talking about ideals, he said, "In America, it is written into our founding documents as 'life, liberty, and the pursuit of happiness.' In France: 'Liberté' … 'égalité, fraternité'" (Obama 2009). Obama disregarded the fact that the values of *égalité* and *fraternité* (equality and fraternity) stand opposed to the absolute superiority of private property, even at the time of the French Revolution, as elaborated below.

"Liberalism" and its related concept of "freedom," as applied to the political system in the U.S., cannot be detached in any way from the extreme individualism of private-property rights. Characterized by these traits, co-optation and the American Dream were crystallized during the very early stages of the Thirteen Colonies.[3]

Thus right from the beginning, a project based on private property provided the foundation for the U.S. political system. This distinguishes it from the Cuban Revolution's social project, which is rooted in socialism adopted for the economic and social well-being of the vast majority of people instead of the unlimited accumulation of private property.

These features of the U.S. model help to explain the motion of contemporary democracy in the U.S., as orchestrated by different sections of the ruling elites. Even though the latter are not homogeneous — indeed, diverse sectors of the oligarchy are often in conflict with one another — the majority of the ruling circles can come to an agreement on certain issues. Co-optation by segments of the real economic rulers favours the participation of a few select individuals. They manage to realize the American Dream and then, as a reward, become part of the machinery to block the participation of the majority. This does not mean that the democratic struggles of the peoples in the U.S. did not — and do not — achieve anything. Noteworthy accomplishments emerged, for example, out of the 1960s civil rights movement and other victories for workers' rights. However, this chapter focuses on the role of co-optation and on how it operates in U.S. politics at the highest levels.

In order to be more fully conscious of the above and delineate all the complexities based on private property, liberty and freedom, it is helpful to review the philosophy of other Enlightenment thinkers, aside from John Locke. The authors of the U.S. Declaration of Independence had rejected others as a source of motivation. For example, Jean-Jacques Rousseau surfaced as one of the most outstanding thinkers of his time, favouring collective and fraternal relationships over the individual, possessive nature of capitalism.

While Rousseau envisaged a new moral and social order based on equality, the new arrangement "did not suppress individual creativity" (Lambie 2010: 85). The Founding Fathers rejected Rousseau for his staunch defence of the collective, even if this did not preclude the importance of the individual.[4]

The rebuff of enlightened thought and events by the American Revolution is a critical feature. In reality, the American Revolution's mottoes of liberty (to accumulate wealth) and happiness (tweaked from "property") are

---

3. See www.democracyintheus.com, "Property, Liberalism and Co-Optation."
4. See www.democracyintheus.com, "Rejection of Rousseau's Enlightened Collectivism in Favour of Locke's Individualism."

the basis of U.S. ideology — and a blunt dismissal of the French Revolution. To the limited extent that the French Revolution opened, albeit in words, toward collectivity and fraternity, the American Revolution rejected this.

Samir Amin (2004) offers some important insights into U.S. liberalism. The French Revolution's radical Jacobin wing recognized the contradiction within rising bourgeois thought, namely, "economic liberalism is the enemy of democracy." In France and other parts of Europe, "equality" and "liberty" were on a par, that is, they occupied the same standing. However, in the U.S., "liberty alone occupies the entire field of political values.... American society despises equality. Given that political culture is the product of history viewed over a long period of time," what are its distinguishing features in the U.S.? Amin holds that U.S. liberalism is based on "the chosen people" extremism, typified by the Protestantism implanted in New England, which was further reinforced by successive waves of immigration from Europe. They were victims of the system existing in the old continent. However, their circumstances as immigrants to the U.S. "led them to renounce collective struggles to change the conditions common to their classes or groups in their own countries and result in an adherence to the ideology of individual success in their adopted land." In Europe, after the French Revolution, the 1871 Paris Commune represented an assault on capitalism based on liberalism. However, the ruling circles in the U.S. manipulated the successive generations of poor immigrants, such as the Irish and Italian, forming them into gangs to kill each other. Amin highlights the extreme U.S. liberalism based on individualism in another original manner. He contrasts the U.S. evolution of political culture with that of Canada, which he correctly warns does not "yet" share American ideology. Canada also had successive waves of immigrants "capable of stifling class consciousness." Yet, Canada "does not share the fanaticism of the religious interpretation of the New England sectarians." He goes on to ask whether another cause of this difference with Canada is due to the large migration of "loyalists" fleeing from New England because they did not want to separate from the English mother country (Amin 2004: 56–67).

It is worthwhile to pause a moment to reflect on this last perceptive point. The extreme liberalism in its New England form outdid even those loyal to the British Crown. Therefore, to infer that U.S. liberalism in any way as something positive is entirely unfounded in history. On the contrary, U.S. liberalism stems from extreme individualism, whose very roots originate in private property. U.S.-centrism even outdoes its mother's origins and thus posits a formidable contradiction with democracy.[5]

The next important phase in exploring democracy in the U.S., following the 1776 Declaration of Independence (for the purposes of the book's focus on participation), is the U.S. Constitution in 1787. The Thirteen

---

5. See www.democracyintheus.com, "The Origins of U.S. Liberalism and Contemporary Democracy."

Colonies in the period from 1776 to 1787 were already divided into the wealthy few and the poor in the cities and in the countryside. The U.S. War of Independence exacerbated this situation, bringing windfall profits to businesspeople in transportation, food and munitions. In his classic book on democracy and wealth in the U.S., author and journalist Kevin Phillips concludes, based on his study, "Every millionaire ... owed a fair part of his wealth to wartime or postwar connections to the new government" (Phillips 2003: 10–15). It is important to draw a clear distinction between the developing U.S. elites and the people. This division dated from the birth of the colonies and continues to the current period. Robert Kagan, a *Washington Post* journalist, wrote a scholarly book in 2006 on U.S. foreign policy from before its founding to the end of the nineteenth century. In Cliff DuRand's (2009) review of the book, he writes that Kagan "embraces it [imperialism] as defining the national character. In effect, he claims that imperialism is as American as apple pie." DuRand then differentiates between the U.S. elites and the people of the U.S. He justifiably argues that if war and aggression were part of the U.S. national character, then why would the elites and the media have to "cajole and trick people into accepting" decisions such as to go to war against Cuba (1898), Vietnam and, more recently, Iraq (DuRand 2009).

From the birth of the U.S. as a blossoming colonial-imperialist country, there were class differences resulting in a test for the ruling elites that many U.S. colleagues rightfully highlight. These contradictions interfered with U.S. ambitions. For example, during the War of Independence, in 1781, the common troops in Pennsylvania revolted, dispersed, killed and wounded officers because the soldiers had not been paid. Then, fully armed and with cannon, they marched on Philadelphia. Other mutinies followed in that period (Zinn 2005: 81). In drafting the Constitution, de facto and de jure disenfranchisement was not merely a question of wealth and connections; it had a political basis derived from the outlook of the Founding Fathers.[6] This heritage contrasts sharply with Cuba's legacy as well as with the recent experiences of Venezuela, Bolivia and Ecuador.

Princeton University professor and author Sheldon S. Wolin, in his classic *Democracy Inc.*, points out that the Founding Fathers were interested in controlling "democratic impulses." They asked themselves "how to manage democracy, or how to exploit division and thereby dilute commonality" (Wolin 2010: 280). In the same way, another U.S. author and academic, Michael Parenti, highlights that Founding Father James Madison "touched the heart of the matter: how to keep the 'form' and appearance of popular government with only a minimum of substance" (Parenti 2008: 43).

The right to elect representatives and to be elected to the Constituent

---

6. See www.democracyintheus.com, "Fear of the Majority and Pluralism as Cornerstones of Exclusion."

Assembly was severely limited, and most people were excluded, acutely curtailing franchise and suffrage. Thus the U.S. Constitution was adopted without the participation of the vast majority.[7]

Most striking is what the U.S. Constitution does *not* contain in comparison with different types of democracies. This is not a case of raising issues from the luxury of hindsight, but rather from the viewpoint of many criteria in vogue at the very time the U.S. Constitution was drafted. The preamble and the entire document are devoid of sentiment and inspiration, unlike the 1791 French Constitution, which arose out of the Enlightenment and the French Revolution. (Note that all references to the Constitution are from Cullop 1984.) It is significant that, in the stern preamble to the U.S. Constitution, the first objective mentioned is "a more perfect union." This reflected the most important preoccupation of the wealthy few: to work out the differences among the states. This concern reverberates to this day in presidential speeches and statements. One of the reasons for this contemporary preoccupation is that it continues to be a problem. On the positive side, the Constitution enshrines the "blessing of liberty," albeit one based on extreme individualism in pursuit of property as defined by the Constitution drafters. They identified liberty and liberalism as limited to this quest for the accumulation of private property. Wolin, in his award-winning book on U.S. democracy, indicates that one of Madison's main concerns was the preservation of unequal abilities in acquiring property. To do away with this difference would be to destroy liberty. Wolin asserts that Madison "posed inequality as both reality *and* ideal against the authenticity of equality" (Wolin 2010: 279–80, emphasis in original). The Western frontier expansion, as described by its apologists, contributed to developing, among other features, individualism (Wolin 2010: 232). Pursuit of property and radical individualism are thus at the very heart of the economic and political system. The absence of two concepts in the U.S. Constitution further highlights this point: the first is the fact that the term "democracy" is not mentioned in it; the second is the non-existence of the progressive notion of that period, namely, that sovereignty be vested in the hands of the people.[8]

There also existed the problem of the states' relationship to the central government. The work of U.S. anthropologist Jack Weatherford (1988) details the positive features of many of the Indigenous peoples in the U.S. Their emphasis on collectivism, for example, was tempered by respectful individualism, equality and respect for nature and environment. However, the only trait that caught the eye of the Founding Fathers was the Indigenous peoples' ingenuity of building federations of nations. Reportedly, the first person to

---

7. See www.democracyintheus.com, "The Constituent Assembly for the New Constitution: The Vast Majority Disenfranchised."

8. See www.democracyintheus.com, "Democracy and Vesting Sovereignty in the People."

propose a union of all of the colonies and to suggest a federal model for it was the Iroquois chief Canassatego.[9]

In summary, with regard to participation, the declaration of principle in the U.S. Constitution states, "We the people." However, as Amin astutely contends, "the conclusions were not drawn from this principle. Quite the contrary, the efforts of the Founding Fathers were focused on the objective of *neutralizing* the impact of this declaration" (Amin 2012a, emphasis added). The entire political superstructure reborn as U.S.-centrism is an offshoot of Eurocentrism: individual property and expanding capitalism, with the added powerful dose of racism applied inside and outside its own borders. These features, in turn, were part of the birth and development of the U.S. This made for a lethal cocktail consisting of an extremely limited participation of the people. There was, however, one exception to non-participation: all, including slaves and ex-slaves, were allowed and encouraged to participate in U.S. expansionist policies by serving in the military.

Foreign Policy Toward Its Neighbours and Democracy Promotion

The birth of the U.S. took place as a self-professed evangelical "beacon of the world." Their U.S.-centric economic and political system, based on private property, would be promoted throughout the globe. As a corollary to this, the separation from Britain was nothing more than being part of the growing global British–French–Thirteen Colonies rivalry. This rivalry, in which the Thirteen Colonies enthusiastically took part, also involved Spain and its colony Cuba.

> The rebellion of the thirteen colonies in 1776 provided new trade opportunities between Cuba and North America. Spain opened Cuban ports to North American commerce officially in November 1776, with appropriate pomp and protocol. The decision was in part inspired by opportunism, in part by self-interest: a gesture of support for the North Americans and a snub to the English. (Pérez 1991: 61)

U.S. democracy promotion, embedded in the U.S.-centric roots of the American Dream, is based on an empire, even though the actual term "democracy promotion" was not always in vogue. From 1898 to 1969, irrespective of which of the two political parties was in power, the same policies of military intervention were followed.[10]

---

9. See www.democracyintheus.com, "A Blind Spot for U.S. Indigenous Peoples' Collectivism."
10. See www.democracyintheus.com, "The Origins and Development of U.S. Democracy Promotion."

The U.S. political system eventually became consolidated, ridding itself of its most grotesque features of slavery. However, this "purging" took place only on a superficial basis. It would make U.S. democracy increasingly appropriate, in the eyes of its beholders, for exportation to countries in the South.[11]

During the period before, and in the initial stages of, World War II, the U.S. was not involved in fighting fascism. When the U.S. finally joined the allies in World War II, Franklin Delano Roosevelt (F.D.R.) articulated the ambition of the U.S. to be the "great arsenal of democracy" (Roosevelt 1940), and this became an instrument for U.S. policy after the war. F.D.R.'s domestic policy, despite the illusions generated by many liberals, had a specific motive. Conrad Black, a conservative biographer of F.D.R., praised him as "the saviour of American capitalism" (Black 2003: 1124). The Monroe Doctrine, Manifest Destiny and Good Neighbor Policy succeeded one after the other from the nineteenth to the twentieth centuries. Followed and developed by presidents of both Republican and Democratic parties, they have as their base the Puritans' "chosen people" concept and policy.[12]

Even though it is a complicated process, in general, the "military–industrial complex" shapes the U.S. elites' worldview. The ruling class does not dominate as "a secretive, conspiratorial, omnipotent, monolithic power … and occasional sharp differences arise in ruling circles" (Parenti 2008: 290). However, despite its non-conspiratorial nature and even with the existence of sharp conflicts, there is a common denominator: it is the worldview consisting of the need to maintain high levels of military spending. One is never to question these enormous expenditures. To confront this militarist policy is to defy the ingrained superiority of the U.S. over the world. This mission of supremacy originates from the time of the Pilgrims. Its raison d'être is to safeguard, anywhere in the world, any serious objection to the unlimited accumulation of private property and U.S. access to it. The rejection of U.S. aspirations and of unlimited accumulation of private property normally emerges from grass-roots movements in favour of democratization of the economy and politics. In the U.S. itself, the "military–industrial complex," in the course of dealing with contradictions in its own ranks, also controls the political system. This necessarily excludes real participation of the people in the daily functioning of its democracy. In addition, at the ballot box itself, exclusion has been handed down from the Founding Fathers to the contemporary U.S. This is the case even though voting is the epitome of the U.S. democratic model.[13]

Further in this chapter, the section dedicated to the rise of Obama

---

11. See www.democracyintheus.com, "Appropriating U.S.-Centrism for Itself."

12. See www.democracyintheus.com, "The Manifest Destiny of the U.S. and Beyond to World War II."

13. See www.democracyintheus.com, "Shaping Global Superiority Abroad and Elections at Home."

("Competitive Multi-Party Democratic Elections: Obama Case Study") deals with political and historical aspects in the context of the competitive two-party democracy in the U.S. as compared with the path of democracy that Cuba has followed. Concerning the role of funding and U.S. election campaigns, it is appropriate to highlight this feature of the political system regarding Obama. On some occasions, the majority of these elites — often the most powerful segments — find common ground. For example, in the 2008 presidential elections, the most important sectors of the "military–industrial complex" fully backed and endorsed Obama.[14]

Newspaper endorsements in U.S. presidential elections are a key to victory, since they represent the consensus among the most important sectors of the oligarchy as to who would best serve their interests. The investigation of endorsements by major news publications (such as *Editor & Publisher* and *Alternative Newsweeklies*) shows that the most powerful segments of the elites chose Obama as president. It is a form of replacing people's participation with behind-the-scenes decisions. During the 2008 elections, newspapers, magazines and other publications wrote election endorsements. Up to the November 4, 2008, Election Day, Obama had received more than twice as many publication endorsements as John McCain. In circulation terms, the ratio was more than 3 to 1. According to *Editor & Publisher* magazine, 273 newspapers endorsed Obama compared with 172 for McCain (Benton Foundation 2008). Obama led McCain by 86 to 2 in college newspaper endorsements. *Alternative Newsweeklies* reported that Obama led McCain by 57 to 0 in endorsements among its 123 member newspapers (Whiten 2008).

"Military–industrial complex" and newspaper endorsements in 2008 set the stage for a similar scenario in the November 2012 Obama electoral triumph.

Founding Fathers' Heritage and Voter Turnout

As previously illustrated in this chapter, right from the early stages of the Thirteen Colonies, de facto and de jure disenfranchisement was not merely a question of wealth and connections. It had a political basis in the outlook of the Founding Fathers and in the Constitution that they produced: the result was barring the right to vote based on race, which specifically targeted African-Americans, who were, at the time, mostly slaves.

After the Civil War, on December 6, 1865, the Thirteenth Amendment to the U.S. Constitution, abolishing slavery, was adopted. On February 3, 1870, with the Fifteenth Amendment, race was no longer an obstacle to voting, thus espousing the right of African-Americans to vote. This amendment, according to the Constitution, stipulates, "The right of citizens of the United States to vote shall not be denied or abridged by the United States or by any State

---

14. See www.democracyintheus.com, "Obama's Funding and Endorsements by the Wealthy Elite."

on account of race, color, or previous condition of servitude" (Constitution of the United States 1984). In the wake of the peoples' democratic struggles, on January 23, 1964, the Twenty-Fourth Amendment, barring poll taxes (a source of revenue based on a head tax often used in order to stop African-Americans and other poor people from voting), was ratified (Constitution of the United States 1984).

On August 6, 1965, the Voting Rights Act was adopted, following the civil rights activism of the late 1950s and 1960s. An important milestone was Martin Luther King Jr. leading the Selma to Montgomery March and bringing to public attention the reality that overwhelming numbers of African-Americans did not have suffrage rights. To this day, African-Americans are still widely barred from voting despite the Civil War, the three constitutional amendments cited above and the 1965 Voting Rights Act.

One of the main juridical instruments to keep this Founding Fathers' heritage alive is the "felony" crime. Several U.S. scholars are carrying out daring, profound research on this issue.

> The term "felon" is derived from the legal classification of crimes. "Felony" is a generic term, historically used to distinguish certain "high crimes" or "grave offences" such as homicide from less serious offences known as misdemeanors.... In the contemporary United States, felonies are considered crimes punishable by incarceration of more than one year in state or federal prison, and misdemeanors are considered crimes punishable by local jail sentences, fines, or both. (Manza and Uggen 2006: 69)

According to Jeff Manza and Christopher Uggen, the two sociology professors quoted above, the number of felons in the U.S. "now [2006] exceeds the entire population of countries such as Cuba" (Manza and Uggen 2006: 9). Felons who have served their time are, in many instances, refused the right to vote, often for life. The authors divulge, by making an important comparison, that "felon disenfranchisement laws in the United States are unique in the democratic world. Nowhere else are millions of offenders who are not in prison denied the right to vote" (Manza and Uggen 2006: 41). The extremely high proportion of African-Americans caught up in the judiciary system "produces the shocking fact that more than one in seven black men are currently denied the right to vote, and in several states over one in four black men are disenfranchised" (Manza and Uggen 2006: 9–10).

Rutgers University (New Jersey) political science professor Elizabeth A. Hull points out that, based on the current trend of incarceration and the Bureau of Statistics reports, 29 percent of the next generation of African-American men are about to lose their suffrage rights for at least part of their lives (Hull 2006: 27).

The massive exclusion of felons, the vast majority of whom are African-Americans, affects in a very noticeable fashion the U.S. voter turnout rate. Another significant part of the voting age population that does not have the right to vote consists of disenfranchised non-citizens, such as the millions of Latinos who are residents of the U.S. However, they "do not have to be a U.S. citizen in order to join the U.S. Military"; the only obligation is that they live permanently (and legally) in the U.S. (Powers 2011). Therefore, Latinos and other non-citizens work, pay taxes and can fight in the military, taking the risk of dying or being injured, but do not have the right to vote.

Dr. Michael McDonald of George Mason University in Virginia has elaborated and compiled figures based on different options, one being the concept of voting age population (VAP). This includes all people eighteen years of age and older, including felons, who are very widely disenfranchised (mainly African-Americans), and non-citizens, who are completely disenfranchised.

In the 2010 general midterm elections, the VAP voter turnout rate is applied to the vote for highest office in that election year, that is, governor, U.S. senator or combined House of Representatives. The VAP voter rate indicates that it was 37.8 percent. That is, among all people eighteen years of age and older, including felons and non-citizens, the proportion of people who voted was 37.8 percent (McDonald 2011b).

Regarding the 2008 presidential elections won by Obama, McDonald indicates that the VAP turnout rate was 56.9 percent. There were 3,144,831 ineligible felons, while 8.4 percent of the VAP consisted of non-citizens not permitted to vote (McDonald 2011a). The November 2012 presidential elections, won by Obama, resulted in a decrease of the VAP voter turnout rate, bringing it to hover around the 50 percent mark (McDonald 2012b). In this chapter, the trend is further explained below in the section entitled "The November 2012 Elections and Obama."

Normally, the presidential candidates roughly split the vote. Therefore, the president and commander-in-chief had a "mandate" in his first term (2008–12) from approximately 28.5 percent of the population eighteen years and older (half of the 56.9 percent VAP turnout rate). In the 2012 elections, the VAP was approximately 50 percent; therefore, Obama's "mandate" was further reduced to about 25 percent of the VAP.

McDonald also coined the phrase "voting eligible population" (VEP). For this option, he does not include non-eligible felons or non-citizens. The VEP, in contrast to the VAP, thus includes only those eligible to vote. Nevertheless, in the 2008 presidential elections that provided Obama with his first mandate, only 61.6 percent of the VEP voted. Therefore, close to 40 percent of U.S. citizens having suffrage rights did not vote (McDonald 2011a). In the 2012 presidential elections that provided Obama with his second mandate, the VEP declined in comparison with the 2008 elections (McDonald 2012b). There are several well-known reasons in the public domain for this high abstention rate. First, there exists the widespread lack of faith or interest generally in the U.S. political system. Second, a sizable portion of the population does not carry any illusions about the "democratic two-party competitive system" as an instrument of change, thus the notorious refrain "They are all the same." Third, the simple act of voting itself encompasses other hurdles such as interminable lineups to vote, at times taking several hours. Fourth, poverty and semi-illiteracy creates an obstacle in view of the relatively complicated ballots placed in the hands of potential voters. Fifth, voting on a working day (Tuesday) hinders suffrage for working people. Sixth, the very stringent and discriminatory voter registration policy in many states severely restrains voter registration for people who otherwise would be eligible to vote.

Making voter registration even more difficult for those who technically have the right to vote is part of the electoral system. For example, with regard to the 2012 presidential elections, according to the Brennan Center for Justice at New York University School of Law, since the beginning of 2011, there have been at least 180 restrictive bills introduced in 41 states, and 25 laws and two executive actions presented in 19 states. In addition, 27 restrictive pieces of legislation are pending in six states (Brennan Center for Justice 2012). Difficulty in obtaining photo IDs is one of the main instruments. For example, according to the same authoritative source, in 2011, the number of states "requiring voters to show government-issued photo identification quadrupled in 2011. To put this into context, 11 percent of American citizens do not possess a government-issued photo ID; that is over 21 million citizens" (Brennan Center for Justice 2012). Thus one can conclude that the Founding Fathers' restrictive heritage on suffrage is being followed today. Even on the simple act of voting, to which "participation" in the U.S. democracy is often reduced, the anti-participative nature is widespread and ingrained in the very nature of the state as it was born at the end of the eighteenth century.

We now turn to other aspects of U.S. presidential elections, such as co-optation and individual opportunism, through a case study on Barack Obama. This analysis of Obama is carried out in the context of competitive multi-party politics, the model expected to be used to measure other systems, such as those existing in Cuba, Venezuela, Bolivia and Ecuador.

Competitive Multi-Party Democratic Elections: Obama Case Study

The previous sections have provided a review of many of the harmful characteristics of the U.S. political and economic system. Juxtaposed with the 2008 presidential elections, they featured the self-promotion of Obama with the assistance of the media as a symbol of change. This was supposedly taking place for the benefit of many peoples in the U.S., especially African-Americans. The Obama phenomenon can be viewed as redeeming change.

On closer inspection, however, Obama is far from breaking with the past. From the beginning of his literary and political career, he has been a fully conscious and willing candidate in service of the financial oligarchy.

It is thus necessary to explore a pivotal component of U.S. democracy, the competitive multi-party (in reality, two-party) system. Readers will recognize many of the factors indicated in previous sections of this chapter. However, U.S.-centric preconceived notions *do* hinder many people from seeing through the multiple filaments forming the cobwebs that surround the U.S. approach to democracy. This contributes to fostering prejudiced and unfounded views against other systems, such as the Cuban one. In the U.S. model, the dishonourable features publicly acknowledged in its political system and in its society are manipulated by elites to *maintain* the political system. This situation also contributes to the lack of existing solid structural mechanisms to defy the two-party system. The U.S.-centric outlook that is promoted covers up the process whereby the system co-opts dissatisfaction in order to preserve itself. In the case of the Obama phenomenon, the objective is to go on an *offensive* internationally and domestically in order to serve the "military–industrial complex."

Co-Optation and Individual Opportunism

Co-optation combines with individual opportunism to create illusions about the two-party system as a vehicle for change. The first feature put forward in this section is the role of co-optation as an important component of U.S. democracy. For example, the common use of the term "military–industrial complex" by Eisenhower and the media is also a means by which opposition to the ruling oligarchy is co-opted and rendered inoffensive. This is accomplished by vulgarizing this concept of the "military–industrial complex." It is proposed as a feature whose *undue* influence is, *of course*, undesirable. However, the "military–industrial complex" maintains the advantage of remaining an integral part of the economic-political landscape with no fundamental alternative possible. The only issue allowed — and even encouraged — to emerge in public opinion is how to deal with its *abusive* influence, not its actual, continued *existence*. The acknowledged destructive features, such as those of the "military–industrial complex," can thus be co-opted in such a way that they are not harmful to maintaining the system; on the contrary, they can serve in this way as an effective instrument in *salvaging* the status quo. The most obvious, atrocious features, whether in the domestic or international arena, are surreptitiously packaged as an "abuse" of an otherwise appropriate system.

"Abuse" in general, whether intentional or not, points to *individual* maltreatment and is often based on "individual ill-use" of a system. It conjures up notions of the exaggerated use of a system, blaming the individual committing the ill-use rather than the system itself. In this case, the desired effect by the people at the base in raising these problems as a challenge to the status quo is converted into its opposite by being co-opted. Let us take a few well-known, recent graphic examples. There are the well-documented tortures carried out by U.S. military personnel in Abu Ghraib and in Guantanamo. There is the assassination of Iraqi civilians from U.S. Apache military helicopters, as exposed by Bradley Manning, and the killing of other civilians in Iraq and Afghanistan over an entire decade. Other examples include scenes of U.S. soldiers urinating on the bodies of dead Afghans and the burning of Qu'rans by the U.S. military. Washington considers these and other "incidents" to be cases of "abuse" or "exceptions."

In March 2012, a U.S. soldier killed sixteen Afghans (nine Afghan children, three women and four men). Obama immediately pointed to the individual, saying, "This incident is tragic and shocking, and does not represent the exceptional character of our military" (Obama 2012b). By using the individual morality card, Obama not only exempts the U.S. and its military, but also strives to become the champion representing the outrage against these atrocities, thus co-opting opposition.

The same emphasis on individual morality and "abuse" is applied to domestic crises. For example, with regard to racist killings of African-Americans, Obama, like any other U.S. president, points to the individuals involved, avoiding the problem of deeply rooted racism in U.S. society and how the U.S. laws and the Constitution provide the framework for this to take place. There is the well-known case of the African-American youth Trayvon Martin who was killed by a white vigilante, George Zimmerman, in 2012. This is the tip of the iceberg, according to the Malcolm X Grassroots Movement's groundbreaking report, cited by author Paul Street. He lists eleven similar cases in 2012. The Malcolm X Grassroots Movement reported in July 2012, "We know of at least 120 cases of black people being killed by police, security guards, and 'self-appointed law-enforcers' (e.g. George Zimmerman) between January 1 and June 30th, 2012. That's 1 killing every 36 hours" (Street 2012). Obama, as the "post-racial America" promoter (as cited in the next section, "The Credibility Gap"), ignores this continual murder. He thus indirectly contributes to it.

In the same way, what were Obama's reactions to mass killings such as Arizona (Congresswoman Giffords' case), Fort Hood, the Colorado Batman massacre and the Wisconsin Sikh temple shooting? The mass shootings are continuing. The increasing international use of force by the U.S. is an extension of the domestic extreme violence inherent in U.S. society itself. There are calls for the individuals to be "brought to justice" and hypocritical weeping for victims and their families. However, in all the cases that occurred during Obama's first term, he never called into question the laws and the U.S. Constitution's Second Amendment on the right to keep and bear arms

(Killough 2012). The problem is rather the "abuse" by individuals of these laws that are otherwise deemed generally acceptable.

In all these cases of "abuse," the entire ruling class and *its* correlating political system are spared. In their place, the U.S. penchant for individual piousness takes centre stage. With this in place, the recuperation of increasingly anti-status quo opposition is ground through the machinations of competitive two-party U.S. democracy. This is the co-optation instrument par excellence stemming from the U.S.-centric bias. Through this process, the system recovers itself. In this sense, democracy in the U.S. *is* in motion. The system can then go on the *offensive* in realizing its ambitions, taking advantage of a created *image* of "opposition," swallowed by segments of the population. The elites consequently salvage widespread opposition in society. This recuperation, or co-optation, is hence one of the two essential components of U.S. democracy in maintaining the status quo.

The second main characteristic of the two-party system is indelibly linked to co-optation. This consists in what is referred to here as "pure presidential political opportunism." Running for president requires the utmost in political speculation. This selfish entrepreneurship does not necessarily apply to those who become candidates and eventually win seats in Congress, such as some members of the Congressional Black Caucus and various other representatives or senators. Nor does this appellation of pure presidential political opportunism pertain to all mayors and local municipal politicians. It is limited here to only the highest office in the country: president and commander-in-chief of the biggest economic power in the world (at the time of writing) and the strongest military force on the planet.

This pure presidential political opportunism arises from the fundamental principle on which the Declaration of Independence and the Constitution are based: the primordial and overreaching role of the individual. Directly related to this, one finds individualism fashioned on private property as the foundation upon which the entire economic, social and political system rests.

Unadulterated presidential opportunism is a political application of the economic notions of liberalism and freedom for the capitalists. It also highlights the concept of the American Dream and its related, isolated rags-to-riches stories, all of this serving as a cover-up for the real situation.

In this sense, it is instructive to conduct a serious examination of Obama's early writing (his first *New York Times* number one bestseller) regarding his political and personal life, his subsequent political discourses and an ensuing second book (his second *New York Times* number one bestseller). They illustrate that, from the beginning, Obama has flashed all the right signals (almost in code) and the appropriate buzzwords to the ruling circles. By so doing, he had clearly indicated that he is the person the oligarchy needs not only to maintain the system, but also to go on the offensive domestically and internationally. This is a rapidly changing world when the U.S. can no longer mark time or tread water. The U.S. certainly cannot continue with its tremendous loss of credibility within the U.S. itself and globally. However, this individual presidential political opportunism is carried out surreptitiously. While Obama is indicating his utility to the ruling circles, he is simultaneously reaching out to the citizens (or at least to the small portion who vote) through appropriate phrases and the suitable "look" fostered by him and faithfully packaged for sale by the media.

It is *not* a conspiracy between the presidential candidate as a speculator and the "military–industrial complex," which would have already chosen their president. Rather, it is the merger of the rising individual presidential political opportunism with the needs of segments of the financial oligarchy at a specific period during the election cycle. The candidate and the elites feel themselves out in the process. The White House candidate has to prove his or her worth, with those who have the wealth and the political power, along with the important sections of media following the lead of the elites, who eventually make their choice. By demonstrating his or her worth, the budding candidate is able to prove allegiance to the system and the needs of the oligarchy for the period in question. *At the same time,* the would-be candidate must be able to project an image. The potential candidate must be the person capable of mustering a certain amount of credibility among both the increasingly skeptical U.S. population and international public opinion. The two aspects (individual presidential political opportunism and the key segments of the wealthy elites) coincide at a certain appropriate moment in order to make their common move. It is the "invisible hand of the free market" applied to presidential politics. Consequently, the main power of the ruling circles, through their campaign's financial funding and mass media, designated Obama as their person when the service he could render became clear to them. A subsequent section examines the role of the "visible fist" in assisting the "invisible hand" of the free market, as applied to the Obama case.

Refusing to recognize how the U.S.-type of democracy actually works can lead to dangerous situations. For example, entire sectors of the population (trade unionists, some African-American and Latino activists, social activists, progressive academics and intellectuals, and people calling themselves liberals or leftists) were extremely dubious about the political system. However, many were ensnared into believing that Obama really represents change. This happened largely in the 2008 elections resulting in Obama's first mandate and repeated itself to a certain measure for the 2012 elections. The heart of the problem is the relentless and intrusive illusion that the competitive two-party system and its corollary, the "lesser of two evils," can actually work in favour of the majority at any given time. U.S. democracy, seen from this perspective, is working exceptionally well at this time. It is able to sustain itself in an incredibly successful manner through the well-hidden camouflage of the two most important threads of the cobwebs surrounding the U.S.-type of democracy: co-optation and pure presidential political opportunism, as the case study of Obama illustrates.

The Credibility Gap

There were innumerable indications by representatives of the U.S. ruling circles that the country had a major problem. This obstacle consisted not only of international credibility, especially after the Bush years, but also of its domestic standing.

Let us initiate this theme beginning with the international aspect. Zbigniew Brzezinski was a former National Security adviser to President Bill Clinton. Brzezinski wrote in his 2008 book *Second Chance: Three Presidents and the Crisis of American Superpower* about the "global alienation from America and worldwide doubts about Bush's leadership." He also expressed a pre-occupation with the "increasing linkage in Latin America between the rise of democracy [in reference to countries such as Venezuela] and the rise in anti-American sentiments." Brzezinski goes on to write about how George W. Bush "misunderstood the historical moment ... and undermined America's geopolitical position." Brzezinski was also apprehensive about Europe being "increasingly alienated." Latin America was "becoming populist and anti-American." He highlighted the "intensifying hostility to the West through-out the world of Islam [and] an explosive Middle East" (Brzezinski 2008: 175–77, 208). During the Democratic primaries in 2007, Brzezinski came out in favour of Obama versus Hillary Clinton. Brzezinski's reason was that Obama "recognizes that the challenge is a *new face* [and has] both the guts and intelligence to address that issue [world affairs] and to change the nature of America's relationship with the world" (Zacharia 2007, emphasis added). Another example of wide-scale fear was expressed regarding U.S. credibility in Egypt and Latin America. It consisted of what was declared at a high-profile panel held in November 2008 featuring the establishment's think-tank, the Council on Foreign Relations, whose representative said, "The election of an African-American had effectively countered propaganda about U.S. racism" (Council on Foreign Relations 2008).

Domestically, the integrity and authority of the capitalist system was a source of distress. The credibility gap is most evident among African-Americans. Michelle Alexander is an African-American civil rights advocate and Stanford (California) Law School professor. She published one of the most impressive books on U.S. society and recent history, bringing the readers into the stark reality faced by African-Americans (Alexander 2010).

The two-party system provides the opportunity for the elites to present one presidential candidate as different and better than the other. The credibility gap among African-Americans was a major preoccupation for the ruling circles before Obama's 2008 election. Obama, as an African-American, thus proved to be the ideal candidate to co-opt this dissatisfaction as manifested domestically and internationally. For example, domestically, Obama served to drastically reduce the credibility gap among African-Americans toward U.S. society. He proclaimed in his 2004 keynote address to the Democratic Convention that contributed to launching his career, "There's not a black America and white America and Latino America and Asian America; there's the United States of America" (Obama 2004b). He identified himself as the symbol of a "post-racist" society in order to gain some credibility in favour of the system. Like other aspects of the two-party system, it served as yet another illusion.[15]

Obama's First Experiences and Reactions

No person evolves in isolation from the ideas, values, concepts and trends in social thought that circulate in society and throughout world. Simultaneously, each person — whether a student, academic, trade unionist, social activist, political actor or other — also learns from personal experiences in society as he or she evolves and matures. As an individual goes forward in society and is invariably exposed to concepts vying for influence, he or she can be radicalized (in the sense of changed, altered, modified or being avant-garde) toward progressive values and actions. Conversely, a person can also move toward those standards that can generally be characterized as conserving the status quo (conformist or traditionalist), that is, stifling progress rather than propelling it. One can conclude that an individual can become a middle-of-the-road person, also at times known as being cautious, compromising, impartial, neutral or non-partisan. This "on the fence" thinking and action is in reality often a hidden defence of the conservative outlook. It is in effect another face with which the latter presents itself for the purpose of self-conservation and turning back the clock of history or hindering its advance. Or, as aptly summarized by the 2002 book title of noted U.S. historian Howard Zinn (1922–2010), "you can't be neutral on a moving train" (Zinn 2002).

Obama has the unique characteristic (for a president) of having been, before his decision to run for the Democratic presidential nomination, an exceptional and accomplished writer of two books. His first book, *Dreams from My Father: A Story of Race and Inheritance* (2004a), was commissioned after Obama was elected as the first African-American president of the *Harvard Law Review.* He graduated from Harvard in Constitutional Law. An academic specializing in African-American culture, Daniel Stein uncovers some of the motivations behind Obama's writing. Stein writes that Obama's goal was to "tell the story of his success as a black professional and academic" (Stein 2011:

15. See www.democracyintheus.com, "The International and Domestic Credibility Gap Facing Democracy in the U.S. Before the 2008 Presidential Elections."

2). According to *The New York Times,* writing in February 2008, it started to sell quite respectably right after its 2004 publication and, by 2008, was in its 81st week on the *New York Times* paperback non-fiction list. It surged in sales with the book endorsement by Oprah Winfrey and Obama's appearance on her show (Hofmann 2008).

Obama's earlier writings indicate clearly that he was already creating an image of himself as an African-American, while at the same time distancing himself from African-American militants active in the 1960s and 1970s. He also distorted Martin Luther King Jr. to serve his own program. This approach made Obama safe for assuring the general status quo in the U.S., at the same time making him the ideal candidate to put a lid on the continuing omnipresent possibility of revolt among African-Americans against racism and the system. Within this spirit of revolt, African-Americans tend to gravitate toward progressive and revolutionary ideas.

Obama downplayed the differences between Republicans and Democrats on international issues, promising to further promote the "free market" and "liberal democracy" in Cuba and Latin America. He skilfully used the illusions about the two-party system in order to simultaneously create the image of change while using the appropriate buzzwords and examples from history. In this way, with these code words, he indicated to the oligarchy that he was not only faithful to the American Dream but could carry it through for the interests of the U.S. elites better than anyone else.[16] Obama explicitly discarded any fear that may have existed among the dominant oligarchy that he would take a stand with those African-Americans who preferred revolt against the system. He clearly indicated that he was on the side of being a slavish servant of the ruling circles to make sure that African-Americans do not get "too much out of hand" and thus "keep them in check."[17]

Obama's two books sent the right signals to the ruling circles, with the vehicle being the two-party system. Through this system, he takes his own personal success for that of African-Americans. Obama equates his own fortuitous situation as proof of the American Dream's viability. However, what is the situation of African-Americans, of the collective? In his groundbreaking book *Slavery by Another Name: The Re-Enslavement of Black Americans from the Civil War to World War II,* Atlanta Bureau Chief of *The Wall Street Journal* Douglas A. Blackmon documents how slavery took on another name during the period covered in the aforementioned title (Blackmon 2008). This era included Amendments to the Constitution, such as the Thirteenth Amendment: Abolition of Slavery (1865) and the Fifteenth Amendment: Voting Rights (1870) (Constitution of the United States 1984: 83, 85). For her part, Alexander devastatingly deals with contemporary, post-World War II

---

16. See www.democracyintheus.com, "The Early Evolution of Obama's Personal American Dream."

17. See www.democracyintheus.com, "What Obama Did Not Like About Malcolm X."

U.S. society, which she calls the "new Jim Crow," indicating that King's dream is far from being accomplished (Alexander 2010: 246).

"Jim Crow" was the name of the racial caste system operating primarily, but not exclusively, in the border southern states, between 1877 and the mid-1960s. One of the features of the original "old" Jim Crow was mass discrimination of African-Americans, including lynching and incarceration. Its goal was to reverse the gains that came about with the abolition of slavery, including the right of African-Americans to vote. Jim Crow sought to undermine these constitutional amendments and reinforce racial discrimination and violent repression such as lynching (Pilgrim 2000).

Alexander cites Martin Luther King Jr.'s 1968 Poor People's Campaign as representing "a shift from a civil rights to a human rights paradigm." She quotes King as elaborating on this thesis in May 1967, when he said, "We have moved from the era of civil rights to the era of human rights.... We moved into a new era, which must be an era of revolution" (quoted in Alexander 2010: 246).

In 1967, King's process of political thought was based on collective action, whose conclusions are in direct opposition to those of Obama. The latter was going through his own development in contact with thinkers and action as expressed in his second book. Obama's evolution does not at all coincide, even in the remotest manner, with that of King. Significant here, for the focus of this book, is how Obama manipulated the King legacy for his own personal purposes. Obama thus gave life to the plausibility of the competitive two-party system for domestic consumption and as the model for the world.

King, as opposed to Obama, became an opponent of co-optation and all attempts to recuperate the movement in order to safeguard the status quo. King warned, seeming to foresee the hurdles, "No Lincolnian emancipation proclamation or Johnsonian civil rights bill [President Lyndon Baines Johnson's 1964 Civil Rights Act] can totally bring [African-American] Freedom." In this context, he spoke out on issues in the same address, cited above. His discourse indicated that he was increasingly groping for revolutionary ideas suited for the salvation not only of African-Americans, but also of all the poor. He was escalating his questioning of the entire system and seeing the need to strive for some kind of political power outside the established structures, still undefined at the time of his assassination: "Why are there forty million poor people in America? Moreover, when you begin to ask that question, you are raising questions about the economic system, about a broader distribution of wealth ... you begin to question the capitalist economy." King went on to conclude, "I'm simply saying that, more and more, we've got to begin to ask questions about the whole society." While he did not support socialism, he was increasingly open-minded in the last years and days of his short life. In the same address, he put forward his interpretation of the Cuban Revolution when he said, "Castro may have had only a few Cubans actually fighting with him up in the hills, but he could never have overthrown the Batista regime unless he had the sympathy of the vast majority of the Cuban people" (King 1991: 246, 249–50).

The democratic rights won, for example, by the struggles of the civil rights movement are of great significance. However, Obama is not a continuation of this or in any way a product of these democratic struggles, and is even less a catalyst to rekindle these battles. On the contrary, he has been recruited by a very important segment of the ruling elites to snuff out the possibility of these democratic movements erupting once again. He stands in opposition to Martin Luther King Jr. and not as an extension of the 1960s democratic struggles.

Obama's second book was widely circulated and promoted after his election to the Senate and before his nomination as Democratic candidate for the presidency. In the epilogue to this book, he responded to the hype being manifested after he was confirmed in 2004 as only the fifth African-American senator in history. He stated, "Some of the hyperbole can be traced back to my speech at the 2004 Democratic Convention in Boston, the point at which I first gained national attention." Obama goes on to say, in his next sentence, "The process by which I was selected as the keynote speaker remains something of a mystery to me" (Obama 2008: 418). Until this period, one can say that the "invisible hand of the free market," as applied to U.S. individual presidential political aspirations, was playing itself out. However, as Amin points out, to guarantee the proper working of the free market, this "implies that the visible fist ... must complete the work of the invisible hand of the market" (Amin 2009: 15). In a different context that is nonetheless applicable to this study, DuRand quotes a 1999 *New York Times* article, admitting that the "hidden hand of the market will not work without a ... fist" (DuRand 2012: 79). In the case of Obama, the "visible fist" to help the "invisible hand" consists of the efforts of his Chicago adviser David Axelrod. He had a Chicago-based consulting firm through which he became known for his capacity to get African-Americans elected and for his use of the media. He employed this talent to create the (at the time) unknown Obama into the image of Obama as an African-American "grass-roots" candidate, the quintessential face of the American Dream come true.[18] This provided a certain regain in validity to the two-party system.

As far as domestic issues, let us deal with those concerning the plight of African-Americans. Obama had to win the support of the most important segment of the ruling elites as a "responsible" African-American. In 2008, he delivered two presidential addresses of interest regarding race: one was a Father's Day speech and the other is known as the "Race Speech." He

---

18. See www.democracyintheus.com, "The Making of a 'New Face' for Democracy in the U.S. and Abroad."

used the opportunities to send subtle messages to the white-dominated ruling oligarchy that he, as a candidate, possessed a certain advantage. He could use racial stereotypes and foster dangerous misconceptions about a post-racial society much more effectively than his adversaries.[19]

An important corollary of being blinded by the workings of the combined concepts of recuperation and political opportunism is the firm belief in, first, the two-party system and, second, the "lesser of two evils" theory (choosing one status quo party over the other). These presumptions combined constitute the lifeline of maintaining the status quo and averting a crisis in the U.S. political system, because these concepts and related actions block people from going beyond the two-party system. These visions forever delay new forms of struggle and political action with the goal of eventually attaining political power, no matter how difficult it appears. Obama gave all the signals (as highlighted above) about his true conservative intentions, which were unfortunately not noticed by many people before the 2008 elections. However, his first term in office indicated his real design. So, what are the lessons to be learned about the two-party system?

Obama's Foreign Policy: The "New Face" and Cuba

One of Obama's initial important foreign policy experiences following his first inauguration in January 2009 was the April 2009 Summit of the Americas, held in Trinidad and Tobago. All 34 of the countries in the Americas were invited except Cuba. It was unilaterally expelled from the Organization of American States (OAS) in 1962 because of its Marxist–Leninist ideology, defined by the OAS as being against its democratic charter. Membership in the OAS determines the invitation list to the Summit of the Americas. However, in 2009, among the issues was Cuba itself, *the* most burning question.

Two days before the summit, countries of the Alianza Bolivariana para los Pueblos de Nuestra América (ALBA — Bolivarian Alliance for the Peoples of Our America) met in Caracas. Hugo Chávez said, "If they want to come with the same excluding discourse of the empire — on the blockade — then the result will be that nothing has changed.... Cuba is a point of honor for the peoples of Latin America" (*Granma* 2009). The next day, Obama's White House adviser for the summit, Jeffrey S. Davidow, held a press conference in which the Cuba issue dominated the majority of the journalists' questions. Some of the journalists were reporting for Latin American media. When asked if Cuba should be invited to the summit, Davidow responded, "No.... It still remains an undemocratic state. The United States still hopes to see change in Cuba that at some point will allow Cuba to rejoin the inter-American community." Another journalist enquired, seeing as Davidow

---

19. See www.democracyintheus.com, "Competitive Democracy Goes Far: Manipulation of Race."

mentioned it, "The U.S. is looking for dialogue, then why not include Cuba [in the summit]?" Davidow skirted the Cuba issue, simply replying, "It's a complex one, and I don't intend to dissect it here." With regard to the lifting of the Bush restrictions on Cuban–U.S. family travel and remittances to Cuba while disallowing travel for all Americans, Davidow responded, "Cuban Americans are the best possible ambassadors ... of our system when they visit that country" (Davidow 2009).

Several days later, on April 13, and only four days before the opening of the summit on April 17, the White House issued its announcement regarding the "series of changes" in U.S.–Cuba policy. (Note that Obama did not deliver the announcement to journalists, a fact that journalists would raise later that same day.) The main feature of the "Reaching Out to the Cuban People" policy change was to "support ... their desire to freely determine their country's future.... President Obama believes these measures will help make that goal a reality" (White House 2009b).

One correspondent's comment provides an indication as to why Obama did not appear for the press conference. The reporter stated, "The Latin American countries are going to be pressuring ... President Obama for greater normalization of relations [with Cuba]. Is this announcement today an attempt to inoculate the President and the White House a bit from this?" The response to this question was a denial (White House 2009a).

Obama's differences with past U.S. policies did not consist of opening up any meaningful change toward normalization of relations. His role, based on the illusions created regarding the two-party system, was to change the tactics because they had "failed to reach the same goal of regime change."[20]

One can deduce from all of the above that, despite the "new face" in the White House, the basic strategic policy toward Cuba has not changed. The blockade against Cuba, the attempts to continue its isolation and the refusal to have diplomatic relations are all part of the explicitly enunciated objective for more than 50 years "to bring about hunger, desperation" (Foreign Relations, Document 499) and force the Cuban people into submission. This policy in turn stems from the age-old (since its inception with the Declaration of Independence) U.S. foreign policy of expansion as the self-appointed "beacon of the world." What has changed are the tactics; this is the "new face." The devices constitute a swing away from the Bush policy against which the only Obama complaint is that it "did not work." This policy was a failed one because it did not succeed in bringing about the desired results for U.S. national interests. The sending of tens of thousands of Cuban-Americans to Cuba for travel purposes, as his spokespersons said, would be in the context of their expected function as the "best possible ambassadors ... of ... our system." Alongside this increased penetration into Cuba, there is also the

---

20. See www.democracyintheus.com, "Obama and Cuba: The Danger of the 'Failed Policy' Concept."

relatively large amount of funds in the form of expanded remittances to Cuban families. These cash resources are available to back up the "proof" that the U.S. system is superior by bringing aid to the "floundering Cuban economy." No one can reasonably stand against the reunification of families or economic assistance to them. The opening up of Cuba to academic and other similar visitors is also beneficial, as long as it lasts, because scholars and students generally return to the U.S. with positive assessments of Cuba. However, it would be naive to think that there is even one ounce of good intention, as can be deduced from the White House citations above. Cuba, for its part, has done everything to promote mutual exchange on various fronts, such as fighting terrorism, combatting drug trafficking in the Caribbean, immigration and other issues. The "changes" carried out by Obama are not "timid"; instead, they represent a rather *bold* attempt to try once again with *other tactics* to overthrow Cuba's political system. The position held by some that the blockade as it stood at the time of Bush "did not work" is a dangerous supposition because it opens the door for new devices that *will* work. It is similar to Obama's opposition to the war in Iraq when he was a senator. He said that it was a "dumb war," thus leaving us to wonder what a "smart war" is. The "new face," moreover, does not consist merely of the U.S.-type of two-party system co-opting opposition to the Bush policies, such as on Cuba, in order to continue with the same goals, safeguarding U.S. interests. Rather, what is unfolding with Obama is not simply a continuation or "more of the same" as transpired with Bush. Obama represents an *offensive* or an increase in the policies of domination, not merely maintaining the status quo. Along with travelling and remittances, Obama is leading other policies geared to subversion and other means in striving to destabilize and eventually overthrow the constitutional order in Cuba. This new assault could only take place with a "new face" in the White House.

With regard to Cuba, the facts show that the Obama administration is following through on the same long-term Bush policies and has the identical long-term objective as the current Republicans, even their most "hawkish" Cuban-American members of Congress. This policy goes back to the first days after the 1959 Revolution, that is, to overthrow the Cuban system. The only issue at stake is the tactics, as illustrated in the following statement by Hillary Clinton. She participated on behalf of the Obama White House in a March 10, 2011, session of the U.S. Congress House Appropriations Subcommittee on State, Foreign Operations, and Related Programs. In response to a Cuban-American Republican member of this subcommittee — who raised a question concerning the feasibility of the Obama changes regarding family travel and remittances in reaching the U.S. objectives in Cuba — Clinton stated, "We can certainly disagree about the tactics, but we have total agreement in what we are trying to achieve in terms of goals" (Clinton 2011c; McAuliff 2011; Terra Noticias 2011). The establishment press usually presents differences between the Republicans and Democrats on the issue of Cuba as being sharply distinct in order to keep the competitive two-party system illusion alive. However, behind the relatively closed doors in the halls of Congress, the discrepancies are more like friendly exchanges on the best tactics in order to achieve the common goal.

This is why the Obama campaign funding from the financial oligarchy and the major media endorsements were carried out to ensure his election in 2008. The elites clearly saw (better than the Cuban-American Republicans themselves) the need to renovate a series of tactics. The ruling circles believed that they would be more efficient in reaching the goals (in this case) regarding Cuba. The 2008 McCain–Palin Republican team and their Republican supporters from Miami did not obtain the elites' approval. They desperately needed new tactics and a new image to fix the Cuba policy, which was "not working." Herein resides the danger of being in any way blinded by U.S.-centric, preconceived notions that the U.S. two-party system can bring about change to improve relations with Cuba. At the same time, the Cuban government, for its part, is correct in attempting to introduce the possibilities of better relations with the U.S., a goal that the majority of the people in the U.S. desire. These contingencies, even if very remote, appear to a certain extent when these tactics change. For example, when Obama alters tactics, there may seem to be an opening in the eyes of U.S. public opinion, which Obama must take into account.

What did Martin Luther King Jr. have to say about the normalization of relations between the two neighbours? In his posthumously released essay entitled "A Testament of Hope," the Reverend offered an almost uncanny glimpse into the future:

> However, we simply cannot have peace in the world without mutual respect. I honestly feel that a man without racial blinders — or, even better, a man with personal experience of racial discrimination — would be in a much better position to make policy decisions and to conduct negotiations with the underprivileged and emerging nations of the world (or even with Castro, for that matter) than would an Eisenhower or a Dulles. (King 1991: 318)

Did Obama (having had personal experience of racial discrimination), who portrays himself as a follower of Martin Luther King Jr. and, indeed, as being his living heritage, ever take into account what King said about relations with Cuba? As the story of Obama has unfolded, one sees that he has turned his cheek on the personal experience of racial discrimination. Rather, from his relatively comfortable socio-economic position, he has viewed the situation of African-Americans as a trampoline for his own personal ambitions, leading him all the way to the White House. This is something that

King would never have done. From the height of the White House, this novel façade in Washington was able to make a dent in the Trinidad and Tobago Summit, even if not to the extent that was desired.[21]

Honduras: The "Reluctant Sheriff"

There was opposition in the Summit of the Americas from Venezuela, Bolivia, Ecuador, Nicaragua, Argentina and other countries to Obama's Cuba policy. However, the overall atmosphere in the summit itself, and emerging from it, was one of mitigated opposition. The conflict over Cuba was tempered by an atmosphere of "change" blowing over the summit, or a new era of positive relationship between the U.S. and Latin America. The summit result was in reality a compromise, since the final declaration was an offence to Cuba. As such, and for other reasons, the attendees did not sign it. The final declaration was made public as *the* summit document with no formal declaration against Obama's Cuba policy. It seemed that Latin America was waiting to see further actions from Obama, giving him the benefit of the doubt with regard to his administration's real intentions. In general, world public opinion on Obama's foreign policy at the time was in the wait-and-see mode — a very dangerous presupposition.

The downside of this proved to be the military coup d'état in Honduras and the manner in which it was carried through to the satisfaction of U.S. interests. It indicates the perilous results of being blinded by illusions regarding the U.S. two-party system. The major deception consists in believing that this system can bring about a change by offering one candidate who is fundamentally different than the other. Obama, in his second book, wrote, "There will be times when we [the U.S.] must again play the role of the world's reluctant sheriff. This will not change nor should it" (Obama 2008: 362). The U.S. is the "reluctant sheriff" in the sense that, in *words,* it is against interfering in others' affairs. However, if Washington judges at any given time that its national interests are at stake in a region or country, it *does* interfere in all manners possible, including supporting military coups d'état.

The coup in Honduras represents an example of Washington's goal to underhandedly continue interfering in and dominating Latin America. The situation in Honduras was complex; there were various U.S. agencies, military commanders and State Department officials involved. However, the Obama administration was also involved in the coup, confirmed by the 2012 WikiLeaks revelation. In 2012, diplomatic cables made public by WikiLeaks revealed that the U.S. Ambassador to Honduras collaborated in the coup and was in contact with the White House (LibreRed 2012).

Obama came in very handy. With his gift for words and the image of

---

21. See www.democracyintheus.com, "Change in Washington and Relations with Latin America: The Sharp Edge of Resistance Slightly Blunted."

"change" resulting from the two-party system, he carried out a high-wire act, balancing between two positions. One position was supposedly against the coup with the wording of this "opposition" changing often to evaporate into a meaningless posture. The other position, in real practical terms, *op-posed* the return of Manuel Zelaya to Honduras as the democratically elected president, which was, in reality, the litmus test of real opposition to the coup. With these tactics, Obama served the goal of striving toward overcoming the disastrous loss of credibility for the U.S. and reducing the anti-U.S. sentiment in the area. It was not the swashbuckling Bush-type attitude that saw the coup through, but rather the more acceptable new face of the "reluctant sheriff" with the appropriate Ivy League discourse. The facts show, however, that Obama fully supported the coup.[22]

In a similar manner as in Honduras, in June 2012, a parliamentarian coup was organized in Paraguay against its left-leaning, constitutionally elected president Fernando Lugo. Irrespective of whether the Obama administration was involved directly or indirectly, the coup was in the interests of the U.S. The very day of the coup, the head of the Paraguayan parliamentary defence committee met with U.S. military chiefs. The goal was to negotiate the establishment of a U.S. military base in Paraguay's Chaco region (Fuentes 2012c; Allard 2012).

The Occupy Movement: Breaking Out of U.S.-Centrism?

Obama was chosen by an important segment of the elites to recuperate U.S. foreign policy credibility and thus forge ahead with U.S. plans for world domination. The establishment media focused on the Republican Party and Tea Party opposition to the Obama health care plan in order to foster illusions about the two-party system. In this way, the mainstream media and both parties kept the critics with progressive perspective out of the limelight. For example, Dave Lindorff, a long-time investigative journalist in economics and other fields, concludes in one of his studies, "Obamacare was to be a plan constructed around the needs and interests of the health insurance industry, not around the needs of the people of the country." This explains why Obama received "truckloads of money from Wall Street" for his 2008 election campaign (Lindorff 2011). In a similar way, author and journalist Mike Whitney divulges that Wall Street and Obama's Wall Street economic team "fingered [Obama] as the pitchman for structural adjustments and belt-tightening." Even before his election victory, Obama talked about "belt-tightening" on Main Street, thus zeroing in on Medicaid and Social Security. "This explains why corporate America and big finance kept his campaign chest overflowing in 2008" (Whitney 2011). Political economist Rob Urie concludes in his investigation, "Barack Obama handed us over to the health

---

22. See www.democracyintheus.com, "Obama and the Military Coup d'État in Honduras."

insurers because doing so created the appearance of providing a public service while actually strengthening the hand of the insurance companies." Mitt Romney as Massachusetts governor "played the same game" (Urie 2012).

The Occupy Movement is not homogeneous and is changing constantly in each city. The relationships among the cities are continually shifting. A total of 7,293 arrests were made from September 17, 2011, when the first occupation was initiated on Wall Street, to June 14, 2012 (*OccupyArrests* n.d.). There are also official U.S. documents indicating that the Obama administration is directly involved in cracking down on the Wall Street Movement (Lindorff 2012). Despite this repression, the movement is raising the issue of political participation and socio-economic justice in U.S. democracy controlled by the 1 percent. However, in some cases, the movement leaves itself wide open to co-optation for electoral purposes by the Democratic Party and Obama. In other cases, there appears to be strong opposition to this. Growing hostility to co-optation is developing. For example, during the September 2012 Democratic National Convention (DNC) in Charlotte, North Carolina, to confirm Obama as their candidate in the elections, Occupy Wall Street organized demonstrations in collaboration with the local Charlotte Occupy Movement. While the Western media focused on the convention floor, they censored the position of the Occupy Movement. *Occupy Charlotte*, sharply criticizing Obama's domestic policies and his increase in wars and international violence, countered to the DNC, "We want a true democracy. A country by and for the People. Not a country by and for the corporations and the 1%. We cannot allow this two-party system and its corporate puppeteers to determine our country's destiny" (*Occupy Charlotte* 2012). In the context of the DNC, Occupy Chicago's statement published by *Occupy Wall Street* proclaimed, "Obama is no different." It went on to chide the ruling circles, "We are often told to select 'the lesser of two evils' without even the slightest hint of humor, and this election cycle is no different." The Chicago groundswell also exclaimed, "End Obama's War on the World's 99%" (*Occupy Wall Street* 2012: Document 14). Furthermore, *Occupy Charlotte* singles out the Obama administration for favouring the 1 percent, trampling on civil liberties, waging wars that have "caused the deaths of millions around the world … through a dangerously expanding imperialistic war economy," refusing to close Guantanamo prison, rejecting true universal health care, deporting immigrants in record numbers and using secret kill lists, and for its "documented systematic effort to quash Occupations throughout the country" (*Occupy Charlotte* 2012).[23]

In 2012, tear gas was used simultaneously against the Egyptian people and those in the Occupy Movement in the U.S. The reaction of the Obama administration was similar in both cases: it excused the repression in both

---

23. See www.democracyintheus.com, "Some Initial Reflections on the Occupy Movement."

Tahrir Square and in U.S. public spaces. Obama feigned sympathy for the Egyptian people during the January–February 2011 revolt that ousted Mubarak, while fully supporting the military regime. In a similar manner, in the U.S., Obama attempted to co-opt the Occupy Movement by "understanding" the "profound sense of frustration" (in his own words) as manifested by the movement (Obama 2011).

Amid this combination of force and co-optation, Noam Chomsky reminds us about one of the great weaknesses in U.S. society blocking change. He targets what the business leaders themselves call "fabricating wants." Their goal is to "direct people to 'the superficial things' of life, like 'fashionable consumption.' That way, people can be atomized, separated from one another, seeking personal gain alone, diverted from dangerous efforts to think for themselves and challenge authority" (Chomsky 2012b). The U.S. grass-roots movement today is challenging authority while striving to avoid being atomized and separated from one another.

The situation is very complex in the Occupy Movement. While some seem to be taking a strong stance against the dead-end two-party system, there seem to be lingering illusions among others about the "lesser of two evils." The situation is in flux and it is an example of democracy in motion at the grass-roots level, where people are experimenting with alternatives. The African-American progressives are carrying out their proud tradition inherited from all the previous struggles since the 1960s. These writers and activists have seen through the Obama-hype created by his media-image makers. For example, *Black Agenda Report* executive editor Glen Ford summarizes the 2012 DNC by listing all the activities that Obama has "inflicted on the nation and the world" over the years. He incisively warns (after also having summarized the real history of Michelle Obama), "The Obamas are a global capital-loving couple, two cynical lawyers on hire to the wealthiest and the ghastliest." Ford gets to the heart of the matter by contending, "The key to understanding America has always been race. With Obama, the corporate rulers have found the key that fits their needs at a time of (terminal) crisis. He is the more effective evil" (Ford 2012). If the influence of these African-Americans spreads, this could be the difference to turn the situation around. Such a new context would substantially widen the movement so that it becomes a massive alternative participatory democracy in opposition to the exclusionary U.S.-centric two-party system.[24]

---

24. See www.democracyintheus.com, "The Occupy Movement and Democracy in Motion."

The November 2012 Elections and Obama

In November 2012, Obama won the presidential elections. The campaign and the election results follow — and even confirm — the facts and analysis presented above in this chapter regarding the Obama case study and the historical context.

First, the voting age population (VAP) turnout rate, as discussed earlier, takes into account the millions of felons, who are in the majority African-Americans. The VAP also includes non-citizens, such as Latinos. They all are disenfranchised. According to the figures, the 56.9 percent VAP in the 2008 presidential elections dropped substantially in the 2012 voting, bringing it close to approximately 50 percent. The VAP 50 percent phenomenon has been in existence since the 1980s. For example, in 1988, George H. Bush (Bush Sr.) won the elections with barely more than 50 percent of the voting age population casting a ballot. In 1996, Bill Clinton became president with less than 50 percent of the VAP actually voting. George W. Bush won his first mandate in 2000 with approximately 50 percent of the voting age population going to the polling stations (McDonald 2012a). In 2012, Obama joined the club of being elected with approximately 50 percent of the VAP voting (McDonald 2012b).

Second, a most significant feature is that the "lesser-of-two-evils" prejudice based on the "competitive multi-party democratic elections" illusion proved to be as influential as the 2008 elections. The euphoria regarding the "change" image projected in 2008 still maintained itself in 2012 among some sectors of the liberals and the left in the U.S., and even internationally. Michelle Obama this time directly contributed to renovating this image that there is a difference between the two parties while at the same time using her platform to promote militarization.[25]

Third, this new stimulus from Michelle Obama provided the opportunity for Barack Obama to further create the chimera of the American Dream while promoting war abroad. His pledge to the elites was fully exhibited for all to see. In his November 6, 2012 victory speech, Obama affirmed that irrespective of colour, class or other distinctions, "you can make it here in America if you're willing to try." He avowed that America is "exceptional" because its "destiny is shared" among Americans who carry "common hopes and dreams," and uphold "patriotism" as "one nation one people." Obama pledged that his goal is for the U.S. to be "admired around the world; a nation that is defended by the strongest military on Earth and the best troops this world has ever known." He confirmed once again, "We have the most powerful military in history." He beamed about his Osama bin Laden exploit by reminding the world about the "SEALs who charged up the stairs into

---

25. See www.democracyintheus.com, "Michelle Obama: The Obesity Concern and Military Recruitment."

darkness and danger." The newly re-elected president concluded his speech by boasting that the U.S. is "the greatest nation on Earth" (Obama 2012a).

Given the economic crisis and other factors, are Obama's activities since 2008 and this 2012 speech a harbinger of things to come, such as fascism?[26]

The next chapter looks at other examples: Venezuela, Bolivia and Ecuador. They are the other Cuban neighbours, in addition to the U.S., that are considered in this book. What is the level of participation by the majority of people in these three political and socio-economic systems?

---

26. See www.democracyintheus.com, "The Red Herring in Two-Party Politics and the Danger of Fascism."

Chapter 3

Exploring Democracies in Venezuela, Bolivia and Ecuador

Venezuela: New Experiments in Participatory Democracy

The Bolivarian Republic of Venezuela, one of Cuba's neighbours, is located on the northern coast of South America facing the Caribbean Sea. For many decades, Cuba was virtually alone in Latin America and the Caribbean with regard to socio-economic and political transformations. Today, however, the region is stirring, and one of the most remarkable changes has come from Venezuela. The Bolivarian Revolution, headed by Hugo Chávez, took aim at key elements of the private sector to convert a portion of it — the privileged elites — in favour of the social and economic well-being of the people. Most important was the oil industry. Based on intensive field research, Iain Bruce provides numerous grass-roots examples from people's living experience in the *barrios* (neighbourhoods or, in some cases, also shantytowns). One such instance recounts his visit to a Caracas shantytown where he met some of the 40 people who were enrolled free of charge in the Ribas mission, "one of a series of adult education programmes paid for directly out of Venezuela's oil income" (Bruce 2008: 17–18). These and the many other missions that Bruce investigated exist because "the Bolivarian government had begun to reassert control over Venezuela's oil industry, the fifth largest exporter in the world" (Bruce 2008: 18–19). By initiating the process of democratizing the economy, this evolution had repercussions in the political system. It is seeking to convert Venezuela's exclusionary U.S. approach, consisting of the competitive two-party system, to a participatory democracy.

A great deal of literature covers the historical background leading to contemporary Venezuela. This also includes momentous events, such as the attempted 2002 U.S.-fostered coup d'état against Chávez, which was defeated in large part due to the masses of people. Aside from works in Spanish originating in Latin America and Venezuela, there are many others (Ellner 2008: 17–109; Raby 2006: 132–58; Wilpert 2007: 9–18; Buxton 2009: 57–74; Golinger 2006; Clement 2005: 60–78).

This section therefore concentrates only on those points covering this book's focus. Venezuela's Bolivarian Revolution broke out of the past by directly opposing the U.S.-centric two-party system, known as the Pact of Punto Fijo. According to this pact, the elites agreed to shuffling political power between the two main political parties while maintaining the status quo. Opposition to this political system grew from the massive discontent among the poor and the middle class. They were hurt by the deteriorating economic conditions overseen by both parties in the institutionalized two-party system (Wilpert 2007: 18–19).

Since Chávez's presidential election breakthrough in 1998, when he was elected for the first time, the Bolivarian Revolution has won every single ballot box contest except one (i.e., thirteen out of fourteen, including the October 2012 presidential elections).[1] It triumphed in the April 1999 referendum, in which it asked the people if they agreed to the need for a new constituent assembly in order to draft a new constitution. The overwhelming popular approval was the key step in the evolution of the Bolivarian Revolution. It concretized the main promise that Chávez had made in the 1998 elections.

The exercise of drafting a new constitution was not merely in the hands of the Constituent Assembly, but also in those of the people themselves. Consequently, because they were involved, the grass roots felt that they were part of the new Bolivarian Revolution. According to an interview with an activist in the process, the new government organized a vast campaign in neighbourhoods and workplaces. The people received assistance in procuring, reading, having read by others (illiteracy was still a problem) and making proposals for changes and modifications in the original draft. Containers with thousands of proposals were sifted through, with the result that 70 percent of the original draft was modified (Interview, Lor Mogollon 2009). One of the main features of the new Constitution was the promotion of participatory democracy, with popular input facilitated by the state. Indeed, the very drafting of the Constitution itself, prior to its adoption, illustrates this approach to democracy. The social movements presented "as many as 624 proposals to the Constituent Assembly, over half of which were incorporated into the new Constitution" (Ellner 2008: 177). Even a relatively critical U.S. political science observer wrote, for example, that "the constitution itself was subject to considerable input from civil society ... and afterward was mass distributed. Chávez never tired of talking about its provisions in his national speeches and *Aló Presidente*, his weekly talk program" (Hellinger 2005: 11).

The Venezuelan Constitution was the first in its history approved by the people, in addition to the actual consultation during the Constituent Assembly. Its clauses thus reflect this. For example, the new Constitution declares Venezuela to be a "democratic and Social State." "Sovereignty resides non-transferable in the people, who exercise it directly in the manner provided for in this Constitution and in the law, and indirectly, by suffrage, through the organs exercising Public Power" (Constitution of the Bolivarian Republic of Venezuela 1999). As examples of direct participation, the Constitution specifies "voting to fill public offices, referendum, consultation of public opinion,

---

1. The following information on the election results is based on data compiled by the author from the Consejo Nacional Electoral [Venezuela] n.d.

mandate revocation, legislative, constitutional and constituent initiative, open forums and meetings of citizens whose decisions shall be binding among others" (Constitution of the Bolivarian Republic of Venezuela 1999). It opposes privatization of the state oil company by requiring that the "State shall retain all shares" of the state oil company, Petróleos de Venezuela (PDVSA — Petroleum of Venezuela). The Constitution upholds the right of the state over PDVSA and thus the use of funds from oil. The document assures basic socio-economic rights, such as health, culture, education, employment and housing. Significantly, several articles focus on the recognition, promotion and protection of cooperatives for the purposes of economic inclusion and the decentralization of the state (Constitution of the Bolivarian Republic of Venezuela 1999).

The implication of the people in the constitutional process and the new Constitution's eventual ratification at the polls were major steps forward for the leadership and the new participating protagonists at the grass roots. This participatory experience contrasts significantly with how the U.S. Constitution came into being: exclusivity based on the protection of the unlimited accumulation of private property.

The new Bolivarian Constitution targeted the supreme and uncontested position of private property, the most important of which was oil, even though it had been "nationalized" in 1974 prior to Chávez. In reality, however, it had been controlled by the same oil oligarchy that had dominated it before the 1974 nationalization. Chávez brought the nationalized oil industry into the service of the population. He also nationalized many foreign-controlled oil fields. Based on the new Constitution, the Chávez government increasingly democratized the oil industry toward the needs of the people. The Bolivarians presented three laws in November 2001 that accentuated the oligarchy's loss of economic and political supremacy:

> The Land Law, which promised to institute a sweeping land reform of all idle lands of over 5,000 acres, the Hydrocarbons Law, which raised royalties on oil exploration by foreign companies [while the Constitution guaranteed state control over its oil company per se, subsidiaries and foreign exploration were still allowed to operate], and the Fishing Law, which forced large fishers to fish further away from the coast so that "artisanal" fishers would have a better chance. (Wilpert 2007: 23)

The removal of unlimited accumulation of private property from its pedestal did not mean that Venezuela cast off the capitalist system. The experiment (like others) is developing in a context where capitalist relations of production are still the dominant mode of economic activity (Ellner 2012: 105). This trial is part of twenty-first-century socialism, which is still vague and will continue to develop over time through practice (Ellner 2012: 97). The debate is inhibited by prematurely defining participatory democracy before the experiments further evolve. Likewise, there is no need to define twenty-first-century socialism while it is still in evolution. In fact, neither concept should ever be described *definitively*, seeing as they are in constant flux and state of experimentation. However, twenty-first-century socialism contains several main principles. First, it rejects the failed, highly centralized model of the Soviet bloc. Second, it opposes capitalism in its most grotesque form with all the importance bestowed on individualism, as it exists in the U.S. model. According to twenty-first-century socialism, within the context of opposing individualism, key sectors of private capital accumulation are limited. Instead, strong nationalism and opposition to the plunder of resources by foreign powers and multinationals place these resources in the service of the people. Social justice and solidarity in favour of the majority of people are replacing the devastating results of individualism. Third, this new orientation, combined with the call for a national constituent assembly, results in the capacity of Venezuela to develop its own form of participatory democracy.

The U.S. model can be compared with that of Venezuela, which is still operating largely under the capitalist mode of production and with an electoral system that is superficially similar to the one in the U.S. In the U.S., as long as the Founding Fathers' maxim of private property (as expressed today in the oligarchy) maintains its control, participatory democracy cannot emerge from the top down. It can strive to impose itself from the bottom up, as is the case with the Occupy Movement and other such stirrings.

The missions are one of the main vehicles through which the Bolivarian Revolution transforms individual private-property values toward the well-being of the people. These missions are best defined by what they actually accomplish, as expressed by someone in one of the missions who declared that Chávez "is helping us students with scholarships" (Bruce 2008: 17–18). Those most in need, about 10 percent of those enrolled in that particular *barrio* mission, received grants of about $100 per month so that, instead of worrying about daily income, they could concentrate on their studies.

Barrio Adentro is one of the most famous missions. It operates virtually throughout the country, with the help of more than 15,000 Cuban medical personnel. In the same *barrio* investigated by Bruce, he emphasized that this mission "for the first time made primary health care easily and freely available in most of Venezuela's poor communities" (Bruce 2008: 18–19). It is interesting to note the case of a *barrio* resident who said proudly in an interview that, as part of the local health committee, he does voluntary work to help the Cuban doctors (Bruce 2008: 18–19). This last comment illustrates that the people are not only on the receiving end of these missions; many are actively participating in them in one way or another. They are thus being empowered. They are politically conscious of the objectives of these missions and the source of funding.

The following missions were inaugurated between 2003 and 2006, and in operation in 2007: health care; literacy; primary, secondary and decentralized university education; communal land titles; human rights for Indigenous groups; assistance to small-scale miners while promoting environmental sustainability; subsidized state supermarkets; endogenous vocational co-ops; housing; land redistribution and reform; elimination of *latifundismo;* sponsorship and dissemination of popular culture in the arts; assistance to marginalized groups; social assistance for indigent mothers and female heads of households; reforestation; and environmental education (Hawkins, Rosas and Johnson 2011: 191). Exhaustive studies of six of the above-mentioned missions confirm that the missions "incorporate Venezuelans into a growing, parallel, state-sponsored economy that competes with the traditional, private sector and ultimately seeks to supplant it" (Hawkins, Rosas and Johnson 2011: 190). This is where the Bolivarian Revolution and twenty-first-century socialism are distinct from both capitalism and the defunct highly centralized Soviet bloc experience.

The different needs of the population necessitate the continual establishment of new missions in response. There are other missions in addition to those inaugurated until 2007, as discussed above. For example, in 2011, the Bolivarian government requested large sums of funds for the social missions, of which close to half will go toward the government's new housing mission. Another substantial portion is earmarked for the employment mission (Boothroyd 2011c). Again, in 2011, new missions were established "to provide economic help to pregnant women, families with children under the age of 18, and families with children of any age who have a disability" (Pearson 2011). A mission established in 2011 expands the number of Venezuelan senior citizens who have access to a pension (Boothroyd 2011a). The rapid extension and deepening of the missions in the last half of 2011 "could contribute to reducing the national rate of extreme poverty from 7 to 3.5 percent in the medium term" (Agencia Venezolana de Noticias 2012). A new mission came into being in 2012 that "aims to incorporate over 800,000 unemployed citizens into the labour market" (Boothroyd 2012a). Plans are under way for the implementation of other missions.

Most importantly in terms of developing the country's experimentation with participatory democracy, Chávez promoted the rapid spread of *consejos comunales* (communal councils), which involve between 200 and 400 families. Ellner concurs with the significance of this promotion, as it "committed the government to providing each one with $60,000 to undertake infrastructural and social projects." In addition, equivalent organizations at the regional and national level were established. By early 2007, about 20,000 communal councils were in place (Ellner 2008: 127, 128, 180). By February 2012, the government announced that 43,600 communal councils had been constituted (Santana 2012).

In February 2011, Wilpert (2011) reported, "Perhaps the most important new form of participation takes place in community self-organization, via citizen assemblies. This has resulted, since 2006, in the creation of more than 30,000 communal councils and dozens of agglomerations of community councils, known as communes." Based on a new law adopted in 2010, communes integrate communal councils into what can become self-governing areas or towns. In addition, along with social movements, the communes can actually get involved in the planning of the national budget and the eventual establishment of a Communal Parliament. The Bolivarian Revolution therefore is "willingly expanding civilian powers and helping to create a challenge to its own power" (Serafimov 2012).

Thus social missions are being established to bypass the private sector. The communal councils, for their part, are officially recognized and have access to state funds. This diverges from the entrenched local and state governments, which are at times seen as being corrupt.

In addition to the missions, cooperatives play a major role in economic decentralization. A cooperative tradition that predated the Bolivarian Revolution already existed in the country. However, with the new 1999 Constitution, a special standing and importance was accorded to this type of worker-controlled local economic entity. The co-op movement exploded after the 2001 Special Law of Cooperative Associations. In 2012, there were 60,000 workers' cooperatives (Serafimov 2012; Piñeiro Harnecker 2005). Cliff DuRand's perceptive remarks illuminate a path for the future economy. He states, "The promotion of worker co-ops is planting the seed of a solidarity economy parallel to the existing capitalist economy" (DuRand 2011: 191). Furthermore, he astutely brings to the fore that "the members assemblies of co-operatives are exercises in direct democracy" (DuRand 2012: 213).

With regard to co-ops, Marx can be quoted either in favour of or against them (Bruce 2008: 60). However, in this second decade of the twenty-first century, one has to look at the reality and go beyond citations taken out of context to coincide in some cases with preconceived notions. The Venezuelan experience shows clearly that co-ops do not harm or contradict socialism. On the contrary, they contribute to the economy and to the self-esteem and feeling of empowerment of the people at the grass-roots level.

In Venezuela, there exist tens of thousands of cooperatives, as well as entities that foster worker input in decision making in both private and public companies. These initiatives, consisting of communal councils and co-ops, exhibit a new experience in participatory democracy. Nevertheless, as Ellner points out, these experiments face major obstacles "and fall short of the expectation of the grassroots purists who celebrate the absolute autonomy of social movements and distrust the central government." However, he concludes that "the Venezuelan state has played a central role in giving form to the grassroots approach" (Ellner 2008: 180). Therefore, the example of Venezuela shows that there is no contradiction between the building of grass-roots instruments of empowerment and the central state.

In Venezuela, the co-op movement is at the heart of an orientation that, by its very nature, goes against the approach based on restricted and all-encompassing state planning. In addition, co-ops built from the bottom up, as in Venezuela, clash with the logic of capitalism. Bruce highlights an important criterion on which to reflect and elaborate. Implanting co-ops in a socialist strategy "is the result less of a momentary political revolution than of the maturing of a more gradual social revolution" (Bruce 2008: 61). This may be viewed as a justified plea to refrain from placing more emphasis on political victories at the polls than on the day-to-day organizing of co-ops and other local economic initiatives. Political ballot victories, such as the October 7, 2012, presidential elections, are, of course, crucial. However, groups of citizens collaborating on a daily basis to develop their local socio-economic entities in relationship to the overall socialist program lay a solid foundation for the defence of the Bolivarian Revolution and socialism. Electoral victories are accomplished within this context.

Ellner explores (in a chapter entitled as such) "the Chávez movement's top-down and grass roots approaches" regarding not only the missions, but also all other aspects, including the communal councils and the workers' co-operatives (Ellner 2008: 175). He concludes that the Venezuelan experience serves as a "corrective to the abstract analyses that have characterized the left's search for new models since the collapse of the Soviet Union. Chávez himself envisions Venezuela as a *laboratory* in which a trial-and-error dynamic" leads to new formulations of socialism (Ellner 2008: 175, 188, emphasis added). Most important to keep in mind is that Venezuela represents an *ongoing* "laboratory" experience. Taking into account socio-economic and political factors, it is a democracy in motion, with the participatory feature at the centre. This motion favours twenty-first-century socialism, defining itself as it develops. The dialectic relationship between the central political leadership and the local communal councils, missions, communes, co-ops and other such grass-roots organizations explains the Bolivarian Revolution's success at the polls. The participation by the people in these local activities (despite their weaknesses) fleshes out, in their minds and hearts, the nature of the new Constitution.

These advances, however, do not mean that everything is working out well. Nuanced conclusions come from on-the-spot political analysts with varying degrees of sympathy for the Bolivarian Revolution. They point to problems such as corruption, government bureaucracy and incompetence. In addition, many elected officials do not apply some important policies. Rather than improving the links between elected and electors, in certain cases, relationships are eroding. Furthermore, the problems of unemployment and insecurity persist. Proactive participation as a goal of Bolivarian democracy, such as the communal councils and other grass-roots efforts, suffers from shortcomings described by observers (Hellinger 2011: 29, 36; Ellner 2010: 7–12; Ellner 2011: 421–49; Wilpert 2010; Golinger 2010b).

The negative features in Venezuela's experience paradoxically also underline and justify the reasons for and the approach to the development of its grass-roots participatory democracy. While there are problems in the functioning of the communal councils, many of the obstacles found are not in the councils themselves, but rather in the electoral system. This is the case especially at the municipal and local state levels. Some Chavista supporters may get elected and wear the Bolivarian emblematic red shirt, but they in fact act as an obstacle. They dominate some of these instances. They are old-line thinkers who do not grasp the new participatory nature of the Bolivarian Revolution. Chávez led the central government to adopt the Communal Council Law in 2006. These councils receive billions of dollars annually (US$5 billion in 2007 alone), the amount depending on the achievements made. The funds allotted to the missions do not consist of "charity," as exists in the U.S. political system. According to this perspective, the elites are forced to concede handouts to the people in the form of social welfare and other programs. In Venezuela, in contrast, funds from the centre toward the grass roots actually serve as instruments of self-empowerment. These monies even go so far as to act as a buffer zone and self-protection against municipal and regional state governments. By using these funds properly, people experience empowerment in their daily lives. This participatory nature is the basis of democracy in Venezuela; it is a growing movement in the ongoing process of democratization. However, the crucial step toward democratization will have been achieved only once the modern-day oligarchy — holders of private property — is forced to give up at least part of its wealth and privileges toward the well-being of the people. By its very nature, this drastic change allows participatory democracy to take further steps toward overcoming the obstacles inherent to representative democracy. Yet, one has to recognize that, in the case of Venezuela, there are elections and representatives, and that this aspect of the political system is set in a wider context that includes daily participatory initiatives.[2] It is important to keep in mind Chávez's insistence on decentralized missions and communal councils as an attempt to bypass the central government and its local tentacles. The constant effort to weaken the local state apparatus can be attributed to the fact that many local "Chavistas" were such in name only.

"The community councils are an effort to bypass the state apparatus and local officials by putting decision-making power in the hands of the people at

2. Errol Sharpe was kind enough to share with me these observations based on his 2011 fact-finding trip to Venezuela.

the grass roots" (DuRand 2011: 191). Chávez directly says so, as evidenced in the announcement of the government financial grants to the communal councils for the year 2007 (one year after the adoption of the Communal Council Law). He is reported to have remarked, "As the Communal Councils spread they will also deepen and will become the new Venezuelan state taking over what he described as the old 'bourgeois state'" (Mather 2007). Along with co-ops and other forms of local initiatives, the main strategy for states such as Venezuela, according to DuRand citing Michael Leibowitz, is using "the old state, now in the hands of revolutionaries, to nurture the cells of a new state below." DuRand goes further into an area that Leibowitz did not treat. He points out, "Whereas in Cuba it took a revolution to create a socialist state, in Venezuela an attempt is being made to create the revolution within the old bourgeois state." Chávez furthermore is carrying this out "against the opposition of sectors of governance ... [and] against the old state and civil society." He is consciously increasing the councils' strength in order "to create a situation of dual power" (DuRand 2011: 190).

Bruce confirms this in another analysis on the co-op movement and co-management of larger workplaces in Venezuela. He considers it necessary to "make a leap from the democracy of the ballot box to the democracy of popular power" (Bruce 2008: 129). This statement applies to all forms of local initiatives, such as missions and communal councils. The comment deserves serious reflection if one is to advance further in conceptualizing participatory democracy. In Venezuela, there are elections and representatives. However, democracy is far more meaningful if the people at the base wield popular power on a daily basis. The process of democratization advances to the extent that real political power displaces representation. Bruce develops this "strategic challenge," which asks:

> how a project for social transformation, or socialism of the twenty-first century, which is elected into office through the mechanisms of the *old* state, can move beyond these institutions to build the structures of a *new* kind of public administration, based on direct democracy and the power of the organized population. (Bruce 2008: 170, emphasis in original)

In order to envisage a new kind of public administration based on participatory democracy, the new strategy points toward the notion of communes. Bruce asserts that the communes could bring together four or five communal councils that could replace the local parishes remaining from the old system, and thus could become "the basic cell of a whole new structure of communal power" (Bruce 2008: 171). These would evolve to communal cities, larger zones and upwards to a completely new national framework of communal authority. Bruce unapologetically acknowledges, however, that while Chávez denied charges that he was trying to bypass locally elected institutions to centralize his own power, the successful development of communal power "would indeed strip away the traditional functions and powers of local and regional administrations." Bruce is not referring necessarily only to *opposition* city mayors and state governors, but to some *Chavista* partisans (Bruce 2008: 171).

Thus one can see the paradoxical nature of the movement: the very forces inhibiting the growth of decentralized programs ("Chavistas" or not) contribute to the central state's need to work out daring new forms of participatory democracy. While often accused of authoritarianism, Chávez is in fact the one leading this attempt to decentralize the state and further empower the people with new forms of participatory democracy.

In order to explore the Venezuelan route of democracy and its electoral process, it is not sufficient to simply label it a competitive multi-party system as it exists in the U.S. To do so would represent a failure to appreciate the full extent of the transformational socio-economic and political processes under way. Nor is it appropriate, despite the long string of competitive balloting from 1998 to date (October 2012), to deny that it is a bona fide multi-party system. To negate the validity of the Venezuelan approach to this system amounts to a blatant acceptance of the U.S.-centric notion of democracy and elections.

The Bolivarian Revolution won at the polling stations in thirteen of fourteen occasions, almost all due to the programs developed at the base. The Revolution's anti-neo-liberal and anti-U.S. domination focus is the very basis for its raison d'être. The elections are thus a vehicle that drives the Revolution, and the grass roots are the fuel. Participatory democracy is a daily way of life for a growing number of people.

Venezuela's participatory political socio-economic democracy as well as its representative democracy are not "representative" in the sense of the U.S. approach. Representation through elections in Venezuela is but one aspect of the Bolivarian Revolution. Venezuela thus does not have a hybrid system composed of both participatory and representative aspects, the latter supposedly based on the U.S. model. We have seen in Chapter 2 how elections and representation really function in the U.S. In order to fully appreciate Venezuela's political system, representation there cannot be viewed with the superficial U.S.-centric optic. As will be seen in Parts II and III, dedicated to Cuba, this country also has elections and the representative aspect; these too, however, are part of the Cuban Revolution.

On October 7, 2012, the Venezuelan presidential elections took place. The role of the Bolivarian Revolution in these elections as such also distinguishes the voting in Venezuela from the U.S. elections. Contemporary Venezuelan elections show that there are many types of democracies and elections. These Venezuelan elections are participatory and can offer some important lessons for those interested in participatory democracy as a concept to be developed.

The Gran Polo Patriótico (GPP — Great Patriotic Pole) is a coalition of like-minded forces in favour of socialism whose immediate tactical goal was to win the October 2012 elections. With the latest GPP Venezuelan innovative move, the main feature is not representative democracy, but rather participatory democracy, even though the purpose is to elect the president as a representative. While the idea of a coalition goes back to the first 1998 elections, in which an alliance of political forces and political parties, the Patriotic Pole, backed Chávez in his successful bid to become president, the current GPP is different.

As a local activist in the formation of the GPP explains, the 2012 edition of the GPP is primarily a coalition of tens of thousands of already existing social movements and collectives at the base, unlike the 1998 Patriotic Pole. The latter was mainly a coalition of political forces. In an interview, Jessica Pernia, a local community activist, offers a lively and realistic account of the 2011–12 GPP. She says there is a need for "regaining the trust of the movements, something that has dwindled in the face of opportunism and reformism in the political spaces." Pernia goes on to say that the Revolution was losing "the trust of movements when it comes to political participation" and that "the biggest obstacle that we have to overcome is apathy." In this sense, they have to "overcome the current weaknesses" within the government and its institutions (Pernia and Pearson 2012).

When the GPP was formed in October 2011, it had registered 35,000 movements across the country — and it continued to grow. For example, in one area, these movements include revolutionary organizations, the Educational Community Socialist Front, the Bolivarian Front of Researchers and Innovators, a student movement, the rural workers' front, the popular educators' network, the women's front, local television collectives and others. While the communal councils register to join the GPP, the latter is focused on "organisations and social movements, given that the communal councils have their way of organising — through the communes, which group them together" (Pernia and Pearson 2012). The social movements, in contrast, do not have that possibility and thus have remained in isolation from each other. These social movements may have different political positions, but they have in common the cause of the socialist revolution. According to Pernia, the GPP is so open-ended and varied in its composition that the opposition is "trying to make people believe that the GPP is an organisation that is hostile to the PSUV [Partido Socialista Unido de Venezuela — United Socialist Party of Venezuela]." However, she continues, the GPP is organized to make proposals to Chávez (Pernia and Pearson 2012).

In fact, it was Chávez himself who called for the formation of the GPP. In October 2010, in appealing for its foundation, he said, "'The PSUV cannot be everything, no, it is just one part'" (Reardon 2010). In a public meeting in August 2011, he claimed that the GPP represents the "unity of the popular movement, as a tool for organisation and the transition to a new form of organisation from the base, as has always been the guiding principle pushing forward the revolutionary process in our country" (Boothroyd 2011b). In October 2011, one year after the initial call to form the GPP and a year away from the actual elections, Chávez called on all individuals, organizations and social movements committed to the Bolivarian Revolution to join the GPP to achieve a victory in the October 2012 elections. He said, "Get ready, all you social, political, patriotic, nationalist, socialist, humanist, and Christian movements ... but above all else the social movements." Chávez said that the GPP "will not come from the top down" but instead is to "surge from the roots, the base ... aimed at consolidating the Bolivarian Revolution for years to come" (Chávez 2011). While the GPP and the PSUV are far from being in opposition to each other, the GPP can even transform the PSUV by widening its outreach and improving its methods of work with the base.

Significant in the GPP movement, apart from the participatory nature of the Bolivarian intervention in the 2012 elections, are the actual long-term goals of this participation. First, the objective, in the words of one GPP organizer, is "*going beyond electoralism* based on bourgeois laws" to "get past electoralism and bureaucracy" (Pernia and Pearson 2012, emphasis added). It is easy to recognize the limits of the electoral system when viewed from a U.S.-centric perspective. In this sense of going beyond electoralism, the GPP basis for increasing participation, according to the vice-president of the National Assembly and a representative of the PSUV, is to "convert itself [the GPP] into a 'historic bloc' in Venezuelan politics ... 'that must definitively displace the hegemony of the imperialist bourgeoisie.'" The elections are thus part of a larger "'strategic, structural battle'" (Robertson 2012). In a phone call to then Vice-President Elias Jaua, President Chávez reiterated the opinion that the GPP should continue organizing beyond the presidential elections, forming part of a new political hegemony in the country (Robertson 2012). Thus the Bolivarian Revolution does not view the role of the party in the traditional top-down, "Leninist" style. Rather, the Bolivarians view the role of the party as an instrument in collaboration with the mass movements. This coalescence stimulates and educates the people so that they themselves can impose their political domination over the bourgeoisie.

Leading up to the October 7, 2012, presidential elections, the national and international pressures against Chávez and in favour of his opponent Henrique Capriles were extremely powerful.

Adding to this, Capriles presented himself as a "moderate," supposedly in favour of maintaining the social missions and explicitly projecting the image of Brazil's left-leaning Lula. This way, he hid the fact that he was actively involved in the U.S.-supported 2002 coup d'état against Chávez and that he comes from one of Venezuela's wealthiest families. However, in contrast to the image, his own party leaked a document signed by him, which laid out a "set of neoliberal rollbacks of social programs" (Hellinger 2012).

Despite the very unfavourable situation, Chávez received 55.25 percent of the votes, while his opponent garnered 44.13 percent. A full 11 percent separated the two, while participation hit a record high of 80.67 percent of registered voters going to the polls. The 11 percent difference was not as great as in the previous presidential election in 2006, when Chávez overwhelmingly won 63 percent against his opponent's 37 percent (Consejo Nacional Electoral [Venezuela] n.d.).

It must be taken into account that the conditions were not the same in 2012. While much has been accomplished by the Bolivarian Revolution for and with the people since 2006, there are still problems of bureaucracy and corruption. These roadblocks result in a cumulative negative effect on the population as time goes on. In other words, bureaucracy and corruption become less and less bearable over the period of several mandates, even though the positive achievements also accumulate. In addition, the anti-Chávez campaign was far more vicious in 2012 than in 2006, as the international oligarchy used the 2008 Obama card as applied to Capriles. He was portrayed as a "progressive" in favour of "change," rather than an openly pro-U.S. representative of the oligarchy. In a sense, the image created was a candidate running virtually within the parameters of the Bolivarian Revolution in order to gain some credibility. Capriles, it was proclaimed, would be able to do away with corruption and bureaucracy, whereas Chávez could not. Given this, the 2012 election results represented a major triumph.

In addition, the Bolivarian Revolution, through the GPP and the PSUV, won a majority in 22 of the 24 states, including in Miranda, where Capriles is governor. This positive Chávez polling also encompasses other traditionally opposition-held states where the Caracas conglomeration states are located, such as Carabobo and Miranda. Even Zulia, on the Colombian border and readily influenced by right-wing elements from that neighbouring country, went to the Bolivarians (Consejo Nacional Electoral [Venezuela] n.d.).

It was a momentous, historic victory for the Bolivarian Revolution and for Latin America and the Caribbean. The election results represented a resounding defeat for the U.S. and its allies not only in Venezuela but also in Cuba and the rest of Latin America who were rooting for Capriles. The principal reason for the victory lies in the social, economic and political work carried out by the Bolivarian Revolution. The majority of the people have a stake in the Revolution. They have become politically mature and able to distinguish, to a large extent, between truth and falsehood in the domestic opposition and international media that still dominate in Venezuela.

October 7, 2012, was the culmination of all the work and sacrifices carried out by the leaders and the grass roots since the 1990s. In the last few months, this heritage of effort was given a new injection of revolutionary fervour in the battle to win the elections. The building of the GPP as a broad front of all forces paid off. People were able to mount impressive activities in the street with up to three million people taking part in a demonstration of force in Caracas just a few days before polling day.

Chávez was elected president and, according to the accepted view in the North, as the presidential level "representative." Thus, from this U.S.-centric optic, the presidential position is merely an organic part of representative democracy as experienced in the U.S. However, like the PSUV as the main political force in Venezuela, he is part of the Bolivarian Revolution. This movement bears no similarity to representative democracy. In social, economic, cultural and political terms, the October 7, 2012, elections reflected one more crucial step in the democratization of the country. Venezuela's democracy in motion spread from the election results on October 7 to the official validation of the victory on October 10, when Chávez outlined the actions for which the majority of people voted. For example, he pledged "that his next 6 year term would mark a period of 'greater advance' towards the construction of socialism as well as 'greater achievements and greater efficiency in this transition from capitalism.'" Furthermore, he "argued that the project of 21st century socialism in Venezuela was something that must be constructed 'in the long term,' and promised that his government would try to respond to citizen's [*sic*] concerns over the next 6 years." In addition to outlining macro-economic policies involving the development of entire areas of Venezuela in collaboration with other South American countries, he is also seeking to build on the success of the missions in order to improve the lives of the people. He termed the deepening of the mission experience as "'micro-missions,' which according to the president will be implemented at a local level by organised communities and focused on those most in need." Chávez asserted, "'They will be applied in towns, regions, factories, schools and the different places where they are needed'" (Boothroyd 2012b).

Of utmost significance is Chávez's admission that there are needs for major improvements in the action and attitude of the government. Chávez said,

> We are obliged as a government and as the state to speed up the administration of efficient responses and solutions to the thousands and thousands of problems that the Venezuelan people still suffer from. We are obliged to be more efficient, precisely so we can continue every day with greater force. (quoted in Boothroyd 2012b)

In this sense, he argued, "In order for these projects to be effective, they must be rooted in grassroots organisation. 'We must keep giving *power to the people*, that is the solution, it's not the power of the bureaucracy and elites that is going to solve the problems of the people'" (Boothroyd 2012b, emphasis added).

This objective is aided by the work already accomplished with the missions, the communal councils and the flowering of the communes toward the top, as well as cooperatives. It is as if the scaffolding has been built, but has yet to be further solidified while ridding itself of the weak links in the structure in the forms of bureaucracy and corruption. Chávez's insistence on the need for more efficiency, as outlined above, is directly linked to, as he emphasizes, opposing "the power of bureaucracy and the elites." Revolutionaries, their organizations and grass-roots involvement have their own features that go beyond the limited, stultified structures of the multi-party political system. This is where participatory democracy absorbs representative democracy. The latter's very nature undergoes a metamorphosis in the process, and thus Venezuela's democracy in motion continues to supersede representative democracy. This motion brings democracy to another qualitative level. Thus in Venezuela, while the political and electoral structures may appear on the surface to resemble representative democracy, it is no longer so. The October 7, 2012, elections put another nail in the coffin of representative democracy based on the U.S.-centric notion.

Nonetheless, the U.S. and its followers cannot be expected to sit back. It must be noted that the oligarchy still exists in Venezuela, even though it has been greatly weakened by the Bolivarian Revolution; they have their own representatives in the form of political parties and individual elite representatives, such as Capriles. The revolutionary process in Venezuela came about from within the capitalist system rather than confronting it head-on. It was the most viable avenue open under existing conditions in Venezuela.

Capriles played upon weaknesses in the government and the PSUV in order to portray himself as the candidate who would maintain the missions while getting rid of bureaucracy and corruption. The majority of the people were not deceived. However, these problems have to be dealt with if the Bolivarian Revolution is to succeed fully.

The exercise in exploring Venezuela's democracy constitutes an avenue to widen horizons on how to view political systems — including the Cuban one — that do not conform to U.S.-centric notions of the two-party system of representation. It also provides some paths to explore for those active in the U.S. grass-roots movements who are seeking alternatives in participatory democracy.

Bolivia's Democracy in Motion: On the Edge

The furthest of Cuba's neighbours under consideration, the Plurinational State of Bolivia, is a landlocked country located in central South America. For the historical context of contemporary Bolivia, including the 1952 Revolution, which was one of the most important in Latin America, as well as the water and gas wars and resistance against U.S. coca leaf policies, see Sven Marten (2011: 13–154) and Waltraud Q. Morales (2012: 49–65).

Before the arrival on the political scene of the Movimiento al Socialismo (MAS — Movement Towards Socialism), led by Evo Morales, Bolivia had a political system somewhat analogous to the Pact of Punto Fijo two-party system in Venezuela, which was undermined by the Bolivarians in 1998. The old Bolivian political system is characterized by two leading academic authorities, John Crabtree and Laurence Whitehead, as follows: "Alternating in power and pursuing similar policies, traditional parties came to be seen more as client machines distributing state patronage.... In Bolivia the genesis of ... [MAS] provided a new mechanism for articulating social discontent" (Crabtree and Whitehead 2008: 107). It was an umbrella organization (but had acquired electoral experience even before 2005) (Crabtree and Whitehead 2008: 107). Party rule was "venal and corrupt," and so Morales's 2005 victory was a "break with the past," "a more direct and participatory scheme of democratic representation" (Crabtree in Crabtree and Whitehead 2008: 1). The MAS arose from the grass roots based on an unconventional experience of direct democracy that already existed in Bolivia outside the normal channels of protest.

The 2005 ballot box accomplishment was significant in the context of the region's five centuries of history. A campaign slogan of the MAS was "de-colonize Bolivia after 500 years of oppression" (Oviedo Obarrio 2010: 98). The election of Morales "reflected the end of a particular Andean form of apartheid that had marginalized the majority of the indigenous population since the Spanish Conquest" (Kohl 2010: 107). For further information on what the 2005 election victory represents, see Fernando Oviedo Obarrio (2010) and Carlos Arze Vargas (2008).

It is pertinent to note the revolutionary manner in which the MAS, its leadership, the *cocalero* and the miners' unions, as well as other grass-roots associations mobilized the masses of people in preparing for the 2005 elections. Many of the latter were illiterate and needed assistance to register and vote. This rise to power of the victims of 500 years of apartheid and complete exclusion put an end to the old-party system, which had been festering for quite some time. The direct participation of the people from the bottom up gave them a real and deserved sense of self-empowerment. The 2005 elections were a crucial first step toward the democratization of the Bolivian political system. In order to achieve success, among other things, the union *cocalero* activists had to overcome a major obstacle by teaching members who were illiterate how to vote. Morales, in addressing a Cochabamba coca union at an electoral preparation meeting, said, "You defended coca, with this experience defending water, then gas, and all natural resources. *Cocaleros* are also from the nations of Aymara, Quechua and Guaraní, the rightful owners of this land." The content of the MAS election theme song appealed for the end of capitalism, in favour of socialism and against Yankee imperialism, constituting another characteristic of the movement (*Cocalero* DVD).

The 2005 elections resulted in Morales winning in a surprising first-round bid with 53.72 percent to the opposition's 28.62 percent. The voter turnout of 84.22 percent was exceptional in a country where so many Indigenous people, a high percentage of whom are illiterate, were voting for the first time, even though voting in Bolivia has been compulsory since the 1952 Revolution. This principle of compulsory suffrage was incorporated into the 2009 MAS-led new constitution (Constitution of the Plurinational State of Bolivia 2009). However, the increasingly high voter turnout since the first Morales victory is not the result of a compulsory vote. For example, observers from Peru (Asociación Civil Transparencia 2005) indicate that the government has traditionally not employed the sanctions accorded by law; in general, the "compulsory" vote is not applied. This is confirmed by the International Institute for Democracy and Electoral Assistance (International IDEA 2009). In the same elections, MAS elected 84 percent of the senators and 55 percent of the Chamber deputies (Tribunal Supremo Electoral n.d.).

One of the main themes of the 2005 MAS electoral campaign was the need for a constituent assembly and a new constitution. A general, progressive and revolutionary current among intellectuals and the *campesinos*/Indigenous peoples for a new constitution had been developing since 1991. This resulted, after the 2005 MAS electoral win, in a Constitutional Assembly convoked in 2006. In July 2006, the MAS won the majority of Constituent Assembly seats, but not the two-thirds majority required to rapidly approve a new draft constitution (Oviedo Obarrio 2010: 99). In the Constituent Assembly, the MAS majority included Indigenous peoples as the greater part of their delegation (Roca 2008: 80). In addition, the gender proposal put forward by Indigenous social organizations resulted in the election of an equal number of men and women from the predominantly Indigenous regions of the Andean highlands. "These gender complementarities (*Chacha Warmi* or man/woman) is [*sic*] conceived in accordance with customs and practices employed in many indigenous districts" (Barragán 2008: 32).

These delegates to the Constituent Assembly wrote the new Constitution. This situation represented a major leap forward from the previous circumstances of exclusion for five centuries to the present day, when Indigenous peoples are drafting their own modern constitution. People writing their own constitution and ratifying it in a popular referendum is one of the hallmarks of a democracy. This experience is especially indicative of the move toward democratization as an ongoing process. The new Constitution as such does not change the system, but it opens the door for major transformations. This was seen in Venezuela, whose new Constitution, which people participated in drafting and approving, provides the scaffolding to, later on, flesh out twenty-first-century socialism. This breakthrough in Bolivia both facilitated and accompanied the democratization of the society as a work in progress. It is therefore not an exaggeration to declare, "Because of the high level of participation and expectations from many spheres of society, the constituent assembly is a major turning point in Bolivian history" (Rousseau 2011: 5). At the same time, if one is to be consistent with the application of the "democratization" norm, one also has to recognize that "Bolivia's constitution has always been a work in progress.... The 1952 Revolution was one democratic watershed." At that time (1952), many democratic rights were recognized (Albro 2010: 74). However, the 2009 Constitution went far beyond anything that previously existed in Bolivia. The delegates elected to the Constituent Assembly were directly involved in the writing of the new Constitution. Given the Constituent Assembly's composition and the manner in which it was elected, it was as if the grass roots constituted itself into this assembly. The proceedings were a public event and thus directly contributed to the evolving culture of a participatory democracy.

During the course of the Bolivian Constituent Assembly proceedings, Morales had to overcome a recall referendum on August 10, 2008. The recall referendum was originally suggested by Morales himself in order to contest the stalling tactics of some local departments (states). They favoured autonomy or separate states. Events took place in the midst of a bizarre, long and complicated Constituent Assembly, an explanation of which is beyond the focus of this section on Bolivia. At stake in the recall were the positions of both Morales as president and Álvaro García Linera as vice-president, as well as most departmental governorships. The No percentage vote in the Referendum — and thus an approval for Morales and his vice-president to continue their mandate — actually increased over the percentage garnered in the original presidential elections, which had taken place a little more than two years before the recall (Tribunal Supremo Electoral n.d.).

In 2009, the new Constitution was ratified by more than 61 percent in favour and less than 39 percent against (Tribunal Supremo Electoral n.d.). The February 7, 2009, Constitution of the Plurinational State of Bolivia contains many important features, but only those necessary for the focus of the book are addressed here. First, the Constitution takes aim at the most savage manifestation of individual private property as illustrated in Bolivia. The Constitution thus asserts that hydrocarbons (gas and oil) are "the inalienable and unlimited property of the Bolivian people" and that "water constitutes a fundamental right for life." Similarly, cultural patrimony provides for protection of ancestral coca. This socialization or democratization of the economy is further entrenched by enshrining the Indigenous concept of *Pachamama* (Mother Earth) (Constitution of the Plurinational State of Bolivia 2009).

This Indigenous value goes beyond and perhaps even predates Western notions of economic considerations for a democracy, or power of the people as defined by Greek tradition. Bolivia and Evo Morales are even putting forward an international demand, on behalf of Indigenous peoples, for the Universal Declaration on Rights of Mother Earth. Chomsky points out, "The demand is ridiculed by sophisticated Westerners." He advocates instead, "We can acquire some of the sensibility of the indigenous communities" (Chomsky 2012b). *Pachamama* indicates the dialectic relationship of the environment (including resources) and the people. They are interdependent. *Individuals* cannot possess the environment or its fruits and products independent of the people's needs. By its very nature, Mother Earth is social and belongs to the people. Once one removes the notion of the right of powerful individuals over natural resources, in favour of the well-being of the majority, the possibility of participatory democracy prevails. This replaces the truncated and exclusionary U.S.-centric democracy that consists of rotating political parties representing competing elites. Thus, based on these incursions against the unlimited accumulation of private property, the political system as such can strive toward democratization. For example, the new Bolivian Constitution declares that sovereignty resides in the people (which the U.S. Constitution does *not* prescribe). Direct participatory democracy and delegated representatives can thus together exercise democracy. In addition to direct participative democracy and representative democracy, there is a third form of democracy. It is, according to the Constitution, "communitarian" based on the "norms and procedures of the indigenous ... farmer nations and people" (Constitution of the Plurinational State of Bolivia 2009). This communitarian democracy is similar to what is known in the North as participatory democracy.

In the first four years of the Morales government (2006–09), in addition to working out the new Constitution, there were improvements in education, the building of new schools and the implementation of a more accessible higher education system. The country made strides in the health care system and achieved a 50 percent reduction of the foreign debt. It introduced an increase to the minimum wage by more than 20 times compared with the previous administration. There was an increase in foreign investment, twice as much job creation and a higher GNP. The reserves increased more than six times over past administrations (Parada 2010). Moreover, in March 2011, Bolivia's government announced another 20 percent increase of the minimum wage and a 10 percent increase of salaries in the fields of teaching, health, armed forces and police (Agencia Púlsar 2011). In August 2012, Morales was able to announce that, since 2006, one million Bolivians have escaped poverty, with a global reduction in poverty rate of 19 percent. This success has arisen from the new policies based on the constitutional recognition of Indigenous territories for agriculture and the production of food (*Europa Press* 2012).

Because of these socio-economic improvements and the increasing empowerment of the people through the drafting and approval of the new Constitution, the Morales ticket overwhelmingly won the December 6, 2009, elections. They triumphed with the highest presidential vote in Bolivia's history, over 64 percent versus less than 27 percent for the opposition candidate.

The voter turnout rate for the presidential and legislative elections was 94.55 percent (Tribunal Supremo Electoral n.d.). According to a United Nations agency, the compulsory vote is "not necessarily the cause" of the increasingly high voter turnout rate (Espejo 2010). Morales's mandate lasts until 2015.

In his January 2010 election inaugural speech, Morales said, "We will also focus on industrialization, not just gas and oil, but also lithium, which requires millions in investments that will be opened to private partners" (quoted in Parada 2010). His vice-president, García Linera, affirmed that the 2009 [elections victory] will "give way to an Integrated State with a socialist horizon, somewhere between a Colonial State and the new Plurinational State we are building" (quoted in Parada 2010). This is Bolivia's challenge. It is a test to create an ongoing symbiosis between a plurinational state that assures the protection of the Indigenous majority's rights and economic development based on expressed aspirations toward modern notions of socialism.

In addition to this colossal, domestic task, one cannot discuss Bolivia's democracy in motion without addressing the role of the U.S., just as the case with Venezuela. This interference has increased since Morales became president in 2006. According to Morales, Washington — or, at least, the U.S. Embassy in Bolivia — was involved in the 2008 attempt to destabilize some eastern regions where white (non-Indigenous), right-wing leaders dominate in some cases with the collaboration of Indigenous political activists. As a result, Bolivia expelled the U.S. ambassador for his alleged involvement. He is an expert with accumulated experience in a series of separatist activities in Kosovo. In April 2009, a similar destabilization and assassination plot was uncovered (Friedman-Rudovsky 2008; Barrionuevo 2009; Carroll 2009). The U.S. denies its involvement, but as seen in Chapter 1, it was directly involved several months later in the June 2009 Honduras coup d'état and is not opposing the 2012 Paraguay coup.

Since 2001, the U.S. presence has been evident in Bolivia through its democracy promotion plan in that country. The U.S. is interfering in the conflict over the Territorio Indígena y Parque Nacional Isiboro-Secure (TIPNIS — Isiboro-Secure National Park and Indigenous Territory) highway project, which would carve through Indigenous territory.[3]

The accusation of U.S. interference in the TIPNIS conflict through Indigenous organizations is well founded. However, a close observer of the Bolivian scene concludes that the issue of the highway and the consultation process may prove to be

> an important step in broadening the necessary debate on how to flesh out the constitution's provisions on indigenous autonomy and land reform. This entails dealing with complex issues, such as how best to tackle poverty and develop Bolivia's economy while protect-

---

3. See www.democracyintheus.com, "U.S. Democracy Promotion in Bolivia."

ing the environment and the rights of indigenous communities. (Fuentes 2012a)

This is the essential issue. In addition, the new Constitution based on the spirit and letter of participatory democracy in fact mitigates heavy-handed activities such as those that occurred at TIPNIS. The Bolivian process represents a difficult balancing act between anti-neo-liberal, sovereign economic development and the rights of the Indigenous peoples, *campesinos* and workers. Both of these considerations stem from the recent Constitution. It is an ongoing problem testing the burgeoning Bolivian democracy as an example of the new democratization movement. Bolivia has to experiment with its democracy and socio-economic development in favour of the majority, who are Indigenous peoples. It is relatively easy to criticize the Morales government from both the left and the right, especially since some Indigenous organization leaders at the grass-roots level are involved in opposing Morales. However, this simplified approach does not take into account that Bolivia is a democracy in motion, a work in progress that has just begun, still fleshing out its new Constitution as it progresses.

The future of Bolivia's fledgling participatory democracy depends on the capacity of the MAS and its leadership to adjust and resist pressures and interference from the right-wing, tied to U.S. interests. It also has to refuse to go along with some segments of the left, nationally and internationally, that simplify the situation by viewing the Bolivian democracy as a static structure. U.S.-centric prejudices on democracy completely obliterate the value of political participation by the people as an ongoing democratization process. Only upon making the first moves consisting of real participation can other steps toward this long-term goal of democratization be taken.

In the context of such a democracy in motion, the groundbreaking phase consisted primarily in involving the people in drafting a new Constitution. Linked to the initial stage, there was also the need to convert the formerly omnipresent property rights of the privileged elites from Bolivia and the U.S. into the common wealth of the people. Political implication allows for a democracy and provides the ability to change, adjust and improve its participatory nature. It must take place along with independent socio-economic development based on the long-term vision of twenty-first-century socialism. This also includes the capacity, as exhibited by the political leadership of Morales and García Linares, to learn from mistakes and adjust accordingly. For example, in April 2012, Bolivian Indigenous peoples participated in the commissions established by the Morales government for consultation on TIPNIS. These commissions had the mandate to decide on the construction of the highway and perspectives of development for the Indigenous communities (Presno 2012). This is in conformity with the Constitution that defends a democracy that is "direct and participative," including the right of "prior consult" (Constitution of the Plurinational State of Bolivia 2009). In October 2012, Morales announced that 45 of the 46 communities consulted through these commissions agreed to the construction of the highway and that the project is now under way (TeleSUR 2012). Therefore, the participation of members elected to the Constituent Assembly in the public drafting of the new Constitution also armed the assembly members and the peoples on how to use the Constitution.

Participatory democracy is not just bottom-up; it also has to be top-down. In this case, it is the close, sincere relationship of the Morales government with the people, an anomaly from the point of view of U.S.-centric, preconceived notions of leadership.

U.S. academic Waltraud Q. Morales (2012) writes that, as long as the social and Indigenous movements continue to support the Constitution's provisions for "land reform and socio-economic redistribution and development," the Morales government "may consolidate its gains in the years to come." She says that Bolivia today remains a country "of instability and conflict, where civil discord has been inherent to democratization and social and revolutionary change." She concludes that the Indigenous peoples and social movements "are an integral part to that ongoing process" (Morales [Waltraud Q.] 2012: 84). Bolivian democracy seems to be on edge due to the strains, some genuine and others flamed by the U.S. and its benefactors in Bolivia. This dynamic makes for a democracy that is necessarily in motion.

Ecuador's New Constitution:
Sumak Kawsay and Participatory Democracy

Cuba's South American neighbour the Republic of Ecuador is bordered by Colombia to the north, Peru to the east and south, and the Pacific Ocean to the west. Ecuador's Indigenous tradition is largely based on *sumak kawsay*, an Indigenous Kichwa concept or principle that roughly means *buen vivir* ("a good life" or "to live well"), not merely "living better." (Kichwa is the Ecuadorian variant of the pan-Andean Quechua language, the only one spoken on a virtually countrywide basis.) *Sumak kawsay* together with pluri-nationalism and environmental protection are three characteristics (among others) of the new Constitution, drafted in the wake of Rafael Correa's electoral victory at the polls.

After Correa was forced to resign in 2006 as minister of economy in a neo-liberal government, he founded the new Alianza PAIS — Patria Altiva i Soberana (Proud and Sovereign Fatherland Alliance) for the elections to be held that year. Running for president, he arrived a very close second in the first round. However, he easily defeated his opponent in the second round, on November 26, 2006, by a score of 56 percent to 43 percent (Consejo Nacional

Electoral [Ecuador] n.d.). One of Correa's main planks was the convening of a new Constituent Assembly to formulate a new constitution in order to found the country anew. The issue of the Constitution and its aftermath are the central points in this section of the chapter, given the underlying tension that prevailed at the time the Constitution was drafted. These strains, related to the level of real participation in the new democracy, are still present today and will probably continue in one form or another in the near future.

In April 2007, following up on Correa's promise, a referendum was held to ask citizens if they agreed to organize toward a new constitution by convoking a Constituent Assembly. More than 80 percent of the registered voters approved its convocation. In the elections for the Constituent Assembly, Correa's new political formation triumphed with a majority of seats, based on close to 70 percent of the vote, while the opposition, led by Lucio Gutiérrez, garnered less than 7 percent. Both these victories at the polls were largely due to support from the very active Indigenous communities (Becker 2011: 49). For further elaboration on the role of Gutiérrez presenting himself supposedly as part of the Latin American "pink tide," along with da Silva (Lula) and Chávez, but in reality later exposed as a representative of the conservative oligarchy and the U.S., see Marc Becker (2012: 13, 120–1). As will be seen later in this chapter, there are legitimate controversies over Correa's administration and his ability to include people from the base in the new democratic process. However, one cannot accuse Correa of going over to the side of the U.S. as Gutiérrez did.

The Constitution worked out by the Constituent Assembly was approved by a strong Yes vote against a very low rejection rate, 64 percent to 28 percent (Consejo Nacional Electoral [Ecuador] n.d.). Surprisingly, in the April 26, 2009, presidential elections, the first held under the new Constitution, Correa won in the first round against Gutiérrez, the former "pink tide" candidate turned pro-U.S. aspirant.

In evaluating the current situation in Ecuador and the formidable test of moving toward an effective participatory democracy, one must consider the following. Between 1995 and 2001, in the context of "anti-neo-liberal protests in Latin America," Ecuador tops the list in the number of arrests, second in the number of protest campaigns, third in protest events and fourth in deaths and injuries. "The indigenous movement has been central to almost every such protest from 1990 to this day, and it is among the most successful indigenous movements in Latin America" (Jameson 2011: 63).

Therefore, it is not surprising that Indigenous rights in Ecuador were on the agenda during the constitutional debates and in their wake, continuing in many ways to dominate the political scene. For an authoritative analysis, on which much in this section relies, see Becker (2011: 47–62).

The controversy over the rights of Indigenous peoples is bound to affect the future of the new movement led by Correa and its quest for a unique type of inclusive, yet dynamic, democracy based on anti-neo-liberal, economic development. The review below of a few issues emerging from the writing of a new constitution concentrates on themes related to democracy.

Becker states, "The 2008 constituent assembly provided a critical juncture for indigenous movements by opening up a historic opportunity to decolonize the country's political structure" (Becker 2011: 48). Evaluating the historical context of the new Constitution, Indigenous leaders

> argued that political parties had failed, people were ready for a change, and now the hour of social movements [had arrived], the victory of the referendum represented a rejection of the neo-liberal economic model that concentrated wealth and power in the hands of a few privileged people. (Becker 2011: 49)

Nonetheless, the jury is still out as far as the capacity to implement the spirit and word of the new Constitution. The goal of applying the Constitution required the implication of all elements of society who were the architects of the new Constitution and its endorsement. The person who received the most votes for the Constituent Assembly, a close ally of Correa, declared during the elections to that body that he pledged to work for the

> principle of *sumak kawsay*, the Kichwa concept of a Good Life (not just living better). It included an explicit critique of traditional development strategies that increased the use of resources rather than seeking to live in harmony with others and with nature [the environment]. (Becker 2011: 50)

The *sumak kawsay* concept was the centre of much debate. Finally, those Indigenous groups that supported the Constitution and the Yes vote coalition in favour of the Constitution's final draft made "repeated reference to *sumak kawsay*, beginning in the preamble ... [It represented] a strike against neo-liberalism and a step toward opening up democratic participation" (Becker 2011: 59). *Sumak kawsay* constitutes a novel input from the South into this process. However, it is new from the prejudiced view of the North, but not from the South. *Sumak kawsay*, according to Ecuadorian economist and university professor Pablo Davalos, is "a new framework of political, legal and natural governance." From the Indigenous peoples of Ecuador and Bolivia, this concept has begun its "voyage into the range of human possibilities" (Davalos 2009). It is therefore contributing toward participatory democracy based on Indigenous concepts and values. New economic and social development models, such as *sumak kawsay*, are opposed to neo-liberalism. These "new" paradigms are inseparable both from governance and from political power and the question of who exercises it. *Sumak kawsay* constitutes an example of the necessity to go beyond U.S. and Eurocentric notions of democracy and history that claim a monopoly from the time of ancient Greece. For further elaboration on *sumak kawsay*, see Davalos (2009).

The new Constitution also stipulates that the "non-renewable natural resources of the state's territory are property of the State, inalienable, non-renounceable and imprescriptible" (Constitución de la República del Ecuador 2008). The Ecuadorian Constitution is the first to enshrine explicitly the protection of the environment as part of this new way of thinking, intimately linked to Indigenous thought and practice. (As noted above, the Bolivian Constitution likewise does so, but was approved after the Ecuadorian one.) The Constitution has a safeguard: "The right of the population to live in a healthy and ecologically balanced environment that guarantees sustainability and the good way of living (*sumak kawsay*) is recognized" (Constitución de la República del Ecuador 2008).

With the concepts of environment protection and *sumak kawsay*, the Correa government and its Constitution further opened up an important breach against U.S.-centric concepts of democracy. The Constitution is, in fact, a hybrid one. Not only does it include the Indigenous notions emerging from some of the most vigorous, sustained and well-organized Indigenous movements on the continent, but it also features some of the basic Western notions of democracy, such as multi-party elections. *Sumak kawsay*, as the community grass-roots way of viewing political power, shares the stage with notions originating from *some* of the countries in the North. For example, the very first article in the Ecuadorian Constitution declares, "Sovereignty lies with the people, whose will is the basis of authority, which is exercised through the organs of public power and through the forms of direct participation set forth by the Constitution" (Constitución de la República del Ecuador 2008).

There is not a straight line running between participatory democracy and a radical reduction in the importance of private property in favour of democratization of the socio-economic base. Venezuela saw a real revolutionary process in action whereby the empowerment of the people through participation is in motion toward increasing democratization. Bolivia is also struggling with this issue, but it is still unfolding.

In Ecuador, the participatory nature of the political system seems to be straggling behind the economic reforms directed against the mighty power of the economic oligarchy. Many left-wing Indigenous peoples evaluated Correa's government as "highly contradictory" (Becker 2012: 124). While the new Constitution included *sumak kawsay* — which consists of a rejection of the traditional economic strategies based on the indiscriminate use of resources — the activists charged that the Correa government approved laws that were against Indigenous communities, such as the expansion of mining concessions, the privatization of water resources and the removal of Indigenous control over bilingual education programs. Oil extraction was also part of this policy. Of particular interest to the focus of this book is that, prior to the new mining initiatives, Becker points out that Correa "refused to grant communities prior and informed consent before mining activities could proceed on their territories." This resulted in massive demonstrations and critiques by Indigenous and social movements against the Correa government mainly for taking these decisions unilaterally and in contradiction to *sumak kawsay* (Becker 2012: 124–28). It can also be argued that Correa's alleged arbitrary decisions are also a violation of the Constitution. It stipulates that Indigenous peoples have the right to "free, prior informed consultation" on the use of natural resources in their territories (Constitución de la República del Ecuador 2008).

One should also take into account that Correa did apply his promises to close the U.S. military base and to cancel $3 billion in foreign debt. According to the president, this debt was "illegal and illegitimate because it had been contracted by military regimes." Correa also substantially increased spending on education, health care and assistance to single mothers and small farmers. Much of the social funding came from oil exports (Becker 2012: 133–34).

Author Federico Fuentes, in a report summarizing Ecuador's recent evolution, points out that the main extractive industry is oil but it has not been entirely nationalized. Therefore, both nationalized and internationally led conglomerates subsist side by side. From 2006 to 2011, the state's share of oil production increased from 46 percent to 70 percent. In 2007, Correa increased the windfall taxes on oil profits (accrued when oil prices surpass those agreed upon in the contracts between the companies and the state) from 50 percent to 99 percent. Correa's government also dismantled some oil funds set up under past neo-liberal governments that directed oil revenue to repay the foreign debt. Government projects are now on the receiving end of the liberated oil revenue. One result of this new orientation was that social spending between 2006 and 2009 has nearly doubled as a percentage of the gross domestic product. Minimum wage has gone up 40 percent in real terms over a recent five-year period. The government, Fuentes emphasized, "has stemmed the flow of oil wealth out of the country and begun redirecting it towards meeting ordinary peoples' needs." However, this positive report also admits, "There has also been a lack of government consultation about these projects" (Fuentes 2012b). Other affirmative accounts also include a caveat indicating that the government policies, such as those mentioned above, were more beneficial to cities than to poorer rural areas (Becker 2012: 130). This is perhaps another symptom of the Correa government's lack of consultation. There is notably ongoing agitation at the grass-roots level against many of his policies.

The reduction in the standing of the former all-important oligarchic private property and the rights of international banks is significant. The seemingly untouchable domestic and international ruling elites' rights were being dethroned by the Correa government in favour of the economic and social well-being of important sectors of the population. This opens the door for participation in contrast with the U.S. model, built on democracy of exclusion in order to protect the ruling elites and its privileges. The Ecuadorian example shows that the reduction of enormous individual property privileges in favour of a more just society does not necessarily immediately translate into meaningful participatory democracy. These economic transformations in favour of the majority cannot be applied in a simplistic manner to exaggerate the real standing of a new participatory democracy. It exists in Ecuador only in an embryonic stage. Nevertheless, in the Ecuadorian case, the Indigenous peoples and the social movements have an exceptionally strong tradition of struggle for inclusionary economics and politics. Ecuador is a relatively small country geographically; however, it is a giant when it comes to grass-roots movements in terms of their long history, determination and radical left-wing political content. In this case, the democracy in motion at the base from the bottom up can merge with the Correa-led democracy in motion from the top down. He has opened the space for inclusion with the policies of increased socio-economic justice and national sovereignty at the expense of unlimited international and domestic accumulation of private property. This was previously viewed as untouchable. The historical tradition and current situation in Ecuador make it increasingly possible to develop participatory democracy, as is happening in Venezuela.

Correa's position in favour of the long-term goal of twenty-first-century socialism contributes to the potential for Ecuador's approach to participatory democracy. His concept of twenty-first-century socialism is still quite vague as far as its content, which may be considered normal and even healthy. It is in the evolutionary stage. Ecuador has a refreshing view on socialism. Correa said that "socialism in the twenty-first century is not one single kind (*no es único*), but rather in constant evolution" (Correa 2009). However, despite its vagueness, at one international forum in 2009, Correa "presented the deepest and most serious analysis of the current economic crisis" compared with other leaders, such as Hugo Chávez, Lula da Silva and Evo Morales, challenging neo-liberalism and capitalism (Becker 2012: 128–29). As this book's exploration of Venezuela, Ecuador and Bolivia indicates, participatory democracy is linked to the actions and aspirations toward a social system (socialism) that negates the sanctity of unlimited oligarchic accumulation of private property.

Given the goals of the Correa government, it is not surprising that the 2010 attempted coup d'état took place against the president. It is significant because it represents a concrete effort to reverse potential anti-neo-liberal policies of natural resource protection and people's participation in their own political system. The U.S. is very aware that political empowerment provides a formidable base from which people can resist U.S. policies. The closing of the U.S. military base grants a sense of dignity to the people, who have been opposing U.S. domination in the country and the region for many decades. This pride of national sovereignty, as expressed both collectively and individually, can lead to yet greater economic and political initiatives in favour of the people. The 2010 attempted coup d'état is recognized by sources, media and international organizations of all tendencies and political orientations: Correa was forcefully kidnapped and held hostage (Ramonet 2011: 183; El País 2010a, 2010b; Brice 2010; CNN 2010; Golinger 2010a; Allard 2010a, 2010b). Among the commentators, there is also ample evidence that the defeated former "pink tide" presidential opposition candidate, Lucio Gutiérrez, was involved in organizing it. It was obviously a premeditated coup. Even Agence France-Presse reported it as follows: "The unrest, which recalled a military-backed coup against the elected president in Honduras last year [2009], rocked Ecuador's neighbors with many leaders swiftly coming out in his support" (Martínez 2010). Other reports link the coup to the Obama administration and Gutiérrez. The latter said on the day of the coup attempt, "'I think the end of Correa's tyranny is near'" (Corcoran 2010; Nikandrov 2010). This was reminiscent of the 2009 Honduras coup. We have also seen earlier the efforts of the U.S. in Venezuela and Bolivia to undermine the constitutional order. The economic and political empower-ment of the peoples is confronting the U.S.

This completes the investigation of Venezuela, Bolivia and Ecuador. They represent examples of democracies, each in their own right, with all factors taken into account and not as simple offshoots of models from the North. They are also at different levels of achieving participatory democracy. The goal of this survey of the three illustrations of democracy is to assist in clearing the cobwebs spun by U.S.-centrism with its severe limitations on examining other types of democracies, such as the Cuban one.

ALBA, CELAC and U.S. Democracy Promotion

Venezuela, Bolivia and Ecuador and other countries, along with the pio-neering experience of Cuba, are extending these values of democracy and associated socio-economic systems beyond their borders. They are moving from the domestic to the Latin American and Caribbean area. The failed coup attempts in Venezuela, Bolivia and Ecuador, as well as the successful ones in Honduras (2009) and Paraguay (2012), show the need for regional defence of these anti-neo-liberal and sovereign-minded policies.

Alianza Bolivariana para los Pueblos de Nuestra América (ALBA — Bolivarian Alliance for the Peoples of Our America; *alba* also translates as "dawn of day") is a regional Latin American and Caribbean integration bloc of a different kind. It was founded following an agreement between Cuba and Venezuela in Havana on December 14, 2004. The role of Fidel Castro and Chávez in initiating ALBA is a historical fact. The leaders met for the first time in 1994 in Cuba. Their political collaboration and friendship has developed since that time. They are "two like-minded individuals, soul brothers, thinking on the basis of anti-imperialism, social justice and what Latin America can be" (Interview, Azicri 2009). With ALBA's creation, this bloc began to blossom with the following new adherents: Bolivia (2006); Nicaragua (2007); Dominica (2008); Honduras (2008; although, following the coup against democratically elected Manuel Zelaya on June 28, 2009, the U.S.-backed military coup regime withdrew from ALBA); St. Vincent and the Grenadines, Ecuador, and Antigua and Barbuda (2009); St. Lucia and Suriname (2012); and Haiti (2012, permanent observer, constituting a step toward the possibility of full membership).

Like its founding members, ALBA does not base itself on the fundamental interests of unlimited accumulation of private capital and dependence on U.S. domination, including its democracy model. ALBA covers a wide variety of mutually beneficial relations and cooperation that has become a model for advantageous relations among neighbouring countries (Azicri 2010). The ALBA countries share myriad relations in the economic, financial, social, medical, educational, cultural, sports, scientific and mass-media sectors (Cole 2010, 2011).

It is of interest to note that ALBA in practical terms opposes U.S.-centric democracy promotion. Each of the ALBA countries has its respective political system. Cuba, Venezuela, Bolivia and Ecuador are following their own paths to socialism or, at least, anti-neo-liberal policies as a first step. Dominica, St. Vincent and the Grenadines, and Antigua and Barbuda have their more traditional systems. However, none of these ALBA member states questions the right of each country to follow their own respective paths. One value that they have in common is their defiance of U.S. domination in the area. ALBA, along with other regional blocs in the area, went further in 2009. In a Brazil-hosted series of meetings, they constituted the first step toward the formation of the Comunidad de Estados Latinoamericanos y Caribeños (CELAC — Community of Latin-American and Caribbean States). CELAC integrates all of the 33 countries situated in the area extending from the Rio Grande on the border between Mexico and the U.S. to Tierra del Fuego, the very southern tip of South America. This constitutes the entire region also known as the "Americas," except the U.S. and Canada. The summit held on December 2–3, 2011, in Caracas, may turn out to be the single most important event in two centuries of attempts at regional unification.[4]

In the April 2012 Summit of the Americas in Cartagena, Colombia, the issue of Cuba came up, taking centre stage. In the period leading up to the Summit, during its proceedings and since then, lingering illusions about

---

4. See www.democracyintheus.com, "CELAC Defines Democracy and Cuba Is Fully Involved."

the U.S. competitive two-party system remain in some Latin-American and Caribbean circles.[5]

The regional integration movements (ALBA and CELAC) have an economical and political effect on Cuba and the entire region. Cuba has made an important contribution as a pioneer and continues to do so in different conditions. However, the new blocs are relatively fragile for many reasons. This growing regional cooperation relies first on the capacity of the countries examined in this chapter, Venezuela, Bolivia and Ecuador, to increasingly advance along the route toward anti-neo-liberal and anti-U.S. domination. The success of the regional cooperation also depends on the progress the countries are making in building their own participatory democracies. Only when people are empowered can they resist pressures from the U.S. and its allies in the region. This also applies to Cuba — the next and principal approach to democracy to be explored — even though it has the advantage of more than 50 years of experience.

---

5. See www.democracyintheus.com, "Lingering Illusions About the U.S. Democracy's Competitive Two-Party System."

PART II

Cuba: Constitutions, Elections and New States

Chapter 4

Participation in Constitutions, Elections and a New State (1868–1952)

This chapter traces the origins and development of democracy at the grassroots level in Cuba. In the second half of the nineteenth century, the Wars of Independence broke out. The goal at that time in Cuba was to shed the Spanish yoke, not to eliminate or even to drastically reduce the unlimited accumulation of private property. However, as the struggle advanced, there was growing opposition to slavery, the most monstrous manifestation of private property and Spanish domination. Given the social and quantitative importance of slavery in Cuban society, even though private property as such was not the target, the goal of abolishing slavery had enormous repercussions. These affected the growing national consciousness and the relationship of the individual to the collective. There developed an increasing demand for social justice and a more just, ethical and cultured society. With the advancement of these tendencies, popular participation was able to flourish in a rudimentary fashion, even in nineteenth-century Cuba.

Private property exists in all Western systems and their colonies. In the U.S., it existed right from the beginning. The U.S. separated from Britain, but never underwent a social revolution. In contrast, in Cuba, a social revolution was initiated in the nineteenth century, and while private property existed there, as it did in the U.S., the conditions were different. In the nineteenth century, Cuba was already witnessing the initial transition from one social system to another, even though this conversion was at first limited and not explicit. A space opened up for mass-based participation in proportion to the advances made in this transition. Indeed, in the nineteenth century, the most marginalized and excluded sectors of society played a leading role in their own growing empowerment. In Cuba, right after the 1959 Revolution, private property continued to exist to different degrees as the transition from one system to another was taking place. However, later on, after 1959, the *social-collective* nature of the new system dominated over the accumulation of private property.

In the U.S. today, as we have seen, it is only from the base that the all-powerful minority of oligarchs is being challenged. The Occupy Movement's goal is to enhance people's participation in the political and economic system. This is because the U.S. has never undergone a transition from one system solidly based on the accumulation of private property to another arrangement based on the collective well-being of the vast majority. In contrast to the U.S., the countries of Venezuela, Ecuador and Bolivia are going through this transition, albeit in early stages and to varying degrees. In Cuba, this conversion began during the second half of the nineteenth century. It was interrupted by U.S. intervention and then rekindled in the 1950s.

The long period under consideration in Cuba, 1868 to 1952, concentrates on the seeds of a participatory political culture — and on opposition to it. It is helpful to keep in mind this participatory heritage when examining, in later chapters, how the Cuban political system evolved after 1976. Likewise, it is instructive to acknowledge tradition when exploring the situation as Cuba continues to undergo major transformations.

Cuba has a rich, homegrown experience and custom regarding constitutions, elections, the state and the battle for democracy that originates in the nineteenth century. There are two common threads: first, the participation of the people, and second, the value of social justice over and above private property as the sole consideration. These motifs have necessarily meant the defence of Cuban sovereignty, at first against the Spanish colonizers, and then U.S. neo-colonial and imperialist interests.

Cuba's First Homegrown Constitutions, Embryonic States and Elections (1868–98)

The emergence of the Presbyterian Félix Varela in the 1820s proved to be a turning point in Cuban political thinking. It became a precursor of the later nineteenth-century Wars of Independence. As Varela evolved in his thinking, he took a stand in favour of Cuban independence against all foreign domination, whether Spanish or U.S. He also opposed slavery. He became known as "the one who first taught us to think [*en pensar*]" (quoted in Torres-Cuevas 2001: 136). By bringing teaching out of the confines of abstract thought detached from daily life, Varela made an important contribution to Cuba. He taught his students to "reason with their own heads" and to "think and decide for themselves" (EcuRed n.d.). Indeed, effective and conscious participation in a political process requires that people be able to think on their own and for themselves. By appealing to all Cubans in this way — without distinction as to rank — he contributed to Cuban political culture at the mass base. This represents the tradition that consists of all Cubans appreciating their own country by opposing slavery as the most grotesque form of private property supported by colonialism. This orientation was linked to the grass-roots bearings of Varela's thinking and action as he rescued thought from the ivory tower of religious institutions. This legacy has proven to be a foundation on which future Cuban leaders have leaned, affecting important sectors of the population. Thus, very early in Cuba's history, anti-dogmatic thought and the pursuit of social justice became part of Cuban political culture. We turn next to the second half of the century, beginning in the 1860s.

In the nineteenth century, various domestic and international factors, including the tightening of the Spanish grip on Cuba, severely affected Cuba's elites. They were composed mainly of sugar plantation owners, coffee growers and ranchers. At this stage, Carlos Manuel de Céspedes came onto the scene. Travelling through Europe, he earned his law degree in Spain and was knowledgeable about the French Revolution.

However, while the French Revolution influenced him, he could not apply the model directly to Cuba, as the situation on the island was different. There were no slaves in France, while Cuba was a slave society under colonial domination. Céspedes had to contribute toward working out novel varieties of a new constitution. On the surface, the constitutions may appear to resemble first the U.S. approach especially and, second, the French. However, concrete conditions in Cuba dictated the need for a roving Republic in Arms guided by a constitution (Interview, Fung Riverón 2009).

Sometime after returning to Cuba in the early 1850s, Céspedes established a sugar plantation and became a slave owner as any other planter. However, he soon openly criticized Spanish domination. On October 10, 1868, Céspedes freed his slaves and called on them to join forces with him. He assembled 500 collaborators in a joint effort to free Cuba from Spanish colonialism. He also announced that those former slaves who did not want to enter into combat could remain free. This historic event did not mean the abolition of slavery. The end of slavery came gradually. However, by taking this first step, Céspedes involved the slaves in their own liberation, thus planting the seed of the Cuban nation. Side by side with military victories, Céspedes initiated the work toward establishing the first, very rudimentary local government in Bayamo as the capital of the Republic in Arms. The local administration began its transformation toward serving the needs of the local community. This was possible because the rebels won for themselves a liberated territory from which they could develop their program. The Republic in Arms transformed the social composition of the local town council, formerly under Spanish dictate, a change that took place through elections. It led for the first time in Cuban history to the election of both a *mulato* and a worker to the local administration. This experience in the context of the Republic in Arms proved to be a formative, mobile state within the colonial system. Céspedes was also an initiator of the Cuban state as an indigenous political entity and a bulwark against Spanish colonialism and, later, the U.S. drive for domination. The itinerant state extended to local organizations at the grass-roots level. Therefore, the kernel of the new state and the unity of the people as the harbinger of the Cuban nation took place at the same time. The elementary Cuban state that evolved within the Spanish colonial structure — including under the occupation by Spanish arms — served as a precedent for a state within the U.S.-backed Cuban Batista state in the late 1950s. The significance of involving the slaves in their own liberation can be fully appreciated by contrasting this with the experience in the U.S. War of Independence, where slave owners, such as George Washington and others, led the war, resulting in a state based on slavery (Interview, Cristóbal 2009).

Céspedes's decision to free his slaves was not based mainly on military or economic considerations. When he freed his slaves, he did not force them into military activity, as some would have it. Céspedes said to his former slaves on October 10, 1868, "'Those who want to follow me can follow me; those who want to remain can remain; all will be as free on an equal basis'" (quoted in Alarcón de Quesada 2002b: 24). Furthermore, it is important to note that Céspedes had only about 20 slaves. This can hardly be seen as a major military threat to the 100,000 well-armed Spanish colonial troops (Alarcón de Quesada 2002b: 26). Thus Céspedes's action goes well beyond any martial or mercantile contemplation. Regarding the evolution of the abolition of slavery, it is true that it involved several steps, not one single activity or declaration. Many plantation owners were not ready for this, seeing as they depended on slavery. This is why, according to the noted Cuban historian Eduardo Torres-Cuevas, the gradual approach used can "be interpreted as a good tactic by Céspedes to win over the slave-owning bourgeoisie" (Torres-Cuevas et al. 1996: 26). Perhaps the best way to evaluate whether or not a political personality is consistent in principles is the manner in which the person lives to the very end of life. In the case of Céspedes, once he was unjustly removed from the position of leadership in the war against Spain, he retired to an outlying area. He dedicated himself in part to teaching illiterate children how to read and write. In 1874, he was found by Spanish troops and killed (Torres-Cuevas et al. 1996: 114–15).

In this context of participation of the slaves and other sectors of the population, the first Cuban Constitution through the Guáimaro Constituent Assembly was established in 1869. Fabio Raimundo Torrado, a Cuban doctor of law and specialist in constitutional history, explains the process. The people and members of the Liberation Army met in the hamlets or villages. There were no property requirements. The people chose their representatives through a show-of-hands vote (Interview, Torrado 2008).

A Constituent Assembly session devoted to rights highlighted participation and the norm of equality, irrespective of property holdings. Citizen Manuel Sanguily, not a delegate but attending the open meeting, rose to make a moving speech in favour of equality for all before the law. This was significant, seeing that the articles on rights did not yet feature equality. Sanguily's intervention resulted in its inclusion in the final draft of the Constitution (Del Carmen Barcia, García and Torres-Cuevas 1996: 45–48; Loyola Vega 2002: 235, 243–46). A further example of participation along with the spirit of social justice and equality took place during another session of the Constituent Assembly. Ana Betancourt publicly made the following statement in favour of rights for women; Agramonte (the main leader along with Céspedes) then read it to the Assembly itself: "Citizens … You have destroyed slavery in the form of colour by emancipating the servants. The time has come to free women" (Torres-Cuevas et al. 1996: 50).

The "Guáimaro Constitution [Constitución de Guáimaro]: Political Constitution that will be in force in Cuba until the War of Independence is over, April 10, 1869" represented the formal establishment of the Republic in Arms. Its structure was similar to those found in the United States and Europe, but it applied to the conditions of a roving Republic in Arms. Furthermore, it stipulated the rights of electors with no mention of property or literacy conditions. The Constitution also declared, "All inhabitants of the Republic are entirely free" (Constitución de Guáimaro 1973: 376–79). This was generally seen as the equivalent of the abolition of slavery. However, abolitionism went through a series of steps before taking effect. This hesitation on abolitionism derives from the October 10, 1868, uprising that led to the 1869 Guáimaro Constitution. Its manifesto accorded only the "gradual elimination of slavery," not its abolition. Furthermore, freedom for the slaves had to include indemnities for the slave owners. After the adoption of the 1869 Constitution enshrining the principle that all inhabitants of the Republic were free, the legislative branch of the Republic in Arms adopted a law in July 1869 that limited the full independence of the slaves. However, Céspedes quickly vetoed this because of its restrictions. The issue of the abolition of slavery was controversial, and it was only in December 1870 that Céspedes fully abolished it by decree (Loyola Vega 2002: 235, 247; Del Carmen Barcia, García and Torres-Cuevas 1996: 48). Annexation to the U.S. also surfaced within the ranks of the Republic in Arms as a measure to defeat Spain (Pérez 1995: 124–25). It was a harbinger of events to come as, to this day, the struggle remains between pro- and anti-annexation to the U.S.

Despite these contrasting positions on many issues, including slavery, the most important lesson is that the Cubans were working out their new path through their own participation outside the realm of Spanish colonialism. This involvement stemmed from its own constitution and seminal state in the form of the Republic in Arms.

Participation was manifested in other ways. When a Spanish military advance on Bayamo forced the people to flee, they decided in a public meeting to burn down their city. It served as an act of defiance to Spain, leaving the city reduced to ashes for the approaching Spanish forces.

At the local level, the Republic in Arms established a system of prefects (*prefecturas*) based on local hamlets or villages in the liberated areas. They organized material support for the Liberation Army. The Army, in turn, through the *prefecturas*, developed the main economic and social needs of the people as best possible. In the process, it provided cohesion and unity.

In order to expand these *prefecturas* further at the grass roots, the House of Representatives, established by the Constitution, elaborated the functions and responsibilities of those mandated to lead the *prefecturas* and *subprefecturas*. The people in their respective *prefecturas* elected them. Among the functions was the application of the laws in their territories, such as free primary education for children and adults. The *prefecturas* and *subprefecturas* encompassed farms, small workshops producing powder for ammunition and repairing armaments, blacksmiths, tinsmiths, carpenters, basic clothing gear, cheese producers, home-based post offices and basic postal services. Some areas were even able to provide small hospitals for giving blood. The main problem that the *prefecturas* and *subprefecturas* faced consisted of continual attempts by the Spanish army and the militia to destroy them. The Spanish realized that they constituted an important base for the insurgent forces (Izquierdo Canosa 1998: 14–33).

The Spanish killed Céspedes and the other main leader, Agramonte. There was opposition to an unfavourable peace treaty signed by the Republic in Arms in 1878, the Pact of Zanjón. The resistance provided another example of participation from the bottom up being increasingly embedded in the Cuban tradition. The pact was considered treason by the most militant separatists for two reasons. First, those who agreed with the pact sanctified the continued control over Cuba by Spain. Second, they refused to abolish slavery altogether, applying abolition only to those who had enrolled in the Liberation Army (Pérez 1995: 125). Independence from Spain and the abolition of slavery were the two main goals of the War of Independence. Antonio Maceo, a humble *mulato,* was the leader of opposition to the pact. His social origins consisted of delivering products and supplies by mule. He worked at this trade with his father, who was a farmer in eastern Santiago de Cuba. Maceo had joined the Liberation Army as a simple soldier in October 1868, just two days after the beginning of the war. He was among the thousands coming from more modest origins in the Liberation Army who moved up in its ranks. As a major general, he, along with his collaborators, did not recognize the Pact of Zanjón. They considered it a capitulation. Maceo told the Spanish authorities that Cubans did not agree with the pact. After ten years of struggle and sacrifice, this was not the way to end the independence fight. Others in the delegation who were not *mulato* or former slaves declared that the pact did "not at all include the terms of [their] program, that is, independence and the abolition of slavery" (Buznego, Loyola and Pedroso 1996: 148). Rather than capitulate, Maceo and his followers defied the Spanish and drafted a new constitution of the Republic of Cuba in Arms (Loyola Vega 2002: 285–92). Known as the Baraguá Constitution, this second constitution was adopted in 1878. It represented the desire to continue what had been initiated in 1868. Its main point was "peace based on independence," which could not be ratified "without the knowledge and consent of the people" (Constitución de Baraguá 1973: 405–6).

The First War of Independence in 1868–78 was a defeat. There were several reasons for this setback. One important debate concerned the decision over which branch of the Republic in Arms would predominate — the military or the civilian. Other negative factors included regionalism and the lack of a clear, consistent program.

José Martí was responsible for the groundbreaking concept of a party to lead the nation and Revolution in order to solve these problems, among others. Martí was born in Cuba in 1853 to Spanish parents. From the early age of fifteen, based on his own experience, he started to oppose Spanish colonialism and the injustices in Cuba. His personal exposure to the cruel treatment of slaves and exploitation of the peasantry led him to reach his own conclusions. These were fostered when, as a youth in 1865, he began to attend a senior boys' school. The school director, Rafael María Mendive, was in favour of Cuban independence from Spain and highly esteemed Varela, who had taught Cubans to be innovative. Mendive had an important influence on Martí, who was coming of age during the First War of Independence (1868–1878). Martí publicly supported the war through his writings, even before he turned sixteen. This stance led to his arrest in 1869 and his conviction to six years of hard labour in prison, where he was to make the decision to fight for independence. After two years in prison, his health was so bad that the Spanish authorities commuted his sentence to exile in Spain. Following the expiration of his sentence and travel, he arrived in New York in 1880. By that time, the First War had resulted in defeat, in 1878. The "small war" (*guerra chiquita*) took place in 1879–80 and was also vanquished. Martí began to prepare for the Third War by organizing those Cubans who had gone into exile, first in New York and then in all the main cities where Cubans were to be found, such as Key West (Cayo Hueso), Tampa, Philadelphia and New Orleans. In 1892, he led the formation of the Partido Revolucionario Cubano (PRC — Cuban Revolutionary Party), which took place after several years of preparation, especially the last months of 1891. He was mainly in the U.S. until 1895, when he led expeditions to Cuba in coordination with supporters on the island who had initiated this Third War of Independence (Kirk 2012: 26–45, 79).

Upon arrival in the U.S. in 1880, Martí was initially quite enamoured with the country and its political-economic structure. However, he soon developed his own critical analysis of its political and economic system. This disapproving view matured with experience. Reality taught him about the U.S. two-party system (Democrats and Republicans), elections and governing. Martí wrote on March 15, 1885, "[Apart from certain distinctions] both govern equally abusively wherever they govern, for both are slices of the same people," providing many examples of how the elections operate (Martí 1988:

65, 71, 86). John Kirk, an authority on Martí, summarizes, "Martí informed his Latin-American readers of the existence of powerful business interests that controlled the official policies of both the Republican and Democratic parties and blatantly manipulated these parties in order to further their own ends" (Kirk 2012: 54).

However, Martí's doubts about U.S. intentions toward Cuba, Puerto Rico and "Our America" emerged well before that. As early as 1882, he began to see the natural spillover effect of expanding U.S. capital and industry into other territories. He wrote in January of that year,

> The descendants of the pilgrim fathers had their celebrations. What a difference, though! Now they are no longer humble, nor tread the snow of Cape Cod with workers' boots. Instead, they now lace up their military boots aggressively and they see on one side Canada and on the other Mexico. (quoted in Kirk 2012: 56)

Kirk emphasizes the perceptive capacity of Martí, who foresaw that the "U.S. industry would ultimately need both a cheap source of raw materials and a market for the resulting surplus of its manufactured goods and Latin America was the obvious choice to satisfy both needs" (Kirk 2012: 57).

As Martí's thinking and practice evolved, he concluded that the establishment of a political party, the PRC, was most necessary. The main goal was to unite all Cubans in the U.S. and in Cuba itself, thus overcoming the principal weakness of the First War. The PRC had to have a coherent political program — a feature absent in the First War of 1868–78 — in order to overcome the political and ideological confusion hovering over the insurgents during this war. He also opposed any annexationist tendency toward the U.S., thus exorcizing from the liberation movement this trend that hampered the First War. Right to the end of his life, he held a strong feeling against the U.S. system and its Goliath-type intentions toward Cuba and Latin America. He wrote on May 18, 1895, the day before he was killed in action: "I have lived in the monster and I know its entrails; my sling is David's" (Martí 2007b: 253).

On the militarist-civilian debate, while Martí opposed a militarist orientation, he learned from the experience of the First War of Independence. The leading force had to be agile and not hampered by unnecessary structures. The establishment of the PRC took place based on voting by, and consultation with, the exiles in the U.S. On April 8, 1892, after reaching agreement, the local associations unanimously elected Martí as delegate (*delegado*). The Spanish term translates best as someone delegated to lead in a participatory manner alongside those who are electing him, rather than being merely a "leader." On April 10, 1892, the PRC was formally proclaimed. It was composed of people espousing varying political convictions. These ranged from socialists (later to be instrumental in forming the first communist party in Cuba in 1925) to those who desired only independence from Spain, with no real social content; all races were present as well as women's clubs and veterans of the First War of Independence. Uniting them into one party was an important achievement (Ibarra 2008: 116–17; Martí n.d.: 25; Kirk 2012: 79–83, 163–64). From its initial stages, the PRC was characterized by Martí's encouragement of people's direct participation in the development of this party.

Martí saw the necessity of solving the *principal* contradiction. This meant the contradiction between the people, on the one hand, and colonialism and the new imperialism as exemplified by the U.S., on the other. By living in the U.S. and examining its economy and society very closely, he discovered imperialism on a rudimentary level. He accomplished this even before Lenin, who evolved after Martí and wrote on the subject later on, in 1916. Martí predicted the rise of the U.S. desire for domination over Cuba and Puerto Rico with the goal of using these islands as a base to conquer the rest of the region in the South. Martí was aware and sympathized with the situation of the working people and peasants under the modes of production existing in Cuba and Florida at the time. However, he felt strongly that Cubans of all classes had to rid themselves of Spanish colonialism and, then, if need be, U.S. imperialism. In those formative years before the founding of the PRC, of interest is Martí's relationship to Carlos Baliño, one of Martí's main collaborators in the U.S. Baliño was later to become one of the two main founders of the first Partido Comunista de Cuba (PCC — Communist Party of Cuba), in 1925. Martí convinced Baliño, who favoured social change above all, to join the struggle to liberate Cuba. After having accomplished the goal, Martí argued, one could examine the contradictions within Cuban society as such (Interviews, Fung Riverón 2008, 2009). According to University of Havana professor and researcher Olivia Miranda Francisco, Martí not only verbally reassured Baliño of this, but also wrote texts indicating that a society of "social justice and democracy could ... only take place with a social revolution. Martí differentiated between the struggle against colonial domination in the first place, and then, with *power in the hands of the Cuban people,* they would start to work and to analyze how to solve the social problem" (Interview, Miranda 2008, emphasis added).

The anti-colonial struggle was linked to the next step, which consisted of social justice, even though it did not aim to eliminate large private property holdings. Rather, it focused primarily on the just distribution of wealth. This program in favour of the most humble Cubans contributed toward stimulating the participation of the people at the base in the War of Independence. Thus the embryonic transition in Cuba from one social system to another was under way.

There is an important lesson to be learned from Cuban traditional thought, spanning from Varela in the first half of the nineteenth century to

Céspedes and Martí. Kirk, who has studied all that Martí had written, concludes that he was unfettered by dogma. "A study of his [Martí's] writings, which include his correspondence and diaries, affirms that he was primarily influenced by the dramatic experience of his own life … [and] not by abstract intellectual influences" (Kirk 2012: 149–50).

Martí recognized the need to have a new methodology, which Kirk identifies as "an approach in which all members would be expected to *participate actively*" (Kirk 2012: 92, emphasis added). This emphasis on participation was reflected in the constitutions and other institutions during the War of 1895–98. The PRC led the establishment of two constitutions for the Republic in Arms and the building of a solid base in the *prefecturas*. They were a source of fighters for the Liberation Army. It actually defeated the Spanish in 1898, three years after Martí's death. Martí often wrote about the "future Cuban constitution" exhibiting the need for this law of all laws (Martí 2007a: 156). He wrote, "I want the first law of our Republic to be the Cuban cult of full dignity for man" (Martí 2007c: 143). After Martí was killed in action in 1895, the next and third Constitution was established after the first two that were written during the First War of Independence. Once again, it reflected the ongoing participatory tradition in Cuban political culture. The elections to the Constituent Assembly took place in the context of the *mambises* (male independence fighters) and *mambisas* (female independence fighters) moving toward consolidating the war by 1895 in three of the four provinces. This represented 70 percent of the national territory. It was being accomplished despite the death of Martí (Loyola Vega 2002: 355). The election of delegates to the Constituent Assembly resulted from proposals for delegates. A show-of-hands vote followed in each of the five Liberation Army Corps in existence at the time, which covered all the territories except the west (Interview, Torrado 2008). Each of the five military corps had the right to propose and elect four delegates, for a total of 20 (Pérez Guzmán 1996a: 450).

This third Constitution was the 1895 Jimaguayú Constitution (Constitución de Jimaguayú 1973: 497–99). Most important to note here is that the Cubans once again wrote it themselves. The Jimaguayú Constitution's preamble was up to the standards of Martí's values and political thought, even though drafted after his death. The Constitution's text "declares the separation of Cuba from the Spanish monarchy and its constitution as a free and independent State with a government of its own, by a supreme authority, named Republic of Cuba" (Constitución de Jimaguayú 1973: 497). The preamble also emphasizes that the Republic emerges in the name of "the elected representatives of the Revolution, in a Constituent Assembly" (Constitución de la Jimaguayú 1973: 496–99).

The major electoral advances took place after the elaboration and adoption of this 1895 Jimaguayú Constitution, followed by the organization of civil life, including two electoral laws for the election of the next Constituent

Assembly. These elections, according to the 1895 Jimaguayú Constitution, were to take place two years later. Therefore, in January 1897, the Governing Council approved the electoral law, which established direct suffrage for all males, sixteen years and older (Interview, Torrado 2008). This is another Cuban creation, because in no other country did people so young have the right to vote. Cuba is today one of the few countries in the world that enfranchises sixteen-year-olds (see Chapter 7). There were once again no property or literacy requirements.

The new electoral law was far more elaborate than the one established during the First War of Independence. It was based on secret ballot voting and overseen by elected voting boards. The delegates were convened for the next Constituent Assembly to take place in October 1897. The goal was to draft the fourth and last Constitution in the 1868–98 Wars of Independence, the Yaya Constitution (Interview, Torrado 2008).

The Yaya Constitution was of historical importance because, among other points, it had already envisioned, on the day of its promulgation, the forthcoming complete independence of Cuba. The Yaya Constitution indicated that, once a treaty was reached with Spain, the basis of the upcoming Cuban victory, the Republic in Arms, would continue, "until such time [as] the definitive Constituent Assembly [took] place" (Constitución de La Yaya 1973: 500–7).

In addition, the most resolute forces made sure to include in the preamble that the Constitution was "ratifying the firm and unwavering purpose of obtaining the absolute and immediate independence of the entire Island of Cuba, to constitute it into a democratic Republic" (Constitución de La Yaya 1973: 500–7). The Constitution assured that in a liberated Cuba "the right to vote [would] be regulated by the Government, based on general suffrage." In addition, "teaching [education] [would be] free in the entire territory of the Republic" (Constitución de La Yaya 1973: 500–7; Loyola Vega 2002: 385–86; Portuondo Zúñiga 1965: 566; Pérez Guzmán 1996b: 506–9).

During the Third War, as in the First War, the local grass-roots participation benefited from some basic socio-economic services. For example, necessities for daily consumption and the war were produced in the workshops of the *prefecturas*, where some workshop directors were elected (Izquierdo Canosa 1998: 37–41). The people had the right to free education. According to one law, "an elementary school for boys and another one for girls [would] be established in each *Prefectura*" (Izquierdo Canosa 1998: 153).

The Republic in Arms had a solid base at the grass-roots level that assured its victory over Spain. The PRC as the political party of the nation and the Revolution oriented the independence struggle. The PRC had solved the problems that had occurred during the First War of Independence in 1868–78. Based on the Yaya Constitution, military leaders Máximo Gómez and Calixto García were preparing the final assault against Spain from their strongholds in the cities. In noted U.S. historian Louis A. Pérez's account, Gómez reported, "The enemy is crushed"; it was just a question of time. Pérez observes, "Cuba was lost to Spain, and if Washington did not act, it would also be lost to the United States" (Pérez 1995: 176–77).

During the Wars of Independence against Spain in 1868–98, Cuba established four constitutions linked to nascent emerging states within the colonial apparatus. This development included elections to the constituent assemblies and to the local apparatus. They highlight some distinguishing features concerning continual participation, a type of democratization at the embryonic stage. Participation by the people and self-empowerment were features that carried through during the entire period of the 1868–98 Wars of Independence. The *mambises* also gave themselves a revolutionary political party. The PRC was not at all election-oriented, but rather fashioned to lead the nation and the Revolution toward social and national emancipation. The U.S. hijacked the 1868–98 Cuban independence struggles in 1898. However, the Wars of Independence influenced the period in the 1950s when the Revolution was rekindled, finally succeeding on January 1, 1959.

Cuba, U.S. Freedom of the Press and Military Intervention (1898)

The U.S. appropriated the Cuban victory and took over Cuba, replacing Spain. The U.S. intervened militarily under the pretext of the explosion and destruction of the USS *Maine* in Havana Harbour on February 15, 1898. The U.S. media played an important role in shaping public opinion in favour of U.S. intervention in Cuba with the excuse "Remember the *Maine*." Despite the lack of any proof that Spain was responsible, on February 17, 1898, the *New York Journal* headlined, "Destruction of the War Ship *Maine* Was the Work of an Enemy."

The headlines continued, "The Journal Offers $50,000 Reward for the Conviction of the Criminals Who Sent 258 American Sailors to Their Death" (*New York Journal* 1898). The USS *Maine* incident and the role of the press indicate clearly that there is no such concept of "freedom of the press" in the abstract. Therefore, in order for people to explore democracy in Cuba today, the preconceived U.S.-centric notions of democracy, including "freedom of the press," promoted by the U.S. and other Western establishment media, must be evaluated in context.[1]

---

1. See www.democracyintheus.com, "'Remember the *Maine*' and U.S. Freedom of the Press."

$50,000 REWARD.—WHO DESTROYED THE MAINE?—$50,000 REWARD.

EDITION FOR GREATER NEW YORK

NEW YORK JOURNAL

AND ADVERTISER.

NO. 5,572. NEW YORK, THURSDAY, FEBRUARY 17, 1898.—16 PAGES. PRICE ONE CENT in Greater New York. Three CENTS within 200 Miles. Elsewhere, Four CENTS.

Copyright, 1898, by W. R. Hearst.

The Journal will give $50,000 for information, furnished to it exclusively, that will convict the person or persons who sank the Maine.

DESTRUCTION OF THE WAR SHIP MAINE WAS THE WORK OF AN ENEMY.

$50,000!

$50,000 REWARD!
For the Detection of the
Perpetrator of
the Maine Outrage!

The New York Journal hereby offers a reward of $50,000 CASH for information FURNISHED TO IT EXCLUSIVELY, which shall lead to the detection and conviction of the person, persons or government criminally responsible for the explosion which resulted in the destruction, at Havana, of the United States war ship Maine and the loss of 258 lives of American sailors.

The $50,000 CASH offered for the above information is on deposit with Wells, Fargo & Co.

No one is barred, be he the humble, but unheralded, woman, who set a few miserable dollars by acting as a spy, or the minion of a government secret service, placing, by any devilish means, to release dastardly mischief or cripple menacing countries.

This offer has been cabled to Europe and will be made public in every capital of the Continent and in London this morning.

The Journal believes that any man who can be bought to commit murder can also be bought to betray his comrades. FOR THE PERPETRATOR OF THIS OUTRAGE HAD ACCOMPLICES.

W. R. HEARST.

Assistant Secretary Roosevelt Convinced the Explosion of the War Ship Was Not an Accident.

The Journal Offers $50,000 Reward for the Conviction of the Criminals Who Sent 258 American Sailors to Their Death. Naval Officers Unanimous That the Ship Was Destroyed on Purpose.

$50,000!

$50,000 REWARD!
For the Detection of the
Perpetrator of
the Maine Outrage!

The New York Journal hereby offers a reward of $50,000 CASH for information FURNISHED TO IT EXCLUSIVELY, which shall lead to the detection and conviction of the person, persons or government criminally responsible for the explosion which resulted in the destruction, at Havana, of the United States war ship Maine and the loss of 258 lives of American sailors.

The $50,000 CASH offered for the above information is on deposit with Wells, Fargo & Co.

No one is barred, be he the humble, but unheralded, woman, who set a few miserable dollars by acting as a spy, or the minion of a government secret service, placing, by any devilish means, to release dastardly mischief or cripple menacing countries.

This offer has been cabled to Europe and will be made public in every capital of the Continent and in London this morning.

The Journal believes that any man who can be bought to commit murder can also be bought to betray his comrades. FOR THE PERPETRATOR OF THIS OUTRAGE HAD ACCOMPLICES.

W. R. HEARST.

"Destruction of the War Ship Maine Was the Work of an Enemy," *New York Journal*, February 17, 1898

U.S. Domination, Interference and
Co-Optation vs. Democracy (1898–1952)

Martí's ethics, the enhancement of social justice and opposition to slavery were cornerstones of this democracy in motion as it was about to take political power on the entire island; this was the movement that was sabotaged by U.S. military intervention.

In the wake of the USS *Maine* pretext, the U.S. occupied Cuba. The island's northern neighbour immediately began to replace the Cuban, anti-U.S.-centric rudimentary democracy model, especially as it developed under Martí, with the U.S. approach to democracy. Thus the Cuban incipient transition toward another social system hostile to unlimited private property, but in favour of social justice, faced an impasse. With this interruption, people's participation also came to a standstill. The best account of this comes from the words and deeds of Leonard Wood, the very person who was in charge of this conversion of Cuba on behalf of the U.S. In his book *Leonard Wood: Rough Rider, Surgeon, Architect of American Imperialism,* Jack McCallum paints a relatively favourable picture of Wood. According to McCallum, Wood completely reversed the advances accomplished by the Cuban independence fighters from 1868 to 1898 in the realm of participation, including constitution writing, elections and suffrage (McCallum 2006).[2]

However, the 1868–98 Wars of Independence resulted in the menacing omnipresence of the *mambises*. The danger of resurgence haunted the U.S. presence in Cuba from 1898 until they were finally defeated 61 years later, on January 1, 1959. Virtually everything that the U.S. and their allies said and did after 1898 had to take into account the nineteenth-century rebellion.

The U.S. imperial policy initiated by Wood on behalf of Washington from 1898 to 1902, combining exclusion, co-optation and military intimidation, was later to face a popular uprising. Opposition continued to grow for many years after Wood's initial establishment of the groundwork for the U.S. route of democracy. We will now turn briefly to another important watershed for the focus of this book. It consists of the 1933 Revolution and the resulting 1940 Constitution, because of the importance that the latter played in the Revolution led by Fidel Castro. The PCC, the unions and the revolutionary students played a key role in the 1933 Revolution. One of the PCC founders in 1925, along with Julio Antonio Mella, was Baliño, Martí's closest collaborator.

The pro-U.S. and conservative forces in Cuba could not fully turn back the 1933 Revolution. This resulted in a new Constituent Assembly and a Constitution. It was the most progressive Constitution in Latin America at that time. It was signed in Guáimaro, where the first Constitution was established in 1869. Significantly, the date of its application was October

---

2. See www.democracyintheus.com, "Imperialism and Democracy in Cuba."

10: the date in 1868 when Céspedes freed his slaves and initiated the War of Independence against Spain. The fact that the 1940 Constitution linked itself to Cuban indigenous heritage is an indication of the avant-garde nature of the 1940 Constitution. It was revolutionary for its time in content as well. For example, Articles 1 and 2 of the Constitution stipulate that Cuba is a "democratic Republic" where "sovereignty resides in the people." Article 20 indicates, "All Cubans are equal before the law." "Latifundia are outlawed" in Article 90. According to Article 97, "Universal, equal and secret suffrage is established as a right, duty and function of all Cuban citizens" (Constitución de la República de Cuba, 1940: 91–92, 98, 133, 136). While these and other articles were very advanced for their time, the enabling laws that were necessary to put them into practice were never adopted. The new movement led by Fidel Castro in the 1950s took up the need for these measures.

Fidel Castro and his movement arose in the following conditions. Presidential and legislative elections were scheduled to be held in 1952. The polls showed that the opposing Orthodox Party presidential candidate was heading for a victory, while the pro-U.S. Batista candidate was a distant third. Fidel Castro was running for a Congressional seat as an Orthodox Party candidate. Even historians who are relatively critical of the Cuban revolutionary process write that Batista, running "a distant third, [was] a likely reason for his staging a coup" (Domínguez 1979: 113). Batista organized the coup d'état in the early morning of March 10, 1952 (Torres-Cuevas et al. 1996).[3]

We have seen how the Cuban Revolution was developing from the nineteenth century until 1952. In this context, the approaches to democracy by the Cuban patriots and progressive forces stood out in contrast with the U.S. route. The two opposing forces were locked in a fierce combat. We will now turn to the period after the March 1952 Batista coup, when the tide began to turn against the U.S.

---

3. See www.democracyintheus.com, "Two Visions of Democracy: U.S. vs. Fidel Castro."

Chapter 5

Democracy, Elections and the New State

A Rebellion Against Dogmatism of the Left and the Batista Dictatorship (1953)

The current international debate concerning Cuba and the issues of democracy, elections and the revolutionary state finds its origins mainly in the period from 1953 to 1962. On July 26, 1953, Fidel Castro led groups to attack the garrisons of Moncada and Carlos Manuel de Céspedes in eastern Cuba. Castro later claimed in his defence that the intellectual author of this act was José Martí, whom he considered to be the "culmination of [Varela's] thinking" (Castro Ruz [Fidel] 2007: 419). Castro was also well versed in the experiences of the nineteenth-century Wars of Independence. At the time, he was likewise familiar with the 1917 Revolution in Russia and many of the works of Marx, Engels and Lenin. The attack against Moncada was the reflection of his ability to fuse all these tendencies into action and thought based on Cuba's concrete conditions. This testified to the innovative nature of the Cuban Revolution. The intention at Moncada was to restart the 1868–98 Wars of Independence. After attempting judicial and electoral avenues, Moncada constituted a rejection of the dogma from the left in Cuba and internationally. The left was incapable of tracing an innovative path out of the crisis. Ernesto Che Guevara, in his capacity as an activist having a perspective based on a broad experience in the international revolutionary movement, wrote, on July 26, 1967, in his Bolivia diary: "At night, I gave a short talk on the significance of July 26, a rebellion against oligarchies and against revolutionary dogmas" (Guevara 2000: 296). A manifesto dated July 23, 1953, just three days before Moncada, was made public. It was intended to be read on radio to the nation had the Moncada attack succeeded. The manifesto stated that the action was "'motivated by the most genuine *criollo* [Cuban indigenous] values [and] ... [came] from the soul of the Cuban people.'" Moreover, it said, "'[The] Revolution declares that it recognizes and bases itself on the ideals of José Martí, the program of the Partido Revolucionario Cubano [PRC]'" and other progressive and revolutionary organizations (Castro Ruz [Fidel] 1972a: 157–58). From Varela to Céspedes, to Martí, to Fidel Castro, the innovativeness of the Cuban Revolution seems embedded in its political DNA. The *criollo* tradition of the *mambises* stemmed from their close ties to the grass roots. Many of the independence fighters arose from the humble base. As the war advanced, some of the important leadership emerged from among the poorest and most marginalized. This expanding base was an important reason for the defeat of the Spanish in 1898. The grass-roots participation was an implicit part of the spirit that animated the new generation of the 1950s. In 1953, the democracy in motion initiated in the previous century was reborn, but under new conditions and with more advanced ideas.

During the Moncada attack, five rebels were killed in combat; a short time later, the Batista regime murdered 56 others (Castro Ruz [Fidel] 2007: 133). After the Moncada assault, Castro and others were arrested and tried. His lengthy self-defence summation on October 16, 1953, became known as "History Will Absolve Me." There is some speculation as to what extent it was radical. However, according to the Cuban researchers and editors of *History Will Absolve Me*, Pedro Álvarez Tabío and Guillermo Alonso Fiel, the "Moncada program of action," as it was later called, responded to "Cuba's concrete circumstances at that time …. [It] was the most advanced set of political, social and economic demands that could rally the broadest sections of the exploited classes of Cuban society, including broad segments of the urban and rural petit-bourgeoisie" (Álvarez Tabío and Alonso Fiel 1998: 19–20). This was Castro's innovative feature. He was able to capture the movement's level based on the aspirations of the vast majority at a given moment. The leader was capable of assessing this motion in order to envision broader horizons in the *process* of a revolutionary struggle. He did this without giving up principle. Castro himself commented in 2007 about "History Will Absolve Me," indicating that it contained "the basic elements of a future Socialist revolution, which didn't have to come immediately — it could be carried out gradually, progressively, but it would be solid and uncontainable." He added, "Although we wouldn't hesitate to radicalize it if necessary" (Castro Ruz [Fidel] 2007: 168). In the same way that the Moncada attack itself was, as Che Guevara pointed out, "a rebellion against oligarchies and against revolutionary dogmas," so was "History Will Absolve Me." This approach explains in part how common ground is found today in the Cuban experience and in that of the developing varieties of twenty-first-century socialism, such as in Venezuela, as well as in Bolivia and Ecuador, where anti-neo-liberal sovereign routes are being followed. They all link principles based on anti-neo-liberal policies, different long-term approaches to socialism and opposition to U.S. domination. They thus represent processes in constant motion, radicalizing themselves according to the conditions. These different roads to socialism share an appreciation of each other because they are commonly opposed to dogmatism and an idealistic, static view of socialism, democracy and revolution.

Castro presented his court summation in a two-hour defence from memory, because prison authorities had confiscated the notes he had carefully prepared. Castro quoted Martí by heart on innumerable occasions throughout his defence.

One of Castro's earliest biographers, Gabriel García Márquez, wrote about Castro, "He knows the 28 volumes of Martí's work thoroughly" (García Márquez 1998: 17). Even during his early high school days, as Castro wrote in a biographical essay in 2010, "The names of Martí, Maceo, Céspedes, Agramonte and others, appeared everywhere and aroused admiration and the interest of many of us" (Castro Ruz [Fidel] 2010: xxv). Martí's humanist and advanced ideas found expression in the ideas of Marxism. Castro was able to fuse the two tendencies in applying them dialectically to Cuba. He thus remains "the anti-dogmatist par excellence" (García Márquez 1998: 17). Like Varela and, later, Céspedes, both of whom cultivated their thought and action on their own, Castro wrote in his biography of his early years, "I had no mentor" (García Márquez 1998: 134). Researcher Concepción Nieves Ayús points out, "Castro was a natural *martiano*" (follower of Martí's thinking). However, he "became a Marxist-Leninist thinker not only through studying [their works] but also by confronting himself with reality." Martí himself "drank from the fountain of reality, but he also drew from the revolutionary thinking that preceded him," such as Varela (Interview, Nieves Ayús 2008). This epistemology is based on a unique manner of combining one's own practical experience with the thinking and action of others, with the principal ingredient being one's own mind and heart.

In Castro's "History Will Absolve Me" court summation, he paid special attention to the four nineteenth-century Cuban *mambí* Constitutions and the 1940 Constitution. He listed "the five revolutionary laws that would have been proclaimed immediately after seizing the Moncada garrison" (quoted in Castro Ruz [Fidel] 1998: 58). They were to be broadcast to the nation. For example, the first revolutionary law "gave sovereignty back to the people and proclaimed the 1940 Constitution as the supreme law of the state" (quoted in Castro Ruz [Fidel] 1998: 58). The second revolutionary law dealt with latifundia (pieces of property covering very large land areas), giving ownership of the land to all farmers who held "five *caballerías* [the equivalent of approximately 67 hectares, or 165.85 acres] or less of land" (quoted in Castro Ruz [Fidel] 1998: 59). He dealt with innumerable questions, such as the rights of workers and peasants in the cities and countryside, housing and the confiscation from embezzlers of all illegal holdings (Castro Ruz [Fidel] 1998: 59–60).

After the trial, Castro reconstructed the summation from memory while in solitary confinement. It was thus prepared for publication. By October 1954, tens of thousands of copies of *History Will Absolve Me* were distributed throughout Cuba (Álvarez Tabío and Alonso Fiel 1998: 12, 15, 17). Even though it was not explicit, the Moncada action program represented a step along Cuba's route to socialism. It clearly targeted the oligarchy's accumulation of private property, especially in the countryside. Unlimited accumulation of private property is the very basis on which the capitalist political system is founded. In combining a major agrarian reform with other measures, such as housing and other urban issues, and the rights of workers and peasants, the very foundation of the Cuban capitalist system was implicitly confronted. As mentioned earlier, the "first revolutionary law gave sovereignty back to the people." This defied the political power held at that time by the U.S.-backed Batista regime. All huge private privileges hinged on this regime, which was the real sovereign power in 1953. The new political democracy in motion initiated at that time cannot be detached from the democratization of the economic and social base. The spark of the transition to democracy in 1953 encompassed both political and socio-economic dimensions.

Participatory Nineteenth-Century Republic in Arms Reborn (1957–58)

Despite the defeat at Moncada, the forces returned, this time to the Sierra Maestra in eastern Cuba, toward the end of 1956. The new July 26 Movement (*Movimiento 26 de Julio*), named after the date of the Moncada attack, and its Rebel Army (*Ejército Rebelde*) spread their influence widely. By 1957–58, based on deepening support in the countryside, the movement and its army established an embryonic state within a state. This was reminiscent of the Republic in Arms and *prefecturas* established in the Third War of Independence (1895–98) (Interview, Toledo Santander 2008). In the nineteenth century, there was no Cuban state; the island was merely an appendage of the Spanish colonial empire. Therefore, the embryonic state at that time was a "state within a colonial apparatus." However, under U.S. domination, the latter established a Cuban state. Thus the Sierra Maestra experience constituted a "state within the U.S.-dominated state." The participation of the people in their own liberation is a heritage of the nineteenth-century struggle for independence and social justice. This tradition of people striving to empower themselves was carried forward in the 1950s Sierra Maestra experience.

The July 26 Movement anticipated the imminent success of the Revolution, and thus the people were acquiring political power to the detriment of the Batista dictatorship. There are many cases of how the embryonic state was being organized. For example, neighbours were appointed to assume governmental functions pertaining to the administration of their territory. This included health, educational and financial support (Fernández Ríos 1988: 220–23).

The 1958 Agrarian Reform Law in the liberated territories was carried out with the full participation of workers and peasants. The first workers' congress in arms and the first peasants' congress in arms took place in the liberated areas (August 1999: 165). Property was granted to those who worked the lands as well as to tenants and sharecroppers (Torrado 1998).

The application of the Moncada program of action, even before the actual seizing of power on January 1, 1959, indicated that the Cuban people were taking the road toward an indigenous type of socialism. It had its roots in international revolutionary traditions as well as Martí's ethical and social justice premises. It was also founded on the participation of the people at the base.

As the Rebel Army advanced from one victory to another, it was obvious to the U.S. that the inevitable would occur unless they took action.

Lessons for Today from 1958: Grass-Roots Democracy vs. Elections, Co-Optation, Dissidence

A close examination of declassified official U.S. government documents from 1958 sheds light on certain aspects of the current Cuban domestic political landscape and relations with the U.S. There are hypotheses promoted in some Western academic circles and all of the U.S. establishment media. These suppositions strive to have the political system in Cuba measured through the prism of the supposed innate superiority of the U.S. competitive multi-party system and its accompanying capitalism. These are not simply ideas. The U.S. also actually endeavours to shape the political and economic landscape in Cuba so that it coincides with the notion propagated by the U.S. In 1958, as the rebel forces were gaining strength and heading toward victory, the U.S. attempted to co-opt forces in Cuba to put a halt to this advance. From 1958 until today, this is the path that the U.S. follows. While the current situation has changed since 1958, the basic U.S. policies in place then and now are very similar. They thus contribute to a truncated view of democracy in Cuba. The review that follows will address how the U.S. also used co-optation and individual political ambitions, in the same manner as we discussed earlier in the Obama case study.

While supplying arms to Batista, the U.S. was simultaneously putting into place its policy of co-optation and recruitment of its first "dissidents." However, the U.S.-organized opposition at that time occupied a different social base and was not known as dissident. Since the 1980s, the term "dissidents" has become known in international public opinion to mean those who proclaim to be in opposition to the former U.S.S.R. and Eastern bloc countries. In most cases, it has referred to individuals or a movement that shared the original ideas and policies of these political systems, but later renounced their convictions. In the Cuban context, the term "dissidents" refers to those who were involved at any time in the revolutionary movement as early as 1953, but who later renounced it. "Cuban dissidents" also refers to those who were not involved or had not sympathized with the Revolution. In this book, "Cuban dissidents" includes both those who are paid (directly or indirectly) by U.S. democracy promotion programs as well as the unsalaried opponents of the Cuban constitutional order. Extensive literature and many websites, originating from both Cuba and elsewhere, prove how the U.S. and European countries, such as Spain, pay their dissidents. U.S. journalist Tracey Eaton, who is *not* a supporter of the Cuban Revolution, has a continually updated website devoted to tracking U.S. funding of Cuban dissidents (Cuba Money Project n.d.). Therefore, this book concentrates not on the funding aspect, but rather on the dissidents' historical context and their common political and ideological content. Dissidence is not a matter of holding opposing ideas. In Cuba, as will be seen in Chapter 6, there has been and continues to be an ongoing vigorous debate on the path to follow and how to apply the changes. This is not the same as the dissident course based on opposing the constitutional order, which foments regime change, with "Castroism" being the main target. Their common complaint, ranging from the left to the right on the dissident spectrum, is the supposed complete lack of democracy in Cuba and the authoritarian or dictatorial nature of the Cuban leadership. This perspective coincides with the policy of regime change worked out by Washington since 1959. This plan is followed at times by some European countries such as Spain.

"Dissidence," as it is used today in Cuban politics, originally arose in the 1958–62 period outlined below, although, as previously mentioned, they were not referred to as dissidents at that time. They were mainly petty bourgeois and bourgeois remnants of the disintegrating Bastista regime. They had either fled to the U.S. or remained in Cuba, working clandestinely to overthrow the regime with U.S. assistance. The U.S. initiated its late 1950s version of what later became known as "fostering dissidence"; it also developed other similar tactics of recruiting alternative elements to avert the revolutionary movement. Simultaneously with this, Batista and the U.S. continued to bomb the revolutionary forces in the Sierra Maestra in eastern Cuba. A February 7, 1958, telegram from the U.S. Embassy in Cuba to the Department of State details how U.S.-trained army personnel and B-26 bombers had been active in the Sierra Maestra in support of the Batista regime. It was considered the legally constituted government of Cuba, which the U.S. had duly recognized (Foreign Relations, Document 11). Unable to repress the Castro-led revolutionary movement, the U.S. began its policy of organizing its own "alternative" to Castro. In an April 2, 1958, memorandum from the U.S. intelligence apparatus to the U.S. Secretary of State, several important points emerged. One was that the "Batista must go" clarion call had pervaded the political landscape, to include even U.S. policy. This major change in U.S. policy took place because, as the memorandum stated, "[The] moderate middle elements have either withdrawn from political activity or aligned themselves with the opposition [the Castro-led July 26 Movement]" (Foreign Relations, Document 47). Therefore, according to the memorandum, there was the need for a *"third alternative"* (Foreign Relations, Document 47, emphasis added). While this option opposed the continuation of Batista, it also fought the installa-tion of a revolutionary regime dominated by Castro. This third alternative "could be the emergence of a military-civilian junta which would oust Batista but not permit Castro a dominant position" (Foreign Relations, Document 47). The basic U.S. foreign policy comes into play once again by replacing a faithful ally such as Batista while co-opting another face in order to avert the Revolution. In this sense, the goal was to recuperate the "Batista must go" movement into a ploy to *maintain* the status quo. Instrumental to achiev-ing this goal was "public opinion," or the role of the press. Its purpose was mainly to sanctify the U.S. hold over Cuba through elections. For example, an April 22, 1958, U.S. memorandum focused on the U.S. press. The goal was "to gain acceptance in the eyes of the American public, press and Congress of his [the Cuban ambassador] Government's intentions to hold elections which would be acceptable to a majority of the Cubans" (Foreign Relations, Document 52). A May 2, 1958, memorandum from the Pentagon confirmed the continued arms shipments to Batista, even if he did "not command the support of a majority of the Cuban people [at that time]." The holding of elections was to be used to legitimize the regime and thus serve as an excuse for continued arms shipments. However, even if the elections were not cred-ible in Cuba, the arms shipment would continue. The U.S. State Department memorandum conceded that arms would flow to Cuba even when Batista "promised free elections in June but had not convinced the people that they would in fact be free" (Foreign Relations, Document 54).

As public opinion in the U.S. continued to be very dubious regarding the Batista regime and its use of arms against the popular rebellion, Washington relied on the elections scheduled for November 3, 1958 (Foreign Relations, Document 55). Elections under Batista returned once again as a main theme, in a May 22, 1958, memorandum declaring, "President Batista had promised free elections." However, while the U.S. complained about the government's real intentions to hold elections, military support to Batista continued. This U.S. memorandum defended the political system (under Batista) in Cuba as exhibiting "one of the purest concepts [of democracy]." In response to the U.S. complaint that Batista came to power by a coup and, therefore, had no legitimacy, the Cuban ambassador to the U.S. stated, "The fact remained that the Batista Government immediately made preparations for elections and was *duly elected to office in November 1954*" (Foreign Relations, Document 58, emphasis added). However, even the critical Cubanologist Jorge I. Domínguez writes that, in 1954, "Batista was 'elected' president without opposition," because the other candidate pulled out due to a lack of confidence in the electoral system at the time (Domínguez 1979: 124). In addition, voter turnout of registered voters dropped from 79.5 percent in 1948 to 52.6 percent in 1954 (Domínguez 1979: 124). It is instructive to keep these U.S. manoeuvres in mind today when examining the issue of elections and democracy in Cuba. We have also seen how the U.S. used elections in Egypt to sanctify its control over the country through the military. However, Cuba has its own tradition of democracy that should be explored based on its own merits and limitations, not through the prism of U.S.-centric democracy promotion.

Elections were to be held initially in June 1958, but were postponed because of complaints from political parties about the lack of guarantees. Nonetheless, preparations continued for what was to become the last election held under U.S. domination, on November 3, 1958, less than two months before the Revolution's victory. According to a U.S. document, it was acknowledged that there "appear[ed] to be little possibility for anything resembling an acceptable election in Cuba" (Foreign Relations, Document 112). What was the answer? The U.S. document further stated, "The only possibility apparent at this moment of minimizing a violent transition in Cuba [i.e., a revolution] is that of effecting a compromise arrangement between the Batista Government and *responsible leaders of an organized opposition*" (Foreign Relations, Document 112, emphasis added). At this point, one witnesses yet again the role of the U.S. in organizing opposition groups, presently known as dissidents.

Two formerly secret documents are available from December 29, 1958, two days before the revolutionary victory — one emanating from the U.S. Embassy in Havana and the other from Washington. The first is a telegram from the U.S. ambassador in Cuba to the State Department. The main proposal was to dump Batista in favour of another puppet regime, but to which even more arms could be funnelled in a last-ditch attempt to defeat the July 26 Movement (Foreign Relations, Document 196).

The second document, a memorandum, reveals that the U.S. elaborated another scenario. It suggested forming "a small informal group of Latin American OAS Ambassadors to study the Cuban situation" and then "encourage the group to ask Batista to invite it to visit Cuba for a first-hand study." This inspection included the evaluation of the elections held November 3, 1958 (Foreign Relations, Document 197). However, what was the credibility of these 1958 elections among the Cuban people? Once again, even from Domínguez, who is rather critical of the Cuban Revolution: "The presidential elections of 1958, a few months before Batista's fall, had two opposition candidates, but the elections were so obviously fraudulent that they served, once again, to undermine the government rather than to strengthen it" (Domínguez 1979: 124).

Despite all the intrigues and military repression, the advance of the July 26 Movement and its allies could not be halted. One of the main instruments in the success of the January 1, 1959, triumph — and in the crucial days that followed — was the use of radio, specifically Radio Rebelde. The Batista regime, right from the first day of the coup on March 12, 1952, suppressed radio transmitters and stations, opposition press and their offices, telecommunications and other media (Pérez 1995: 288–89). Radio Rebelde was virtually the only radio not controlled by Batista.

A week after the power generator and the first radio equipment arrived at Che Guevara's Sierra Maestra command post, the guerrilla leader founded Radio Rebelde, on February 24, 1958. By the end of the war, each Rebel Army column had its own radio equipment, with the result that 32 local rebel stations joined forces with Radio Rebelde for simultaneous transmissions (Radio Rebelde n.d.). People, especially the youth, cheered the radio reports of rebel victories. Radio Rebelde was used to halt the plots to stop the imminent success of the Revolution. To do so, the radio station directly addressed the Cuban people (Dorschner and Fabricio 1980: 222–23, 132, 296). The establishment and outreach of Radio Rebelde, shielded from the Batista forces, would not have been possible without the collaborative participation of the people.

The Provisional Revolutionary Government and Constitution (1959)

Batista fled in the early morning of January 1, 1959. That day, Castro made a proclamation through Radio Rebelde. He declared that the revolutionary forces (the Rebel Army) and the people should be alert against any coup attempt (Castro Ruz [Fidel] 2008a: 8–9).

Later that same day, Castro addressed the people of Santiago de Cuba through Radio Rebelde, pointing out that the city was not completely liberated and, once again, cautioning against the coup in Havana. Indicating the importance of staying oriented by listening to the radio, Castro broadcast to the people: "Stop work and come out in solidarity with the [liberation] fighters.… The history of 1895 will not be repeated! Today the *mambises* will enter Santiago de Cuba"[1] (Castro Ruz [Fidel] 2008a: 10; Castro Ruz [Fidel] 1972c: 446–47).

Once again, later that same January 1, through Radio Rebelde, Castro declared that, while Batista had escaped the country, his accomplices had stayed. Castro therefore appealed to Cubans "for freedom, democracy, and the triumph of the Revolution, [to] *support the general revolutionary strike in all territories that [had] not been liberated*" (Castro Ruz [Fidel] 1972b: 448–49, emphasis in original). A few hours later, through Radio Rebelde, Castro ordered all columns to advance onto the main cities in the centre and in western Cuba, including Havana, to control the entire country (Castro Ruz [Fidel] 2008a: 13).

---

1. In reference to the refusal of U.S. troops led by Wood to allow the *mambises* to enter Santiago de Cuba at the end of that Independence War in 1898 in order to recuperate the victory against Spain for U.S. interests.

On January 1, late at night, Radio Rebelde convoked people to Céspedes Park for a public meeting (Buch and Suárez 2004: 43). Castro said, "We have finally arrived in Santiago! ... The Revolution is beginning now. It will not be an easy task" (Castro Ruz [Fidel] 2004: 44). Triumphant, on January 2, 1959, in Santiago de Cuba's Céspedes Park, Castro declared, "The Revolution will lead to its real conclusion; it will not be like [18]95" (Castro Ruz [Fidel] 2008a: 14). By the evening of January 2, the military columns of Camilo Cienfuegos and Che Guevara succeeded in liberating the centre of the island and advanced to Havana. In the early hours of January 3, all of the arms in Havana, including the Colombia garrison, were under the control of the July 26 Movement (Buch and Suárez 2004: 48–49).

The experience in 1958 and the first few days of 1959 make it difficult to separate the leadership from the participants at the base. It seemed to consist of one wave.

The new Provisional Government constituted itself on January 3, 1959. Manuel Urrutia had been nominated as provisional president in December 1957, as he was a progressive lawyer and president of the Santiago de Cuba Penal Court. The members of the first Council of Ministers of the Provisional Government were designated. Urrutia, as provisional president of the Republic, appointed Castro as commander-in-chief of the armed forces (Buch and Suárez 2004: 49–50). A charter forming the legal basis for the foundation of the new revolutionary government was drafted. It stressed the need for a legislative body to replace the Congress dissolved by Batista and to adopt a constitution on a temporary basis (Acta de constitución del Gobierno Revolucionario 2004: 172–74). The next day, on January 4, the Council of Ministers met again and decided to "approve the Fundamental Law of the Cuban State, essentially based on the 1940 Constitution, with the modifications required by the current circumstances and needs of the Revolution" (Buch and Suárez 2004: 52–53).

On February 7, 1959, this Fundamental Law of the Republic was promulgated. It served as the Constitution until the 1976 Constitution, elaborated and approved by the people, as will be explained later (Constitución de la República de Cuba 1976). One of the principal problems with the 1940 Constitution was that no enabling legislation was ever passed by U.S.-influenced governments in order to put the Constitution into practice. One example is land reform. In 1959, the Council of Ministers had given itself legislative authority combined with executive obligations. Thus it had the right to adopt laws based on the Fundamental Law in order to apply its most urgent provisions in line with the objectives of the Revolution (Interview, Toledo Santander 2008).

Two important changes in the Fundamental Law are among the most controversial. The first relates to the death penalty. The old 1940 Constitution stated in Article 25, "[The] death penalty may not be imposed. However, crimes of a military character committed by members of the armed forces, and treason or espionage in favour of the enemy in time of war with a foreign nation, are excluded [from the ban on capital punishment]" (Constitución de la República de Cuba 1940: 100). A new article in the 1959 Fundamental Law expanded exceptions to the death penalty prohibition to explicitly include the Batista henchmen, the "repressive corps of the Tyranny" (Constitución, *Ley Fundamental de Cuba* 1959). The Cuban revolutionaries considered that, since the Allies at Nuremberg had judged and sentenced to death Nazi war criminals, Cubans also had this right regarding the Batista murderers. Even the U.S. admitted to Batista's crimes, which were notorious. In a 1960 speech, John F. Kennedy stated, "Fulgencio Batista murdered 20,000 Cubans in seven years — a greater proportion of the Cuban population than the proportion of Americans who died in both World Wars" (Kennedy 1960). In the same vein, the U.S. government concluded in a 1969 investigation, "It is clear that counter terror became the strategy of the Batista government. It has been estimated by some that as many as 20,000 civilians were killed" (Graham and Gurr 1969: 582).

Fidel Castro responded to a question by one of his biographers in 2007 about possible errors in the manner the trials were carried out. Castro explained why they had used public places: "[to allow] the proceedings to be attended by a great number of our countrymen who were justly outraged by the thousands of crimes that had been committed…. We lost no time in rectifying what was unquestionably a mistake" (Castro Ruz [Fidel] 2007: 220). Castro also elaborated on how the July 26 Movement modelled itself after the Nuremberg trials, thus avoiding the lynching of Batista collaborators (Castro Ruz [Fidel] 2007: 220–21).

The other important change in the 1959 Fundamental Law regards latifundia and land reform. The old 1940 Constitution dealt with the problem of land concentration by outlawing latifundia. It stated, "The law shall restrictively limit acquisition and possession of land by foreign persons and companies, and shall adopt measures tending to give the land back to Cuban ownership" (Constitución de la República de Cuba 1940: 133). In the 1959 Fundamental Law, the above-mentioned article was retained entirely, without any changes. However, keeping in mind that the 1940 Constitution was never applied by means of a law as required by the Constitution, the 1959 Fundamental Law further stipulated how to go about eliminating latifundia: "In cases of forceful expropriations used for Land Reform to take effect … it shall not be mandatory that a prior compensation payment be made in cash" (although other forms of payments, such as bonds, were allowed) (Constitución, *Ley Fundamental de Cuba* 1959). Of significance is that the added stipulation explicitly allowed for "land reform."

The Council of Ministers, acting as the Provisional Government with legislative authority, enacted the first Agrarian Reform Law on May 17,

1959. It limited land holdings and expropriated the remainder with compensation (Franklin 1997: 21). This affected U.S. interests in Cuba. According to a 2008 U.S. Department of Agriculture Report, in the late 1950s, "U.S. interests owned … 75 percent of the arable land" (Foreign Agricultural Service 2008). With this land reform, land ownership was henceforth limited to 1,000 acres with some exceptions based on its usefulness for the economy. Expropriated land and state-owned land were distributed free of charge to co-ops or individual agricultural workers. The U.S. objected to the terms of compensation, which to date have never been settled, while other governments successfully negotiated their respective compensations (Franklin 1997: 21).

The first Agrarian Reform Law and nationalizations in the urban area, especially of U.S. companies, laid the basis for a socialist orientation placing ownership of the main means of production in the hands of the new state.

Elections: Who Rejected Them?

After the Revolution triumphed on January 1, 1959, the issue of elections was on the agenda, both for the revolutionary government and the U.S. The latter had just lost Cuba. The debate over elections in the immediate, post-1959 period carries with it repercussions even today. It is bound to continue.

The chronicle of the post-1959 election controversy is also one of the best examples of participatory democracy. At one point in a mass meeting with citizens, almost immediately after the January 1 victory, Castro himself introduced the possibility of holding elections. The people attending the mass rally actually booed down the proposal. Urrutia, who had been president of Cuba since January 3, 1959, and who had participated in the meeting held at Marta Abreu Central University in Las Villas, Santa Clara, later made the following comment:

> The first time I heard the promise of elections repudiated was when Castro and I attended the opening of the library at Marta Abreu University at Las Villas. At the end of the meeting, Castro mentioned elections and a large number of his listeners shouted against them. After the speech, Castro asked me, "Did you notice how they opposed elections?" (quoted in Pérez 1995: 321–22)

Soon after, on March 16, 1959, Castro asked at another large gathering:

> Which of us here has said anything against elections? No one.… However, such is the weariness that people feel, such is their repugnance at the memory of that verbiage, at the memory of those rallies with hypocrites parading from one platform to the next … We are favourable to elections, but elections that will really respect the

people's will, by means of procedures which put an end to political machinations.[2] (Castro Ruz [Fidel] 2006b: 122)

On another occasion in June 1959, Castro asked:

> Do you want to have elections right away, tomorrow? Shall we call on the people to vote tomorrow? [The audience shouted "No!"] … What really is odd is that those who have no popular support talk about elections.… There is democracy in the Government. The Government at the service of the people, not of political cliques or oligarchies.… We have democracy today, for the first time in our history. (Castro Ruz [Fidel] 2006a: 122)

The next year, on January 4, 1960, in an interview with NBC (National Broadcasting Company), the moderator asked Castro, "Do you think there will be elections in 1960? … Castro [response]: It depends on the people. This is a matter that is in the hands of the people" (Cuba-L Direct 2011).

In a 1960 May Day interactive speech with thousands of people, Castro said, "Democracy has prevailed today in this direct form because we are in the midst of a revolutionary process.… The Cuban people voted, not with a pencil, but with their blood and the lives of 20,000 compatriots" (quoted in August 1999: 193–94).

During this debate on elections, in the period immediately following January 1, 1959, the Cuban revolutionary government carried out radical, wide-ranging socio-economic transformations. For example, it nationalized large U.S.-owned industries in the urban and rural areas. It removed privileges of absentee and other big real-estate owners, who were gouging tenants, in favour of the people. Despite all the difficulties, such as the loss of most of its doctors, who fled to the U.S., Cuba initiated its network of free health services in both the urban and rural areas. It was also developing free education for all. This included the 1961 Literacy Campaign, which resulted in over 700,000 people learning to read and write (Kapcia 2000: 111). Culture and sports activities started to flourish. The revolutionary transformation of the state made all of this possible.

The Batista state's armed forces were defeated in the battlefield. The majority of the people rejected attempts by the U.S. to put those few intransigent elements into action against the revolutionary government. Along with this groundswell of rejection, the old U.S.-controlled political system

---

2. I am very appreciative of Professor D.L. Raby's many hours of research in Havana. She meticulously translated passages from the newspaper *Revolución* containing the views of Fidel Castro on elections as expressed in the first few years after January 1, 1959. Combined with my previous research and that of other writers, the compilation of Castro's views, though far from complete, is intended to provide a picture of how the situation evolved from 1959 to 1960 with regard to this theme, and especially the participatory role of the people.

deteriorated rapidly. For example, as shown by the declassified April 1958 State Department documents cited earlier, "Moderate middle elements ... either [withdrew] from political activity or aligned themselves with the opposition [the Castro-led July 26 Movement]." This tendency developed further after the January 1, 1959 victory. The new provisional revolutionary government drew from representatives of some "established political parties" (Pérez 1995: 313). After January 1, 1959, several thousand people closely associated with Batista left the country. They departed partly of their own accord, partly because of the provisional revolutionary government and partly by U.S. inducement (Domínguez 1979: 139–40). The remainder of the Batista forces, the worst assassins and torturers, went on trial and met with severe consequences.

However, the old U.S. model multi-party system did not completely disappear in one fell swoop. While the political elites in the main were no longer in the picture in 1959–60, they still attempted to resurface politically through violent clandestine activities. Therefore, the dismantling of the old party system was still a high priority. The most important factor in disassembling it, as indicated above, was the people themselves in the meetings with Castro on the theme of elections. They knew by instinct and political experience that the multi-party system was not viable.[3] Thus the new state arose. The new socio-economic and social orientations based on, and arising out of, the new state encouraged the people to retain a political system to their liking. The grass roots expressed the will to reject the U.S. model right from the beginning. Above all, there was fear that anything foreign to the Cuban political process would interfere with the transformations going on at the economic and social base. The simultaneous and radical democratization of the political and economic systems as a revolutionary process could take place only because of the socialist orientation of the Revolution. This socialist character was announced in April 1961. The dividing line was the pre-eminence of the accumulation of private property for the extremely small minority versus the economic, social and cultural needs of the vast majority. Democracy was in rapid motion.

Elections Analysis: Then and Now

Regarding elections in the early post-1959 period, one Cuban-American Cubanologist, Marifeli Pérez-Stable, wrote about those years: "In May 1960, before a million Cubans in Havana, Fidel Castro officially announced that the government would not hold elections. His audience shouted that the people had already voted, and they had voted for Fidel" (Pérez-Stable 1993: 77).

---

3. Regarding this conclusion, I am indebted to researcher Olga Fernández Ríos, who has dealt extensively with this period. In reading the manuscript, she pointed out to me that the old pre-1959 party system cannot be considered to have disappeared in one stroke.

Pérez-Stable does not acknowledge the revolutionary nature of the elections issue that unfolded after January 3, 1959, as outlined above. Furthermore, Pérez-Stable's account of that May 1, 1960, mass meeting is inaccurate. The "Castro Speech" database contains the full-text translations of speeches, interviews and press conferences by Castro, based upon the records of the Foreign Broadcast Information Service (FBIS), a *U.S. government agency* responsible for monitoring broadcast and print media in countries throughout the world. These records are in the public domain (Latin American Network Information Center n.d.).

This U.S. account on Castro's May 1, 1960, speech reports:

> Castro said the [former] rulers had created a democracy and despite the tremendous force and sacrifices of the people, they had created a democracy in which the majority did not govern and did not count for anything. However, in a real democracy, the majority counts for something, in a real democracy the interests of the majority are protected, and man has the right to bread, to work and to culture. This is democracy and this is the democracy of the Cuban Revolution, Castro said. At this point gathered masses broke out into loud and long cheering. Shouts of Fidel, Fidel, Fidel, and what seemed to be revolutionary slogans continued for approximately [the number of minutes not recorded] minutes. Following this Fidel resumed speaking. We are all sacrificing and yet our enemies vilify us and demand elections. At this point, the crowd broke into shouts of "No, Fidel!" This shout was followed by a chant, which was unintelligible. The chanting lasted for about five minutes. Fidel then said: "Yes, these enemies demand elections," and the people began once again to shout "No, no, no, Fidel." The second outburst lasted about two minutes. (Latin American Network Information Center 1960, minor grammatical changes for clarity)

Pérez-Stable ignores the development of the post-January 1, 1959, public debate on elections as exhibited by the participatory synergy of Fidel Castro with millions of people. It constituted an example of the Cuban Revolution's innovative nature, resulting in a unique form of participation. Moreover, regarding this mass meeting, even the U.S.-monitored database highlights the polemic relationship between Castro and the citizens. This is groundbreaking in the annals of revolution, whereby leaders publicly exchange with the people in mass meetings and a dialectic bond is created in order to make decisions.

Also providing a skewed perspective, Cubanologist Jorge I. Domínguez writes, "On April 9, [1959,] Prime Minister Castro called off elections, long promised as an integral part of his rebellion and challenge to Batista" (Domínguez 1979: 144). This is in contrast with Castro's account of the mass meeting. He recalls that when he said at that mass meeting that there was the issue of elections, the people interrupted by saying, "We do not want elections." He responded, "Why has a reaction been produced among the people against the elections? Because everyone remembers what politics has always been in Cuba" (Castro Ruz [Fidel] 1959). It is thus inaccurate to claim, as Domínguez does, "Castro called off elections." All the emphasis is wrongly placed on Castro as the individual. This focus results in denying the role of the people in the evolution of the situation until that meeting and in the gathering itself, as well as in the months that followed. There is a blind spot regarding the participatory nature of the Cuban Revolution.

In contrast with the Cubanologists' views, Ernesto Che Guevara, who had actually experienced this participatory democratic process, makes some valuable comments. He writes about Fidel Castro and the people as follows: "At the great public mass meetings one can observe something like a dialogue of two tuning forks whose vibrations interact, producing new sounds." Furthermore, highlighting how the people participated in decision making, Guevara remembers, "Fidel and the mass begin to vibrate together in a dialogue of growing intensity until they reach the climax in an abrupt conclusion." He concedes that "for someone not living the experience," it is a "difficult thing to understand," referring to the "close dialectical unity between the individual and the mass in which both are interrelated." Faithful to his appreciation of the individual's role, Guevera concludes, "The mass, as an aggregate of individuals, interacts with its leaders" (Guevara 2006: 6).

When elections take place in Cuba today, the U.S. establishment media often cite these Cubanologists in order to publicize their views. Based on the above, it would be prudent to consider that these analyses are only one side of the coin in evaluating Cuba's democracy. Chapter 7 deals with these and other Cubanologists' views on contemporary Cuban elections.

Regarding the immediate post-1959 period, there is an important conclusion to make with regard to U.S.-centrism and people's participation. For the Cuban people at that time, it was only natural to oppose U.S.-style elections or any elections, for that matter. This was the feeling at the grass roots even though the new political system of elections in that period had yet to be developed. However, the rejection by Cubans of U.S. pressure was a significant step to overcome. Here lies a basic contradiction between the vision from Cuba and the U.S.-centric notion of democracy and elections. For the Cubans, there was no major issue in rejecting elections under these circumstances. It arose as a natural, indigenous view. Similarly, the vast majority refused to accept capital accumulation and foreign domination as being innate to Cuban society.

Participatory Democracy and U.S. Frustrations

As seen in the previous section, in the first few years after January 1, 1959, the Cuban leadership and the grass roots participated actively in bringing about socio-economic transformations while developing their own unique political interaction system. The U.S. admitted through its State Department in 1960, "The majority of Cubans support Castro" and "there is no effective political opposition." Therefore, the conclusion was the imposition of the blockade against Cuba with the goal "*to bring about hunger, desperation and overthrow of government*" (Foreign Relations, Document 499, emphasis added). With this objective, the U.S. had hoped to create conditions to "prove" that socialism does not work, while building its own political opposition to spearhead regime change. This policy was a continuation of what the U.S. attempted to carry out in 1958 in the face of the advancing revolutionary forces. On what foundation was the political opposition to be based? "Castro [has] *betrayed* Cuba.... [There is the need for] a definite program in accord with the *original aims of the peoples' Revolution*" (Foreign Relations, Document 607, emphasis added, note capitalization of "Revolution" in original). At first glance, it may seem that the quotation regarding betrayal, while co-opting "the original aims of the Revolution," may originate from certain trends among the current opposition groups and dissidents. However, the source is a November 7, 1960, *U.S. Department of State* memorandum (Foreign Relations, Document 607). The 1960 U.S. pretext of "betrayal" is the guideline for present-day dissidents from just about all tendencies. One of their main targets is the supposedly "authoritarian Castro regime" and the lack of democracy and elections (U.S.-approach) in Cuba. This theme is examined in the chapters on contemporary Cuba. The purpose here, however, is to show the political basis and the historical origins of the organized opposition to the new democracy. There are many other such U.S. documents and appeals from that early period based on the "betrayal" theme, whereby the U.S. based their hopes mainly on liberals.[4]

The "betrayal" theme, as worked out by the U.S. immediately after January 1, 1959, is currently a key political pretext for dissidents. One of the most promoted dissidents, often honoured by Obama, is Cuban blogger Yoani Sánchez. She responded to a question on her assessment of the January 1, 1959, Revolution by saying, "It was a process that sparked a lot of hope, but that *betrayed* the majority of Cubans" (Lamrani 2010, emphasis added). This is the betrayal theme that both right and left dissidents have in common. For example, Yoani Sánchez places herself on the right, openly in favour of capitalism. She said in the same interview, "We can create a *sui generis* [unique] capitalism" (Lamrani 2010). Meanwhile, those from the left, who claim to be in favour of socialism, also allude to betrayal. For example, they write in the

---

4. See www.democracyintheus.com, "'Betrayal': Common Denominator of Cuban Dissidents."

dissident *Havana Times* website that they are "true to the revolutionary principles that guided the struggle against the Batista dictatorship" (Fernández 2012). The same "leftist" dissident website defends the pro-capitalist Yoani Sánchez (Robinson 2012). There are innumerable examples of cross-referencing between "left" and right dissident websites. Side by side with the betrayal theme, and completing their common foundation, is opposition to what they call "the authoritarian or dictatorial rule of the Castros." Both the betrayal theme and the leitmotif of pro-democracy anti-authoritarian/dictatorship find their common origins in the 1958–61 period. These are the years when the U.S. initiated its regime change policy toward Cuba. There even exists complicity between Yoani Sánchez, a "moderate," and those "hardliners" who openly promote U.S. military intervention in Cuba as the only path for regime change and democracy.[5] However, how did the development of democracy unfold in Cuba after the January 1959 victory?

Democratization Through Mass Organizations and Participation

In 1959 and the early 1960s, the U.S. carried out its interventions, initiated the blockade and considered further "USS *Maine*-type" pretexts. Washington also elaborated its orientations, such as the "betrayal" theme and U.S.-organized opposition. All of these courses of action and guiding principles had as a goal the subversion of the Cuban constitutional order. These policies set the basis for Washington's orientation, which it still employs today. However, in the early 1960s, Cuba continued its democratization process despite external threats from the U.S. and the opposition it attempted to manufacture.

The innovative participatory feature of the Cuban Revolution, as illustrated by the example of how the people reached a decision in the immediate post-1959 period regarding elections, continued in other forms as well. There was a direct link between this political process and the socio-economic transformations taking place at the time. Another notable, avant-garde concept related to the embryonic participatory nature of the Cuban political system was the creation of the Comités de Defensa de la Revolución (CDR — Committees for the Defence of the Revolution).

On September 28, 1960, approximately one million people congregated in front of Havana's former presidential palace. The occasion was Castro's return from a trip to New York on United Nations business. In the course of this mass meeting, participants heard a bomb explode, which the crowds met with defiant, patriotic shouts. After a second bomb went off, Castro declared that there was a need to establish a system of "collective, revolutionary surveillance (*vigilancia*)" (Castro Ruz [Fidel] 1960). He pointed out

---

5. See www.democracyintheus.com, "'Democracy Promotion' Through U.S. Military Intervention."

that every neighbourhood, apartment building and street block in Havana was represented in the mass meeting (Castro Ruz [Fidel] 1960).

Thus the people in the neighbourhood spontaneously started to organize their own committees, known later as the CDR, which has since developed committees throughout the country. In the initial months and years after its 1960 formation, the CDR network of neighbourhood committees acted as virtual local governments carrying out social and political activities as well as surveillance. The CDR committees became de facto organizational channels for people's participation. One year after their founding, more than 800,000 Cubans became active members, even though membership was, and continues to be, voluntary (Interviews, Lezcano 2008b and Martínez Canals 2009).

Another example of the participatory tradition in Cuba's political system consists of the Milicias Nacionales Revolucionarias (MNR — Revolutionary National Militias), formed in the fall of 1959. The goal was to defend the nation against U.S. terrorist-led activities taking place virtually everywhere on the island. Membership in the militia rapidly became a badge of honour. People received arms to defend the country against possible invasion (Interview, García Brigos 2009b). These brigades were formed in the image of the *mambí* Republic in Arms and the Sierra Maestra Rebel Army. The past historical participatory experiences consisted in recruiting and arming people in local areas in the course of extending the liberated territories.

One of the most important factors of change contributing to social and political participation materialized in the groundbreaking Literacy Campaign, initiated in 1961. The campaign took place in the face of U.S.-organized provocations against literacy campaign activists (Interviews, Rojas Hernández 2009a and Castro Espín 2009). Literacy as a problem to solve and the way people participate in its resolution constitute some of the best examples of a democracy in motion. The inventive Cuban approach to involving the people resulted in life-changing results for those who learned to read and write. Just as importantly, the grass-roots participation of the young and old alike who carried out the Literacy Campaign resulted in a lasting impact on their lives and values. This countrywide activity became a source of bonding among the people and helped to reinforce the cause of the Revolution. One of the main forces spearheading this campaign was the Federación de Mujeres Cubanas (FMC — Federation of Cuban Women), founded in August 1960.

The formation of the CDR, the Militias, the FMC and other mass organizations, combined with the Literacy Campaign, served to encourage the process of people's empowerment. Cuban society was innovatively being democratized as a process based on its own tradition and thinking. People felt part of the revolutionary movement because they were participating in it. This was possible only because there were parallel transformations in the socio-economic system in favour of the people and to the detriment of unlimited accumulation of private property closely tied to U.S. domination.

Initial Attempts to Establish
Local Governments and Elections

In 1959, local governments headed by commissioners replaced the former Batista-led municipalities and provinces. In 1961, these in turn were substituted by more highly developed grass-roots institutions composed of local representatives of mass and political organizations. They also included individuals designated by the central government. This first attempt at local government had as its goal the coordination of the national and local activities at a time when major changes were taking place, such as nationalizations of big U.S. and other major foreign enterprises. It strove to involve people in the work of the government (García Brigos 1998: 45–47), but they were lacking in structure and experience (Roman 2003: 64; LeoGrande 1981: 275–78).

In 1966, this local system underwent changes to improve the systematic and organic participation of the people in government activities. Elections were organized for delegates from neighbourhoods, work centres and local administrations. Nomination meetings took place in which people proposed candidates and then voted on them by a show of hands (García Brigos 1998: 47–48; Roman 2003: 65–66). While this Local Power, as it was known, represented a significant experiment in improving participation, pressures of daily life and activities related to production and providing services absorbed much of the delegates' energy (García Brigos 1998: 49). However, despite its drawbacks and limitations, it was a "significant phase in the development of Cuban political participation ... [and] the first systematic attempt to create government institutions with some degree of accountability to the public" (LeoGrande 1981: 279). People participating actively in the political process found its antecedents to an extent in the nineteenth-century *mambí* experiments with the Republic in Arms. A forerunner of grass-roots participation was also practised during the late 1950s in the Sierra Maestra territories liberated from Batista by the revolutionaries. Both these experiences in the nineteenth century and the late 1950s were embryonic, but they provided familiarity with a process on which to build in the future. For an analysis from another perspective of Cuba's roots in experimenting with government and elections, see Peter Roman's exceptional work *People's Power: Cuba's Experience with Representative Government* (Roman 2003: 9–59).

In addition to the weaknesses of local government experiments in the 1960s and their eventual demise, there was the failure to reach the ten-million-ton sugar harvest target in 1970 based on mass mobilization. These problems and others resulted in a test that Cuba had to face. This trial consisted in seeking means to further enhance a more effective participation of the people in the political system.

Origins of the PCC: Yesterday and Today

Simultaneously with the developments of the mass organizations and the attempts at local people's power from 1959 to the late 1960s, the new Partido Comunista de Cuba (PCC — Communist Party of Cuba) was taking its first steps. It eventually took shape by the fusion of three organizations: the July 26 Movement, the Partido Socialista Popular (PSP — People's Socialist Party) and the Directorio Revolucionario 13 de Marzo (DR-13-M — March 13 Revolutionary Directorate). These were the three main groups that took part in the Revolution and post-1959 activities.

Of the three, the July 26 Movement was the most important, as it led the Cuban revolutionary movement to break away from the dogma and the inertia exhibited by the communist party. Were it not for the July 26 Movement, the Cuban Revolution would not have been rekindled in 1953, which in turn led to the 1959 victory. Nonetheless, this was not accomplished alone. Other organizations, including the communist party, rallied to the cause once the path opened. The July 26 Movement was always a *movement* — never a party. It emerged from the 1953 Moncada operation against a dominant tendency in the international communist movement and the communist party in Cuba itself. Both considered Moncada adventurist and putschist. The second organization involved in the integration, the PSP (formerly known as the PCC), eventually also rallied to the cause, even though it did not agree with Moncada at the beginning. The DR-13-M was the third important organization implicated in the synthesis to establish the new party; it had fought against Batista mainly in the central region.

A concerted effort took place to unify the three organizations. In 1961, the first step resulted in the Organizaciones Revolucionarias Integradas (ORI — Integrated Revolutionary Organizations). Following a series of complex situations, this gave way to the second step at amalgamation, the Partido Unido de la Revolución Socialista (PURS — United Party of the Socialist Revolution). It was not until 1965 that the new and current PCC was established. Its founding First Congress took place in 1975 (Kapcia 2008: 31–35; Kapcia 2000: 124; LeoGrande 2008: 50–51; Interview, Cristóbal 2009).

The new PCC (resulting from this integration in 1965) arose out of various forces, but principally out of the July 26 Movement. Despite obstacles in uniting, such as problems of sectarianism, those involved persevered until they accomplished their goal. The Cuban value of unity, which finds its source in Martí, played an important role. In this context, the gesture by Blas Roca (a PSP leader) and the PSP to unite with the July 26 Movement was of historic significance (Interview, Fernández Ríos 2008).

This innovative approach to building a new communist party has its origins largely in the Cuban political tradition. The 1940s generation of Castro was raised on Martí's thinking and legacy. Most youth who were able to attend school studied Martí and many were aware of his main teachings:

first, unity; second, the need for a political party to lead the nation and the Revolution; third, the requirement of conscious popular participation; and, finally, ethics and social justice. In addition, one of the initial founders of the old PCC in 1925 was Baliño. He was a colleague of Martí in the founding of the Partido Revolucionario Cubano (PRC — Cuban Revolutionary Party). Roca, a leader of the PCC since the 1930s, also followed Martí. Roca led his party in the 1960s to unite with Castro's movement under the latter's leadership, an extremely important action (Interview, Gómez 2008; Fung Riverón 1982). It is very unusual for a leader of a communist party to integrate the organization into another formation that is not communist; in addition, Roca conceded the leadership role to Castro and his movement.

The formation of the party in 1965 under the leadership of Castro was not a concession to the U.S.S.R., with which Cuba had been developing economic relations. According to Kapcia, the party's foundation, "more importantly reflected the Cuban leaders' growing identification with communism and their developing belief that the Revolution should be advancing well on its way toward a communist society" (Kapcia 2008: 74). The Cuban leadership's view opposed the post-1945 Moscow attempt to impose its policy. This line consisted, as applied in Eastern Europe, in calling communist parties something else. This alternative terminology was to reflect a kind of "people's democracy," "secondary in importance" compared with the "communist system," to which only the U.S.S.R. had a claim (Kapcia 2008: 74). George Lambie agrees with the evaluation of Cuba holding a relatively independent stance. He says that while Cuba was moving closer to the U.S.S.R., "it did not become a proxy state and its 'Sovietization' was only partial" (Lambie 2010: 159). Lambie offers several examples. However, one of the most significant for the focus of this book is Cuba's insistence on the importance of "participation and the formation of political consciousness … despite the constraints resulting from the closer relationship with the Soviet Union, and the adoption of some of its practices" (Lambie 2010: 159). The origins of the PCC and the development of the Cuban Revolution are reminders that Cuba never became a satellite of the U.S.S.R.

Elections, New State Structure and Constitution (1970–76)

Not long after its founding in 1965, the PCC took up the need for effective participation of the people in the political system. In 1970, the PCC leadership organized a program to work out suggestions for a more participatory and effective electoral system. This exploration also included the search for a formal state structure from the highest level to the grass roots. The democratization that came about through the Revolution itself and the early years after 1959 had to move to another level. Following the PCC's suggestions, in

1974 in the province of Matanzas, a pilot project was launched by the PCC and the government to test a new political system. If successful, it would be applied to the entire country and at all levels of government.

A document on the Órganos del Poder Popular (OPP — Organs of People's Power) was worked out based on studies of electoral systems in different countries, including the U.S.S.R. and the U.S., and on Cuba's own experience. A pilot project was then elaborated involving municipal and provincial elections held in the province of Matanzas in the summer of 1974 in order to test the new system (Interviews, Lezcano 2008a, 2008b; García Brigos 1998: 29, 49, 52). On August 22, 1974, Raúl Castro spoke to the 1,046 elected delegates at the closing session of a seventeen-day Seminar for Delegates of the OPP in preparation for them to take up their functions in the municipalities and at the provincial level in Matanzas. He said:

> In the early years of our Revolution, the necessary conditions required to set up these institutions did not exist, nor was there an urgent or pressing need for them; they weren't decisive in carrying out the tasks, which faced the Revolution during the early period. In order to operate in such a situation and face the tasks of the moment, we needed a state apparatus, which both was functional and could be quickly mobilized....
>
> In the first years of the Revolution, we were not equipped to face the task of setting up representative institutions. At that time, we did not have a strong Party, the mass organizations were not sufficiently developed, in short, we did not have the organizational tools available to us now.... To all these factors, we should add a certain lack of experience and understanding on the part of many of us regarding the importance of these representative institutions and the role which they are to play.... The setting up of representative institutions of the state constitutes a tremendous step forward in the revolutionary process.... At the beginning, during the early years of struggle for survival, they [representative institutions] were neither necessary nor vital parts of the state and, indeed, they might well have put a brake on the state, which then needed to be quickly mobilized. (Castro Ruz [Raúl] 1974)

Based on the Matanzas pilot project of the summer of 1974, a special commission of the PCC was established in the fall of that year comprising constitutional experts as well as representatives of mass organizations such as the CDR. Their responsibility was to produce a draft constitution that would include the basic outline of a new electoral system. It would later be elaborated in detail by a new electoral law. The draft also defined the role of the state. It was completed by February 24, 1975. Beginning on April 10, it was taken to the public for discussion. This was followed by a two-month debate at workplaces, in educational institutions and in the countryside, with the direct involvement of all mass organizations at the local levels. Debates were also held at the local PCC units. The CDR reported 70,812 neighbourhood discussion meetings with 2,064,755 participants. Based on observations by Chilean author Marta Harnecker, the lively input and debate was evident. The press and television were also involved by providing information and question-and-answer sessions. Harnecker reports that, in July 1975, the

> PCC Commission responsible for the debate tabulated that close to 170,000 assemblies took place, making its way into many of the twelve chapters comprising the draft Constitution. More than six million people participated. Suggestions from the debates led to changes in 60 of the proposed articles. (Harnecker 1980: 44–55)

The PCC First Party Congress adopted the revised version of the draft constitution by the end of 1975. A referendum on the Constitution by universal, secret suffrage was held on February 24, 1976, with a voter turnout of 98 percent. Of these voters, 97.7 percent voted in favour of the Constitution. Based on this Constitution, elections took place later that year, in October, for the first time throughout the country at the municipal level. This was followed in November with the election by municipal delegates of the provincial delegates, who, in turn, elected the deputies to the national level. This national level was constituted on December 2, 1976; the electoral system has since been reformed (Interview, Lezcano 2008b).

The Asamblea Nacional del Poder Popular (ANPP — National Assembly of People's Power, or Parliament) is the highest level of the revolutionary state, which finds its inspiration to a certain extent in the nineteenth-century Republic in Arms and the Sierra Maestra experience of 1957–58. The *mambí* flag of the Wars of Independence is displayed alongside the official current Cuban flag during ANPP sessions. In addition, it is significant to note the date chosen for the inauguration of the new ANPP mandate after the elections in Cuba, which has since at least the 1940s thrived in a culture that places emphasis on historical anniversaries (Kapcia 2000: 170). The ANPP's investitures invariably take place on February 24, the anniversary of Martí's initiation of the 1895 War of Independence.[6]

---

6. This is why I prefer not to use the term "parliament" for the ANPP. The expression "parliament" derives from the fourteenth-century English parliament based on tedious procedures, the old Anglo-Latin "The *Modus Tenendi Parliamentum*" (English: Method of Holding Parliaments). The terminology "parliament" also finds its origins in the Old French *parlement*, from *parler* ("to speak"), or parley. In modern day, we would call this a "talk shop." Thus the Spanish acronym ANPP reflecting "People's Power" (National Assembly of People's Power) is employed in this book. It is the equivalent to the appellation "parliament" at times used inside and outside of Cuba.

The PCC held its Second Congress in 1980, its main theme being the further advancement of social and economic development. The Third Congress took place in 1986 and was marked by the process known as the "Campaign of Rectification of Errors and Negative Tendencies." This "Rectification Process," as it was also termed, related to Cuba's own problems, not to the issues that were about to erupt in the U.S.S.R. after 1986. In essence, the Rectification Process began in December 1984, when Fidel Castro gave two important speeches dedicated to negative tendencies related to economic efficiency. Furthermore, it became a more mass-based social process starting in April 1986, after Castro's speech on the same topic. This led to the final session of the Third Congress at the end of that year.[7] The Fourth Congress took place in October 1991. It was preceded by public debates at the grass roots in order to obtain the input of the people at that important juncture of the Cuban Revolution. Such a wide-scale discussion had not taken place since 1976, when citizens had been involved in the drafting of the new Constitution. In 1991, many issues came to the floor, including reforming the electoral and state systems in order to democratize them. This resulted in constitutional reforms and a new electoral law in 1992. (Other reforms were brought to the Constitution in 2002.) The Fifth Congress was held in 1997. On the political front, it elaborated the PCC's vision of democracy in the post-U.S.S.R. period with a document entitled "The Party of Unity, Democracy and the Human Rights We Defend: Fifth Congress of the Communist Party of Cuba" (Castro Ruz [Fidel] 1990a; *Granma* 1990; García Brigos 2005: 113; Reed 1992; Congreso del Partido Comunista de Cuba n.d.; Constitución de la República de Cuba [1976] 2003: 3–4).

As seen in this chapter, the PCC has never been an electoral party. Yet, it provides leadership in the development of democratic institutions and electoral processes. Furthermore, as of 1953, the Cuban Revolution developed mainly on the basis of its own traditions and heritage. Thus it has been able to overcome major challenges and survive — and even flourish — on many fronts. However, as we will see in Part III, the most colossal test for the future of the Revolution is taking place now. Will it be able to emerge victorious?

---

7. In reading a draft manuscript of this book, Cuban researcher Jesús García Brigos pointed out the historical background to the Third Congress. It started to emerge in December 1984. A careful reading of these two December 1984 speeches by Fidel Castro indeed shows that the basic features of the Rectification Process were initiated in December 1984. It developed further in April 1986, before the main session of the Congress in December of that year. Azicri cites other Cuban sources, who trace the initial stirrings to 1982. However, December 1984 and April 1986 remain the main precedents (Azicri 2000: 329).

PART III

Contemporary Cuba:
The Test for Democratization

Chapter 6

The 2011–12 Communist Party Congress and Conference: Democratization and the Press

Democratization Through People's Control and the Press

In light of the examples provided in Chapters 2 and 3 regarding democracy in the U.S., Venezuela, Bolivia and Ecuador, there is clearly more than one way to view democracy. Contemporary Cuba constitutes yet another instance.

To explore democracy in Cuba, the electoral process and the functioning of the state must be investigated in conjunction with the other main features of the political and economic system. This chapter reviews an aspect that is, according to some preconceived notions, the antithesis of democracy: the role, in the system, of the Partido Comunista de Cuba (PCC — Communist Party of Cuba). The function of the PCC constitutes one of the important strands of the U.S.-centric cobweb that surrounds democracy in Cuba. The PCC is portrayed as the epitome of dormancy — static and stuck in a time warp — as well as, by its very nature, "authoritarian." However, in the case of Cuba, the PCC arose entirely differently than other communist parties, especially those in the former U.S.S.R. and Eastern Europe, as explained in previous chapters. By its very nature and heritage, founded partly on José Martí's tradition of what constitutes a political party, the PCC is striving to foster democracy in motion through participation. Indeed, in many ways, the PCC opens up new paths. Its policies on people's participation leading up to the Congress stimulate the debate on enhancing participatory democracy in the entire political process and at all times. The contribution of several Cuban social scientists toward this endeavour to further people's empowerment is also briefly considered.

From the perspective of preconceived U.S.-centric notions regarding "freedom of the press" in Cuba, democracy in Cuba is non-existent. This prejudice constitutes yet another significant filament of the cobweb constantly spun around Cuba's democracy. Simultaneous to Cuba's effort aiming toward further economic and political democratization has been the debate on the appropriate role of the press that has erupted from the grass roots and all levels. These deliberations relate directly to people's capacity to participate and control their own destiny.

Today's Cuba is undergoing a transition from one development model to another. Transitions like these that are taking place within socialist systems such as Cuba's constitute one of the most complex problems in the world today, according to Cuban researchers Concepción Nieves Ayús and Jorge Luis Santana Pérez. Regarding the current transformations in Cuba, while "official political discourse is calling ... this change the updating of the economic model ..., in fact this is an integral social change." In other words, these changes are related to the "functioning of socialist democracy" (Nieves Ayús and Santana Pérez 2012).

In examining the renewed Cuban model currently under adoption, certain factors regarding democratization must be taken into consideration. Most significant is the role of people's participation in enhancing democratization in this newly evolving situation. In the previous chapter, we reviewed the background to the current Cuban situation up to the 1976 reforms that brought about, for the first time, the expanded Cuban political system of People's Power. There were, however, important junctures in Cuba's post-1976 evolution that have had a direct impact on the current situation and the debates surrounding the updating of the Cuban economic model.

First, there was the 1980s "process of rectification of mistakes and negative tendencies." Second, the collapse of the U.S.S.R. and Eastern Bloc (on which Cuba was almost entirely dependent economically), which started in 1989, resulted in Cuba's biggest test since 1959. This was the Special Period, which began in the early 1990s and was designed to safeguard Cuban socialism in the face of the Soviet–Eastern European collapse. The U.S.'s tightening of the blockade against the island compounded the dire situation in which Cuba found itself. Washington saw the new situation that resulted from Cuba's abandonment by the former U.S.S.R. as the ideal opportunity to put an end to the Cuban Revolution.

Several scholars, such as Max Azicri, consider that the process of rectification began in the early 1980s, several years before the crumbling of the U.S.S.R. The goal was to undo the policy of "having assimilated uncritically European socialist political and economic modalities, without considering Cuban idiosyncratic and development differences" (Azicri 2000: 55–56). The rectification process, according to an official PCC document, would have "'definitely distanced the Cuban revolution from the U.S.S.R.'s and Eastern Europe's erroneous conception of socialism'" (Azicri 2000: 329). However, because of the Special Period and the tightening of the U.S. blockade, the rectification process "lost momentum" (Azicri 2000: 329). In order to focus on today's major transformations in Cuba, Nieves Ayús and Santana Pérez argue that two "successive models of socialist development" have transpired since 1959. The first corresponds to the period from January 1, 1959, to the rectification process in the 1980s. During this period, indigenous revolutionary actions took place while Cuba also "incorporated into its physiognomy basic traits of so-called 'real socialism'" (U.S.S.R. and Eastern Europe). However, the 1980s rectification process based on eliminating economic errors was abruptly affected at the beginning of the 1990s with the Special Period. The two scholars therefore consider that the 1980s rectification is the "genesis of the necessary social change that is blossoming today in our country [Cuba]" (Nieves Ayús and Santana Pérez 2012). This analysis highlights the importance of today's debate on the influences of the former Soviet Union and Eastern Europe. It directly affects the quality of people's participation, as the heritage from the former U.S.S.R. is very different than the participatory political culture that is indigenous to Cuba.

Bureaucracy is one of the enemies of participatory democracy. As these chapters on contemporary Cuba deal with bureaucracy, it is necessary to provide a brief definition of the term. Bureaucracy, as a general concept of administration, has a long history that traces back to Western civilizations and to ancient ones such as those that existed in Egypt, China and cultures indigenous to Latin America. Max Weber and others have studied bureaucracy extensively in the West since the end of the nineteenth and early twentieth century. In the Cuban context, bureaucracy existed before 1959 under the capitalist system and now subsists as well under socialism.

In 1963, Ernesto Che Guevara (2005) provided perhaps the sharpest and most concise concept of bureaucracy, which also encompassed its pejorative connotation of bureaucratism (or *burocratismo*). His vision is valid today even though the conditions are different. The "original sins" of the Cuban pre-1959 government bureaucracy had their share of "hangers-on and opportunists" (179). Thus, as Guevara elaborated, bureaucratism existed in the capitalist society. What was critical for Cuba after January 1, 1959, in his view, was the matter of transforming the early "guerrilla" stage of management into the centralized state. Guevara explains that Cuba's "swing went too far" under the influence of the socialist camp. The high level of centralization resulted in placing "too many restrictions on the initiative of administrators" (178). There was also a shortage of trained, middle-level civil servants and the lack of a control mechanism to spot and correct errors. Both the most conscious and apprehensive civil servants "curbed their initiatives in order to adjust them to the sluggish motion of the administrative machinery" (178–79). Others "continued doing as they pleased, without feeling obliged to respect any authority" (179). To face this situation, the Cuban government then had to introduce "new control measures" (179). Along with other characteristics, "this is how our revolution began to suffer from the evil called bureaucratism" (179). He then adds to old features new problems such as lack of motivation. Not all civil servants are the same. Many are also victims of bureaucratism. It is "like a ball and chain weighing down the type of official who is trying as best he can to solve his problem but keeps crashing time and again into the established way of doing things, without finding a solution" (180).

Since the 1960s, and because of accumulated problems, *burocratismo* has, to a certain extent, merged with corruption, as we will see in this chapter. Participatory democracy is the main potential combatant against bureaucratic practices and dishonest or corrupt bureaucrats at all levels.

Since 1976, in addition to, first, the 1980s rectification campaign against bureaucracy and economic inefficiency and, second, the 1990s Special Period, there was a third important turning point. The 1992 reforms in the political system — directly related to democratization — also constitute an important juncture. These 1992 changes will be discussed further in Chapters 7 and 8.

Opening the Debate

This current process of change, as part of the "transition from one development model to another within the same social system," is centred on the decisions made by the PCC's Sixth Congress in 2011. The current stage of transition is also evident in different categories of legislation and resolutions issued and adopted before and since the Congress. What is the role of people's participation in this entire debate, which is so crucial to the future of the country and socialism? What are the prospects for the necessarily enhanced grass-roots participation in overseeing and controlling these major modifications and their successful implementation? In this context, how are social scientists intervening and what are their views? These are significant questions, given that some of these changes are relatively new to the Cuban experience and move beyond any other previous transformation.

This current process, according to several Cuban social scientists, including one who is cited below, began in 2005 with comments by Fidel Castro. In a public meeting, he dealt mainly with problems of bureaucracy and corruption. Castro concluded, "This country can self-destruct; this Revolution can destroy itself, but they can never destroy us; we can destroy ourselves, and it would be our fault" (Castro Ruz [Fidel] 2005). If measures are not undertaken, the Revolution will be at risk. In an interview conducted on this theme and others with Cuban political scientist and University of Havana professor Emilio Duharte Díaz, he affirmed that this was the first time that the self-destruction of the Revolution was openly presented in an official public speech, which, he said, "had an extraordinary impact" (Interview, Duharte Díaz 2009).

While this appears to be so, it is important to understand the speech in its context.[1] There were many unresolved problems festering since the 1980s, including bureaucracy. The solution to this was aborted in the 1990s with the Special Period. The 2005 Fidel Castro speech was groundbreaking in the sense that proof of corruption had been investigated prior to the speech

---

1. Much of what follows in this paragraph stems from a series of email exchanges in 2012 with Cuban researchers Olga Fernández Ríos and Rafael Alhama Belamaric in the context of their reviews of a manuscript of this book.

and was found to be anchored in the system. In addition, the 2005 speech did not reflect a momentary insight; rather, Castro founded his conclusion on his observation of an accumulation of problems.

After Fidel Castro's 2005 speech on the possibility of the Revolution's self-destruction, Raúl Castro followed up on the debate. On July 26, 2007, the first vice-president of the Council of State at the time, Raúl Castro (while Fidel Castro was recuperating from his illness), delivered an important public speech in Camagüey. He detailed the people's many economic and social problems and concerns, which the PCC and government leadership had been studying comprehensively. Of utmost importance was his comment about the difficulties encountered: "We need to bring everyone to the daily battle." Furthermore, he pledged, "All of us, from the leaders to rank-and-file workers, are duty-bound to accurately identify and analyze every problem in depth" (Castro Ruz [Raúl] 2007).

In September and October 2007, based on this speech and as a follow-up to it, meetings were organized for all citizens at the grass-roots levels in neighbourhoods, work centres and educational institutes. These local gatherings were "not limited to the subjects dealt with in that speech… [but also encouraged] the people to express themselves on any issue of their interest" (Castro Ruz [Raúl] 2009).

Elena Martínez Canals is president of a Comité de Defensa de la Revolución (CDR — Committee for the Defence of the Revolution) in the municipality of Plaza de la Revolución, Havana (at that time, in 2007, called the province of Ciudad de La Habana). Her CDR covers two street blocks. She explained in an interview how these discussions took place in her CDR block (Interview, Martínez Canals 2009). First, by the time that her block meeting took place, most of her immediate neighbours had already participated in the discussions in their respective places of work, educational centres, and PCC or Unión de Jóvenes Comunistas (UJC — Communist Youth League) nuclei. Second, Raúl Castro's speech had already been broadcast on TV and radio. Therefore, her CDR decided to get right down to the *planteamientos* (suggestions, complaints, proposals) without reading the Castro speech. Martínez Canals went on to explain that there was a very high rate of participation. Many participants worked out "clear *planteamientos*," which were presented by attendees in the spirit of "changing everything that had to be changed and transformed." It was a "productive (*rico*) debate," in which concrete problems were raised, such as food prices, availability of certain products and pensions for retirees. In addition, many gave their opinion on the "difficulties, successes, strong and weak points in the revolutionary process, and the role of mass organizations in the neighbourhoods." Each *planteamiento* "was recorded almost textually in a formal document (*acta*), without mentioning people's names, and presented to the superior level of the CDR." From there, the *actas* were forwarded up into the structure to be processed (Interview, Martínez Canals 2009).

Emilio Duharte Díaz, during an interview, declared that the 2007 speech by Raúl Castro was what "awoke that spirit of polemic in the population" (Interview, Duharte Díaz 2009). Duharte Díaz writes in a political analysis that the criticisms that arose in these public meetings touched, for example, on inadequate wages, low agricultural production, regulations and prohibitions on citizens, poor housing standards and the press. The information from these meetings in the fall of 2007 "was systemized and classified for consideration by the government." Duharte Díaz's comments were based on his analysis of measures taken by the state and speeches delivered by Raúl Castro between the fall of 2007 — when the debates took place — and 2009 (Duharte Díaz 2010: 58–59).

One measure that Duharte Díaz refers to is Decree-Law No. 259, enacted in July 2008. It provides for the distribution of fallow state land in usufruct and rent-free to individuals and their families. This is part of the program geared to increasing food production, variety and distribution, while lowering prices (*Gaceta Oficial de la República de Cuba* 2008: 93–95). The goal of this decree-law consists in addressing a major problem as quickly and as effectively as possible: that 60–80 percent of Cuba's food is imported (Pável Vidal 2012). The rapidly rising cost of imported food, due to the international economic crisis, must also be taken into account. This has been draining the Cuban economy even further. The goal is to replace these imports, where possible, by domestic agriculture. This program of distributing usufruct, rent-free land to individuals was one of the first implemented as part of the updating of the Cuban economic model. It was decreed almost three years before the 2011 Congress.

Duharte Díaz concludes that these measures, such as distributing rent-free fallow land, "correspond to the essential needs of Cuban society and demonstrate a political will to change. Many of them reflect demands put forward by the public in the national political debate [in September–October 2007]" (Duharte Díaz 2010: 59). Due to these measures, among others, in the period from 2007 to 2008 alone, the "country has been in a permanent debate" (Interview, Duharte Díaz 2009).

On August 1, 2009, Raúl Castro reported that, in September and October 2007 (following his 2007 public call to debate and put forward suggestions on all issues and problems facing the people), more than 5.1 million people participated in these workplace, educational institute and neighbourhood meetings. In November, "the collection of information and the elaboration of the summary were carried out." There were 3,255,000 separate entries recorded (the *actas* taking into account all individual interventions as described by Martínez Canals in the above-cited interview), including 1,301,203 concrete proposals. Of these suggestions, 48.8 percent were criticisms. By December, Raúl Castro said, "[they] were able to examine the final report in the Party." He concluded, "The product of this activity was not thrown into a bottomless basket [bottomless pit]." On the contrary, it would prove to be "very useful for the subsequent work of the country's leadership" (Castro Ruz [Raúl] 2009).

The 2011 Party Congress Deliberations: Input and People's Control

In reality, the PCC Congress as such began in 2010. The 2010 Draft Guidelines for the Party Congress in general reflected the debates that took place among the population in the fall of 2007 with regard to many of its concerns, expectations, demands and dissatisfaction.[2] In the perspective of the Party Congress convened for April 2011, the 291 Draft Guidelines for Economic and Social Policy were published on November 1, 2010 (*VI Congreso del Partido Comunista de Cuba* 2010). The following information originates from the May 2011 summing-up document (*VI Congreso del Partido Comunista de Cuba* 2011a).[3] People at all levels, from the grass roots to the Asamblea Nacional del Poder Popular (ANPP — National Assembly of People's Power, or Parliament), discussed the November 2010 Draft Guidelines from December 1, 2010, to February 28, 2011. There were 163,079 meetings with 8,913,838 participants. They contributed to 3,019,471 separate inputs.

The discussions and ensuing suggestions resulted in a second draft of the Guidelines. In this version, 68 percent of the original 291 guidelines were modified. Along with other alterations, this resulted in 36 new guidelines, totalling 311. During the Congress, held from April 16 to April 19, 2011, discussions took place in five commissions, composed of the 986 attending delegates and 97 invited guests. This led to another modification; this time, 28 percent of the second draft of the Guidelines was changed. Two guidelines were also added. The third and last draft thus included a new total of 313 guidelines. This version was finally approved by the Congress on April 18, 2011 (*VI Congreso del Partido Comunista de Cuba* 2011b).

The following is a brief compilation of only a few of the approved guidelines. They serve to illustrate the procedure and level of participation. The collected data represents the product of *all* the debates at *every* level (from the grass roots to the leadership), that is, from December 1, 2010, to April 17, 2011, resulting in the third (final) draft.

2. Information provided by Elena Martínez Canals and Emilio Duharte Díaz, as cited above, concerning the debates, the forwarding of grass-roots input and its immediate effects, contribute to this conclusion. I am also indebted for this supposition to a series of email exchanges with other Cuban colleagues from the time of the publication of the Congress documents in November 2010 to the April 2011 Congress. In 2012, researcher Olga Fernández Ríos was kind enough to follow up on a series of email communications to elaborate on this issue.
3. I relied on my own translation into English, since no official Cuban version was ever published in English. However, the translation carried out by Marce Cameron was extremely useful. I am very grateful to him for the monumental task that he took up.

The assembling is based on information provided in the party document *VI Congreso del Partido Comunista de Cuba* (2011a), including the final Guidelines. Changes to some guidelines reflected the desire for more control by the workers and population, and for administrative decentralization in cities and the countryside. For example, in a guideline dealing with the increase in the powers of enterprises in the newly decentralized structure, people added that this must take place "with the necessity to require accountability from those enterprise managers whose decisions, actions or omissions damage the economy" (379 opinions, Guideline No. 8).

The Congress brought about changes on decentralization of state economic plans and other activities. For example, it introduced an amendment to include the involvement not only of provincial administrative councils, as the draft originally stated, but also of the municipal levels (160 opinions, Guideline No. 121). Another amendment explicitly made more flexible the procedures for modifying the system of administration, distribution and commercialization of agricultural products. It expanded the initial guideline to include the possibility for the producer to bring products to the market on his or her own initiative (1,295 opinions, Guideline No. 18).

Education and health also went through many modifications, reflecting the growing preoccupation regarding the quality of these services. For example, on raising the quality and rigour of the teacher training process, the revised guideline makes "teaching enhancement [capacity to teach properly]" explicit (13,126 opinions, Guideline No. 145). Regarding the concern for health services, the original wording referred to, among others, improving the quality of services. A modification to this incorporated "satisfying the population, improving working conditions and providing attention to health [services] personnel" (16,600 opinions, Guideline No. 154).

The Congress also dealt with other important issues bearing far-reaching political and social implications. For example, the rations booklet is an instrument that has been in place since the 1960s. At present, it provides for approximately 40–50 percent of food requirements at prices highly subsidized by the state. Before the Congress, there was widespread opposition by the population to a rapid elimination of the rations booklet. Thus, while the original guideline stipulated only its "orderly elimination" and other conditions, the input added "gradual" elimination, in order to assure individuals and families against any precipitated move. (This issue registered the highest number of interventions: 54,979 concerns and reservations, in addition to the 925 opinions for Guideline No. 174.)

Regarding the sale and purchase of homes, the original stipulated only the need to "apply more convenient procedures to home exchanges, purchases, sales and leases in order to facilitate solutions to satisfy the demands of the population for housing." This was modified to widen the notion of home sales so as to "allow the buying and selling of housing, while other forms of ownership transfers (exchanges, donations and others) among individuals were to be made more flexible." The new version also highlighted the need to simplify "procedures for renovations, restoration, construction, leasing and the transfer of property ownership, with the goal of contributing solutions to the demands of the population for housing" (10,942 opinions, Guideline No. 297).

Concerning car purchases and sales, a *new* guideline was introduced. It allowed for "the purchase and sale, between individuals, of existing vehicles. The priority of improving public transport is maintained" (13,816 opinions, Guideline No. 286). Another new guideline required "first-rate attention to urban, rural, intermunicipal and interprovincial passenger transport" (16,875 opinions, Guideline No. 283). While the international press focused on the new right to purchase and sell cars, this same guideline still concentrated on the need to give priority to public transport. In addition, people's participation added a new guideline to improve passenger transport in urban and rural areas. This guideline received far more input than the one concerning car purchases and sales (approximately 16,000 compared with 13,000).

Other guidelines not mentioned above include some relating to self-employment and individual usufruct land users, and cooperatives for both rural and — for the first time — urban areas. In addition, emphasis was placed on local municipal development and new tax regulations for the self-employed in order to fund, among others, local development in the municipalities.

The practical application of the guidelines provided above as examples, along with other amended and new guidelines, remains a problem to overcome. Rafael Hernández is the director of *Temas* magazine, which offers a useful perspective based on "the critical reflection and debate of ideas" (Temas 2002). Hernández also serves as a visiting lecturer at Harvard University. In a post-Congress interview in the U.S., he said that the guidelines, as adopted by the Congress, naturally have certain "deficiencies, empty spaces (*espacios vacíos*)." The existence of these gaps, which often relate to the actual application of the guidelines, was "raised during debates held by millions of people … during several weeks" (Hernández 2011). Hernández said that one could not appreciate the ultimate application of the guidelines

> if this is not accompanied by the Inaugural Speech [Central Report] to the Congress by Raúl Castro …. [Castro] clearly said that, without transforming the political work style, without changing the manner of conceiving the role of the party, without also transforming the democracy within the party, participation, the party's work style in its relations with the population, without these changes, the reforms would not succeed. (Hernández 2011)

Hernández also judged that the axis running through the guidelines, even though it is socio-economic, is in fact political. For example, there is the need for decentralization, removing the state's omnipresence (*desestatización*), de-bureaucratizing society and other political changes (Hernández 2011). Likewise, researcher and author Olga Fernández Ríos from the Havana-based Instituto de Filosofía indicates that this process should be viewed in its full dimension. The course of action has important political repercussions on the entire political and legal systems (Olga Fernández Ríos, email message to author, June 19, 2012).

The Dialectics of Discrepancies and Consensus: Democracy in Motion

In addition to the controversial removal of the rations booklet, the reduction of bloated payrolls (i.e., overstaffing or inflated payrolls) also resulted in discrepancies across the population. Raúl Castro raised the issue of bloated payrolls on April 4, 2010, when he said, in reference to the state sector, "Some analysts estimate that the surplus of people in work positions exceeds one million. This is an extremely sensitive issue that we should confront firmly and with political common sense" (Castro Ruz [Raúl] 2010a). This was not the first time that the issue of bloated payrolls had been raised. For example, Fidel Castro also raised the problem in 1990. He said, with regard to factories and all work centres, "The bloating of payrolls is taking place." He qualified this by saying, "[We] are not going to say from one day to the next that we are going to apply staff reductions" (though this had been a focus of evaluation in the context of the Rectification Process in the 1980s) (Castro Ruz [Fidel] 1990b).

Returning to the current period of bloated payroll reductions, on September 13, 2010, the Central de Trabajadores de Cuba (CTC — Workers' Central Union of Cuba) newspaper, *Trabajadores,* announced the plan to reduce bloated payrolls in the state sector by more than 500,000 jobs. Completion of the first phase of this initiative was slated for the first quarter of 2011. The objective included the rapid introduction of a much larger number of new jobs in the private sector, namely, self-employment possibilities with 250,000 new licences. Overall, the goal was to improve the economy (*Trabajadores* 2010). However only a few days after the CTC's announcement, its secretary-general, Salvador Valdés Mesa, was reported to have said on September 17, 2010, in a union meeting, that the payroll reduction plan had shown that "the workers and [the] population [had] many concerns" (Rodríguez Gavilán 2010).

On October 25, 2010, special tabloid-sized newsprint issues of the Official Gazette (*Gaceta Oficial de la República de Cuba* 2010a, 2010b), dated October 1 and 8, 2010, were made public on a massive scale. They provided details of decisions made by the Council of State and Council of Ministers and some ministries. These outcomes took the form of decree-laws, decrees and resolutions to deal with both the bloated payroll plan and the significant extension in the definition of "self-employment" that was designed to absorb as many state employees as possible. This announcement took place six months before the Sixth Congress (*Gaceta Oficial de la República de Cuba* 2010c: 73–88; *Gaceta Oficial de la República de Cuba* 2010d: 89–168). However, the workers' concern, as expressed by the CTC, deepened once the resolutions and decree-law were made public. This was apparent in the Cuban press.

For example, *Juventud Rebelde* journalist Luis Sexto reported for a second time in as many weeks in September 2010 about irregularities in the process. In this second concrete example, there was an attempt to "confirm that a worker may remain on the payroll because it was convenient [for management] and not for production considerations or the specific position [*ocupación*]." The journalist also alluded to some workplaces where those not directly related to production tinkered with the procedure to save their respective positions (Sexto 2010a). The bureaucratism that Che Guevara warned about in 1963 is embedded in, and is acting as a dissuasive factor against, the implementation of the plan.

In an expanded session of a Council of Ministers held on February 25, 2011, on the issue of reducing overstaffing, *Granma* reported Raúl Castro declaring about the plan, "It cannot be undertaken within inflexible time limits; the pace of its progress will depend on preparing the conditions" (Martínez Hernández and Puig Meneses 2011a). According to journalists Leticia Martínez Hernández and Yaima Puig Meneses, Castro took "into consideration the delay in launching this process, [and] directed that the time frame for its execution be adjusted" (Martínez Hernández and Puig Meneses 2011a).

After the April 2011 Congress, *Granma* indicated that a May 14 Council of Ministers expanded meeting "approved a proposal to extend the time frame for the process of reducing overinflated personnel rosters" (Martínez Hernández and Puig Meneses 2011b). In order to minimize the negative impacts, the leadership has since changed its mind regarding the *pace* of applying the plan to reduce bloated payrolls. The tempo follows the feelings expressed by the people, while respecting their interests. Cuba's tradition of social justice predominates over taking unpopular measures. The policy is not being carried out according to the original time frame. In general terms, therefore, a consensus emerged since the Congress, at least on the pace of the process. It is an example of how participatory democracy works in Cuba, even — or especially — in the most adverse circumstances. This traditional policy contributes to consensus.

Since the second half of the nineteenth century, the seeking of consensus and unity has been characteristic of Cuban political culture. At the same time, differences of view also define this tradition. Cubans are expressive about their opinions. There is a dialectic relationship between consensus and discrepancies. Consensus is not permanent, but rather temporary. It changes and varies as events take place. In the same manner, discrepancies are not constant and they transform as a situation evolves. They are also found at many levels within the Cuban system. For example, the Instituto de Filosofía, which is related to the Ministry of Science, Technology and Environment, hosted a July 2012 workshop on the transition process. Reflecting these discrepancies, Cuban researcher Rafael Alhama Belamaric presented a paper to the workshop. He wrote about the basis of staff reduction as pointed out in one of the Congress guidelines. It is based on "suitability" of maintaining a post and "availability" (the term used to indicate that the person would be more useful to the economy in another employment). However, he admitted that these criteria are neither sufficient nor adequate. The problem of workforce reorganization can only be part of a full "economic, productivity and employment restructuring." Otherwise, the ongoing saga of bloated payrolls may continue because of a policy that, over the decades, does not take into consideration the overall economic situation (Alhama Belamaric 2012).

Just as a dialectic relationship exists between consensus and discrepancies, there is likewise a dialectic bond between the leadership and the people. A continual, reciprocal bottom-up and top-down process takes place. Taken together, these two dialectic connections (consensus and discrepancies, leadership and the people) constitute an important innovative feature of the Cuban political system. The system is also inspired by the long-standing democratic political culture of participation and mutual exchange between the base and the leadership. This characteristic has taken on very different forms and qualities from 1959 to the present. This latest example represents another illustration of Cuba's creativeness, which provides it with the ability to be flexible while upholding principles. However, the outcome of the current changes is not yet determined.

Congress Guidelines: Application and People's Participation

In general, the economic plan was agreed upon formally in the April 2011 Congress, including amendments to the guidelines. However, there remains the question of implementation. The situation must contend with two hurdles. The first concerns the pace of change. The second relates to the problem of how to contest those who oppose these transformations for selfish interests. The test is how to avoid a post-Congress situation that leaves the people with only structural intentions of local participation, but no actual further amplified involvement. The debate concerns how the people can control negative features — such as bureaucracy and corruption — that are impediments to the new adjustments.

Fernández Ríos raised significant points to consider. In the first of three articles about the PCC April 2011 Congress, she writes that there is "widespread conviction" to throw overboard the "influences of structures and practices of the state-centred and bureaucratic model derived from so-called 'real socialism' [former U.S.S.R. and Eastern Europe]." Despite the two previous PCC Congresses (1991 and 1997) and ensuing rectifications and reforms, these U.S.S.R.-style, "real socialism" influences "have been basically maintained." She argues that the current situation required of the PCC is to use methods that are "more democratic, especially regarding people's participation in decision making, [a process] that requires a permanent revitalization." In reference to consultations and debates, which took place before the 2011 Congress, the decisions made at this Congress do not exclude new adjustments and changes to roles played by the state. On the contrary, the decisions require "maintaining consultation and participation of the people as a permanent feature." Fernández Ríos, in dealing with Marxism, claims that Cuba has to uphold this ideology, but as a "guide to action," as seen by Engels and Lenin. In this sense, she highlights the need to work out the application of this ideology, as Fidel Castro has done, along with the "most advanced Cuban traditions of thinking and action." The Congress was not detached from the problem of confronting factors "that conspire against the full realization of individuality and its correlation with the social ... [a concept] which needs more analysis and attention" (Fernández Ríos 2011c).

In the second article, she addresses the discussion procedure that took place preceding the Congress. The pre-Congress debates served as a testament of the need to involve the people. However, she adds, "At stake is to maintain and further broaden it [the debate process] as a prerequisite for increased development toward a socialism that requires transparency of public management, permanent evaluation and legitimization by the people" (Fernández Ríos 2011b). She stresses the need to constantly engage people's participation as a general principle. Fernández Ríos also raises another important concern: the necessity to take into account the new generations that did not themselves experience the first decades of the Revolution's momentum. The Revolution's earlier phase involved the people's direct participation. She suggests the need to increase, as a stable structure or format (*de forma estable*), people's participation. This involvement should cover local public management, local initiatives and community projects, as well as the innovation of decentralized forms of government (Fernández Ríos 2011b).

In the third article, Fernández Ríos traces the development of bureaucracy over several centuries in capitalist countries, as well as in the former U.S.S.R. From the Cuban perspective, she holds that copying the highly centralized

Soviet model led to negative effects, such as an increase in the middle layers of civil servants. Fernández Ríos points out in this regard the link between the bureaucratic mentality and corruption. This is especially characteristic of those who do *not* want to change the system of prohibitions and delays. She claims that, if this system is eliminated, corrupted bureaucrats will lose possibilities of *mordidas* (bribes or kickbacks). *Mordidas* serve as the condition for the citizen's paperwork to be "completed" (Fernández Ríos 2011a).

The focus is thus on strongly rejecting old dogmas and habits from the former U.S.S.R. In their place, an emphasis on decentralization is needed, accompanied by *effective, regular* and *ongoing* popular participation. This is the instrument for the people to control the situation's evolution and concretely oppose bureaucrats. No illusions can be harboured about dishonest bureaucrats. Fernández Ríos stresses the need for the "improvement (*perfeccionamiento*) of democracy" (Fernández Ríos 2011b).

Two of Cuba's eminent economists, Omar Everleny Pérez and Alejandro Pável Vidal, confirm Fernández Ríos's concern about bureaucracy. They go somewhat further by issuing a warning regarding the "opposition [to the changes] by the bureaucracy, which tries to defend its position at all costs." Other economists raise the following weakness in the current process: "Ambiguities and uncertainties" are indicating that the process is "taking place without a profound critique of the Soviet model to which it owes so much" (Arreola 2012). Noted historian Eusebio Leal Spengler, currently one of the main figures among the Cuban leadership, issued a significant warning regarding the changes. He said, "I have no doubt that there are … elements that are terribly reticent to change" (Leal Spengler 2012).

Increasingly, the press has raised the problem of bureaucracy. To provide but one example, in a November 2010 article, a *Juventud Rebelde* journalist deals with the non-productive sector in some workplaces. The correspondent does not temper his words in describing some of the bureaucracy. He calls it the

> infernal institutionalized machinery that, in order to justify bloated payrolls, has invented a period [a daily time frame] to spend on time-consuming and cumbersome paperwork to bring suffering — I imagine with a certain morbid delight — to the common citizen. The worker's wasted workdays could otherwise be productive and fruitful. (Rius 2010)

Nieves Ayús and Santana Pérez claim that, in order to carry out the transformations, it is necessary to foster "the active participation of the population." They cite another researcher, Miguel Limia David, who claims that the best approach is to combine the top-down and bottom-up outlook and practice (Nieves Ayús and Santana Pérez 2012). However, what are the obstacles to overcome in order to arrive at this active participation? Another Havana-based social scientist places the responsibility on each individual and society. Maritza Moleón Borodowsky, director of Centro Félix Varela, claims, "It is necessary to change the civic culture. The citizens must be more proactive and conscious of their role in society." To achieve this, it is necessary to dialogue. It is likewise important to not be reluctant to "show disagreement" (Chappi Docurro 2012). In the heat of the debate on the economic transformations taking place in 2010, Rafael Hernández writes that the issues being discussed, among others, are "participation and effective political control by People's Power over the bureaucracy" (Hernández 2010). Cuban political scientist Dario Machado Rodríguez sees the importance of bringing into play fundamental concepts of the Cuban political system, such as "broadening of the forms available for citizen participation and the mode to exercise political control" (Machado Rodríguez 2012). Social scientists and journalists are increasingly raising the need to enhance people's control.

The 2012 PCC Conference and the Press: Trials and Tribulations

Citizen participation and control are largely dependent on the press. To participate fully, the citizen has to be aware, and thus fully informed, of what is transpiring. "Freedom of the press" is a source of confusion, as the U.S.-centric notion strives to impose its definition onto the world. In the U.S. Constitution, in its First Amendment on "freedom of the press," there is no explicit restriction on "freedom of the press" (Constitution of the United States 1791). However, as seen in Chapter 2, which deals with democracy in the U.S., the entire political superstructure, including the press, is based on the unlimited accumulation of private property. In the U.S., the press is in the hands of private property that controls the media (Chomsky and Herman 2002: xxii–xx, 1–35, 297–302). Therefore, the press must respond to the interests of media magnates, who are part of the ruling oligarchies. The 1898 "Remember the *Maine*" incident featured in Chapter 4 is the most glaring proof of this. It continues today in different, somewhat more sophisticated, forms.

In the Cuban Constitution, Article 53 indicates (concentrating only on this theme) that "citizens have freedom of … the press." It is stipulated that this freedom must be "in keeping with the objectives of socialist society" and "can never be private property" (Constitution of the Republic of Cuba [1976] 2003).

Regardless of how closely tied U.S. "freedom of the press" is to the interests of the monopolies, the Cuban press cannot simply be ipso facto idealized because it is not in private hands. There have been and still are many problems regarding the Cuban press.

Who are the journalists in Cuba? How does the press operate with regard to its own role in society? A local journalist explained that Cuban correspondents are not separate from the citizenry. They participate in neighbourhood activities, they do not drive fancy cars and they earn the same salary as everyone else. As far as he is concerned, correspondents exercise their profession as journalists as a "way of life (*sentido de vida*), not only to make a living, which is different" (Interview, Chirino Gamez 2008).

The January 28, 2012, PCC First National Conference dealt with many issues. However, the focus here on the Conference will be from the perspective of the relationship between the media and the people as part of the potential to strengthen a democracy in motion. The extent to which the updating of Cuba's socialist system is successful depends, in large part, on the transformation of the press.

In the basic draft document released on October 13, 2011, in preparation for the PCC's January 2012 Conference, one of its original 97 objectives, Objective No. 67, suggests the need to

> stimulate mass communication media to become an effective platform of expression for culture and debate, and offer avenues for knowledge, analysis and permanent exercise of opinion; develop objective and investigative journalism that would enable it to rid itself of (*desterrar*) self-censorship, mediocrity, bureaucratic and artificially sweetened (*edulcorado*) language, mechanical attitude (*facilismo*), rhetoric, triumphalism and banality. (Partido Comunista de Cuba n.d.[a])

These and other political issues were discussed in the local nuclei of the PCC and the UJC before the National Conference. Members made more than one million suggestions. This resulted in the modification of 78 of the 96 objectives up for debate as well as the addition of five other themes (Barredo Medina and Puig Meneses 2011). Consequently, a new second version was drafted.

During the first day of the proceedings, the National Conference, which was held from January 28 to January 29, 2012, was divided into four commissions. Delegates and invited guests discussed different aspects of the new second draft document. It emerged from prior discussions held by PCC and UJC members at the base.

One of the four commissions (No. 2) dealt with political and ideological work. The role of the media is part of this theme. The detailed Cuban television retransmission of large parts of these debates, over a period of four consecutive evenings, and the reports by the printed press served as important sources. The quality of the media is a major preoccupation. For example, delegate Abel Falcón (a local radio journalist in the province of Villa Clara) "transmitted the concern of many journalists regarding the

necessity to evaluate the creation of a legal instrument to facilitate the fulfillment of the policy of providing information" (Puig Meneses and Menéndez
Quintero 2012). Invited guest Lazaro Barredo Medina, editor-in-chief of
the PCC daily *Granma*, said that the media is facing a "very serious and grave
problem" that involves "the entire society" (from Cuban television, February
1, 2012; notes taken by author). He criticized the situation whereby journalists have difficulty in accessing information from functionaries. He strongly
condemned those civil servants who "hinder and build obstacles to access
information, the consequence being that a journalist gets fed up, killing
himself week after week in order to get some data [or] to get an evaluation
[of a situation]." He went on to explain how some civil servants "do not
want to give explanations; they avoid the press." He also rebuked the work of
some journalists who do "not verify the sources of information," but rather
repeat what they are told; they "listen to some civil servant but do not review
or verify and, as a result, at times misinform [the population] and provide
false information." He reached the conclusion that to "lose the credibility
of the population in the press is a great danger to the Revolution and to the
policy of the party" (from Cuban television, February 1, 2012; notes taken
by author). It was determined that the Final Report (*Dictamen Final*) would
include the necessity for both the press and the sources of information to
fulfill their respective roles in order for Cuban journalism to improve (Puig
Meneses and Menéndez Quintero 2012). It also confirms the opinion of
Rafael Hernández, who, while underlining the important recent increase in
public debate, concludes that this development is "still not reflected in the
communication media" (Hernández 2011).

The Final Report that emerged from Commission No. 2 included the
suggestions on the issues of the press (*Granma* 2012b). Conference delegates
approved the final document entitled "Objetivos de Trabajo" (Working
Objectives) on January 29, 2012. After the commission deliberations, the
conference organizers added some points to the original text cited above.
These additions are reflective of the debate, namely, to "demand that the
press and sources of information" take up their responsibilities of providing
information so as to "ensure the development of a more newsworthy, objective and investigative journalism."

In addition to the issue of the press, Objective No. 46 in the final PCC
Conference document called for the "encouragement of real and effective
participation by the population in the making of decisions and the execution
of projects." In the context of the fight against corruption, Objective No. 53
pointed out the necessity to "strengthen people's control." This objective also
called for the appropriate organs to confront impunity. Objective No. 76 suggested a maximum term limit of two consecutive mandates for all political
and state responsibilities (Partido Comunista de Cuba 2012).

In his closing speech to the conference, Raúl Castro emphasized the role of the press among other topics. He directly solicited the support of the Unión de Periodistas de Cuba (UPEC — Union of Cuban Journalists). Castro contended that the PCC must "encourage more professionalism among press workers." He also declared, "Institutions … must provide them [the journalists] with reliable and appropriate information" (Castro Ruz [Raúl] 2012a).

Many correspondents themselves are protagonists at the centre of this debate. UPEC is a professional association established in 1963. In preparation for UPEC Congresses, delegates are elected from among the more than 4,000 correspondents in their local media centres in order to raise issues and make proposals for UPEC's National Committee (Marrero 2006: 5, 24; Interview, Chirino Gamez 2008).

Immediately following the January 2012 PCC Conference, during the month of February, UPEC president Tubal Páez Hernández and other leaders of this professional association toured the provinces to meet their colleagues. The necessity for institutions to provide information, as expressed by Raúl Castro and the UPEC president, does not seem to have affected the attitude of many administrators. On the contrary, according to the director of the Cienfuegos provincial weekly newspaper, journalists still (one month after the party conference) continued to face either long delays or "silence" from administrative organs or enterprises. The "silence" and deferrals concern complaints by readers in the form of letters to the editor. This is an embarrassing situation, said another correspondent, since the people consider the journalists "social entities" with the responsibility to guide and inform the population. For this reason, he countered, journalists should be the "first to know" what is taking place in the province and the nation (Chaveco 2012).

In the province of Sancti Spíritus, reporters also highlighted the problem, namely, that some sources of information refuse to divulge data under the pretext, as journalists disclosed, of "not providing information to the enemy" (Morales [Gisselle] 2012). This "*secretismo*" has to be unearthed "if [Cuba is] going to involve the people in the economic transformations" (Morales [Gisselle] 2012). In the province of Las Tunas, journalists said that there is a need to change the way of thinking, both among the journalists and those administrations that hold back information that the press should provide to the people (Rosendo González 2012). There were similar comments in other provinces calling for changes in both the source of information and the work of journalists. For his part, the UPEC president expressed the need for legal norms (*normativas jurídicas*) applicable to the profession (Beatón Ruiz 2012).

The problem of secrecy goes back to at least 2007. A resolution of the Political Bureau of the Central Committee of the PCC in that year points out that there is a tendency for "state organizations to give themselves the right to divulge or not information that is not secret or strictly internal but that nonetheless contains real public interest." The resolution goes on to stipulate that the "prerogative to decide what is to be diffused in a press organ corresponds exclusively" to those responsible for the journalistic work. It goes on to say, "State leaders and civil servants at all levels avoid contact with the press" and "fabricate pretexts to justify their secrecy" (quoted in Barredo Medina 2012). The articles and published debates illustrate that many bureaucrats and enterprise managers have the upper hand and are as arrogant as ever. Journalists do not seem to occupy the place they deserve in society. In addition, according to their own association and to some writers quoted above, many journalists are also at fault. This situation has come about not because of *secretismo* by bureaucrats, but rather because of their own unwillingness to break out of the old style. The people at the grass roots, therefore, also do not have the information that should be in the media. This access is critical to the improvement of the citizens' participation in the current process of economic change. In order to enhance people's participation, it is necessary for them to be aware of all that is happening. Just as the press is the main instrument for keeping people aware of what is going on, social scientists are also seeking to further be an instrument in the empowerment of the people.

Participatory Democracy, the Press and Social Scientists

There are several important points to make concerning the relevance of the press and social scientists as real and/or potential instruments in further developing participatory democracy.

The press carries the challenge to contest the intentional domestic bureaucratic roadblocks to the transformation of the economic model. These impediments beckon the need for people to exert their control over the situation. This people's predominance contributes to assuring the most rapid and orderly application of the economic changes according to the schedule and real possibilities. In order to overcome this internal bureaucratic blockade, the press is one instrument that should be available to the people. Either it is the people's press or it is not.

In this sense, Cuban journalists at this time have the most difficult, yet crucial, task. They are forced to break through the deterrents erected by those who may have the most to lose because of economic and political changes. Those who hold back information from the press may be the same figures found in the structures targeted for change. It is thus a vicious circle.

It is ironic that, in the U.S., "freedom of the press" is in theory unlimited, but is in reality controlled by media monopolies. In contrast, Cuba is unpretentious in its framing of freedom of the press with socialist objectives. There is likewise an expectation of the press to develop within the need to defend the sovereignty of Cuba. Independence is the *sine qua non* of socialism in the Cuban context. The paradox is that what is presently limiting freedom of the press in Cuba is *not socialism*. Instead, the anomaly lies in the current constraints on freedom of the press originating from, among other factors, those bureaucrats and corrupt individuals who are *fighting against updating socialism*. The goal of the economic changes is to make socialism more efficient and responsive to the needs of the people; it thus directly infringes on the mode of living and material benefits of those bureaucrats who have slid into corruption. What Che Guevara said about this phenomenon holds true today. Some officials, he wrote, just "curbed their initiatives in order to adjust them to the sluggish motion of the administrative machinery" (Guevara 2005). However, others "continued doing as they pleased, without feeling obliged to respect any authority" (Guevara 2005). The path of a renewed Cuban socialism is paved with radical changes that the revolutionary leadership — and the grass roots — are attempting to establish. Opponents embedded in the bureaucracy or elsewhere know very well what is at stake; if this updating program succeeds, it will result in a direct confrontation with their privileged position. It is based upon, and cloaked in, the old Soviet-style, highly centralized state. This is the poison affecting the society, as commented on earlier regarding the "subtle" Cuban bribe (*mordida*). In addition, some journalists, as acknowledged by Barredo Medina in the PCC National Conference and cited above, also have to face their own inertia.

Adding to the pressure against the Cuban press is the work of dissident bloggers from the "left" and the right, both inside and outside of Cuba. They generally base themselves on the high moral ground of "freedom of the press" or "freedom of speech" in the abstract (as it exists in the U.S. Constitution). This is invariably coupled with the U.S.-centric view of the PCC and the resulting dissident demand for the multi-party system likewise inspired (implicitly or explicitly) by the U.S. model. They advocate that these concepts be applied to Cuba.

For example, in an August 2012 document entitled "Call for a Better Cuba," signed by Cuban dissidents residing in Cuba, North America, Latin America, the Caribbean and Europe, the first point is a demand for freedom of "expression and information" in Cuba. Another appeal consists in the "formation of political parties" on the island (Chaguaceda 2012e). The list of signatories includes figures from the "left" and from the right.

Among the signatories, the list of "left" dissidents is very visible. They claim to be in favour of socialism in Cuba. For example, there is *Havana Times* (officially for "open-minded writing," but with a noticeable penchant toward "anti-Castro" "left" dissidents) such as the author cited above, who implores readers to sign the "Call for a Better Cuba." The lineup also includes the self-proclaimed best-known "left" dissident Haroldo Dilla Alfonso. His Wikipedia page, to which he contributes and assists in maintaining up to date, claims, "He is considered one of the leftist intellectual opponents to the Castro government with the greatest influence in the cultural life of his country and of the exile community" (Wikipedia n.d.)[4] In addition, Dilla Alfonso promotes the call in *Havana Times* (Dilla Alfonso 2012c). He also advocates it on the website in which he is directly involved, *Cuba Encuentro* (Dilla Alfonso 2012b). The merger of the "left" and the right is demonstrated by *Cuba Encuentro* itself, of which Dilla Alfonso is one of the main stalwarts, along with overtly right-wing correspondents. *Cuba Encuentro* admits receiving funding and support from the Spanish government (*Cuba Encuentro* n.d.). It is documented that *Cuba Encuentro* saw its Spanish funding increased substantially while the "socialists" formed the Spanish government, compared with the period when the overtly right-wing party was in power. This financing to *Cuba Encuentro* was supplemented by the Washington-based National Endowment for Democracy (NED) (Serrano 2009). Also listed in support of the "Call for a Better Cuba" is another avowed "socialist," Pedro Campos (Chaguaceda 2012e).

Dissident Yoani Sánchez appears among the signatories from the right (as pointed out in Chapter 5, in favour of capitalism for Cuba). Another outstanding signee on the openly right-hand side of the political spectrum is Carlos Alberto Montaner. He is known for his long-standing terrorist activities against Cuba and CIA links (Allard 2005). The right-wing *Miami Herald* boasted the signatures of Yoani Sánchez and Montaner (Chávez [Juan Carlos] 2012). When accessed on August 15, 2012, the *Miami Herald* had accumulated 1,938 entries on Montaner since 1983, either commenting in favour of his positions or as articles signed by him (*El Nuevo Herald* 2012). The overtly right-wing Cuban dissident Ernesto Hernández Busto, who declared to be in favour of armed military intervention to get rid of "the Castros" (see Chapter 5 of this book),[5] also promoted the call on his website, inviting people to sign for, among other demands, freedom of "expression and information" (Penúltimos Días 2012).

Chávez's and the Bolivarian Revolution's October 7, 2012, election victory resulted in widespread international debate on the issue of democracy and elections. This created havoc among the Cuban "left" dissidents. The triumph contributed to exposing the true nature of their demands for "freedom of the press" and the "multi-party system" for Cuba, as expressed in the "Call for a Better Cuba." We recall that it was signed by both "left" and right Cuban dissidents. Thus the effect of the Bolivarian victory also further designated the "left" and right dissidents as two sides of the same coin.

As seen in Chapter 3, in the section covering the Venezuelan October 2012 elections, the domestic and international establishment press created a favourable image for opposition leader Henrique Capriles. Simultaneously,

---

4. The original Spanish reads: "*Es considerado como uno de los intelectuales de izquierda opositores al gobierno castrista de mayor influencia en la vida cultural de su país y del exilio*" (Wikipedia n.d.).
5. See www.democracyintheus.com, "'Democracy Promotion' Through U.S. Military Intervention" (as cited in Chapter 5).

television and newspapers, controlled by the Venezuelan oligarchy and supported by the U.S.-controlled international press, increased their demonization
of Chávez. In contrast, his candidacy had the support of some of the smaller
non-oligarchy and new media created by the Bolivarian Revolution. In this
situation of "freedom of the press," where did the Cuban "left" dissidents
stand on the two opposing candidates? In addition, and related to this, how
did they interpret the Venezuelan "multi-party system" with regard to Cuba?

The "left" dissident position surfaced very clearly in a *Havana Times*
article by Armando Chaguaceda, three days before the October 2012 elections and first published on another favourite Cuban "left" dissident website
(Chaguaceda 2012a, 2012b). The author admits that "the gaze of more than
a few democrats and social activists is focused on preventing the victory of
Chávez, whose victory … threatens to radically capture and transform the
political arena, negating the possibility of representing political plurality." In
contrast, the "leftist" dissident continues, "if Capriles wins, he would have to
incorporate those popularly recognized policies of the current government —
social missions and community participation — and govern with a style and
program of national (re)conciliation." The *Havana Times* regular contributor
comes out in favour of the alternative Capriles under the pretext "that [he]
objectively would have to negotiate with its opponents and the rest of society
to lay better foundations for the exercise of citizens' rights and autonomy and
political pluralism." As a backdrop to his support for Capriles, the dissident
correspondent lists what he terms all the negative features of Chávez in a
similar manner to which opponents of all stripes do with "the Castros." In
Chaguaceda's own words, the Bolivarian Revolution and specifically Chávez
are characterized by "increasing personal ambitions," "hyper-presidential
regime," a "dominant political organization (the United Socialist Party of
Venezuela [PSUV])," "discretionary use of state resources [oil for missions?],"
"usurpation of … party politics … and the media," "authoritarian and statist
tendencies," "concentration of power … in Chávez," "control and surveillance of the press," "a government anchored in power for 14 years" and
"his [Chávez's] authoritarian manner" (Chaguaceda 2012a). This position
was reproduced by many opponents of the "authoritarian Castro regime"
such as U.S.-based adviser to the Cuban dissidents Ted Henken (Chaguaceda
2012d). Another *Havana Times* regular contributor and part of the dissident
"socialist" *Red Observatorio Crítico*, Erasmo Calzadilla, went even further than
Washington itself. He raised the spectre of civil war and disaster affecting
Cuba and Venezuela after the October 2012 elections if the results were very
close. He evoked the scenario that the "leaders of Cuba [would send] troops
[to Venezuela]: firstly in special secret missions, and later, regular troops if
the conflict is internationalized" (Calzadilla 2012b).

After the October 7, 2012, elections won by Chávez, the Cuban "left"
dissidents found themselves in crisis. They carried a variety of positions,

but all their roads led to Rome. They used the elections to advocate against "the Castros" and in favour of "freedom of the press" and especially in favour of a U.S.-style multi-party system for Cuba. For example, in another *Havana Times* article, Cuban "left" dissident Chaguaceda could not hide his disappointment by alleging fraud (even though the opposition candidate Capriles himself recognized the legitimacy of the election procedure and the result, as indicated in Chapter 3). However, it is significant that the Cuban dissident, in this post-elections article, begins his campaign for the Venezuelan opposition in view of the elections held in December 2012 for state governors and deputies; he does so by advising the pro-U.S. opposition in Venezuela "to turn today's morning [*sic*] ["mourning" per Spanish original *duelo*] into effective action in the regional elections ahead, relying on the best candidate that Chávez has faced and an alliance forged during the process" (Chaguaceda 2012c).

In the same *Havana Times*, in yet another article also written by a member of the "socialist" *Red Observatorio Crítico*, Pedro Campos "congratulate[s] the Venezuelan people, the United Socialist Party of Venezuela (PSUV) and especially Comrade Hugo Chávez for this victory" (Campos 2012a). Readers may be wondering if there is a rift in the ranks of the Cuban "left" dissidents because one of these dissidents supports Capriles against Chávez while another in the same camp congratulates Chávez. There would be a difference if one ignored the conclusion reached by Chávez "supporter" Campos, applying the Venezuelan experience to Cuba. However, by taking into account his wind-up, the roads taken by both dissidents lead to the same Rome. In this case, Rome consists of both varieties of "left" dissidents attempting to use the Venezuelan October 2012 election results to oppose the Cuban constitutional order. For example, Campos asserts that Cuba can learn from Venezuela, Ecuador and Bolivia and their "democratic processes, referenda, freedom of the press and association, free access to social networking websites, respect for different ways of thinking, recognition of the role of peaceful and democratic opposition, the direct election of their presidents" (Campos 2012a). This is confirmed by another article in the same online newspaper pleading that Cuba can learn from Venezuela in opposition to the Cuban "one-party system" (Aquique 2012). Chapters 7 and 8 address the role of Cuba's PCC in its political system.

The role of the "left" dissidents is the most dangerous for Cuba because this program is camouflaged with the cover of "socialism" and "socialist democracy." In addition, these dissident bloggers use an eclectic approach. This is carried out by combining some isolated posts that can be considered positive toward Cuba in order to gain credibility inside Cuba and among some of the left outside of Cuba. This façade thus provides the numerous, very negative articles focused on the "authoritarian" nature of the Cuban political system and "the Castros" with the enhanced possibility of believability. This approach has been making headway among some intellectuals and youth inside and outside Cuba. Eclecticism is a disease infecting these sectors of society with regard to Cuba, both on the island and off. However, Cuba is developing a wide variety of its own bloggers who do not fall into the trap of eclecticism and thus contest the dissidents on a daily basis. The Cuban press and journalists are operating in these complicated and difficult conditions since the holding of the 2011–12 PCC Congress and Conference. The press must improve their work while at the same time keeping an eye on their flank situated among Cuban "left" dissidents and some others on the left in the international arena.

Cuba is going through major changes. However, in the North, the view available to most social scientists, parliamentarians and activists is distorted due to preconceived notions. Cubanologists covering a wide and varied spectrum of hostility to the Cuba Revolution are provided with platforms. In addition, dissidents enshrouding a vast array of views from "left" to right (but anchored to the common-denominator "anti-Castro" invective) monopolize Western radio, television, printed press and the Internet. While there is a virtual censorship on the work of social scientists in Cuba, the latter are engulfed in vigorous debates and exchange of ideas on the current changes and their political ramifications. Some are capable of being critical and expanding new horizons, while at the same time defending the path of the changes being brought about to improve socialism and participatory democracy.

One such example is Olga Fernández Ríos. She has a master's degree in history and doctorate in philosophical sciences. She is an associate University of Havana professor. Her specialties include political power, the state and democracy, people's participation and other related subject matters. She has written on these themes as well as participated in academic events in Latin America, Europe and the U.S.

Fernández Ríos presented a paper on June 19, 2012, in a Havana seminar focused, among other themes, on "socialist renewal" (Fernández Ríos forthcoming). In her presentation, she points out the work of academics in virtually all realms of social science, encompassing more than ten research institutes and the University of Havana. These studies and research are made possible through the efforts of the leadership and the people at the base to transform the situation.

Based on the experience of the 2010–11 consultations leading up to the Party Congress, she specifically advocates deeper grass-roots participation. By this, she means going beyond deliberations and providing views. She expounds on the need to convert this 2010–11 exposure to consultation not only into a *permanent* instrument for making decisions, which is in itself very significant, but also to another level. She suggests the need for the people to be involved by "empowering" themselves as "protagonists" in "putting forward policy projects." This would contribute toward filling a void in the Cuban political system, that is, a lack of permanent participation of the people in overall decision making and proposals for new projects. In this context, she points out that bureaucratism and other negative features dovetail with "the refusal to take advantage of, and the underestimating of, participative spaces" available in the political system. This, in turn, is occasionally due to "bureaucratic actions." Taking a fresh look at the current Cuban situation, she claims that the "approaches and forms of people's participation can be renewed in accordance with the new requirements of society." This analytical approach highlights the potential importance of scholars contributing toward further expansion and extension of participatory democracy. This fertile and vibrant exchange of opinions among many Cuban academics is very far from the image projected about them in the North.

In Fernández Ríos's paper, she perceives the current period in Cuba as a further step initiated in 2007, with the speech delivered by Raúl Castro to promote debates at the grass-roots level on all problems facing the people. This phase culminated in the 2011 Party Congress. Given the fact that Cuba is at a crossroads in the development of its new economic model, it is only logical that participatory democracy rises to the occasion. As Fernández Ríos suggests, it must renew itself in order to elevate itself toward the level required and in tune with modern needs.

Capitalism, Socialism and Cuba's Errors

The major changes occurring in Cuba raise the question of errors. According to Fernández Ríos's paper, the Cuban system has unfolded as a dialectic process of continuity and rupture. Continuity is expressed in the strategic advance toward socialism, while the ruptures are derived from a combination of successes, failures and errors regarding tactics. Of interest here is her testimony in the context of the erratic path of breakdowns, mistakes and accomplishments. There has been criticism of this state of affairs from both the leadership and the base. However, this opposition from all levels of society to repeated cycles of continuity and rupture "is meant to be a manner of assessing the Revolution." It does not have as a goal to undermine and discourage the Revolution. Therefore, Fernández Ríos insists that this ongoing appraisal is not an intellectual exercise, but rather "an instrument of change."

According to Raúl Castro, several errors were made, namely, an "excessively paternalistic, idealistic and egalitarian approach instituted by the Revolution in the interest of social justice" (Castro Ruz [Raúl] 2010c). It violated the Marxist principle "'From each in accordance with his ability and to each in accordance with his labor'" (Castro Ruz [Raúl] 2011a). This refers to the false notion of "equality," in which, irrespective of the quantity and quality of the contribution to society and the collective whole, everyone receives the same benefits.

Another error acknowledged by Raúl Castro is "the excessively central-ized model characterizing our economy at the moment." The goal is to "move in an orderly fashion, with discipline and the participation of all workers, toward a decentralized system." In this new system, "planning will prevail, as a socialist feature of management, albeit without ignoring the current market trends" (Castro Ruz [Raúl] 2011a). Learning from the negative centralized model inspired by the former U.S.S.R., Castro concludes, "We do not intend to copy from anyone again; that brought about enough prob-lems for us because, in addition to that, many a time we also copied badly." He further clarified by introducing a caveat, "We shall not ignore others' experiences and we will learn from them, even from the positive experience of capitalists" (Castro Ruz [Raúl] 2010c).

He considers the 2010–11 period as follows: "We are fully aware of the mistakes we have committed and the Guidelines we are right now discussing precisely mark the beginning of the road to rectification and the necessary updating of our socialist economic model." However, it is his conclusion that distinguishes the current Rectification Process from others in the past: "We either rectify — because we no longer have time to keep on skirting around the precipice — or we will sink" (Castro Ruz [Raúl] 2010c).

Castro's view on errors, very briefly outlined above, and the urgency to which he attaches the application of the solutions, shows good judgment. Does the situation negate the thesis that Cuba is a laboratory and that its resilience is in part due to its trial-and-error innovative nature? Not necessarily. There is a need, warned Raúl Castro, to advance while "avoiding committing errors of *strategic* importance" (Castro Ruz [Raúl] 2012b, emphasis added). What *has* changed is that there is presently a substantial reduction in the margin of manoeuvre for "trial and error." This is why Castro recognizes, as cited above, that Cuba is at the edge of the cliff and that, if Cuba cannot leap over it, the Revolution will sink into the abyss below. In addition, the need to reject new pressures from some on the "left" and the right to accelerate and expand the pace of change, without taking the necessary measures to maximize the chances of success, is aggravating this situation. The goal of these critics is to lead Cuba down the road to failure. From some on the "left," this would serve as "proof" that enhancement of socialism in the context of the current constitutional order and the leadership of "the Castros" is not possible. The other objective, that of the right-wing skeptics, is to plunge the island into capitalism and, once again, U.S. domination. While coming from supposedly opposite sides of the political spectrum, the ultimate aim is the same.

Does the 2011 Party Congress represent a shift from socialism to capi-talism and, therefore, from the point of view of the North, eventual "de-mocracy" for Cuba? Alternatively, does this process initiated in 2007 denote another route? Does it signify an eventual strengthening of a new approach to socialism and, in its wake — and as part of the solution — enhanced people's participation and empowerment? In Chapter 1, we briefly reviewed the notion of socialism as applied in this book. It consists of some common denominators comprising varieties of socialism, since, in the twenty-first century, there is no longer only one approach to socialism. Fernández Ríos deals quite extensively with socialism in her paper. While she highlights many worthy aspects, one in particular stands out. "The model that is being implemented demands the repositioning of the role of individuality in socialism." It is necessary to "demystify one of the most harmful dogmatic interpretations regarding socialism: the one claiming that, in [socialist] society, the individual is negated in order to subordinate it in absolute form to the social [collective]" (Fernández Ríos forthcoming). If this concept of recuperating the importance of the individual in society is followed through, it can result in important positive repercussions on the economy. For example, it will facilitate the increasing reliance on individual efforts both in the state and non-state sectors. This vision of combining the individual and collective roles will contribute to socialism, rather than undermine it.

The updating of Cuba's economic model is *not* a rejection of socialism. On the contrary, it is another experiment to *safeguard* socialism. The main means of production remains in the hands of the state. The Cuban economy is geared to improving the satisfaction of the people's basic needs in the realms of food, housing, education, health, sports, social security, social assistance, culture and all other aspects.

The number of self-employed people and individual rural and semi-rural landholders is increasing. In addition, they are now encouraged to form co-ops in the rural areas and, for the first time, in the urban areas as well. Market mechanisms of supply and demand co-exist with a planned economy. To label the current major changes as a renunciation of socialism and a path toward capitalism has many roots. One such source is those who are stuck with the old "Marxist–Leninist manuals," quoting isolated passages from Marx or Lenin. If Cuba were heading toward capitalism, then the leadership would not have rejected recommendations to the 2011 Party Congress that "openly contradicted the essence of socialism, as for example 45 proposals advocating the concentration of property" (Castro Ruz [Raúl] 2011a). The acceptance of these proposals would have facilitated the corroding of Cuba's struggling participatory democracy. A concession to these demands would have provided far more weight in the political system to those who are the benefactors of the accumulation of private property. In an extreme case, such as U.S. capitalism, property concentration is the base of its exclusive non-participatory democracy. In addition, the firm rejection of attempts to undermine Cuba's values of consensus and unity (while enhancing discrepancies and debate) by replacing them with the U.S. approach to the competitive multi-party system is an indication that Cuba is clearly *not* moving toward capitalism.

With regard to the debate about Cuba supposedly turning capitalist, let us briefly examine the concrete conditions in Cuba. Take, for example, a non-party member who is a self-employed entrepreneur or a small farmer. This person is exemplary of those who work hard, pay all taxes and licences, follow all the legal requirements and share the Cuban spirit of social justice, solidarity and patriotism. This individual may also be active in building co-operatives to increase production and the marketing of goods and services. This Cuban is far more valuable to the future of socialism than a party member who is bureaucratically blocking the road to change or, worse, involved in embezzling and corruption. The extent to which the positive characteristic and trend in Cuban society can — and does — dominate over the negative parasitic sections is yet to be decided.

Repatriating the role of the individual in socialist society, as proposed by Fernández Ríos, can also open the path for amplified and reinforced individual participation in the democratic process. It would contribute toward supplanting the old notion of "counting on others," including elected representatives, to carry out responsibilities on behalf of the citizens. Individual empowerment has important repercussions on the strengthening of sovereignty that is vested in the people.

The next chapter, concerning the Cuban electoral system, will look at, among other points, how electors and the elected see their roles in a socialist democracy.

Chapter 7

Elections in Contemporary Cuba

The Cuban Electoral Process: An Overview

The Cuban electoral process is lengthy and unique. Therefore, this chapter begins with an overview of the elections in order to provide a broad perspective. This will serve as the context for the detailed description and analysis, as well as the constructive criticism, that follow.

Elections in Cuba are based on its Constitution, as adopted by a referendum in 1976 and as reformed in 1992. The new 1992 electoral law was approved to enable the latest constitutional clauses on elections to take effect with all the rules and regulations clearly laid out.

The preceding chapter focused on the need for Cubans to tackle enhanced people's participation and on the roles of the Communist Party, press and social scientists. These pursuits compose one part of their democracy in motion; elections are another important aspect to consider in exploring the Cuban approach to democracy.

The PCC is not involved in either nominating candidates or electing them. Elections take place at three levels: municipal, provincial and national. Voter registration is automatic for all citizens sixteen years and older. This ex officio approach to suffrage rights means that, by virtue of being a citizen, the right to vote is recognized by the state without any effort required by the voter.

There are two types of elections: general and partial. General elections take place every five years. They consist of two phases, which together last about seven months, such as from July 2012 to February 2013.

The first of the two phases involves the nomination and election of "delegates," as they are referred to in Cuba, to the municipal assemblies. For nomination purposes, each local *circunscripción* (a very small "riding," "district" or "constituency") of a municipality is demarcated into very compact neighbourhood "nomination areas for assemblies." Each area is composed of a geographical delimitation according to street blocks. In each of these areas, during the course of the nomination area assembly, the neighbours directly nominate people from among themselves by a show-of-hands vote. Citizens then elect the delegates from among the nominees to the municipal assemblies by secret-ballot universal suffrage. These elections do not involve candidate expenses or campaigning. The delegates are elected for a term of two and a half years. These delegates carry out their functions on a voluntary basis after their regular work hours. Once the municipal assemblies are constituted, they elect their officials (presidents and vice-presidents) from among themselves. These presidents and vice-presidents are the only ones who are full-time, earning the same salary as they received at their place of work. There are likewise no perquisites.

In the second phase, elections take place for candidates to be elected as delegates to provincial assemblies and as deputies to the Asamblea Nacional del Poder Popular (ANPP — National Assembly of People's Power, or Parliament). (For the sake of simplicity, regarding this second phase, only the national ANPP is discussed here. The provincial elections, which follow a similar procedure as the national elections and take place simultaneously, are not dealt with.) The ANPP is the supreme body of state power, also known as the Parliament.

There are six principal mass organizations (see fig. 7.1 on page 168), and they are all directly implicated in the nomination procedure for elections to the ANPP. Candidacies commissions, composed of members of the mass organizations, are also involved in the nomination procedure.

Delegates elected to the municipal assemblies account for up to 50 percent of ANPP deputies. Once nominated and elected to the ANPP, they are informally known as *de base* deputies, because they are originally nominated by individuals at the base in the neighbourhoods (and not by any organization). This is one reason that the two phases of the Cuban electoral system cannot be separated — the municipal delegates elected to the national level continue their work as delegates while also fulfilling their responsibilities as *de base* national deputies. Therefore, they have a dual role. At the national level, just as the delegates at the municipal level, *de base* deputies exercise their functions on a voluntary basis after work or study hours. There are some exceptions to this rule when the responsibilities of an elected person are far too time-consuming to be carried out only after regular work hours. For example, delegates who are elected as presidents of municipal assemblies work full-time at this elected position while receiving the same salary they had earned while working. If they are subsequently elected as *de base* deputies to the ANPP, they constitute part of the very small proportion of deputies who are full-time. This requirement of reserving seats for *de base* deputies is one aspect that sets the Cuban system apart from all others.

The other 50 percent or more of the ANPP deputies are composed of *directos*. These *directo* deputies come from all walks of life. For example, *directos* can be political personalities, economists, trade unionists and other mass organization activists, educators, doctors, scientists, sports and cultural figures, or students. They are informally known as *directos* because they are originally nominated directly by organizations, rather than through the grass-roots procedure employed for the municipal delegates. This distinguishes them from the *de base* deputies, who have a dual function: they are delegates to the municipal assemblies *and* deputies to the National Assembly. Anyone can be proposed as a *directo* deputy, except those who have already been nominated and elected to the municipal assemblies. It is from this source (i.e., the municipal assemblies) that *de base* deputies are chosen.

The ANPP candidates are elected from municipalities even though there is no requirement that these *directo* candidates live in that municipality. This is different from the prerequisite applied to the municipal *de base* candidates for the ANPP, who must reside in the municipality in which they are nominated and elected. The municipal assemblies approve or disapprove the candidacies commissions' list of candidates proposed for their respective municipalities. There are no electoral expenses. Instead of campaigns, "meet-the-candidates" sessions are organized in the neighbourhoods, work centres and educational institutions. Unlike multi-candidate municipal elections, there is only one candidate for each seat available in the ANPP. To be elected to the ANPP, 50 percent plus one vote is needed.

The ANPP deputies (both *directos* and *de base*) are not paid for their work as elected representatives; they carry out this work on a voluntary basis after their work hours. There are, however, some exceptions, which include the president, the vice-president and the secretary of the ANPP; the principal leaders of the Council of State; and most presidents of permanent working commissions, along with the municipal assembly presidents, elected as *de base* deputies, who are professional because of the delegate responsibilities at the municipal level. Even then, they all receive the same salary they had earned before being elected. Deputies are elected for a five-year mandate, unlike municipal delegates, who are elected for a two-and-a-half-year term of office. If a *de base* deputy is not re-elected at the municipal level after his or her two-and-a-half-year mandate (for whatever reason), this person can continue to sit as a deputy for the remainder of the five-year mandate.

After the elections, the ANPP formally constitutes itself on February 24, 2013. February 24 is the date that marks the beginning of the Third War of Independence in 1895 under the leadership of José Martí. On this day, the candidacies commission leads the nomination process for the elections of the ANPP president, vice-president and secretary and the Council of State from among the deputies. This includes, for example, the election of Raúl Castro as an elected *directo* deputy to the post of president of the Council of State and Council of Ministers. The ANPP officials and the Council of State are in turn accountable to the ANPP. The Council of State may nominate new members to the Council of Ministers (government). As the government, the Council of Ministers has the responsibility, for example, of conducting foreign affairs led by the minister of foreign affairs. The members of the Council of Ministers are not all necessarily deputies. Unlike the Council of State, the Council of Ministers is not renewed every election cycle. The Council of Ministers is accountable to the ANPP.

This summary of the two-phase municipal and provincial/ANPP general elections indicates how the two steps are interrelated. Up to 50 percent of the ANPP deputies come from the municipal assemblies, whose nomination and election constitute the first phase.

However, municipal elections take place again (on their own and not as part of the national elections) approximately two and a half years after previous municipal elections that took place as part of the first phase of the general elections. This is so because municipal delegates' mandates are limited to two and a half years, as opposed to the five-year terms for all ANPP deputies.

These municipal elections that take place in alternating years between general elections are referred to in our discussion as "municipal partial elections." We will examine the details and consider an analysis of the two-phase general elections and the municipal partial elections later in this chapter.

The Soviet Political Model: A Cuban Import?

The prevailing U.S.-centric prejudice against elections in Cuba assumes that they are entirely controlled by the PCC. This narrow-mindedness perpetuates the preconceived notion that participation by the people is absent or, at best, minimal. This view is fostered by the common perception of the former U.S.S.R. acting as the lens through which the Cuban experience is examined. This mechanical approach does not take into account major differences between the former U.S.S.R. and Cuba. It is a concept that promotes the view that Cuba copied its political system from the U.S.S.R. This hypothesis also attempts to provide credence to the claim that Cuba was merely a satellite of the U.S.S.R. In order to further explain how these misconceptions operate, the example of Venezuela is pertinent. The discounting of people's participation in the Venezuelan example, examined in Chapter 3, arises from the U.S.-centric notion that focuses the attention on Chávez as an individual. Thus the vibrant grass-roots participatory political culture being developed there, based on socio-economic advances, is virtually unknown to the outside world.

In order to help shed light on this issue of the Soviet political model for Cuba, Jorge Lezcano agreed to be interviewed on three occasions with regard to this theme and others. He is an adviser to Ricardo Alarcón de Quesada, president of the ANPP. Lezcano was a participant in the 1974 Matanzas Seminar on the new People's Power (Mesa 1974) and the national coordinator (1973–79) of the CDR.

Lezcano explained that, as head of the CDR, he was sent to the U.S.S.R. on several occasions from 1974 to 1975 as part of a Cuban delegation. The Cubans' mission was to strengthen bilateral relations and exchange experiences. The context of these trips was to assist in preparing the 1974 Matanzas Seminar (explained in Chapter 5) and related activities geared to establishing the new Cuban political system. In order to highlight the importance of the CDR, he revealed, "Given that Cuba had not yet established its political system of People's Power, as head of the CDR, I was received by the secretary of the U.S.S.R. Supreme Soviet [Parliament], who considered the CDR their counterpart."

Furthermore, he conceded, "I was sent to head the CDR delegation to the U.S.S.R. in 1974–75 with the goal of studying how elections were held in that country. We examined this experience of the U.S.S.R., but never had the intention to copy it." Other Cuban delegations, he noted, studied electoral systems in the U.S., the U.K. and France. Lezcano also divulged, "Some aspects of the Soviet system appealed to us … but we did not view other aspects positively, such as the role of the party in selecting candidates." He elaborated by providing examples from the U.S.S.R. concerning the party's role in nominating candidates and carrying out campaigns in favour of candidates. He explained, "The party had a real omnipresence in that aspect of the political process. This, we really did not like" (Interview, Lezcano 2007).

Following further questions on this same theme in a subsequent interview, Lezcano disclosed another aspect with which his delegation was not pleased. This was the quality of contact between candidates and electors. He states, "They were really formal. I personally witnessed them. Deputies brought written speeches, which they simply read. It was very political. There was no polemic, no question period. And then everyone applauded" (Interview, Lezcano 2008a). Based on the evolving experience in Cuba with regard to the role of the ANPP, he made a distinction between the permanent working commissions in the U.S.S.R. Supreme Soviet and the ones in Cuba's current ANPP. Cuba's ANPP involves the people in the actual elaboration of some legislation, from the stage of draft bills to law. This was not the case in the U.S.S.R. (Interview, Lezcano 2008b). In Cuba, this involvement by the people in legislating applies especially to proposed bills that are controversial and thus require direct citizen input. The legislative involvement of citizens also includes bills initiated by mass organizations, as well as, on some occasions, decrees or decree-laws. (This role of the ANPP in legislating and its permanent working commissions are examined in detail in Chapter 8.)

Another participant of the 1974–76 Matanzas experience contends that the Cuban system did not copy from anywhere, including the former U.S.S.R. Current deputy Tomás Victoriano Cárdenas García and president of the ANPP Permanent Working Commission on the Organs of Local People's Power disclosed in an interview that no other country in the former socialist camp had a system in which citizens directly proposed candidates, as is the case in Cuba (Interview, Cárdenas García 2007).

Cuban researcher Concepción Nieves Ayús concedes that there was a certain amount of copying in the 1970s. However, she asserts, "Our Revolution was not imported from anywhere. No one came here to make the Revolution for us" (Interview, Nieves Ayús 2008). The assessment of Cuba's independent path in drafting its 1976 Constitution is supported by the eminent Cuban jurist Fernando Álvarez Tabío. He participated in the 1970s commission that was responsible for drafting the Constitution, before it went to the people for their input. He was also involved in drafting the final version based on citizens' opinions and judgments (Roca 1985: 10). Álvarez Tabío points out that the Constitution drafters received instructions to base the "project on the socio-economic reality established by the Revolution ... taking into account the experiences of fifteen years of revolutionary power [1959–74]... [as well] as the experiences of countries following the road toward socialism and communism." The frame of reference included the necessity to take into account "the progressive and revolutionary traditions of our people" (Álvarez Tabío 1985: 26). In this sense, the 1976 Constitution is the "result of accumulated changes that the country had produced during the provisional period" since 1959 (Prieto Valdés 2000: 33). All the laws adopted between 1959 and 1963 (e.g., agrarian reforms and nationalizations) represented the application of the 1959 Fundamental Law, which served as the Constitution. These laws became part of the "constitutional framework" that influenced the new 1976 Constitution (Vega Vega 1997: 105, 136). Other Cuban constitutional experts provide many examples of how the 1976 Constitution finds its sources and inspiration in the four nineteenth-century *mambises* constitutions as "the constitutional expression of the Cuban nation," which finally realized itself in 1959 (Peraza Chapeau 2000: 23). The indigenous origins of the Cuban political system and new 1976 Constitution explain in part Cuba's relative independence from the former Soviet system. George Lambie argues that, although Cuba was close to the U.S.S.R., "it did not become a proxy state and its 'Sovietisation' was only partial." He provides several examples of Cuba's autonomy, one being the continued priority accorded to people's participation and political consciousness (Lambie 2010: 159).

The 1992 Constitutional Reforms and Their Impact on Elections

In 1991, the PCC held its Fourth Congress, preceded by a wide-scale debate among the population based on a document that dealt with economic and political issues. In these grass-roots discussions and in the Congress itself, various weaknesses in the political system were raised. This resulted in several resolutions to reform the Constitution and elaborate a new electoral law. As far as elections are concerned, one of the two most important constitutional reforms was related to the election of deputies to the ANPP. Before the reform, deputies nominated to run for elections were not elected directly by the voters. At that time, before 1992, the proposed nominees were presented to the municipal assemblies, who then elected the ANPP deputies. Thus the municipal assemblies substituted for direct suffrage by the citizens. The ANPP deputies were therefore elected indirectly. However, since the 1992 reform, deputies nominated for the ANPP are elected directly by the citizens (Constitution of the Republic of Cuba [1976] 2003).

The second important reform is found in the 1992 electoral law No. 72 (Electoral Law No. 72 1992). Before the 1992 reform, the PCC participated in, and presided over, the candidacies commissions responsible for nominating candidates for the ANPP. In the new electoral law, the participation of the PCC in these commissions is eliminated altogether. The mass organizations are the only entities represented in the candidacies commissions (Electoral Law No. 72 1992).

It is instructive to take note of the following 1992 reforms to the Constitution, even though they are not directly or exclusively related to elections. These changes widen the base and the outlook of the PCC and the notion of democracy. For example, the guiding ideas of Martí were added to those of Marx, Engels and Lenin. Sovereignty lies in the "people" rather than the "working people." The PCC is perceived as a follower of Martí's ideas and not just of Marxism–Leninism, as was the case previously. The PCC is defined as the organized vanguard of the "Cuban nation" rather than that of the "working class." Martí's notion that Cuba should be organized "with all and for the good of all" was added. The Constitution eliminates "democratic centralism" as an explicit principle on which the political system operates, replacing this concept with "socialist democracy." However, the relationship between the higher and the lower bodies remains similar even though the term "democratic centralism" is no longer employed. References to the U.S.S.R. in the context of internationalism were eliminated in the reformed Constitution (Constitution of the Republic of Cuba [1976] 2003).

Elections, Constitution and Political System

As we have seen in the U.S.-centric model, the most important feature of democracy is elections. It is the quintessential element. While Cuba does hold elections, the relationship of elections to the overall political system is far more complex and profound. The Cuban state emerged from the 1957–58 Sierra Maestra experience and the Revolution's triumph on January 1, 1959. The Revolution took place and it is still ongoing to a large extent, striving to include and involve the vast majority of the people and to improve its brand of socialism. Elections take place in the context of a multifaceted democracy in motion. Furthermore, this is inclined toward a participatory democracy, rather than being only representative. For example, we have seen in the previous chapter how the PCC and the revolutionary leadership involved the citizens at the grass-roots level to participate in debates since 2007 on the problems facing the society. Moreover, these discussions carried on in 2010, leading up to the PCC 2011 Congress. The policy decisions emerging from the Congress were then proposed to the ANPP, along with the Council of State and Council of Ministers, which could convert these proposals into different types of legislation and resolutions. As will be seen in the next chapter, the citizens, far from being excluded after elections, participate in many ways in exercising power.

As discussed previously, Cuba's participatory heritage played a role in the revolutionary state during the 1959–62 activities. In fact, Cubans themselves directly rejected elections at that time. They thus avoided being distracted from carrying out major economic and social transformations. After 1959, unlimited accumulation of private property and U.S. domination started to give way to the social and economic well-being of the vast majority of the people. Participation increased accordingly. The revolutionary state is currently fighting to defeat bureaucratism and corruption as one of the main dangers to the Revolution. This same state is also ready to repulse any U.S.-backed military intervention or provocation today, as it did in 1961, when U.S.-trained aggressors were defeated on the battlefield in Playa Girón. Therefore, while elections are important in Cuba, they do not represent the entire political system. They are not based on competing programs or platforms. Decisions on policies, overall orientation of the Revolution and legislation are not an outcome of elections. Conclusions, courses of action and laws are worked out in other ways.

As mentioned above, the 2007–12 period of people's participation in legislation incorporates an example of Cuba's approach to democracy. The next chapter deals in detail with the role of people in legislation. The Cuban political culture, developed over many decades going back to the nineteenth century, seeks consultation and consensus while not neglecting the importance of discrepancies.

This is distinguishable from the U.S.-centric notion, which the U.S. and its dissident allies attempt to impose on Cuba. The U.S. course is based on fierce competition and infighting, all in the name of elections. The same atmosphere exists in the U.S. Congress, where virtually nothing is accomplished unless it serves the common interests of different segments of the oligarchies. Elections in Cuba, on the other hand, have as their purpose to choose the best individuals to discuss, elaborate, make and carry out decisions. This is not to suggest that there is not room for improvement in this electoral system. However, this will be addressed later in the chapter.

In Chapter 3, we looked at the participatory nature of the Venezuelan Bolivarian Revolution, even though elections take place there to elect representatives. They are part of a participatory revolution, as the October 2012 presidential elections illustrated. These examples and others, such as in Bolivia and Ecuador, are to be distinguished from the U.S.-centric model of non-participatory democracy, designed to protect the oligarchies.

In Cuba, the electoral process and the functioning of the Órganos del

Poder Popular (OPP — Organs of People's Power) as the organs of the state at all levels (municipal, provincial and national) are nevertheless important. In the same manner, the Órganos Locales del Poder Popular (OLPP — Local Organs of People's Power) constitute the municipal and provincial levels of state power within the OPP. They are just as crucial.

The Cuban electoral system is part of the political system based on the Constitution. The indelible imprint of the Cuban tradition is recognizable in the Constitution's preamble. It declares that Cubans as the heirs are responsible for continuing the creative work and traditions of combativeness fostered by the Indigenous peoples, the slave rebellions and the nineteenth-century Wars of Independence. The Constitution also refers to the struggles of the workers and peasants, the formation of the first Marxist–Leninist organizations while under U.S. domination in the twentieth century and the new movement emerging out of Moncada, Sierra Maestra and Girón. The Preamble closes by declaring that the Constitution of the Republic "be guided by the following strong desire of José Martí, at last achieved; 'I want the fundamental law of our republic to be the tribute of Cubans to the full dignity of man.'" The document states that it has been adopted by a free vote in a referendum (Constitution of the Republic of Cuba [1976] 2003).

General Elections — First Phase: Municipal Elections

According to the Constitution, the Council of State convenes the general elections. There is no fixed date aside from the fact that the mandates for the people elected at the national and provincial level are for five years. Normally, the general elections are called in July, simultaneously specifying the dates for the first phase, at the municipal level. The exact date of the second phase (national elections) is determined later on in the process. For example, the 2007–08 and 2012–13 general elections were called in July 2007 and 2012 respectively, for municipal elections to be held three months later, in October 2007 and 2012.

Once the elections are called, the members of the Comisión Electoral Nacional (CEN — National Electoral Commission) are then designated by the Council of State. The CEN oversees the elections, while the candidacies commissions, briefly mentioned in the overview at the beginning of this chapter, are composed only of mass organizations members. These candidacies commissions actually participate in the nomination procedure. The CEN, on the other hand, does not participate at all in the elections. However, it is responsible for surveying and inspecting the entire election procedure to ensure it conforms with the Constitution and the electoral law. In the 2007–08 general elections, the Council of State designated Minister of Justice María Ester Reus González to head the thirteen-member CEN. This was Reus González's first experience. She leads the commission, not in her function as minister of justice, but rather as a person who is knowledgeable about the laws and procedures; on a previous occasion, the vice-president of the Supreme Court served as president of the CEN. For the 2012–13 general elections, lawyer Alina Balseiro Gutiérrez was designated president of the CEN. The CEN appoints the Comisión Electoral Provincial (CEP — Provincial Electoral Commission) members in their respective provinces. The CEP then goes through the same procedure with all the municipalities located in their respective provinces to designate the members of the Comisión Electoral Municipal (CEM — Municipal Electoral Commission). These, in turn, likewise lead the formation of the electoral commissions at the grass-roots level.

The CEN, in collaboration with these other electoral commission levels (provincial, municipal and grass-roots), is responsible for assuring that the elections take place according to the law (Interview, Reus González 2008).

Decentralization

An innovative feature of Cuba's electoral and political system is its decentralization. It is dispersed to the extent that non-Cubans normally have a difficult time understanding it. At the time of the 2007–08 elections, there were fourteen provinces and one special municipality, Isla de la Juventud. Following new legislation, in 2010, Cuba comprised fifteen provinces and the same special municipality.

The "city" of Havana is not a city, but, rather, is classified as a province in order to decentralize it into cities. The current province of Havana (also known as the "city of Havana") has a population of 2,135,498. This is approximately equivalent to the population of the U.S. city of Houston, Texas. The province of Havana is divided, in turn, into fifteen municipalities, or cities. According to the Constitution, these municipalities "are invested with the highest authority for the exercise of their state functions within their respective boundaries. To this effect they govern in all that is under their jurisdiction and the law." Their administrations, moreover, "direct the economic, production and service entities locally subordinated to them, with the purpose of meeting the needs for economic, health care, assistance, educational, cultural, sports and recreational services of the collective in the territory" (Constitution of the Republic of Cuba [1976] 2003). Municipal assemblies are the local state organs, which exercise the act of governing. They are part of the OLPP (municipal and provincial levels), which, in turn, are integrated into the OPP (all three levels — national, provincial and municipal). The municipal assemblies are, in principle, responsible for most aspects concerning their territory. The municipalities are thus not simply boroughs existing as subdivisions of a city with very limited powers, such as is the case in New York, London and Montreal.

The province of Havana, in terms of population, can be thought of in terms of the city of Houston as a U.S. *state* divided into fifteen cities. One of these fifteen cities or municipalities in the province of Havana is Plaza de la Revolución, which will be examined here as a case study.[1] This municipality has a population of 152,318, or 7.1 percent of the total number of inhabitants of the province of Havana. Plaza de la Revolución is composed of 108 *circunscripciones*, which elect one delegate each. There are approximately 1,450 voters in the typical, urban *circunscripción*. There is an enormous difference between the number of inhabitants in a district, riding or constituency in the Anglo-American world and the 1,450 or so voters in a *circunscripción*. These are clearly two very different types of local political structures. This very condensed local *circunscripción* is one of Cuba's unique contributions to political systems.

Circunscripción No. 12, where the election and other research fieldwork for the case study were carried out, is typical of the 108 *circunscripciones* in this municipality. It consists of eight compact, highly populated street blocks ("a space in a city or town bounded by four streets," which in this area are quite short). The 1,450 registered voters in the *circunscripción* during the 2007 elections were eventually represented by one elected person, the delegate. This is reminiscent of the Cuban tradition going back to the nineteenth-century *mambises* and the 1957–58 Sierra Maestra participatory political culture. It was characterized by its close ties between the leadership and the base. This tradition of mutual interaction is currently being solicited to activate itself further as a permanent feature of the Cuban political system's necessary renewal. These appeals and analyses for renovation stem from all levels in society. The views were reviewed in Chapter 6, where Cuba was perceived as presently being at a crossroads in its history.

Voter Registration

The compilation of voters' lists begins as soon as elections are called in July. Throughout the year, the booklet of registered addresses is continually updated by the government ministry in charge of the citizens' birth and address archives. It contains the name, date of birth and address of each person in every *circunscripción*. The voters' list in each *circunscripción* is based upon, and compiled from, the booklet of registered addresses (Electoral Law No. 72 1992). The voters' list is easily verifiable by the residents. In the cities, no one has to walk more than one block to verify the voters' lists. During the 1997–98 and 2007–08 elections, in both the urban and rural areas, it was observed that citizens had easy access to these lists. The electors can propose

---

1. The 2010 changes mentioned above with regard to demarcations, which went into effect in 2011, dealt with only a small number of street blocks in the municipality. Therefore, these adjustments did not at all affect the case study. No further transformations have taken place for the 2012–13 general elections.

adjustments or correct errors. The final updated version of the voters' list is prepared for election day.[2]

The minimum voting age is sixteen. In order to be elected to the municipal and provincial assemblies, the required minimum age is sixteen, and to the ANPP, eighteen. (This youth suffrage finds its origins in the nineteenth-century *mambises* elections. Anyone who was fighting the Spanish also had the right to vote.) Those declared legally "mentally disabled" or who are serving time for having committed a crime cannot exercise this right (Constitution of the Republic of Cuba [1976] 2003).

The Comisiones Electorales de Circunscripciones (CEC — *Circunscripción Electoral Commissions*) comprise the fourth and lowest level of the electoral commissions, below the national, provincial and municipal echelons.

Circunscripción No. 12 in Plaza de la Revolución is divided into five polling stations (*colegios electorales*) for the duration of the electoral process. The number of polling stations in each *circunscripción* depends on the population. The objective of this further decentralization, designed for electoral purposes, is to make the electoral process more accessible to the citizens. One advantage to this proximity is the ease in verifying the updated and corrected voters' lists. Since Circunscripción No. 12 comprises eight city blocks, each polling station extends not more than one or two blocks. A polling station is composed of five voluntary electoral board members (*mesa electoral*), normally provided by mass organizations.

Nominating Candidates for Elections to the Municipal Assemblies

For the purposes of holding candidate nomination assemblies, each *circunscripción* is divided into two to eight areas. The goal is to allow nomination meetings to be very compressed and based on the grass roots. The number of nomination areas is determined by the population in the *circunscripción*. In rural and semi-rural areas, access and extension of territory are also taken into consideration. There is a minimum of two nomination areas because, according to law, at least two candidates must present themselves for election. The maximum is eight because, given the small population at the *circunscripción* level, none of these *circunscripciones* requires being divided into more than eight smaller areas.

In the case study, there were five nomination areas worked out by the CEC of Circunscripción No. 12. It relies mainly on local committees of the Comités de Defensa de la Revolución (CDR — Committees for the Defence

---

2. It is instructive to note the condescending tone of the U.S.'s plan should it ever realize its dream to take over Cuba: "Establish procedures for voter registration that are effective, impartial, and non-discriminatory, and ensure that voting is equally accessible for all those qualified.... train election officials in voter registration, maintenance of voting lists" (Powell 2004). Contrast this to the U.S. tradition of limited suffrage and discriminatory voter registration.

of the Revolution) to publicize the dates and places of these meetings. The CDR is the backbone of the process, in conjunction with the local CEC, since the nomination areas coincide with one or a few CDR committees. In each of these five nomination assemblies, people have the right to participate, nominate and vote only in the nomination area in which they live.

Normally, these nomination area assembly meetings are held at eight o'clock in the evening on weekdays or during the day on a weekend. The venue in the urban areas is an impromptu space, such as on the sidewalk and part of the street in front of a house or at the ground level of an apartment building. The average participation rate (i.e., the proportion of those who have the right to attend actually being present) for the entire *circunscripción* in the September 2007 study was 81.17 percent. This participation is representative, in very general terms, of the whole country.

The neighbourhood nomination assembly is presided over by the local *circunscripción* electoral commission. The floor is open for nominations. Individuals who attend because they live in that nomination area have the right to propose anyone who lives anywhere in their entire *circunscripción*. In other words, it is not necessary for the nominee to reside in the nomination area where the assembly is held. However, the person proposed must indicate that he or she is willing to be nominated, and the person nominating must give the reasons for the nomination. Such reasons generally focus on the person's personal accomplishments and characteristics, history, contributions and ties to the local community. Whether or not the person is a member of the PCC or the UJC is not generally raised or mentioned.[3] Others also have the right to argue against a nomination.

The first to be nominated was Javier Izquierdo. He was not present, as he did not live in that nomination area. However, he had indicated to the person proposing his name that he would accept. A second nomination was Jesús García Brigos, an incumbent who lived in that nomination area and was present. He indicated his agreement to be nominated. After verification that no other proposals were on the agenda, a show-of-hands vote was taken and counted by the electoral commission.

The person who garners the most votes becomes the nominee from *that* nomination area. In this case, it was Izquierdo. In the four nomination assemblies held on other evenings in different areas, either Izquierdo or García Brigos, or both, were proposed. García Brigos won the majority in a show-of-hands vote in one area. These nomination assemblies produced two nominees to run for the election of delegate for Circunscripción No. 12 of the Plaza de la Revolución Municipal Assembly.

---

3. During the proceedings, some members of the PCC were present. However, they were conversing and in contact only with the electoral commission members in order to ensure that there were no deviations from the Constitution and the electoral law. They had no contact with the electors.

It is quite common to have only two. However, in the 108 *circunscripciones* in Plaza de la Revolución, 30 *circunscripciones* nominated three candidates, seven proposed four and one even had seven.

Concerning the show-of-hands voting procedure, it is one of the main dissident complaints of the municipal election procedure. They find it too "public." Their logic is that it puts dissidents at a disadvantage because, publicly, citizens would not like to associate themselves with these dissidents. However, by all indications, it seems that the overwhelming majority of Cubans do not want to associate themselves either publicly or otherwise with these opponents.[4]

The PCC in the Nomination Process

The PCC does not have the right to propose candidates. Dissidents and most of the Western media claim that, on the contrary, the PCC controls everything and therefore there are no viable elections in Cuba. The nomination procedure described above contradicts this assertion. Nonetheless, in 2007, as part of the case study, this issue of whether or not there exists PCC interference in nominations was further observed and investigated.

Five Plaza de la Revolución Municipal Electoral Commission members explained that they had received training and careful preparation prior to the nomination assemblies. According to the commission members, the PCC has no right to interfere in the proposing of candidates (Interview, Municipal Electoral Commission 2007). It is common practice for verification to be carried out by higher-level electoral commissions to ensure that nomination procedures at the base are being followed according to the Constitution and electoral law. For example, the Havana Provincial Electoral Commission (whose members include a lawyer with experience in jurisprudence and electoral procedures) makes surprise visits to the nomination meetings to ensure that the law is not violated. This includes verifying that the restriction against the PCC taking part in the elections is enforced (Interview, Comisión Electoral Provincial 2008).

Perhaps the most eloquent indication of the non-participation of the PCC may be seen in the case study experience of Circunscripción No. 12. One of the people nominated, Izquierdo, is a PCC member, while the other nominee, García Brigos, is *not* a party member. There was no visible pressure in favour of Izquierdo. The neighbour who nominated García Brigos did so publicly and presented his case. Likewise, when it came time for each neighbour to express their respective views by voting, it also was carried out openly for all to see. In order to see through preconceived notions of

---

4. As I wrote in my 1999 publication based on my experience at that time, this is the dissidents' problem, not that of the electoral system. If support for the dissidents were as widespread as they claim (they often say that they represent the majority of Cubans), they could easily win any nomination in a show-of-hands vote.

the party's role, it is important to keep in mind that the PCC finds its source mainly in the Martí tradition, a heritage based on Martí's critique of electoral political parties in the U.S. This Martí legacy is also found in the concept of the Partido Revolucionario Cubano (PRC — Cuban Revolutionary Party) as a revolutionary party to lead the entire nation. Its goal was not necessarily to participate in electoral politics. Nonetheless, the Western establishment media and dissident bloggers persist in disinforming international public opinion regarding the role of the PCC in the nomination process.[5]

Debating the Improvement of Nomination Assemblies

The red herring concerning the dissident claim that the PCC controls everything is of interest to a small handful on the island along with their media and political sponsors abroad. This is the disinformation to which non-Cubans are often exposed. However, for the vast majority of Cubans, the interest is to *improve* the nomination assemblies in an effort to enhance the OPP, and not to replace the latter with another political system in the image of the U.S.

Improving the nomination procedure has been on the agenda for some time now and is a concern at all levels, from the grass roots to the ANPP leadership. For example, ANPP president Alarcón acknowledged in 1995, "It is necessary to aim for better quality in nomination … It is necessary to achieve a genuine, collective reflection and to think about those neighbours who are most apt, exhibiting the best qualities." He linked this to enhancing the conscious participation in the nomination and election process in order to improve the work of the municipal assemblies (Alarcón de Quesada 2002a: 99). The purpose is for people to develop a better understanding of the delegate's role, among other aspects. In this way, the objective is to facilitate both the quality of nominations and the conscious acceptance by potential nominees (Interview, Lezcano 2009).

In another interview, García Brigos added some arguments that provide substance to the ANPP preoccupation as expressed by Lezcano. García Brigos pointed out that Cuban television presents so many news items on people involved in economic, sports or cultural endeavours. However, he divulged that "there is hardly ever any news about the delegates" or the municipal assemblies, which also play a key role. He gave the example that, even when certain areas are affected by hurricanes, news focuses on the role of local party secretaries. Their function is important, he affirmed. However, with the media virtually ignoring the work of the municipal assemblies and delegates, how can people be expected, García Brigos implored, to appreciate the role of the delegates, to be more informed about whom to nominate and why, and to know whom to vote for? (Interview, García Brigos 2009a). Indeed, as

---

5. See www.democracyintheus.com, "Dissidents in the Nomination Process as Part of U.S. Democracy Promotion."

observed by the author over the last few years, Cuban television news and the printed press certainly seem to have inadvertently fostered the perception that the delegates' role is insignificant. However, the reality is that, in general, the delegates are not aloof and are in fact involved. The paradox is that, despite their sacrifices in the majority of cases, there is very little news about their engagement and activities.

On August 30, 2012, a round table primetime TV program, *Mesa Redonda*, dealt with the 2012–13 general elections. Anchor Arleen Derivet Rodríguez read a question from a viewer to one of the guests, ANPP president Ricardo Alarcón. In response to the question of whether enough time and importance is devoted by the Cuban press to the elections, he conceded, "Frankly, no." He went on to say that in the Cuban media, more time is provided to the U.S. elections than the Cuban ones (*Mesa Redonda*, August 30, 2012, notes taken by author).

University of Havana political scientist (and former delegate) Emilio Duharte Díaz wrote that the entire process has to be improved, including the nomination procedure (Duharte Díaz 2008: 56, 121–31). In an interview, Duharte Díaz argued,

> Some nomination assemblies are well organized. Others are not well organized … There are, in addition, many assemblies in which formalism predominates … This takes place as though there is no real awareness that these nomination assemblies are the very basis of the political system. As a result, there are quite a few people who prefer to get it done rapidly — [*in an imitative tone*] "We are in a hurry" — and therefore the quality of these assemblies suffers. There is a need to pay attention to this in future elections. I believe that, in addition to the people involved in the OPP, we, as specialists, and others can assist substantially in contributing to the public debate on this theme. (Interview, Duharte Díaz 2009)

With regard to the quality of the nomination assemblies, there are major differences from one place to another. For example, in rural areas such as in Abreus, Cienfuegos, where the author carried out a case study in 1997, the nomination assemblies were more outgoing and spontaneous. In rural Abreus, a citizen suggested someone, providing the reason that the individual is revolutionary. The electoral commission member presiding over the assembly "asked [the proposer] sarcastically: 'What else, any other criteria?'" in the sense that in Cuba most people consider themselves to be revolutionary. The participants fully understood the message and "the meeting broke out in laughter," forcing the person to provide more arguments according to the electoral law (August 1999: 271). In contrast, in that same year, in urban areas (such as Havana), some of the assemblies showed signs of formalism. Moreover, when comparing the 1997 nomination assemblies in urban Havana with those of 2007 in the same nomination areas, it appears that what Duharte Díaz calls "formalism" and the anxiety to "get it done" are increasing.

Rafael Hernández believes that the "deficiencies of the nomination process have nothing to do with the structure as such, even though it surely can be improved. The problem is rather how people perceive the delegate." Regarding improvements to the nomination assemblies, Hernández, like Duharte Díaz, claims that there is a problem of "formalism and a ritual manner" in carrying them out (Interview, Hernández 2009).

The discussion, even relatively limited, over the need to improve the nomination assemblies' quality is itself a feature of Cuba's democracy in motion.

Elections to the Municipal Assemblies

Once candidates have been nominated (e.g., García Brigos and Javier Izquierdo in the Circunscripción No. 12 case study), the local electoral commission obtains a short, biographical profile and a photo from the candidates. These are circulated and/or posted in local public places for easy access to electors. This is the only publicity permitted under the electoral law (Electoral Law No. 72 1992). Electors are expected to read the profiles in order to make their choice, having been accorded more than sufficient time between the posting and the voting. There is no electoral campaign or funding permitted.

Duharte Díaz is of the opinion that the posting of biographies and photos "is not sufficient." He says it is necessary to think about working out exchanges between electors and candidates so that electors "learn more about the candidates before voting" (Interview, Duharte Díaz 2009). Hernández holds a similar opinion, namely, that the simple posting of biographies on the doors of local shops is not the way to develop personal interaction between candidates and electors (Interview, Hernández 2009).

The electoral law takes into consideration electoral ethics, such as the opposition to "all forms of opportunism, demagogy and cheap politicking [*politiquería*]." However, the same Article 171 also provides for candidates to participate together in activities, conferences and visits to work centres to "exchange opinions with the workers." The condition for participating *together* in neighbourhoods and work/educational centres is to ensure that there is no individual politicking. This joint participation, according to the law, would allow workers and other citizens "to become acquainted with the candidates." However, according to the law, "this should not be considered as a propaganda electoral campaign" (Electoral Law No. 72 1992). While these joint "meet-the-candidates" meetings take place for the election of ANPP deputies, they are not carried out for the election of municipal delegates. This lends reason to Hernández's concerns.

On the day of the vote, held always on a Sunday, electors confirm their voting eligibility by presenting their identification cards, which all Cubans hold in their possession. The polling station board members explain the voting procedure to the voter, who is then handed a ballot. The ballot, in the case study, had two names, Izquierdo and García Brigos. Voting, of course, is secret.

Analyzing Municipal Election Results

There were 1,450 electors in Circunscripción No. 12 in the October 2007 elections to elect one delegate to the Municipal Assembly. To be declared the winner, a candidate must obtain 50 percent plus one of the votes. In this case, there were only two candidates and they did not end up in a tie vote. A second round was therefore not necessary. While Izquierdo had more support in the nomination assemblies compared with García Brigos, the latter won the elections, though it was quite close (51.80 percent vs. 48.16 percent) (table 7.1). García Brigos, not being a member of the party, was one of approximately one-third of the municipal delegates across the country who were *not* party members (Interview, Reus González 2008). The voter turnout rate in this local *circunscripción* was 90.35 percent. There were 2.20 percent blank ballots and 2.88 percent spoiled ballots. This was lower than the average for the entire province of Havana (at that time called the province of Ciudad de La Habana). Special attention is given in the tables that follow to voter turnout as well as to the proportion of blank and spoiled ballots. As is the case with the dissident campaigns for nomination, there is significant disinformation in the foreign press on this issue, as will be seen in more detail later in this chapter. However, suffice it to mention here that many people record their opposition to the political system by depositing blank or spoiled ballots, although not all of these ballots are indicative of this. Some isolated spoiled ballots are nullified by mistake.

TABLE 7.1   Election results of secret ballot for Circunscripción No. 12, Plaza de la Revolución, October 21, 2007

Polling station	Voter turnout (first round) (%)	Blank ballots (%)	Spoiled ballots (%)	Candidate García Brigos (%)	Candidate Izquierdo (%)
1	87.50	2.08	3.33	52.79	47.20
2	91.74	3.67	2.75	40.30	59.67
3	90.65	1.40	3.73	66.10	33.87
4	93.16	3.04	3.80	61.20	38.76
5	88.62	0.81	0.81	38.78	61.20
Total	90.35	2.20	2.88	51.80	48.16

Source: Comisión Electoral de Circunscripción No. 12 (data provided to author).

The province of Havana (the former Ciudad de La Habana) comprises the city of Havana. It is traditionally the area showing the highest rate of blank and spoiled ballots. It is also where most of the dissidents operate, often calling for people to deposit blank or spoiled ballots. Therefore, in the 2007 municipal phase of the general elections, the rate of 3.90 percent and 4.58 percent for blank and spoiled ballots respectively was slightly higher than the norm for the country (table 7.2).

TABLE 7.2   Election results of secret ballot for province of Ciudad de La Habana (currently province of Havana), October 21, 2007

Voter turnout for first round (%)	Blank ballots (%)	Spoiled ballots (%)
94.52	3.90	4.58

Source: Comisión Electoral Municipal Plaza de la Revolución (data provided to author).

According to CEN president Reus González, in terms of the entire nation, close to 20 percent of the total 15,236 *circunscripciones* had to go into a second round, for two reasons: first, for the overwhelming majority, none of the three or more candidates collected the minimum 50 percent plus one required for election as delegate; and, second, in seven *circunscripciones,* due to technical issues (table 7.3). In the second round, there were four ties, which led to a third round, in which, in all four cases, one person finally got the minimum 50 percent plus one (Interview, Reus González 2008). The proportion of blank and spoiled ballots together at the national level (7.01 percent) was lower than in Havana (8.48 percent).

TABLE 7.3   Final national results, municipal elections for first round, October 21, 2007

3,027 *circunscripciones,* or close to 20%, into second round on Sunday, October 28		
4 *circunscripciones* into third and final round on Wednesday, October 31		
Voter turnout (%)	Blank ballots (%)	Spoiled ballots (%)
96.49	3.93	3.08

Source: Granma 2007b.

The April 2010 partial elections for municipal assemblies were held in order to renew the two-and-a-half-year mandate of local delegates previously elected in October 2007. On October 21, 2012, the municipal first-phase elections of the 2012–13 general elections took place. There was an increase in the number of blank and spoiled ballots from the 2007 municipal first-phase elections (i.e., the first phase of the general elections) compared with the 2010 municipal partial elections. For example, in Ciudad de La Habana, blank and spoiled ballots increased respectively, from 3.90 percent and 4.58 percent in 2007 to 4.67 percent and 6.56 percent in 2010 (tables 7.2 and 7.4). A similar trend appears on the national scale. Blank and spoiled ballots rose correspondingly from 3.93 percent and 3.08 percent to

4.59 percent and 4.30 percent in 2010 (tables 7.3 and 7.4). The combined total blank and spoiled ballots in 2010 (8.89 percent) was the highest compared with any previous year in recent election history, aside from 1995. In that year, a combined blank and spoiled ballot rate of 11.3 percent was registered. A similar tendency transpired from 2010 to 2012. As table 7.4 indicates, in the municipal first-phase elections in October 2012, compared with the 2010 elections, the voter turnout at the national level decreased to 94.21 percent, the lowest in history. The Havana turnout decreased slightly. However, in Havana, the stronghold of the dissidents, the blank ballots were almost the same, while the spoiled ballots actually decreased, albeit slightly.

TABLE 7.4   First-round municipal partial elections, April 25, 2010, and municipal first-phase general elections, October 21, 2012

	Voter turnout (%)		Blank ballots (%)		Spoiled ballots (%)	
	2010	2012	2010	2012	2010	2012
Ciudad de La Habana	94.71	93.12	4.67	4.99	6.56	6.26
National total	95.90	94.21	4.59	4.97	4.30	4.45

Sources: Granma 2010, 2012a; Hernández S. 2012.

As indicated in table 7.5, with regard to voter turnout, there was a very small decrease from the 96.70 percent participation rate in 2007 to 95.90 percent in 2010. From the first municipal elections, held in 1976, until 2010, voter turnout has remained very stable, with the lowest at 95.20 percent in 1976 and the highest at 98.70 percent in 1984. However, the 2010 voter turnout rate (95.90 percent) was the third lowest since 1976. This trend continued from 2010 to 2012, with the voter turnout decreasing to 94.21 percent. This is the lowest since the initiation of the elections in 1976.

TABLE 7.5   Municipal elections, voter turnout, 1976–2012

Year	Voter turnout (first round) (%)	Year	Voter turnout (first round) (%)
1976 [first-phase]	95.20	1997 [first-phase]	97.60
1979 [partial]	96.90	2000 [partial]	98.10
1981 [first-phase]	97.20	2002 [first-phase]	95.80
1984 [partial]	98.70	2005 [partial]	96.70
1986 [first-phase]	97.70	2007 [first-phase]	96.70
1989 [partial]	98.30	2010 [partial]	95.90
1992 [first-phase]	97.20	2012* [first-phase]	94.21
1995 [partial]	97.10		

Sources: Oficina Nacional de Estadísticas n.d.(a); *Granma* 2012a.

Among the ballots duly classified as spoiled, most are marked purposely and explicitly against the system. As table 7.6 indicates, aside from 1995, the total number of blank and spoiled ballots has remained stable. However, there was a notable increase in 2010 compared with the 2007 elections.

It is quite possible that the increase in blank and, especially, spoiled ballots in the 2010 municipal partial elections is a reflection of growing dissatisfaction among some of the population with the economic situation and/or political system. The voter turnout decreased slightly once again from 95.90 percent in 2010 compared with 94.21 percent in October 2012. This, however, was caused partly by hurricane Sandy approaching the eastern and central provinces before the elections. The electoral commissions allowed the polls to remain open for an extra hour (from 6 p.m. to 7 p.m.) in order to take into account the difficult situation. Thus a cautious conclusion regarding decline in voting turnout is in order. Nevertheless, the total blank and spoiled ballots increased from 8.90 percent in the 2010 elections to 9.42 percent in the 2012 elections, the highest rate since 1995, as table 7.6 indicates. However, it is also instructive to analyze the situation in which this trend took place. Between 2007 and 2012, the context was characterized by major domestic and international changes and setbacks and by anxiety about the potential success of the measures aimed at updating the socialist model.

Taking into account the overall voting trends from 2007 to 2012, it is difficult to ignore the discontent existing among segments of the population regarding the pace and efficiency of economic changes. The voting tendency also reflects some doubts about the capacity of the political system to increase people's effective participation on a regular basis, as it had accomplished from 2007 up to the 2011 Congress. At the same time, the voting trend in no way dovetails with the aspirations of the U.S. and its allies for regime change in Cuba.[6]

TABLE 7.6   Municipal elections, percentage of total blank and spoiled ballots, 1995–2012

Year	Blank and spoiled ballots (%)	Year	Blank and spoiled ballots (%)
1995 [partial]	11.30	2005 [partial]	5.30
1997 [first-phase]	7.20	2007 [first-phase]	6.00
2000 [partial]	5.90	2010 [partial]	8.90
2002 [first-phase]	5.30	2012 [first-phase]	9.42

Sources: Roman 2003; *Granma* 2005, 2007a, 2010, 2012a.

6. See www.democracyintheus.com, "Analyzing 2010 and 2012 Municipal Blank and Spoiled Ballots: Hope for Democracy Promotion Advocates?"

General Elections — Second Phase: The National ANPP

The procedure for the nomination and election of candidates for the provincial and national assemblies is different from the municipal first-phase elections. While this study focuses only on the Asamblea Nacional del Poder Popular (ANPP — National Assembly of People's Power, or Parliament), the two phases have in common consultation and input from the people in nominating candidates, without the involvement of the political party, the PCC. As mentioned in the overview at the beginning of this chapter, up to 50 percent of the national deputies are composed of delegates who have been elected to the municipal assemblies. These are known as *de base* candidates or, eventually, deputies, if they are elected. Those who are so nominated and elected hold *two* positions — those of municipal delegate and *de base* national deputy. This is why the first phase (i.e., the municipal elections) of the general elections cannot be separated from the second phase (i.e., the national elections). The other half of the ANPP deputies are *directos*, or those proposed directly by mass organizations, and not by the voters themselves. Each deputy to the ANPP, whether *de base* or *directo*, is elected from a municipality. *De base* candidates are elected to the ANPP from the municipality in which they live and were first elected as municipal delegates, while *directo* candidates can live in any municipality in the country. However, a consultation process (further explained below) provides for *directo* candidates to be paired with any municipality, irrespective of whether they live there. This is carried out for electoral and political purposes, thus allowing for them to be elected from this assigned municipality. As for *de base* nominees from among the municipal delegates, they are, of course, always presented for election from the municipality in which they were elected as delegates at the grass-roots level.

Individual deputies in the ANPP represent between 10,000 and 20,000 inhabitants in the municipality. This municipality is then considered to be the deputy's constituency. The functions of deputies, whether *de base* or *directos*, are also considered by the electoral law to have a national character. The number of deputies per municipality depends on the size of the population of the respective municipality within which they are elected. Each municipality has the right to have a minimum of two deputies. Some municipalities (e.g., in Havana or Santiago de Cuba) have a very high population density compared with others in rural areas. In order to have a just proportion of elected representatives per population across the country, municipalities with a population of over 100,000 are temporarily divided into *distritos* (districts). These *distritos* are not to be confused with electoral districts in the U.S. system or with the compact *circunscripciones* of the Cuban variety. They are temporary in the sense that the demarcations are only for electoral purposes. Thus the elected deputy in these highly populated urban areas is considered to have been elected by the entire municipality and not the temporary *distrito*.

The Candidacies Commissions and Nominations

The national, provincial and municipal candidacies commissions, composed entirely of mass organization representatives from their respective levels, lead the nomination procedure. Representatives of the six mass organizations — CTC, FMC, ANAP, FEU, FEEM and CDR (fig. 7.1) — form the candidacies commissions. They are established respectively under the supervision of the electoral commissions at the national, provincial and municipal levels (fig. 7.2). However, once organized, the candidacies commissions function independently. In order to refine the investigation and analysis of the complex nomination procedure for the ANPP, the author undertook various interviews in 2008 with the Comisión de Candidaturas Nacional (CCN — National Candidacies Commission).

Mass Organizations	
CTC	Central de Trabajadores de Cuba (Workers' Central Union of Cuba)
FMC	Federación de Mujeres Cubanas (Federation of Cuban Women)
ANAP	Asociación Nacional de Agricultores Pequeños (National Association of Small Farmers)
FEU	Federación de estudiantes universitarios (Federation of University Students)
FEEM	Federación de Estudiantes de la Enseñanza Media (Federation of Pre-University Students)
CDR	Comités de Defensa de la Revolución (Committees for the Defence of the Revolution)

Fig. 7.1. Mass organizations.

One interview took the form of a round table with the participation of six of the sixteen full CCN members. The president of the CCN, Amarilys Pérez Santana, was the designated representative of the CTC National Secretariat delegated to the CCN. Yanira Kuper Herrera was appointed to the CCN by the national leadership of the Federación de Mujeres Cubanas (FMC — Federation of Cuban Women). Twenty-four-year-old Rosibel Osorio Arias was the representative of the National Secretariat of the Federación de Estudiantes Universitarios (FEU — Federation of University Students). Nineteen-year-old Julio Carlos Fariñas Pérez was representing the Federación de Estudiantes de la Enseñanza Media (FEEM — Federation of Pre-University Students). Finally, Pedro András Aguila Tejera, a farmer from the Asociación Nacional de Agricultores Pequeños (ANAP — National Association of Small Farmers), and another CTC representative, Héctor Raúl Fardo Marin, also contributed to the round table interview.

CCN president Pérez Santana explained that the CCN was constituted right after the establishment of the Comisión Electoral Nacional (CEN — National

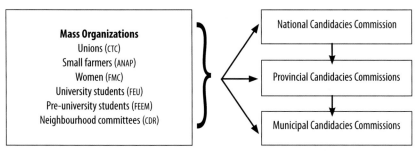

Fig. 7.2. Six mass organizations and three candidacies commissions.

Electoral Commission). As figure 7.2 illustrates, while the grass-roots mass organizations horizontally furnish the candidacies commission at all levels, the actual constitution of these commissions follows a vertical top-down approach. For example, the CCN oversees the fulfillment of the candidacies commissions' composition in each of the provinces based on the same procedure. The sources for provincial representatives come from the respective mass organizations' provincial secretariats at that level. These provincial level candidacies commissions then oversee the establishment of the 169 municipalities (in 2007–08) to complete the full candidacies commissions at all three levels (Interview, Comisión de Candidaturas Nacional 2008).

The CCN members explained that, in order to propose people as candidates for elections (for the present discussion), each of the six mass organizations assembles at all three levels in plenary sessions. For example, the FEU National Council has 185 members who meet in plenary sessions to propose candidates from among the population. These proposals are sent to the candidacies commissions to be considered for nomination for election to the National Assembly.

The goal is to obtain a pool of potential candidates representing a wide cross-section of the population. Therefore, each of the six mass organizations at all three levels (national, provincial and municipal) has the right to propose at least three times the number of candidates needed for each municipality to be represented in the ANPP. The municipal candidacies commissions and mass organizations' municipal plenums concentrate mainly in proposing *de base* candidates for the ANPP. However, the provincial and national candidacies commissions (for the present discussion) focus their attention mainly on proposing *directos* for the ANPP.

These lists of proposed nominees that the provincial and municipal candidacies commissions received from the mass organizations at those levels are funnelled to the CCN. The CCN then is able to first pare down the long list, as well as address various territorial and provincial considerations, while also taking into account gender, skin colour, age, education and occupation. For example, there may be many proposals for people from Havana, but there may not be enough municipalities in that province to accommodate all the suggestions. Therefore, the CCN must propose to place some of them in other provinces, which must eventually be executed with the consent of the local municipality. Others in the CCN interview noted age-related issues, pointing out that 60 percent of the population was born after the Revolution. Therefore, that population must also be taken into account in order to ensure the continuity of the Revolution. With regard to gender, the FMC representative on the CCN indicated that in the 2008 elections, women were expected to have reached a record number (Interview, Comisión de Candidaturas Nacional 2008).

In another interview, this time with CCN president Pérez Santana only, the question was raised as to how the CCN prepares the final list of 614 candidates for the same number of seats in the ANPP. Pérez Santana revealed that the CCN received a total of 5,457 proposals for nomination from all six mass organizations at all three state levels (municipal, provincial and national), including both *de base* and *directo* candidates.[7] The 5,457 proposals were for the ANPP (taking into account the present discussion), and thus did not include those suggestions for the provincial assemblies. This list was eventually pared down to 614 by, for example, eliminating redundancies (those nominated at least twice) and retaining only the most popular. Thus there remained 3,787 proposals for candidates at the national level. In collaboration with the other candidacies commissions at the provincial and municipal levels and with the delegates at the municipal level, mass consultations regarding the quality of the proposed candidates took place at their respective places of work, in their neighbourhoods and in educational centres. The nominated candidate for deputy must obtain 50 percent plus one vote to be elected.

The objective of these mass consultations is to evaluate whether the grass roots considers the potential candidate to be appropriate or not as a deputy, be it a *de base* or *directo* nominee. The goal also consists in finding out whether or not the municipality accepts the proposal for a certain *directo* candidate to run for elections from that municipality, even though the person may not live in the municipality. The final list, once reduced to the number of seats in the ANPP, must be approved by the municipal assembly.

She explained that the list is divided into municipal lists and presented to each municipal assembly, which can reject candidates. This grass-roots level has the final say, seeing that all deputies are elected from a municipality. In view of possible rejections, in addition to prioritizing the CCN choice of 614 nominees, the CCN also retains a reserve list to substitute for potential rejections by the municipalities.

It is at the municipal assembly level that formal nominations are made for both the municipal *de base* and *directo* candidates to the ANPP. In the 2007–08 elections, only one municipality rejected the proposal. The CCN then had to propose another nomination from their list of reserves as an alternative.

---

7.   I am grateful to Amarilys Pérez Santana for providing me with this information.

The entire procedure of consultation, as illustrated above, takes about two months of intensive activity with CCN members, who have often worked until two or four in the morning and slept in the CCN headquarters during the process. The lists were presented to the municipal assembly sessions across the nation on December 2, 2007. Once they were approved, the 614 individuals became the candidates for the 614 seats available in the ANPP (Interview, Pérez Santana 2008).

Improving the Candidacies Commissions

The enhancement of the nomination procedure for the ANPP elections is important. Whereas in the municipal elections, there are at least two candidates from which to choose, in the national elections there is only one candidate per seat. The nomination procedure is effective in many ways, as will be seen below. In addition, the candidate must garner at least 50 percent plus one vote, a condition that may have some meaning in the future, as indicated in the analysis in the section below entitled "One Candidate for Election per ANPP Seat: Talking Figures."

Duharte Díaz, a PCC member, carries strong views on Cuba's political system from a critical, yet constructive, perspective. He claims that many Cubans think like him and he has already published many of these views (Interview, Duharte Díaz 2009). In general, his opinions and suggestions to further enhance the candidacies commissions seem worthy of consideration. Despite his critical stance, he says that the multi-party system will not resolve the problems. He is of the opinion that it is necessary to rethink the composition of the candidacies commissions. He concedes that it is very significant that the candidacies commissions are composed of representatives from all the mass organizations and that there is no PCC participation. The mass organizations are part of the political system and represent the widest cross-sections of the population. However, he argues, the candidacies commissions can be improved. Duharte Díaz's investigation has shown that the candidacies commissions have been enhancing their work, developing a system of interviews with people from all walks of life and extending the search for potential candidates. They are doing a better job than before.

However, this is not sufficient. Duharte Díaz hypothesizes about also including specialists in the commissions. These additional people should enjoy recognized prestige and authority at the local, provincial and national levels. The makeup of the commissions could also include those who have both practical experience and socio-scientific training. He adds that other potential members of the candidacies commissions could be legal specialists, anthropologists and psychologists specializing in the study of political systems.

Duharte Díaz reveals a weak link in the nomination procedure that other Cuban specialists also highlight. While very few people raise it publicly, it is the Gordian knot of the current candidacies commission nomination system. Municipal delegates are elected in the first phase of the general elections in the month of October. The nomination procedure for the ANPP elections then accelerates immediately following these elections. The problem is that approximately half of the incumbents do not return as delegates for a variety of reasons, one being the difficulty in carrying out their responsibilities on a volunteer basis after work hours. This high turnover means that half of its members are newcomers after any election. The positive side is obvious: there is no development of an election-related elitist group or the accumulation of privileges. Unfortunately, however, this also means that half of the municipal assemblies' delegates thus have no experience in their post and in many cases do not know each other or the re-elected incumbents. This latter half — the re-elected incumbents — enjoy at least some experience, but they have only just been introduced to the new delegates. This is the context in which the candidacies commissions find themselves immediately after the municipal elections.

The candidacies commissions begin approaching all of the delegates after these October elections. The commissions seek the delegates' input as to whom they think should be nominated from the ranks of their own municipal assemblies as their *de base* candidates for ANPP elections (as part of the up to 50 percent of eventual deputies).

Duharte Díaz questions how local delegates can appropriately make a judgment in these circumstances. As a solution, he proposes that a longer period be fixed between the first phase of the general elections (i.e., the municipal first-phase elections) and the second phase of the general elections (i.e., the national elections), which starts with the nomination procedure for candidates as deputies to the ANPP. The goal would be to allow grassroots delegates to accumulate experience and get to know each other. He stresses the fact that these local delegates are proposed for the highest level of state power, thus the importance of rethinking the process (Interview, Duharte Díaz 2009). García Brigos suggests something similar (García Brigos 1998: 105; Interview, García Brigos 2007). This problem of excessive turnover affects the functioning of the municipal assemblies and not only the election procedure. ANPP deputy and president of its Permanent Working Commission on Local Organs, Cárdenas García, confided in an interview, under questioning about the problem of two-and-a-half-year mandates, continuity and the functioning of the municipalities, that there has been discussion on expanding the mandate to five years as is the case for the national deputies. However, there are differing opinions and, so far, the discussion has not been elaborated further. There has been serious discussion but no consensus, as it is a delicate issue concerning the responsibility of committing oneself to be a volunteer delegate for five years (Interviews, Cárdenas García 2007, 2008b).

In Duharte Díaz's opinion, the fact that, in 2008, the CCN reported that only one municipal assembly rejected the nomination proposal by the candidacies commissions leads one to wonder about the credibility of the candidacies commissions' final step in the process. It may be a sign of what Raúl Castro calls the "false tradition of unanimity, or I would go further, '*unanismo*'" (Interview, Duharte Díaz 2009).

García Brigos agrees with this. He provides an example from the 1990s, when the candidacies commission insisted on imposing a *directo* as candidate on a local assembly. This local assembly rejected the proposal; however, the candidacies commissions returned on several occasions to try to convince its assembly delegates to accept their proposal. It came to the attention of Fidel Castro that the candidacies commission insisted on imposing a candidate. In a meeting of the municipal PCC activists, Castro said that the candidacies commission had no right to impose anyone against the wishes of the municipal delegates, who have the last word (Interview, García Brigos 2009b).

As he divulged in an interview, Rafael Hernández considers that people may get the impression that the candidacies are being controlled, because the procedure is so tightly linked to being balanced according to a cross-section of society. It would appear, he insinuates, as a filtering process (*proceso de filtraje*). With this perspective, even if everyone votes in the polling stations, he implies that the very high voter turnout rate is not as meaningful as it could be. Hernández argues for quality, not quantity. The candidacies commissions must take their time and consult directly with grass-roots members of the mass organizations. It is not sufficient to involve only those elected to positions in these associations, even if elected democratically. It is necessary, Hernández continues, to decentralize the nomination procedure even further, with no limits on the number of people nominated. Nominations, he urges, have to take place based on the active and open role played by the grass roots; if not, there will be no improvement in the political atmosphere and culture. The validity of the vote does not come from the approximately 96 percent who vote, but, rather, from the real possibility to first participate in the nomination of those candidates (Interview, Hernández 2009).

The controversy over the candidacies commissions seems to be going quite far. For example, University of Havana law professor and expert on the electoral and constitution procedures Martha Prieto Valdés holds a novel view. She reasons that, in addition to the candidacies commission and the mass organization plenum making nomination proposals, individual citizens and ordinary members of the mass organizations should also be able to make proposals.[8]

---

8. This view resulted from comments made by Martha Prieto Valdés in a series of email consultations I made with her, following her reading of a draft manuscript of this book. Her email on this particular option is dated June 5, 2012.

Elections to the ANPP

In December and at the beginning of January 2007–08, in the context of the ANPP elections called for Sunday, January 20, 2008, meetings between candidates and electors were held in places of work and in the neighbourhoods.[9] In addition, the only other publicity or "campaign," for lack of a better term, consisted of a photo and biographical profile of each of the candidates. Electors had ample time to consult them.

The population of the municipality of Plaza de la Revolución (the focus of the case study) is very high (152,318), compared with a rural area or a small town, each forming a municipality. The temporary electoral districts are thus delimited in order to ensure that constituencies do not exceed the constitutional requirement of a maximum of 20,000 inhabitants voting for candidates. The particular district focused on in the case study had three candidates: one was a municipal *de base* delegate and two were *directos*. In other municipalities or temporary districts, there may be, for example, three *de base* candidates and four *directos* out of a total of seven. This is the case so that the total number of *de base* elected deputies for the 614 ANPP seats comes as close as possible to the 50 percent maximum allotted for *de base* candidates.

Elections are carried out entirely on voluntary labour. In the 2008 elections, half a million people were involved. This included polling station board members, electoral commissions and all of the support staff, from drivers to those preparing and delivering food to the polling stations to youth who guarded the ballot boxes. Part of this voluntary support staff also encompassed computer personnel who had just recently (for the 2007–08 elections) upgraded the digital tabulating system (Interview, Reus González 2008). The voters' registration lists were, as in the municipal first-phase elections (i.e., those leading up to a general election), updated and conveniently posted prior to the elections.

Based on the case study of one temporary district in Plaza de la Revolución, there may be several candidates' names on a ballot, as in all temporary districts and municipalities. In the case study, the three candidates on this ballot together were considered the slate, or a list of three. Two of them were *directos* and the third, a *de base* candidate. The government, the PCC and mass organizations called for the *voto unido* (united vote), or a vote for the entire slate. The logic is as follows: if people vote only for relatively well-known personalities, it would be unfair to other candidates, mainly *de base* ones. There is also the desire to inculcate a collective and collegial spirit of work in the ANPP among all deputies, whether *de base* or *directos*. Selective voting is contrary to the slate vote. In a selective vote, a citizen votes for one or more candidates on the ballot, but not all of them. In the district under examination, *directo* candidate Ricardo Alarcón was, of course, *very*

---

9. While, as some commentators claim, there is room for improvement as far as the extent and quality of these meetings (Interview, Duharte Díaz 2009), the ones I attended in 2008 (as was the case in 1998) were at least spontaneous.

well known, unlike the other *directo,* who was not well known, as he was a civil servant not highly exposed to public attention. The *de base* candidate was a municipal delegate, acknowledged in the *circunscripción* where he lived, but not necessarily throughout the municipality.

People have the right not to vote; this is abstention. Another option is to vote for the slate — in this case, all three candidates. Yet another possibility is to vote selectively, that is, for one or more candidates, but not for the full slate of three. There is also the option to deposit a blank or spoiled ballot. In order to be elected, a candidate needs a minimum 50 percent plus one of the valid votes.

The neighbourhood — in the case study, as part of the temporary electoral district — is divided into the very same five condensed polling stations as in the municipal elections. Once voting is over, the ballot boxes are opened and the votes are counted in public.

The author's personal observations and notes taken for the five polling stations are presented in table 7.7. These figures roughly reflect the results for the entire country.[10]

TABLE 7.7   Results for polling stations in Plaza de la Revolución case study, January 20, 2008, for national elections

Number of voters at the five polling stations	
Polling station	Registered voters
1	239
2	209
3	208
4	264
5	252

Voting results in one polling station			
Voter turnout (%)	Blank ballots	Spoiled ballots	Blank and spoiled ballots (%)
99.56	5	6	5.37

Blank and spoiled ballots for all five polling stations		
Blank ballot	Spoiled ballots	Blank and spoiled ballots (%)
44	30	6.60

Source: Personal observations by author.

---

10. The fact that I, as a foreigner, was allowed to observe the counting of ballots is an indication of the transparency of the Cuban voting process.

The Slate vs. Selective Vote:
A Rejection of the Government?

The disinformation by the U.S. media regarding ANPP election results is similar to that witnessed in the municipal first-phase elections. The election outcome data are manipulated and distorted to give the impression that there is a massive move against the political system and the constitutional order in Cuba. For example, *The New York Times* reported, the day after the January 2008 ANPP elections, that voters

> send subtle messages at the polls. In the last election, more than a million voters submitted blank ballots, nullified their ballot in some way or voted for some but not all of the candidates, said Jorge I. Domínguez, a Harvard professor who follows developments in Cuba. (Lacey 2008)

In September 2012, Cuban "socialist" dissident Pedro Campos and others, through *Havana Times*, carried out the same calculations as Jorge I. Domínguez and *The New York Times* (*Havana Times* 2012). Let us take the *New York Times* assertion that the selective vote ("voted for some but not all of the candidates") constitutes part of a message against the government. In two polling stations where the vote counting was observed by the author, Ricardo Alarcón was the known personality and thus "representative of the government and state." According to the *New York Times* insinuation, he would supposedly be at the receiving end of a "subtle message," in the words of the newspaper. However, an examination of the results tells another story.

As table 7.8 indicates, Alarcón received more votes than the other two candidates. The same applied to all polling stations in that neighbourhood. Alarcón would perhaps be dissatisfied with these results, because he was one of the leaders promoting the slate vote. He may have preferred that the unknown candidates obtain more votes than he did, at least in some polling stations. If voters wanted to send a "subtle message" to the government, they would have voted for the other two candidates, *not* Alarcón.

The same trend was seen across the island. Of sixteen Council of State members — therefore relatively well-known political personalities — twelve arrived in first place (*Granma* 2008: compiled by author). If there had been a concerted, conscious campaign at the polls against the Revolution's leadership — even a subtle message — then it seems that these well-known leaders would have received fewer votes, not more, than anyone else. Therefore, it is not possible to analyze the Cuban election results on the basis of the U.S. establishment media. Their sole purpose, along with the assistance of the dissidents, is to manipulate figures to fit their preconceived notion that the majority of people in Cuba are against the "dictatorship" and "the Castros."

TABLE 7.8   National ANPP elections, January 20, 2008, slate vs. selective vote, results for polling stations in Plaza de la Revolución case study

Polling Station No. 3	Slate votes: 162	Selective votes: 33
Of the 33 selective votes, Ricardo Alarcón received 17 votes; of the other two candidates, one received 10 votes and the other 6 votes.		
Source: Personal observations by author.		

Polling Station No. 4	Slate votes: 196	Selective votes: 33
Of the 33 selective votes, Ricardo Alarcón received 13 votes; the other two candidates received 10 votes each		
Source: Personal observations by author.		

Plaza de la Revolución Municipal Electoral Commission results for the entire municipality	
Slate votes: 33,713	Selective votes: 6,401
Alarcón garnered 93.92% of valid votes, compared with 88.88% and 88.85% respectively for the other two.	

Sources: Notes taken by author; Comisión Electoral Municipal Plaza de la Revolución (data provided to author).

It is useful to delve into this *New York Times* disinformation further, as similar disinformation surfaces after every ANPP election (e.g., 2013).[11] One cannot, as the newspaper did, add the selective votes with the abstentions and the blank and spoiled ballots to come up with a figure that gives the impression that a large number of people, albeit a minority, are voting against the Revolution. An analysis of the election results from the four recent national elections (1993, 1998, 2003 and 2008) reveals that there are important indications that should, however, be recognized, with a view to improving the system.

There are several points worthy of mention with respect to the voter turnout and the blank and spoiled ballot rates over the four elections tabulated in table 7.9. The year witnessing the highest rate of spoiled ballots was 1993, at the very height of the crisis and Special Period following the collapse of the former U.S.S.R. However, the spoiled ballot rate decreased significantly in the next elections (1998) and dropped again in 2003, with only a slight increase in 2008. Blank ballots have remained relatively stable over the four elections, hovering between 3.00 percent and 3.73 percent.

Examining the election results from the point of view of constructive debate, there are some important signs. For example, the voter turnout rate, as table 7.9 indicates, has decreased every year, from 99.57 percent to

---

11. See www.democracyintheus.com, "The 2013 Election Results in Cuba and U.S. Desire for Regime Change."

TABLE 7.9 National ANPP election results, 1993–2008

	1993 (%)	1998 (%)	2003 (%)	2008 (%)
Voter turnout	99.57	98.35	97.64	96.89
Slate votes	95.06	94.45	91.35	90.90
Selective votes	4.94	5.55	8.65	9.10
Blank ballots	3.04	3.36	3.00	3.73
Spoiled ballots	3.99	1.66	0.86	1.04

Sources: Granma 1993, 1998, 2003, 2008; Mayoral 2008. (Data compiled by author.)

96.89 percent. This is not very substantial, but it may be an indication of some dissatisfaction. However, what is more remarkable is the slate versus the selective vote rates. The percentage of people voting slate, that is, for the party and government-promoted option rather than selective preference, has decreased notably over the four elections: from 95.06 percent in 1993 to 94.45 percent in 1998, to 91.35 percent in 2003 and to 90.90 percent in 2008. Some Cubans on the island have analyzed this with a view to improving the political system. For example, Duharte Díaz writes about this noticeable drop in the slate vote:

> Can this change in the voting patterns be interpreted as a persistent increase in what some call the "critical revolutionary vote"? Does it [the decrease in slate voting] indicate a position that, *while not stepping outside the revolutionary boundaries,* tends to draw attention to some possible fissures, insufficiencies or failures in the elaboration of candidacies and the nomination of candidates? This should be taken into account during the next process of improving the electoral system. (Duharte Díaz 2008: 121–31, emphasis added)

The "critical revolutionary vote" is not the same as blank and spoiled ballots. The vast majority of these invalid votes consist of a rejection to one degree or another of the economic and/or political system. The "critical revolutionary vote," on the other hand, confirms the validity of the political system. However, the vote reflects a certain reticence about the candidacies commission procedure or some other aspect of the political system. The steady decline in slate voting, and increase in the "critical revolutionary vote," is also a reminder that Cuba's democracy is in motion. As part of this movement, there is a wake-up call, as Duharte Díaz warns, for improvements in the candidacies commission procedure.

One Candidate for Election per ANPP Seat: Talking Figures

The disinformation from the U.S. monopoly media and the "left" and right dissidents concerning the Cuban electoral process concentrates on the fact that there is one candidate per seat for the ANPP. The nomination process is ignored. Only those Cuban dissidents on and off the island, who call for the competitive multi-party U.S. system for Cuba have received the attention of the media.

One of the features of the Cuban electoral system that virtually all observers of these tendencies fail to see as relevant in relation to the ANPP is the following: for a deputy to be elected to the ANPP, at least 50 percent plus one of the vote must be garnered. However, a close look at some of the data reveals an emerging trend.

Table 7.10, dealing with this tendency, provides details of the results from the last four national elections examined. The table has been elaborated in the following manner. For each election, the number and percentage of elected deputies out of all the ANPP seats (approximately 600 deputies) are calculated into three categories: first, those who received 91–100 percent of the vote; second, those with 81–90 percent; and third, those with 71–80 percent.

TABLE 7.10   Number and percentage of ANPP deputies' vote per bracket

Election results	March 11, 1993	February 4, 1998	February 1, 2003	January 30, 2008
Votes 91–100%	588 (99.49%)	592 (99.50%)	589 (95.93%)	579 (93.54%)
Votes 81–90%	3 (0.51%)	3 (0.50%)	25 (4.10%)	29 (4.68%)
Votes 71–80%	0 (0.00%)	0 (0.00%)	0 (0.00%)	5 (0.81%)

Sources: Granma 1993, 1998, 2003, 2008. (Data compiled by author.)

As clearly indicated in table 7.10, the percentage of deputies winning 91–100 percent has remained stable since 1993. The exceptions are 2003 and 2008, when there was a small, but noticeable, decline in popular support. However, if compared with the 1993 elections, this trend is more evident. The percentage of those candidates polling more than 90 percent of the popular vote decreased from 99.49 percent (1993) to 93.54 percent (2008).

The 81–90 percent popular vote category, generally considered a necessary respectable minimum, shows a perceptible reduction in polling for some candidates. In the 1993 and 1998 elections, only about 0.50 percent of the deputies fell into this category. However, in the 2003 balloting, this figure of popular backing decreased appreciably to the extent that 4.10 percent in 2003 and 4.68 percent in 2008 of the deputies slipped into the 81–90 percent bracket.

However, the 71–80 percent classification is most distinguishable. For each of the 1993, 1998 and 2003 elections, not one single deputy received less than 80 percent of the votes. In comparison, in the 2008 elections, five deputies (0.81 percent of the total ANPP) received 71–80 percent of the vote. This percentage (0.81 percent) for the 71–80 percent classification is not a large number. However, in comparison with the previous elections, it seems to indicate a tendency toward a critical evaluation of nominees. Nonetheless, no candidate received less than 71 percent of the vote.

This latest trend only vindicates the Cuban system of posing a condition that, in order to be elected, a 50 percent plus one vote is required. This minimum requirement *is* thus relevant. It is not accurate to assert that the electors do not have any choice at all. They can defeat a candidate who is not judged worthy by simply not voting for him or her. Electors can thus bring the vote to less than 50 percent. This forces the candidacies commission to present another candidate from their reserve list.

On this issue of one candidate per seat, Duharte Díaz is of the opinion that to have more than one candidate per seat would result in a very complicated situation. Many candidates would get less than 50 percent, since there would be a risk of the vote being divided. This would result in a series of second-round elections. He goes on to explain his principal preoccupation, namely, that the pressure on Cuba to have multiple candidacies is part of the U.S.-led campaign for the imposition of the multi-party political system in Cuba. Duharte Díaz re-emphasizes that everything depends on the quality of the candidacies commissions' work. If this is faulty or lacking in-depth and grass-roots consultation, then the "one candidate per seat" becomes an electoral straitjacket. This issue, he concludes, depends on a full examination of the entire electoral system, especially the candidacies commissions (Interview, Duharte Díaz 2009).

Who Are the Deputies? Talking Quality

The author's fieldwork among the deputies in the ANPP concentrated mainly on the presidents and members of the permanent working commissions. This study revealed that, despite the weaknesses in the nomination process, it is mainly effective. In the controversy over the one-candidate-per-seat option for the ANPP, the most important issue is the *quality* of those elected. In the U.S.-centric definition of democracy and elections, mirrored by the dissidents, all the emphasis is placed on the lack of choice for voters. In so doing, though, a most important criterion is completely overshadowed: in the nomination process, despite its shortcomings, there is consultation. In addition, who are those finally elected to the ANPP? Where do they come from? What do they do? This is "talking quality." Unfortunately, this is rarely discussed by observers and journalists inside and outside of Cuba.

Let us take four examples from among all the sitting deputies (in 2008). Again, a preconceived notion is being promoted behind criticism that the ANPP meets in full plenary session only twice a year. In reality, the ANPP's work is far more extensive (in both quantity and quality) than it receives credit for. It carries out its work year-round through its permanent working commissions, which are required under the Constitution. The brief presentation below of deputies' biographies, combined with an initial outline of the ANPP permanent working commissions, serves to illustrate an important focus of this book. The reference here is to the participatory nature of the ANPP and its links to the grass roots as part of a democracy in motion. The life and work of these deputies go a long way to illustrate the soul of the ANPP, which is censored by the Western establishment media and the dissidents.

Approximately half of the deputies, including *de base* deputies, belong to one of these permanent working commissions. According to Lezcano, they are not at all similar to the commissions in the former U.S.S.R.'s parliament, which had very few links, if any, with the population. In Cuba, the people are directly involved in many key pieces of legislation (Interview, Lezcano 2008b).

Many of the members of these ANPP commissions work throughout the year in a multifaceted fashion. Most, including *de base* deputies, are part-time volunteers but, even with their limited availability of time, they participate. The endeavours of these commissions and the individual deputies composing them are unfortunately entirely unknown outside of Cuba.

A series of four interviews with deputy Leonardo Eugenio Martínez López was held from January to December 2008. He is the president of the ANPP's Permanent Working Commission on Food and Agriculture. He was born in 1953 into a *campesino* family in central Cuba. With the help of scholarships, Martínez López was able to complete his education to become a textile engineer. He worked for many years in the textile industry, a key component of Cuba's industrial strategy. He later became a director of the important plant in which he worked in Havana. He was proposed by the mass organizations and candidacies commissions and then nominated to run as a deputy from a Havana municipality in the 1993 elections. Despite being a director in his place of work, he was suggested as a nominee for election by the local union of the CTC; this came about because of his close ties to the other workers and his intense efforts to constantly improve the working conditions and the production of the plant. Right from his first mandate as deputy in 1993, he was approached to be president of the Permanent Working Commission on Productive Activity, which included industry and other related sectors. His experience in industry was an attribute to take into account. He was re-elected every five years and has remained president of this commission all this time. He is one of the few professional deputies, working full-time at this function. However, he receives the same salary as he earned as director of the plant. Later on, in the newly elected 2008 ANPP, changes were made to the permanent working commissions in order to take into account important new strategies, such as the need to increase domestic food production to replace costly imports. Martínez López was recommended for president of the new Permanent Working Commission on Food and Agriculture. His *campesino* origins and close bonds that he still maintains with his seven brothers and hometown proved to be advantageous characteristics (Interviews, Martínez López 2008a, 2008b, 2008c, 2008d). Throughout the many hours of interviews, it was impressive to witness his intimate knowledge of agriculture, industry and the needs of the people and the economy. Also noticeable is his devotion to contributing toward solving Cuba's problems.

De base deputy and municipal delegate Carlos Liranza García was born in 1963 into a working-class family. He is the president of the ANPP's Permanent Working Commission on Industry and Construction. He studied and graduated in electromechanical engineering and works in a firm dedicated to research and investigation. In 2003, he was nominated for and elected deputy to the ANPP as part of the close to 50 percent of deputies who are locally elected *de base* deputies from the municipal assemblies. When the new Permanent Working Commission on Industry and Construction was established in 2008 (in part to strive toward the solution of the serious housing problems), Liranza García became its first president. Of interest here is that he continues his employment in the engineering research enterprise. He thus assumes his post as president of the commission on a non-professional, voluntary basis. However, he is afforded time off from his workplace when necessary to manage the commission's heavy workload. He is also a local municipal delegate, further assuring his grass-roots links.

In the first interview, held in July 2008, Liranza García was proud to explain some of the plans that his commission had worked out to improve housing construction and renovation throughout the island. By the time the second interview took place, five months later, in December 2008, three hurricanes had hit Cuba. These caused immense destruction, especially in housing. In many senses, his commission, whose members had visited all the affected areas since the first interview, then had a double task. They were forced to target the original housing goals as well as repair the structures destroyed or damaged by the hurricanes (Interviews, Liranza García 2008a, 2008b). Despite this, he appeared calm and assured of their capacity to overcome this situation.

Deputy and world champion runner Ana Fidelia Quirot Moret was born into a poor Santiago de Cuba family. She is a member of the ANPP Permanent Working Commission on Health and Sport. Her family was characterized by two parallel traditions: revolutionary and athletic. In addition to her father being a boxer, most of her brothers and sisters are also involved in sports. She studied physical education at university. This provided her with the opportunity to develop not only as an athlete, but also intellectually and culturally. She won national and international fame by winning world championships on several occasions in the 800 metre race, her specialty, and, on occasion, the 400 metre race. She contends that the ANPP is composed of municipal delegates, ordinary workers, artists, athletes, doctors and intellectuals; as far as her case is concerned, Quirot Moret asserts that she was recommended, nominated and elected for her merits, for her attitude toward society — inside and outside the country — and for her principles. When she was first elected deputy from a Havana municipality, she became part of the Cuba–Bolivia ANPP Friendship Association. In a later mandate, she became a member of the Permanent Working Commission on Health and Sport. As part of this work, they have regular programs throughout the year to advise and assist sport and health centres across the island. (In the 2012 London Olympics medal count, Cuba ranked 16th, the first in Latin America, and even ahead of its former colonizer Spain and developed countries with higher populations.) She also used her experience in the athletic realm to visit neighbouring Venezuela to exchange experiences with athletes there.

In response to a question on her reaction to the fact that many athletes in countries such as the U.S. are multimillionaires, Quirot Moret responded:

> Well, we, Cuban athletes, are also multimillionaires from the following point of view: there are many millions of people living in Cuba — eleven million — and so, since we, the athletes, are loved and admired by millions, we are also millionaires in that sense.... Even today, when I am no longer active in racing, when I go into the streets, people show their love and affection.... In the municipality in which I was elected, San Miguel de Padrón in [present-day province of Havana], I got 96.59 percent of the votes. (Interview, Quirot Moret 2008)

Interviews were conducted with deputy Jorge Jesús Gómez Barranco, founder and director of the Moncada musical band. He is the vice-president of the ANPP Permanent Working Commission on Education, Culture, Science and Technology. His activity and attitude also serve to illustrate that the "one candidate per seat" option cannot be viewed without examining the quality of the deputies. Known by his stage name, Jorge Gómez, he was born into a poor family in a town east of Havana. His father, even though a teacher by profession, often received only about half of the paltry, full salary. The pre-Revolution government often left until last those living outside the capital when it came to fulfilling their salary commitments to employees. Even when the family, including his mother, brothers and sisters, moved to Havana to improve their situation, housing rental was so expensive that the family situation actually worsened. The family was shaken by the loss of Gómez's uncle Raúl Gómez García, who was killed in the Moncada assault on July 26, 1953. After the Revolution's victory, the young Gómez was able to go to university; however, his main interest was music. In 1972, he and some of his fellow students formed a band under his leadership. It later took on the name of Moncada and is successful to this day. In addition to criss-crossing the island, the group has also travelled on many concert tours to Canada, the U.K. and China, and twice to the U.S. Regarding the U.S. tours, Gómez disclosed that the Moncada musicians travelled with all their prejudices imaginable into the "land of the enemy." However, they all quickly learned that the "enemy" (government) was one thing, but the people were something else; the audiences were "sensational and explosive" in expressing their appreciation for Moncada's performances. At the time of the interview (2008), he was into his second term of office as deputy. He thus is able to employ his experience nationally and internationally to contribute to the country's policies on culture.

Cuban deputies from the artistic world have a tradition of making their mark, according to outgoing deputy Maria Josefa Ruíz Mederos (2003–08). She was secretary of this same permanent working commission during her mandate. As an example, she recalled how Cuba's best-known singer-composer and deputy (at the time) Silvio Rodríguez stood up to speak in the ANPP. He suggested that he and other artists do a concert tour of prisons for the benefit of the inmates and their eventual reintegration into society. This was taken up by several permanent working commissions and presided over by the president of the ANPP at the time, Ricardo Alarcón. The suggestion was effectively applied. Both Ruíz Mederos and Jorge Gómez provided many other examples. One is deputy Carlos Alberto Cremata, director of the children's theatre group La Colmenita. It tours Cuba and many countries of the world, the latest being a successful 2011 friendship tour of the U.S. On a local level, deputies are also involved in resurrecting the tradition of establishing local musical bands in small towns to play in Cuba's central parks. Virtually every town and village has a central park. In addition, right after one of the three major 2008 hurricanes hit Cuba, Jorge Gómez and Moncada travelled to the hardest hit areas. The band members organized makeshift concerts to raise the spirits of the inhabitants (Interview, Gómez Barranco and Ruíz Mederos 2008; Interview, Gómez Barranco 2008b).

Composition of the ANPP

There exist several other barometers to measure the nature of the ANPP. Table 7.11 indicates that *de base* delegates formed 46.42 percent of all deputies at the beginning of the ANPP mandate.[12] The table also shows that, taking

---

12. The mandate for delegates is two and a half years and the turnover rate is approximately 50 percent. Thus there are always a certain number of *de base* deputies whose municipal mandate is not renewed. However, these deputies have the right to continue their five-year ANPP mandate. As a result, the *de base* percentage normally falls below the initial 46.42 percent, as was the case in 2008. While some observers both inside and outside of Cuba pay close attention to this, I believe that the most important issue is the quality of the municipal nomination meetings and the role of the candidacies commissions and the mass organizations in national elections.

into account all deputies, whether from among *de base* municipal assemblies or from *directos,* a cross-section of society is represented. The ANPP features deputies who are workers from all sectors, trade unions and student federations (including one 18-year-old pre-university student). In addition, as we saw above, there are many artists, such as Jorge Gómez, and sports figures, such as Ana Fidelia Quirot.

TABLE 7.11   2008 ANPP mandate: Municipal, profession and education

Municipal *de base* delegates (a requirement according to law, up to 50% of deputies)	46.42%
From among all deputies, *de base* and *directos:* production workers, small farmers, social service, teaching and health services workers	28.50%
CTC (trade unions)	26 deputies
FEU (university students)	8 deputies
FEEM (pre-university students)	1 deputy

Source: Asamblea Nacional del Poder Popular (data provided to author).

Regarding the age of deputies, as table 7.12 indicates, there is no major tendency shift from 2003 to 2008, except for the *decrease* in the 18–40 age bracket and the *increase* in those deputies over 60 years of age. These figures explain the leadership's preoccupation with reversing this negative trend by increasing the youth presence in all sectors of the state, including the ANPP. However, on the positive side, 5.85 percent of the deputies in 2008 were between the ages of 18 and 30, unusual for any parliament in the world.

TABLE 7.12   Turnover by age group elected to the ANPP, 2003–08

Age	2003 mandate (%)	2008 mandate (%)
18–30	3.77	5.85
18–40	30.37	21.33
41–60	58.94	61.14
60+	10.67	17.26
Average age	47	49

Source: Asamblea Nacional del Poder Popular (data provided to author).

Cuba's high level of education is reflected in the ANPP composition (table 7.13). A representative of the Asociación Nacional de Agricultores Pequeños (ANAP — National Association of Small Farmers) in the candidacies commission indicated in an interview that many *campesinos* have university degrees in order to specialize in cultivating certain crops and in the raising of livestock (Interview, Comisión de Candidaturas Nacional 2008). The same applies to workers.

TABLE 7.13   2008 ANPP mandate: Level of deputies' education

University graduates	78.34%
Currently pursuing pre-university or university degrees	20.68%
High school graduates	0.98%

Source: Asamblea Nacional del Poder Popular (data provided to author).

Table 7.14 on women deputies represents a noticeable trend. In the ANPP mandate of 2008, women made up 43.20 percent of all deputies in the ANPP, ranking them third in the world for women's representation in parliament. These figures are based on accessing the website of the Inter-Parliamentary Union on May 31, 2012. The first two countries are Rwanda and Andorra. The U.S. is ranked 79th. The work of the candidacies commissions is largely responsible for this increase. Despite advances in Cuba in the realm of gender as far as deputies are concerned, the Cuban leadership is not satisfied. This is especially so, given that the ANPP composition does not yet reflect itself in the Council of State.

TABLE 7.14   Proportion of women deputies in the ANPP: Evolution in mandates, 1998–2008

1998 (%)	2003 (%)	2008 (%)*
27.60	35.95	43.20

Sources: Asamblea Nacional del Poder Popular (data provided to author); *Inter-Parliamentary Union n.d. (accessed May 31, 2012).

The role of women in decision making — and thus effective participation — is the subject of an ongoing and frank debate. For example, *Granma* journalist Anneris Ivette Leyva, on the March 8, 2012, International Women's Day, wrote a profound article on this issue in the Cuban context. The focus is reflected in her piece entitled "Women Under-Represented in Decision-Making Positions" (Leyva 2012).

Thus, despite the record-breaking number of women deputies in the ANPP, this can only be considered as part of an ongoing process of democratization of society. The content of the *Granma* article itself, along with the facts provided, constitutes another example of a democracy in motion.

Table 7.15 indicates a small increase for the overall black and mixed (mestizo) population. However, this rate falls short of the objectives, especially with regard to the composition of the higher bodies elected by the ANPP. This was a subject of debate during the 2012 PCC Conference as a problem to be solved.

TABLE 7.15   2003 and 2008 ANPP mandates according to skin colour, in comparison with 2002 National Census

Year	White (%)	Black (%)	Mestizo (%)
2002 census	65.00	10.10	24.90
2003 mandate	67.16	21.84	11.00
2008 mandate	64.33	19.22	16.45

Sources: Oficina Nacional de Estadísticas n.d.(b); Asamblea Nacional del Poder Popular (data provided to author).

Thus, as far as ANPP composition is concerned (as reflected in tables 7.11 to 7.15), there are some negative and positive features. Yet, to compare the Cuban ANPP's composition with the vast majority of individuals sitting in the U.S. Congress — so as to tip the balance in favour of Cuba — would be far too simplistic. Each body represents entirely different and opposed approaches, as well as levels of people's participation, because they are based on two contrasting social systems. In the final analysis, the ANPP composition can only be measured by raising the bar of its own criteria.

"Almost All Deputies Are Communist Party Members"

The PCC and its youth wing, the Unión de Jóvenes Comunistas (UJC — Communist Youth League), do not participate in the elections at any level. The PCC is not an electoral party. These organizations do not propose candidates for elections. No one is presented as a candidate for these political organizations, nor does any candidate speak in the name of a political organization, either for elections or in the ANPP work. However, approximately 97 percent of the deputies are members of the PCC or the UJC. Following the 2008 elections, 598 of the 614 elected deputies were members of either the PCC or the UJC; in the previous ANPP mandate (2003–08), the proportion was the same (ANPP, email message to author, February 6, 2008).

There are approximately 800,000 members in the PCC and 500,000 in the UJC (Castro Ruz [Raúl] 2012a; Partido Comunista de Cuba n.d.[b]). In order to arrive at a realistic proportion of this membership in society, as reflected in the ANPP, census figures for people over 20 years of age have been taken into consideration. This is the closest age range available that can be elected to the ANPP (eighteen years and older). According to the December 2009 Census, there are 7,875,302 citizens 20 years and older (Oficina Nacional de Estadísticas 2009). The PCC membership is thus around 10.16 percent and the UJC approximately 6.35 percent of the total population in this age bracket. Therefore, the total combined communist members (PCC and UJC) of the population is around 16 percent of those eligible to become deputies, compared with the 97 percent of the deputies who are members of either the PCC or the UJC.

Deputy Jorge Gómez, the musician cited above, is one of the very few ANPP deputies who are *not* PCC members. His comments, conceded in an interview dedicated to this controversy, are instructive. The question was raised as to what he thinks about the fact that 97 percent of the deputies are either PCC or UJC members. He made it clear that, in responding, he was providing his *own personal* opinion, not that of his ANPP permanent working commission or of the ANPP. To say that 97 percent of the deputies are communists while the percentage of PCC and UJC members in the population is only 16 percent, he countered, is "misleading" (*engañoso*). Gómez holds that the "criteria should be that those among the population who are PCC or UJC militants go through a process to be part of the vanguard, as a result of being nominated by the people in their respective workplaces or educational institutes." Therefore, the first point to keep in mind is that individuals become PCC or UJC members in their respective work or study institutions. They do not necessarily request membership; their peers nominate them because of their "prestige as workers." This process has nothing to do with being proposed and elected to the ANPP. The individuals have acquired a well-earned reputation among their peers at their respective places of work and thus can become PCC or UJC members. However, he points out, these *individuals' qualities* are the same ones that come to the fore and are recognized as conditions for nomination to ANPP elections; the nominations are not based on their political affiliations as such. Gómez affirmed that he wanted to elaborate on this complicated issue because it is important "that you understand, that you see how it works" (*por donde están los tiros*). When he considers the PCC, he does not see it as an electoral party, stressing once again how people become members through their own merit in their respective places of work. It would be contradictory to have an ANPP with only a very small number of deputies who are communists. If this were the case, it would raise doubts about the extent to which the PCC is actually a vanguard organization. Asked about the issue of proposing members for the Council of State, he confided, "Do you want me to tell you the truth?" When he (Jorge Gómez) proposes someone, he never questions whether the deputy is a party member. Giving the example of deputy Eusebio Leal (a well-known historian and the soul behind the renovation and restoring of Old Havana), he explains, "For me Eusebio Leal is Eusebio Leal, with or without party membership. If he is a member, fine; if he is not a member, this is also okay."

In order to illustrate further his point of not examining a phenomenon with preconceived or distorted views, he related an anecdote that took place in the U.S. This occurred during a workshop as part of his band's concert tour. One person from the U.S. audience asked, "If Cuba is so much against racial segregation, why are your band members positioned to give the 'white' musicians more prominence than the 'black' instrumentalists?" He answered the query by snickering, "Excuse me, I am going to give you an unusual answer. You just brought it to my attention that they are black. As far as I am concerned, they are all my university comrades." He elaborated that the band members were positioned according to musical criteria and capacity to speak English, and that he would not change their placement, as this would be "a concession to your mentality and your struggle, which is not mine" (Interview, Gómez Barranco 2008a).

In order to appreciate the nature of the ANPP, it is necessary to go beyond the mechanical, prejudiced view one may have of the PCC and its liaison to the political system. The PCC and its relationship to society and the state is not a major problem for the vast majority of Cubans.

Looking at the situation from a political–constitutional point of view, does the non-electoral and non-administrative characteristic of the PCC, on the one hand, and the extremely high proportion of deputies who are communist, on the other hand, constitute a contradiction? Furthermore, Article 5 of the Cuban Constitution states that the PCC "is the highest leading force of society and of the state" (Constitution of the Republic of Cuba [1976] 2003).

In Cuba's democracy in motion, there exists a complex ongoing and changing relationship. This liaison is between the PCC as "the leading force of society and of the state" and its non-participation in both elections *and* the administration of the state. This relationship comprises one of the most intricate issues in the continual process of improving the political system, including in contemporary Cuba. The U.S.S.R.'s inability to deal successfully with this was one of the reasons that the Cubans, as outlined in Chapter 5, spurned the U.S.S.R. model on that issue right from the beginning, in 1974. From the initiation that year of the Órganos del Poder Popular (OPP — Organs of People's Power) system in Cuba, the Cubans have summoned themselves to contest this thorny issue of the party–state relationship. For example, in the 1974 Matanzas Seminar, where Raúl Castro outlined the guidelines on this concern, he reasoned, "[The] Party must never take over purely administrative procedures that do not fall within its jurisdiction. Undue interference will make its relations with people's power organs ineffective" (Castro Ruz [Raúl] 1974).

In the 2012 PCC Conference and its aftermath, this issue continues to be addressed. Does this mean that Cuba cannot solve the dilemma? This would not be the appropriate conclusion to reach, as the ongoing effort is yet another indication that Cuba's democratization is faithful to its innovative tradition. Where others have fallen, Cuba retains the need for a Marxist–Leninist Party to lead. At the same time, the Revolution also encourages the application of another article in their Constitution, Article 3: "Sovereignty lies in the people, from whom originates all the power of the state" (Constitution of the Republic of Cuba [1976] 2003). Sovereignty does not lie in the PCC, but in the people, who have this right. The party cannot interfere with it. However, the party as leader, on the one hand, and sovereignty vested in the hands of the people, on the other, is not an easy balance to maintain. As we have seen in Chapter 6, on the 2011 Party Congress, the revolutionary leadership of the PCC guides the current path to experiment with new features of social-ism in order to improve the people's situation. However, it is not merely a top-down approach; we have seen the input of the grass roots. The party is also the most stalwart defender of Cuba's independence and sovereignty. This resistance faces the continual attempts by the U.S. and its allies, includ-ing dissidents, to undermine the constitutional order and thus bring Cuba back to its pre-1959 situation. This continual endeavour to increase people's empowerment also includes the leadership taking a stand on the future of the Revolution. Indeed, Raúl Castro is reported to have strongly declared, "Corruption is now equal to counter-revolution" (Barredo Medina and Puig Meneses 2011). In the context of this book, any positive mention of the party excludes those party members who are engaged in corruption and active, obstructive bureaucracy.

If anyone wants to know why the "Castro brothers" and the PCC are so maligned and hated by the U.S. and its dissident allies from the "left" and right, here lies the answer: Despite all the shortcomings in the system and real people's power, there is a continual striving to make it more effective, so that sovereignty is truly vested in the hands of the people. This stance is directly linked to a people who have at their disposal a party that, as Ernesto Che Guevara said, cannot trust imperialism an iota (*ni un tantico así*) in the face of constant pressures from the U.S. and its dissidents (Centro de Estudios Che Guevara n.d.).[13] The PCC heritage is anchored in Martí's vision of the party, that it is an instrument *of* the people for revolution and *not a substitute* for the people in their ongoing quest for social justice and national independence. Martí's party was not a communist party, yet it was based on social justice, equality and the sovereignty of Cuba. As we examined in Chapter 4, Martí was a staunch opponent of the party substituting itself for the people. This is crucial because, even with the party leadership standing firm in the face of imperialism and in defence of socialism, if the people do not actively identify with this project, the party would become an empty shell. The goal of the PCC consultative deliberations leading up to the 2011 Party Congress and the content of the 2012 Party Conference consisted in strengthening and improving the symbiotic relationship between the party and the people.

Therefore, the dividing line is not the U.S.-centric, artificial dichotomy between the "one-party system and the multi-party system." Some systems are dedicated to vesting sovereignty in the people, such as the Venezuelan Bolivarian Revolution and the Cuban Revolution. Others, such as that of the U.S., are based on the parasitic use of the people for the vested political-party interests of a tiny minority. Countries such as Cuba, Venezuela, Bolivia and

---

13. Readers can view the original Guevara speech with English subtitles at www.youtube.com/watch?v=MsUv7UohLds.

Ecuador uphold their own independence while respecting that of others. The people participate directly in defending this sovereignty. This is why Washington and its allies complain that the PCC is not giving up its "monopoly." The reference to the "monopoly" of the PCC reflects Washington's frustration that Cubans are not giving *ni un tantico así* to the U.S. on questions of principle. This refusal to capitulate applies to Cuba's independence, political system and approach to socialism.

Elections: ANPP Officials, Council of State and Its President, Raúl Castro

The newly elected ANPP has a five-year mandate. As a first step before initiating the new sessions, it meets to elect from among its members its officials (president, vice-president and secretary) and then the Council of State. The Constitution (Constitution of the Republic of Cuba [1976] 2003) states that the ANPP "is the supreme body of state power and represents and expresses the sovereign will of all the people" and that it "is the only body in the Republic invested with constituent and legislative authority." The ANPP "elects from among its deputies [its] president, vice-president and secretary." From among the deputies, the ANPP then elects the Council of State. It consists of the Council of State president and first vice-president, other vice-presidents, a secretary and 23 other members, totalling 31 members. The president of the Council of State is also the head of state and head of government (Council of Ministers). (The current president of these two bodies is Raúl Castro.) Finally, the Constitution states, "The Council of State is accountable for its action to the National Assembly of People's Power, to which it must render accounts of all its activities" (Constitution of the Republic of Cuba [1976] 2003). Cuba does not have a "presidential system" nor does it pretend to have one. The president of the Council of State is elected from among the deputies, who are elected by the citizens.

The Comisión de Candidaturas Nacional (CCN — National Candidacies Commission) is responsible for organizing the nomination and elections of the ANPP's officials and the Council of State. It initiates consultations with the deputies as soon as they are elected. In the 2008 elections, they were elected on January 20, and in the 2013 elections, exceptionally about two weeks later, on February 3, as a result of disruptions from Hurricane Sandy during the October 2012 municipal elections. In any case, the electoral process is completed by February 24; this is the day the newly mandated ANPP meets to constitute itself. Each deputy has the right to propose any deputy to any post among the ANPP's officials and Council of State. Prior to the February 24 constitution of the new ANPP mandate, the CCN provides each deputy with a tabloid containing the biographies of the 614 elected deputies, as well as those of the outgoing Council of State members (Interview, Reus González

2008). This procedure was further explained in a separate interview with the CCN, which, at the time (January 30, 2008), was initiating the process. When the deputy arrives at the CCN office, after having had ample time to review the tabloid, he or she is provided with two blank sheets — one for the Council of State proposals and one for the ANPP's officials. The person can then elaborate a personal list of suggestions, also including the preferences for specific posts, such as presidents and vice-presidents of the Council of State and officials of the ANPP. The list is unsigned and is deposited in secret (Interview, Pérez Santana, Marchante Fuentes and Fajardo Marin 2008).

Deputy Daniel Rufuls Pineda elaborated on this procedure. He reported that the CCN personally provided him with the list of 614 biographies several days before his February 7 appointment at the CCN headquarters. He thereby had "the total freedom to make [his] decision in private" (Daniel Rufuls Pineda, email message to author, March 15, 2008).

Deputy Jorge Gómez related his experience on this process. It also provided an interesting inside account of the period from January to February 2008. At that time, Fidel Castro had already temporarily relinquished his presidency position to first vice-president Raúl Castro, in 2006. On February 19, 2008, Fidel Castro publicly released his announcement of the previous day: "I will neither aspire to nor accept the positions of President of the State Council and Commander in Chief" (Castro Ruz [Fidel] 2008b).

According to Jorge Gómez, in his private session at the CCN headquarters, which took place before the above-mentioned announcement by the Cuban leader, the deputy had proposed Fidel Castro for president of the Council of State. He also listed the name of Raúl Castro as first vice-president and José Machado Ventura as the next-in-line vice-president, along with his other choices for that body. Jorge Gómez also indicated his choice for the ANPP's officials on the other sheet handed to him. Following a question on the continuity in the Revolution's leadership, the "non-PCC" deputy was of the opinion that, in the absence of Fidel Castro having a formal position in the Council of State, it was necessary to "reinforce the historical leadership of the Revolution." On another query as to a February 2008 *Granma* article reporting that Fidel Castro suggested to the CCN that Machado Ventura be nominated as first vice-president, Gómez responded that this was Fidel's logical preoccupation. His goal has been to make sure at all times that the essence of the Revolution is not lost. Gómez was of the opinion that Machado Ventura, as one of the historical leaders of the Revolution, with long-standing experience, should be nominated (Interview, Gómez Barranco 2008a).

Once all the deputies had gone through this process of proposing candidates for the ANPP's officials and the Council of State, the CCN then tabulated the ballots on sheets of paper. According to the number of votes, it elaborated the list of 31 Council of State members, including its leading positions. The CCN formulated another list of the three ANPP officials (Interview, Pérez Santana, Marchante Fuentes and Fajardo Marin 2008).

Based on the author's attendance at the 1998 constitution of the new ANPP mandate at that time and the interviews regarding the 2008 mandate, the final steps of the elections took place in the following manner. On the day of the constitution of the ANPP mandate (February 24, 2008), CEN president Reus González presided over the ANPP until its officials were elected. The list of the three proposed officials was presented to the deputies: Ricardo Alarcón for president, Jaime Alberto Crombet Hernández-Baquero for vice-president and Miriam Brito Sarroca for secretary. A show-of-hands vote followed to determine whether the deputies agreed with these three nominations or whether they had any other proposals. There were no other proposals. Therefore, the list of three nominees became official. The ANPP session was then adjourned for a secret-ballot vote in the lobby, outside the main meeting hall. Once the three nominees were elected and announced as such by the CEN, the new officials took over the presidency of the ANPP. The same procedure ensued for the 31 members of the Council of State. Raúl Castro was elected president of the Council of State and ipso facto president of the Council of Ministers, therefore head of state and head of the government (according to Article 74 of the Constitution) (Interview, Balseiro Gutiérrez and Amarón Díaz 2008; Interview, Pérez Santana 2008).

With this, the general elections — which had begun in July 2007 with the municipal first-phase elections — ended on February 24, 2008. The 2012–13 general elections followed the same procedure (aside from some modifications as indicated above as a result of Hurricane Sandy), beginning in July 2012 and ending in February 2013.

The nominations and elections of the ANPP's officials and the Council of State may seem quite formal. This is in fact true, especially when compared with the elections to the municipal assemblies and the ANPP itself. It would be naive, however, to believe that the Revolution's leadership is not involved in choosing the leaders of this highest level of state. Even if this is the case, the issue is once again the quality, a point dealt with further in the next chapter.

Regarding the roles and positions of Fidel Castro and Raúl Castro themselves, it is also a question of quality and not — as often charged by the U.S. and their dissident spokespersons — a question of nepotism. Raúl Castro assumed the leadership on a temporary basis in 2006 when Fidel Castro fell ill. He took up this position, according to the Constitution, as first vice-president of the Council of State. On February 24, 2008, Raúl Castro was elected president of the Council of State and Council of Ministers. Several factors should be taken into account. First, he has been involved in the struggle without let-up since the Moncada attack in 1953. He has made his own innovative contributions, even before the 1959 victory. One such breakthrough was organizing the liberated territories in the II Frente Oriental

"Frank País" (Frank País Second Eastern Front). This amounted to a virtual state within the state, as described in Chapter 5. It served as a precedent, to a certain extent, for the new revolutionary government established in January 1959. There have been many other examples of Raúl Castro's role since that time, such as the institutionalization of the People's Power system of government in 1974–76. The enterprise improvement system in the 1990s was inaugurated under his leadership through the ministry of the Fuerzas Armadas Revolucionarias (FAR — Revolutionary Armed Forces), of which he was the minister until 2008. Since his 2008 election as president of the Council of State and Council of Ministers, and while retaining his position as general of the FAR, he has been further institutionalizing the collegial leadership. He is doing so by holding regular (almost monthly) expanded sessions (including other people aside from the official members) of either or both the Council of State and Council of Ministers. Raúl Castro is also at the forefront in the attempt to put a stop to bureaucracy and high-level, white-collar corruption. At the same time, he is leading, along with others, innovations to preserve and improve socialism. This is done with an increasing focus on the participation of the people.

Thus, to conclude this chapter on elections, contrary to the dominant view in the North, the issue in Cuba's political system is not the party, nor "the Castros." The question is rather the quality of all those elected at the local and national levels and the opinions on improving the electoral system. In the next chapter, we will deal with how the state operates at the national and local levels after elections have taken place.

Chapter 8

The ANPP and the Municipality: Functioning Between Elections

Are Democratization and Revolutionary Leadership Compatible?

The Cuban political system cannot be explored through the narrow limits of the U.S.-centric separation of powers. This division of responsibilities refers to the supposed checks and balances between the legislative, executive and judicial branches. The ANPP is the sole body responsible for approving legislation. However, legislating is part of the wider scope encompassing the entire Cuban political system. The ANPP, its Council of State and Council of Ministers, in a manner of speaking, share this legislative task. They also do so, for example, in some cases directly with mass organizations and the grass roots.

In Chapter 7, the section entitled "Who Are the Deputies? Talking Quality" explored part of the life and work of a cross-section of elected citizens. This serves as an introduction to the first sections of this chapter on the functioning of the state between elections at the national level (ANPP). However, to place the ANPP in its context, it should be noted that it is part of the single state existing at all levels. The Cuban state is composed, among others, of the Órganos del Poder Popular (OPP — Organs of People's Power). The OPP is a single, intertwined power from top to bottom and bottom to top. It encompasses all levels of state power, the ANPP and the provincial and municipal assemblies. In contrast to these levels, according to the Constitution, only the judicial branch has relative "functional independence." The courts "only owe obedience to the law" in the administration of justice (Constitution of the Republic of Cuba [1976] 2003).

The PCC cannot propose or approve legislation. However, it can recommend overall policies to the ANPP. The latter can then translate the proposal into legislation, in its entirety or in part. The Cuban system is not based on the separation of powers. In such a checks-and-balances approach, each division jealously, and often in a competitive manner for partisan political purposes, guards its own respective prerogatives.

The ANPP, on the one hand, and its Council of State and Council of Ministers, on the other hand, comprise a Cuban innovation. They are characterized by agility and revolutionary action in order to act swiftly when necessary and on issues that are popular and require a decisive response. However, they adopt a participatory method in consulting with the people in order to get their input on issues that are controversial or that involve discrepancies. The Council of State issues decree-laws and the Council of Ministers delivers decrees. However, this does not take place in the manner the North views it; that is, it is not arbitrarily imposed. This approach to legislation is often the result of a popular groundswell. One example of such decrees was the 2008 Council of State Decree-Law No. 259 on allotting rent-free fallow land in usufruct (cited in Chapter 6). The goal is to increase the quality, quantity and effective distribution of food to the people in the context of the international and national economic crisis. This is a major preoccupation of the people.

Another example concerned the important expansion of the number and variety of self-employment categories that are eligible for licensing by the government in order to operate legally. For example, new licence possibilities increased in the domain of food preparation to the public and transportation. This took place in October 2010 because of an initiative of the Council of State and Council of Ministers. It took the form of a Council of State decree-law and related Council of Ministers rules and resolutions (cited in Chapter 6). Their purpose was to deal with both the reduction of bloated payrolls and the significant expansion of self-employment. The latter was designed to absorb as many surplus state employees as possible. Self-employment was a popular demand, while the reduction of overstaffing was controversial. In the years since 1959, there have been changing policies by the government in regard to legal self-employment. A general undercurrent has long existed among some sectors of the population that prefer to work on their own initiative. One of the reasons is to increase their income, given that, if their chosen self-employment is successful, the income derived thereof is higher than state employment salaries. The popularity of this demand went beyond those interested in self-employment to a greater cross-section of the society. For example, from among the population in general, many welcomed the possibility to obtain from the self-employed sector goods and services that the state sector was not able to offer or to present properly. Another factor consisted in many people carrying out self-employment illegally, since no licences had been available for their particular categories. Therefore, another factor fuelling the popular demand was from those who have wanted to come out of the shadows in order to operate legally, a situation that was made possible by the new Council of State decree-law. Therefore, the self-employment expansion decree went ahead, and self-employment has been flourishing ever since, despite problems of bureaucracy and other issues. In contrast, the pace of the bloated payroll reduction, as we have seen in Chapter 6, has slowed down considerably in order to take into account the controversies and dissatisfaction made evident at the grass-roots level and in the unions.

One other such example of popular legislation is the Council of Ministers Decree No. 292, which, for the first time, legalizes the sale and purchase of cars. The newly enacted right to buy and sell cars is another instance of how legislation is effected by the base, on the one hand, and the ANPP and its Council of State and Council of Ministers, on the other hand. This right was not in the original Guidelines sent to the people for pre-Congress consultation. However, citizens raised it and, thanks to popular input, the buying and selling of cars was introduced in a subsequent draft. This led to the Council of Ministers Decree No. 292 in September 2011, approximately five months after the Congress (*Gaceta Oficial de la República de Cuba* 2011a).

Similarly, Decree-Law No. 288 was issued in November 2011 by the Council of State to allow, for the first time, the sale and purchase of housing (*Gaceta Oficial de la República de Cuba* 2011b). The base had a direct role in the legislation even though it was a decree-law. This is how the phenomenon occurred. In the PCC April 2011 Congress, an original guideline existed for the sale and purchase of housing, itself a result of relatively broad public opinion. However, because of the debates organized by the PCC leading up to the Congress and in the Congress itself, this guideline was expanded to be more flexible. This amended guideline was applied through Decree-Law No. 288 approximately seven months after the Congress.

There exists an additional indication that these decrees and decree-laws are part of the wider concern by the leadership to quickly put popular demands into practice. These grass-roots appeals on cars and housing were being acted upon even *before* the Congress took place. On April 16, 2011, in his opening report to the PCC Congress, Raúl Castro announced, "Without waiting to have everything worked out, progress has been made in the legal regulations associated with the purchase and sale of housing and cars" (Castro Ruz [Raúl] 2011a). Thus demands that were either entirely or partially a result of bottom-up efforts were acted upon with the same vigour as if they had originated with the leadership itself. Therefore, the terms "decree" and "decree-law" cannot be viewed with the U.S.-prejudicial notion of authoritarian or dictatorial orders against the popular will. In fact, the opposite is true. Similarly, the leadership did not wait until the end of the Congress proceedings to make modifications to Decree-Law No. 259, which allowed for "expanding the limits of fallow land to be awarded in usufruct to those agricultural producers with outstanding results and ... granting ... credits to self-employed workers and to the population at large" (Castro Ruz [Raúl] 2011a).

The grass-roots participation also resulted in a new Congress guideline to facilitate access to construction materials for renovations and other such activities at non-subsidized prices. This new guideline emerged from opinions expressed at the base and arising from the pre-Congress debates. In January 2012, approximately nine months after the Congress, the Council of Ministers acted in conjunction with the appropriate ministers. They applied this popular demand by issuing a resolution that allowed bank subsidies to assist individuals in housing renovations (*Gaceta Oficial de la República de Cuba*

2012a). This need for renovation and monetary restoration assistance was not proposed by the leadership in the original PCC Congress document; rather, it was introduced from the bottom up and executed rapidly by the Council of Ministers. There are other similar examples of combined bottom-up/top-down legislative interaction, such as the right of farmers to sell their products directly to tourism enterprises (e.g., hotels).

In October 2012, one of the most controversial pieces of legislation was made public. It concerned the decade-long popular demand to update the migration policy, making it more flexible to leave and return to Cuba. This is a very complex situation. It is not possible to consider this outside the parameters of the U.S. policy since 1959 of luring Cubans to the U.S., in a bid to undermine Cuba's economy and services to the population. However, on August 1, 2011, Raúl Castro announced to the ANPP session that the Council of State and Council of Ministers were working on new legislation (Castro [Raúl] 2011b). On October 16, 2012, the Council of State Decree-Law No. 302 and related Council of Ministers and ministries decrees and resolutions were made public. Among other stipulations, it eliminated the need for a costly and cumbersome Travel Permit and Letter of Invitation from abroad to leave the country, while preserving certain restrictions to protect Cuba from the U.S. brain-drain policies (*Gaceta Oficial de la República de Cuba* 2012b). This constitutes another example of Cuba's legislation in the form of decreed laws during this new period of change, combining popular demands with national interests and sovereignty.

Non-decreed laws, in contrast, are either debated in the ANPP before adoption or come from the base and are later adopted by the national body. They can also originate from the Council of State and likewise be adopted as law, but only after consultation with the citizens. For example, legislation such as the Social Security Bill, which will be examined below, came from the top down, but was not adopted as a decree or decree-law. Consultation at the base was required with input from the citizens on the final draft of the bill before it was enacted.

These examples serve to illustrate that the Cuban legislative experience cannot be viewed from the U.S. approach to division of powers and checks and balances. The Cuban course combines consultation with swift action, depending on the situation and, in general, in response to the people's demands. The main difference between the U.S. and Cuban course is people's participation. The U.S. route is very limited in participation because, if allowed to flourish, real participation could upset the rule of unlimited accumulation of private property as the basis of the political system. Rather than taking a channel of participation, U.S. citizens are supposed to have faith in the checks and balances, along with the separation of powers and the right to vote every few years.

Who Legislates?

In addition to the notion of decrees and decree-laws not being divorced from popular demand, there is another option that further exemplifies Cuban democracy's participatory nature. Not all citizens can be elected to the ANPP, but the ANPP as a body and its deputies can and do involve the people in decision making and drafting legislation.

Participation at the grass-roots level and of the mass organizations in the drafting of legislation predates the establishment of the current political system. The mass organizations have the right to initiate legislation. The 1974–75 consultation on the 1975 Family Code was an initiative of the Federación de Mujeres Cubanas (FMC — Federation of Cuban Women) (Interview, Castro Espín 2009; Interviews, Rojas Hernández 2008, 2009b). Let us look at a few examples of this type of participation by the people and mass organizations.

In the first few months of 1994, in the context of the severe economic crisis caused by the fall of the U.S.S.R. and accumulated domestic problems, the ANPP and the Central de Trabajadores de Cuba (CTC — Workers' Central Union of Cuba) took a stand. They agreed to bring to the workers the issue of what to do before any legislation was proposed and adopted in the ANPP. The vast majority of workers participated in thousands of work centre meetings in order to vent their feelings and make proposals; these meetings became known as "Workers' Parliaments" (*Parlamentos Obreros*). ANPP president Ricardo Alarcón is a longtime advocate of the "parliamentarization of society." In April 1994, as these Workers' Parliaments had just completed their proceedings, he wrote about his own experience attending 36 of these local "parliaments." Alarcón cautioned that, while the quality of the participation and debate was not the same in all work centres, he saw how workers confronted the problems facing their respective work centres and society as a whole. He said that it was unfortunate that some comrades lived with the "illusion that some things can be carried out from the top [*desde arriba*]... that they are going to create miracles." Alarcón was of the opinion, rather, that "the participation of all is the source of performing miracles, or there will be no miracles" (Alarcón de Quesada 2002d: 92–97). In June 1994, in philosophizing about the imperative mandate in Rousseau's tradition and the Paris Commune, Alarcón wrote — once again in the aftermath of the Workers' Parliaments — that this problem of imperative mandate can be "resolved by the parliamentarization of society." He elaborated on the 1994 experience of the Workers' Parliaments as an important episode. While he acknowledged it was of course not possible to gather all Cuban workers across the island in one large meeting hall, he stated, "You can incorporate all the workers in the discussion of a specific problem" (Alarcón de Quesada 2002c: 75–87). In 2003, with the advantage of hindsight, Alarcón cited the Workers' Parliaments as the best example in which "the entire Cuban society participated in reflecting profoundly and openly upon the general and concrete problems of our economy in the worst period of the crisis (1993)" (Alarcón de Quesada 2003).

Emilio Duharte Díaz provided some additional information based on his own experience in the Workers' Parliaments. He related how, when the deputies in the ANPP were unable to reach a consensus on orientation and measures to take to confront the crisis, "they thought of a brilliant solution … a convocation of all work centres, all organizations, to discuss the reform package.… I do not know of any other experience in the world like this one" (Interview, Duharte Díaz 2009). U.S. political science professor Peter Roman, who attended many Workers' Parliaments in 1994, concluded, "It is undeniable that workers were consulted.… Much of what the workers requested and suggested was later adopted [in Parliament]" (Roman 1995: 43–58).

Perhaps one of the best examples of how the people are directly involved in some legislation is the Agricultural Cooperatives Bill. In 2002, the proposal for a new bill was put forward to the ANPP by the Asociación Nacional de Agricultores Pequeños (ANAP — National Association of Small Farmers). The ANAP made this decision in their Ninth Congress, held in 2000. This was effected in accordance with its right as spelled out in the Cuban Constitution.[1] The same year, two permanent ANPP working commissions — the Permanent Working Commission on Productive Activities and the Permanent Working Commission on Constitutional and Legal Affairs — issued an August 2002 report, which outlined the background. A special working group was established in the ANPP made up of deputies from both working commissions, the presidents of the different forms of rural co-ops and other specialists. They were all responsible for studying the existing law and drawing up a new draft bill deemed necessary to replace the old one. A massive number of discussions took place in the co-ops and the special ANPP working group (Asamblea Nacional del Poder Popular 2002). When the deputies toured the co-ops to consult on the draft bill, these visits alone resulted in 500 amendments to the original version (Interview, Martínez López 2008a).[2]

Case Study: Participation in Drafting the Social Security Bill

The involvement of the workers in the 2008 discussion over this draft bill took place in the wake of a series of discussions and debates in 2005–07, as explained above. This led right into the 2008 debates on the new Social Security Bill in all workplaces, from industrial to educational centres. One

1. Article 88 reserves the right to legislate for deputies, the Council of State and Council of Ministers, the CTC and other mass organizations. The ANAP operated under this article.
2. For the seminal detailed work of a non-Cuban on this type of bill, see Peter Roman's examination of the legislative process. He concludes his study by writing that the legislative process, based on its own criteria, is "both democratic and effective" (Roman 2005: 1–20).

of its aspects was to increase the retirement age from 60 to 65 for men and from 55 to 60 for women, with some additional benefits, including a higher pension. The new law was to be applied gradually and a transitional period was allotted for people in the retirement age brackets.

This case study of the Social Security Draft Bill does not explore the bill as a piece of legislation unto itself. Rather, the bill is surveyed with the measuring rod of the potential to make these types of popular consultations a *permanent* part of the next step of a democracy in motion. For example, Cuban analysts Olga Fernández Ríos, Concepción Nieves Ayús, Rafael Hernández and Dario Machado Rodríguez (quoted in Chapter 6) and others refer to the involvement of the entire population in the PCC pre-2011 Congress debates. Fernández Ríos proposes "maintaining consultation and participation of the people as a permanent feature" (Fernández Ríos 2011a). Duharte Díaz, in referring to the Workers' Parliaments, declares that these types of activities "should be repeated more frequently" (Interview, Duharte Díaz 2009).

The debate over the controversial Social Security Draft Bill did not achieve unanimity or general satisfaction. However, the participation of the workers from all fields of activities in *modifying* the draft bill is another indication of Cuba's innovative nature. The experience highlights Cuba, once again, as a laboratory, always ready to experiment with new methods of involving the grass roots in decision making, even in the area of legislation. This participation is seen as necessary in the case of this Social Security Draft Bill, which, by its very nature, is not appealing. It is the continual striving to come within reach of — as much as may be possible — the seemingly unachievable merger between the bottom-up and the top-down approaches.

The Constitution guarantees social security and social assistance, with the state as the guarantor. This guarantee is similar to those for the rights to free health services and education. The procedure for the draft bill was initiated in a July 2008 regular legislative session of the ANPP, according to an interview with the general secretary of the CTC, Salvador Valdés Mesa, a deputy and a member of the Council of State. Valdés Mesa went on to explain the genesis of this process.

Deputies participated in the proposal from the Council of State that the procedure for a new Social Security Bill be initiated, given that the situation had changed since the last law was adopted in 1980. Seeing that the law was so important and affected all workers and their families, agreement was reached that the CTC, according to Valdés Mesa, "would develop a process of consultation with all workers in the country." ANPP president Alarcón then suggested that two permanent working commissions (first, the Permanent Working Commission on Economic Affairs, and second, the Permanent Working Commission on Constitutional and Legal Affairs) act in coordination with the CTC and the Ministry of Labour and Social Security. Valdés Mesa stated that the CTC counted on the collaboration of the two working commissions and the government ministry. However, the CTC would be "leading this whole process." Immediately following the ANPP decision, a series of seminars was initiated to train and inform all the people who would be responsible for spearheading this procedure (Interview, Valdés Mesa 2009).

In that July 2008 ANPP session when the procedure was initiated, Raúl Castro in his closing speech referred to the new draft social security legislation and consultation. He quoted from the "Executive Report on the Calculation of the Life Expectancy Rate in Cuba." He said that it had been completed by the National Statistics Office just a few days prior to the ANPP session, but was not yet published: "In the period 2005–2007, Cuba attained a life expectancy rate at birth of 77.97 years for both genders; 76 for men and 80.02 for women." The retirement age of 60 for men and 55 for women had been established in 1963, but the situation had since changed radically. Between 1950 and 1955, before the Revolution, life expectancy at birth had been a little over 59 years, but as Raúl Castro stated, "[It] has increased by almost 20 years, despite the difficulties imposed by the blockade.… Without any doubt, it is a great victory of the Revolution." The birth rate has been decreasing regularly over several decades. As a result, along with the increase in life expectancy, the working age population has been declining. Castro noted, "Social security and assistance costs stand at 13.8%" of the budget. (The state assumes an important portion of pension contributions.) These and other demographic problems "cannot be solved in the short term, and time passes rapidly!" (Castro Ruz [Raúl] 2008).

The Social Security Bill is an example of a proposal that comes from the top down. On the other hand, the Agricultural Cooperatives Bill is an example of a bottom-up approach of consultation initiated from the base by the National Association of Small Farmers (ANAP). The raising of the retirement age is not popular. How has Cuba's participatory democracy fared in this difficult situation? Did it pass the test? Did it contribute to the further democratization of society?

Deputy Osvaldo Martínez Martínez is president of the Permanent Working Commission on Economic Affairs and director of the Havana-based World Economy Research Center. He explained that at the July 2008 legislative session, the Social Security Draft Bill (*Anteproyecto de Ley de Seguridad Social*) was drawn up by the Ministry of Labour and Social Security, the CTC and the two working commission deputies involved. It stipulated that this *draft* bill was to be discussed by the workers.

Meetings in the workplaces, he explained, were called and presided over by the local CTC section. He expected that 80,000 such assemblies would be held. The deputies who were members of either of the two commissions involved were required to follow all the local union meetings. Martínez insisted that the deputies visit as many union assemblies as possible in their respective municipalities. In addition, those who were not professionals (full-time) were also expected to attend their own work centres' meetings. The structures for holding the meetings were created by the local unions at the places of work within the union's own framework, such as being presided over by the union representatives. Also present were representatives of the Ministry of Labour and Social Security and the PCC. Martínez reasoned, "Everyone participates. It is a large national parliament" (*un gran parlamento nacional*). All opinions, suggestions and complaints are gathered and recorded (Interview, Martínez Martínez 2008).

On August 5, 2008, several days after the ANPP had adopted the draft bill and worked out the consultation plan, a special eight-page tabloid-size publication containing the entire text of the bill, with accompanying explanations, was sold to the people at a token price. This allowed for the population to study it and exchange ideas with their fellow workers and families.

Luis Manuel Castanedo Smith has been a deputy since 1998 and is a member of the CTC. Having gained experience on economic questions through union activism, Castanedo Smith found his natural place as vice-president of the Permanent Working Commission on Economic Affairs of the ANPP, working side by side with Martínez. The draft bill, Castanedo Smith elaborated, was adopted in July 2008 and union meetings were scheduled to take place in September and October to consider this draft. Therefore, the month of August, normally a vacation period in Cuba, was used for training seminars with deputies, CTC militants and other specialists across the country.

In an interview with him soon after the union assemblies, he explained how two major hurricanes — one after the other, at the end of August (Gustav) and the beginning of September (Ike, one of the worst to hit Cuba) — completely unsettled the planned union meetings. This was especially the case in those parts of the country most devastated by these natural disasters. Therefore, 80 percent of the meetings were held in October. Looking back at the union meetings, the CTC deputy revealed, "We cannot say that the approval was unanimous.... There were places in which there were very strong discussions (*discusiones muy fuertes*). But this was good, it strengthened us." He said that the main preoccupation of the workers was the additional five years of work. There were many who agreed with the overall draft bill and the necessity to deal with the reality related to demographics, but who nonetheless proposed changes to the draft. He summarized the issue as follows:

> A minority was against the draft bill. However, I do not believe that this was bad, because democracy does not mean everyone is in agreement with everything being said. It is necessary to have discussions, to express opinions and to allow argumentative discussions to take place.... People were given the opportunity to make proposals and the overwhelming majority showed their support to modify the draft bill. This way, we were able to go to the ANPP with a more refined,

more complete bill.... This was the fruit of a process of participatory democracy. (Interview, Castanedo Smith 2008)

Another interview was held with Bernardo Castell Cobol, the general secretary of the local union of teachers and manual workers in Havana's Raquel Pérez primary school. National and municipal CTC activists of the Education, Science and Sports Union were also present at the interview, along with the school principal. Castell Cobol explained that seminars were held for them regarding all the macro-economic and demographic features, as well as the raising of retirement ages and the new benefits.

There was much debate in the local union meeting regarding the requirement to work an additional five years. However, the union participants took into account demographic factors, as part of the phenomena that also exist in North America and Europe, along with the benefits, such as higher pensions. In the school, workers unanimously voted in favour. The national and municipal CTC representatives confirmed, however, that, on a countrywide basis, "it was not unanimous" (Interview, Castell Cobol et al. 2008).

CTC general secretary Salvador Valdés Mesa explained that there were several important changes to the draft bill. These modifications emerged out of the 85,301 local workers' assemblies (such as the one described above), in which 3,085,798 workers participated (93.8 percent of the total workforce). Of these, 99.1 percent voted in favour of the draft bill. In 90 work centres, the majority voted against it.

One of the most important amendments among many that Valdés Mesa outlined in order to illustrate the role of the grass roots in legislative participation concerned the maximum number of years used to calculate pension rates. It is important to consider that there are salary stimuli in Cuba based on performance, production and attendance at work. In addition, the draft bill proposed an increase in pensions. Initially, the draft indicated that, at the time of retirement, pensions were to be calculated on the best five annual salaries of the last ten years of work before retirement. Because of workers' input, the period was changed to the last *fifteen* years. The workers reasoned that, as they approached retirement age, productivity could decline due to age and related factors, such as health and looking after aging parents, thus affecting the work attendance record (Interview, Valdés Mesa 2009).

How significant is the very high rate of approval, of over 99 percent? Rafael Alhama Belamaric is a researcher at Havana's Instituto de Estudios e Investigación del Trabajo (Institute of Studies and Investigation on Labour), related to the Ministry of Labour and Social Security. He specializes in labour economics and is a critical author. In his forthcoming book on some current issues, he provides significant observations on the Social Security Bill's legislative ANPP process and related concerns. His investigated opinions indicate that, given the situation, the 99 percent approval of the draft bill in work and educational centres and the unanimous approval by the ANPP of the amended bill was an accomplishment. However, he cautions that these figures cannot simply be viewed as cold statistics. They do not reflect the underlying problems and lack of satisfaction that are currently being addressed (Alhama Belamaric forthcoming).[3]

All of the changes to the original draft bill resulted in a second draft bill in preparation for the next plenary session of the ANPP. The first step toward this plenary session was the holding of the ANPP working commissions several days before the full session of all the deputies. (It is significant to note that the author of this book was able to attend the permanent parliamentary working commissions that preceded the plenary session of the ANPP.) In the context of the case study, it is useful to highlight some of the proceedings of a joint session of both commissions responsible for seeing through consultations with workers along with the CTC. It was held on December 24, 2008, three days before the ANPP plenary session. The morning agenda termed it a joint meeting of the two commissions dealing with the results of these consultations in the work centres and the latest documents and draft of the bill. In attendance were the deputies of the Permanent Working Commission on Economic Affairs and the Permanent Working Commission on Constitutional and Legal Affairs, ANPP president Ricardo Alarcón, Minister of Labour and Social Security at the time Alfredo Morales Cartaya and ANPP secretary Miriam Brito Sarroca. One week before the joint commission session, each deputy received a copy of the second draft in order to prepare for the session. This draft bill included the new articles that had resulted from the debates in the work centres.

The ANPP commission proceedings would have been expected to be a mere formality, given that the issues had already been addressed and a new draft bill elaborated and printed. However, the deputies raised several other questions. For example, one proposed that self-employed workers be listed as part of those involved in the social security plan. Indeed, in the second draft bill, self-employed workers had been included under the new social security protection, but only as an adjunct to the provisions. Given the increase in self-employed workers since 2008, her proposed and accepted amendment was important. Several other points were proposed and approved. It was decided that a draft report or evaluation (*dictamen*) of the opinions expressed in the joint commission session for further amendments to the second draft be presented to the ANPP plenary session for discussion and approval.

The Social Security Law was on the agenda of the regular plenary session of the ANPP, held on December 27, 2008. A draft report presented to the deputies summarized the entire procedure of consultation and amendments as an annex to the December 15, 2008, second draft version. These

---

3. Researcher García Brigos also pointed out in reviewing the manuscript that workers often vote in favour of such a draft bill even if they have misgivings regarding some clauses. Therefore, these statistics cannot be seen as raw figures.

documents together formed the basis of the final law that would be drafted after the session. The draft document also included an annex in which all the points raised and adopted in the December 24, 2008, joint commission of deputies were recorded in order to be included in the final law. In the ANPP plenary, both the Labour and Social Security minister and the CTC general secretary addressed the deputies, summarizing the experience and the basis of the new third and final version of the law. Following input by several deputies, the law was put to a vote and adopted unanimously.

Law 105 on Social Security was published in the *Gaceta Oficial de la República de Cuba* on January 22, 2009, less than one month after the ANPP session. An examination of the law indicates that the second draft bill and the draft report, resulting from the proposals for changes by the joint parliamentary commission, were included (*Gaceta Oficial de la República de Cuba* 2009).

Workers were directly involved in proposing changes to new drafts of the Social Security Bill. In the process of these workplace debates on the draft bill, workers were made aware of the stark demographic realities facing Cuban society as a collective.

The relative discontent surrounding the Social Security Bill co-exists with consensus. Together, they are in movement and in a dialectic relationship. There are no individual capitalists as a class or oligarchies that can profit from social security modifications, even relatively radical changes as contained in the bill under scrutiny. Therefore, as the Cuban economy improves — if it does — in the years that follow the adoption of the Social Security Bill, it will result in other changes. For example, salary increases are to be expected and thus pension boosts. If the economy develops, improvements can take place with regard to the availability and price of necessities, such as food, housing and transportation. Therefore, in the Cuban case, consensus can flourish side by side with discrepancies and lack of agreement. Indeed, the co-habitation of consensus and discrepancies is what contributes to a lively society — without falling into internecine conflicts and squabbling.

However, no matter how different — or how far worse, as some would argue — the situation is in capitalist countries such as the U.S., this precarious and dire situation does not serve to justify overlooking the problems existing in Cuba. The Cuban situation has to stand on its own, not in comparison with the U.S. approach. It has to have its own criteria based on the quality and quantity of the people's participation and the justness of the economic and social measures. It is not a consolation to Cuban workers that U.S. workers are never consulted in any legislation. Cuba's democracy in motion, based on its evolving socialist system, has to have its own values and measuring rod. The case study illustrates in another way the advantage of having a revolutionary Cuban state. The two massive, successive hurricanes at the end of August and the beginning of September 2008 interrupted the consultations with workers on the social security draft bill. The same revolutionary state that organized the 1994 Workers' Parliaments also led the successful evacuation before the hurricanes hit. The state did this in collaboration with the local municipal assemblies, mass organizations and the PCC. This prevented the loss of lives, and then the central state immediately led the effort to restore damaged and destroyed housing and schools. The state's effort transpired simultaneously with the reorganization of the social security draft bill consultation in 80,000 workplaces to ensure that, despite the situation, workers could carry out their role as legislators.

The media in the West, by ignoring the substantive consultative processes pointed out above, from the beginning of this chapter until now, would have us believe that the ANPP is merely a rubber stamp. For example, the Miami newspaper *Herald* (in English) and *El Nuevo Herald* (in Spanish) write that the ANPP meets "only twice a year, on each occasion for two or three days" (Tamayo 2012). The BBC, in its report on the ANPP session held on December 27, 2008, writes that in a "synthesis, the Parliament approved the new Social Security Law, which increased the retirement age to 65 years" (Ravsberg 2009). A U.S.-born dissident supporter living in Nicaragua and operating *Havana Times*, a self-described "open-minded" bilingual website, but open mainly to "left" dissidents, writes, "The 600-plus legislators meet for only two very brief sessions a year" (Robinson 2011). *Havana Times* dismisses the ANPP in another article by declaring, "Every six months, during the plenary session of the National Assembly, we have the opportunity to confirm whether democracy exists in Cuba. For me it is clear that it doesn't" (Calzadilla 2012a). *Havana Times* "socialist dissident" journalist Pedro Campos asserts that the ANPP acts as a "rubber stamp" where all laws are "executive orders" (Campos 2012b). Some others on the "left" write that the ANPP is "another rubber stamp for decisions taken at the top" (Van Auken 2010). Cubanologists — such as Marifeli Pérez-Stable, cited in Chapter 5 on the period from 1959 to 1962 — are sought out by major media such as the Associated Press to give credibility to their assertions that the ANPP "rubber stamps official party policy" (Associated Press 2008). *The New York Times* writes that it is "little more than a rubber stamp" (Lacey 2008). *Time Magazine* finds that "there's rarely anything newsworthy in the stultifying proceedings of Cuba's rubber-stamp National Assembly" (Padgett and Mascarenas 2008). To provide a pretext for not reporting on the Social Security Law and the full proceedings, the BBC writes, "The [Cuban] national and foreign press had dealt with this abundantly" (Ravsberg 2009). More recently (2012), the same BBC correspondent in Havana, completely ignoring the legislative activities described above, wrote that the ANPP adopts laws as a mere formality and complained that the members of the PCC "fill 90 percent of the parliamentary seats," even though, as outlined above, this is not the issue in the ANPP. To make sure that foreign readers get a negative image of the ANPP, and thus please the BBC editors, the BBC published a photo of a plenary session with the caption "Cuban deputies applauding during one of parliament's two annual meetings" (Ravsberg 2012). In the same vein, Haroldo Dilla Alfonso, one of the top "left" opponents to the Castro government, takes pleasure in constantly attempting to ridicule ANPP president Alarcón. Dilla Alfonso writes about "the colorless National Assembly, where he [Alarcón] can convene their brief sessions that meet twice a year" (Dilla Alfonso 2012a). The BBC and the "left" dissident Dilla Alfonso's writings, as well as others, are all translated into English by *Havana Times* and disseminated on the Internet in English and Spanish.

What all the above have in common regarding the Cuban political system are implicit U.S.-centric prejudices in favour of the supposed inherent superiority of competitive multi-party representative democracy, separation of powers and checks and balances. Thus any person seriously interested in exploring Cuba's democracy in motion cannot rely on these sources for even an approximation of the Cuban system. These detractors promote very similar prejudices against the Hugo Chávez-led Bolivarian Revolution and, to a somewhat lesser extent, the current Bolivian and Ecuadorian experiences.

Unanimity in the ANPP

In Cuba, as we have seen, many important and controversial issues, debates and discussions take place in public. This contrasts with the U.S., where debates take on a very partisan flavour as members of the two parties compete for electoral points. The case study on the Social Security Bill provides the opportunity to explore two issues: unanimity in the ANPP and the parliamentarization of society.

On the issue of unanimous votes in the ANPP, all the new laws we have dealt with, including the case study, were approved unanimously. The Cuban legislative process must be viewed from an angle different from that which other parliaments are perceived. In general, if the leadership feels that there is no consensus on a law, consultations take place and continue until an accord is reached, as was the case, for example, on the Agricultural Co-op Bill. In 1994, the Workers' Parliaments were held because it was obvious that the deputies were unable to reach a common conclusion on their own, without having direct input from the workers. On the Social Security Law, had the leadership not provided improvements in order to avoid a shock-therapy type of situation, the bill would not have reached the ANPP and been adopted.

Reaching a conclusion regarding unanimity and the parliamentarization of society, as seen in the Social Security Bill case study, is a complex issue. Several of the people interviewed in the consultation process pointed out the preoccupation workers have regarding salaries, as does researcher Alhama Belamaric. For example, CTC National Secretariat member and deputy Castanedo Smith said that salaries were brought up as a problem in work-centre assemblies, and asserted, "It is a preoccupation, and we take this into consideration" (Interview, Castanedo Smith 2008). While the vote was unanimous in the ANPP — and virtually unanimous (99 percent) at the grass-roots level — there remains an underlying current desirous of change.

Some revolutionaries in Cuba, and many academics outside the country who are sympathetic to Cuba, raise the question as to whether Raúl Castro's often-repeated remarks against "false unanimity" and "formalism," and in favour of fostering "discrepancies," are applicable to the ANPP. Only the deputies themselves and those who have elected them can answer this question. On the other hand, it would be counterproductive, if not ridiculous, to vote against a law just for the sake of opposing "false unanimity." The adoption of a bill reflects a general, temporary consensus until issues are raised again, and debated, with the goal of seeking further solutions to the ongoing improvement of Cuba's socialism. The ANPP carries out legislation in a multifaceted manner. At times, consultations are lengthy when they are required to reach a consensus. However, we have seen how the ANPP's Council of State and Council of Ministers act quickly to elaborate and adopt complicated decrees and decree-laws, responding to popular demands. While they may be popular — such as those for self-employment expansion, land in usufruct, housing purchases and renovations, and a new migration policy — their application is by no means unproblematic. Moreover, relative popular support does not signify that there is consensus on all aspects of these measures; there is room for improvement and enrichment in the ongoing process of Cuban democracy as an instrument of these socio-economic changes.

The striving for consensus in the Cuban political culture is tenacious. If a draft bill cannot reach this stage of agreement, it is simply not tabled on the agenda of the ANPP plenary session until there is a consensus. The new Family Code is an example of this. Since the mid-1990s, a new code has been debated to replace the outdated one. (At the time of writing, this has been going on for more than seven years.) The mass organization FMC is deeply involved in drafting the new code. It is evident that there is a difference of opinion on some themes, such as same-sex marriage. The latter would require a constitutional reform, seeing as the Constitution recognizes marriage only between a man and a woman. There are other similar issues. Throughout this ongoing legislative struggle on the new Family Code, the U.S. is investing "democracy promotion" funds to try to destabilize the situation.[4]

The ANPP and Cuba's Foreign Policy

So far, we have dealt only with the domestic role of the ANPP. According to the Constitution, the president of the ANPP has the responsibility to "organize the international relations" of that body (Constitution of the Republic of Cuba [1976] 2003). The ANPP has developed relations with parliaments

---

4. See www.democracyintheus.com, "Women Legislating vs. U.S. Democracy Promotion."

and parliamentarians around the world. This includes some members of the U.S. Congress who have visited Cuba on several occasions. International positions on a variety of subjects are more often than not adopted in the ANPP as resolutions or statements. One of the twelve permanent working commissions, International Relations, is dedicated to this.[5]

The Cuban ANPP and its Permanent Working Commission on International Relations are faced with an important issue. The Cuban Ministry of Foreign Affairs, as part of the Council of Ministers, is also involved. The entire Cuban population desires the normalization of relations between Cuba and the U.S. This is also the case for an increasing number of people in the U.S., including a growing segment of the Cuban-American population, even in Florida, and especially the younger generations. However, two principal issues have to be resolved. The first, the U.S. blockade against Cuba, is well known. The second is far less familiar to people in the U.S., since it is virtually censored by the media. It concerns the release of those men known internationally as the Cuban Five and imprisoned in the U.S.: Gerardo Hernández, Ramón Labañino, Antonio Guerrero, Fernando González and René González. They are five Cubans who were sent to Florida to do the work that the U.S. refused to do. This task consisted of stopping the terrorist activities being organized in that state against Cuba. The Cuban authorities had previously fully informed their U.S. counterparts of these activities, but they did not put a halt to them. When the five Cubans collected full proof of the terrorist plans, the information was provided to the FBI. However, in 1998, instead of arresting the Cuban-American terrorists, they arrested the five Cubans. They were subsequently condemned to lengthy prison terms after a prejudicial trial held in Miami. Four are still in prison, while a fifth is detained in the U.S. under probation.

Meanwhile, Alan Gross, a U.S. prisoner in Cuba, was tried and convicted for violating Cuban laws with the goal to subvert the constitutional order in Cuba. His case, of course, is publicized in the U.S., while the real reasons for his detention are distorted and generally censored. The U.S. government holds that Gross is innocent and demands his release. The release of the Cuban Five and their unconditional return to Cuba is a demand of the Cuban population. This demand is part of Cuba's soul. Thus the problem of the prisoners and the role of the ANPP and its Permanent Working Commission on International Relations is an ongoing test, as the latter strive toward normalizing relations between Cuba and its neighbour to the north.[6]

---

5. Its president, Ramón Pez Ferro, is one of the 1953 Moncada assailants (*asaltantes*) and has been deputy of the small municipal rural town of Rodas in the province of Cienfuegos since 1986. As I was about to have dinner with him and his wife at their apartment in 1998, it was natural to wonder what it would be like to share this moment with a Moncada *asaltante*. As it turned out, it was like talking to almost anyone else in Cuba, regardless of his or her history, age or position. The unassuming Pez Ferro was much like any other Cuban.

6. See www.democracyintheus.com, "U.S. Democracy, the Cuban Five and the ANPP."

Municipal-Level Participation: Limits and Perspectives

According to Article 102 of the Constitution, "The municipality is the local society having, to all legal effects, a legal personality." The municipal assemblies are responsible for all the economic, production and service entities in their territory, with the goal of meeting the economic, health care, assistance, social, cultural, educational, sports and recreation services in their territory (Constitution of the Republic of Cuba [1976] 2003). Municipal assemblies take place according to its rules as many times as are deemed necessary, but a minimum of four times a year (Reglamento: Asambleas Municipales del Poder Popular 1998: 11).

In an effort to clarify how municipalities function, the author attended two sessions of the Plaza de la Revolución Municipal Assembly in January and December 2008. The following example is based on observations made during one of these two sessions. The regular municipal assembly session of its 108 delegates, who represented the same number of decentralized, compressed *circunscripciones,* took place in December 2008. Among other points on the agenda, it dealt with an entity under its jurisdiction, the famous Coppelia ice cream parlour (a popular Havana landmark). It serves 15,000 people per day on average. It is one of Havana's favourite social and family venues. Any non-Cuban who has visited Havana probably knows it.

All delegates were issued a document containing the detailed evaluation by the Municipal Permanent Working Commission on Basic Services with regard to Coppelia. This December 2008 report was drafted after interviews were carried out from 2007 to 2008 with the Coppelia administration and workers, as well as with the population in the municipality and the delegates. The report indicated that its work was a follow-up on complaints received by the assembly delegates from the electors. These grievances included the insufficient quantity, variety and quality of ice cream available. The survey also unearthed complaints regarding the quality of service offered to the public. Poor cleanliness and hygiene standards, as well as illegality (the illicit sale of ice cream in the vicinity with apparent impunity), were also discovered. According to the report, one weakness in Coppelia had been the constant turnover in administrative staff and its main directors, which led to instability. Other problems, pointed out by the press, such as the illegal sale of ice cream, persisted. The working commission reported that, in trying to solve the issue, it was collaborating with the Ministry of Food Industry, which was responsible for Coppelia.[7]

In the assembly, the first to speak was the president of the permanent working commission, who read and elaborated on the report and their work. A spirited debate took place. The delegate from Circunscripción No. 60 said

---

7. Document from the Municipal Assembly: "Valoración de la Comisión permanente de servicios básicos sobre la fiscalización y el control a la Heladería 'Coppelia.'"

that the report was closer to what was desirable than to the reality. He warned, "We cannot yet tell our electors that there has been a qualitative or quantitative change in Coppelia." Several other delegates spoke in the same vein.

These problems in Coppelia (also existing in other municipalities regarding other socio-economic bodies) were not settled at that time. They had still not been resolved by the end of 2012, even though the delegates are striving to keep on top of the situation. Can problems such as those exhibited by the Coppelia example be resolved? The solutions depend on the capacity of the people to enhance their control not only through their elected delegates, but also by their direct involvement in these entities. It raises important issues regarding representation and participation, which have been the subject of discussion and analysis throughout this book.

This Coppelia study leads to several conclusions based on applying the analyses presented in Chapter 6 by some Cuban social scientists and political leaders who foresee the need for permanent forms of citizens' participation. Thus "representatives" in the U.S.-centric sense cannot be accepted in a revolutionary state. Participatory democracy should dominate over the concept that the elected "represent" the electors, who maintain a relatively passive role. Sovereignty vested in the people takes on real and effective meaning only when direct participation of the people, along with the elected delegates, intervenes in entities such as Coppelia. The mutation of representation into participation is a key feature of participatory democracy. If this does not take place, the Coppelias in Cuba can carry on with impunity for those who profit from this situation.

The relationship between electors and municipal delegates is demonstrated in the accountability meetings (*rendición de cuentas*), literally "rendering of accounts," or accountability sessions. These take place, according to the municipal regulations, at least twice a year (Reglamento: Asambleas Municipales del Poder Popular 1998: 21). For this purpose, each *circunscripción* is normally divided into small areas about the size of the nomination meeting area demarcations in order to facilitate an intimate atmosphere and discussion. The goal is for a delegate to render an account to the electors of his or her work, as well as that of the municipal government. The electors have the right to raise issues or make complaints. In addition, the goal is for the delegate and the citizens to exchange with each other in order to find avenues to govern collectively. This includes questions of national interest.[8]

These sessions are increasingly being criticized from all sides, pointing to the need for major improvements. For example, in 2012, one of Alarcón's ad-

---

8. On this latter subject, my more extensive experience in the 1997–98 *rendición de cuentas* meetings indicates that often the participants are not interested in discussing issues of national significance. However, on occasions, even the delegates are not aware that these topics should be on the agenda. I attended several of these accountability sessions, from 2008 to 2009, all in municipality of Plaza de la Revolución.

visers, Jorge Lezcano, made an important comment following a report based on the work of municipalities across the island. He said that the delegates' accountability reports are dominated by technical language and formulas that no one understands (Rodríguez Gavilán 2012). The PCC *Granma* daily provides another example. It reported on all the attempts by local railway administrators in Villa Clara province to put a stop to individuals littering the railway tracks in the Santa Clara central train station (which was an eyesore and presented a danger to the public). One attempt entailed the participation in the municipal accountability sessions. However, "nothing came of" these efforts (Pérez Cabrera 2011). Another *Granma* journalist wrote in favour of putting an end to the boring and mechanical accountability sessions. Félix López expressed that they should be replaced by sessions in which the neighbours could really intervene in decisions relating to all the entities in their territory (López 2011). *Juventud Rebelde* commentator Luis Sexto wondered what had become of many accountability sessions that once took place in an "eminently democratic and socialist" environment. He claimed that many, but not all, were lacking an atmosphere of exchange and debate that had been replaced by "cold rhetoric" (Sexto 2009).

In an accountability meeting held on December 16, 2008, in a Plaza de la Revolución *circunscripción*, the proceedings illustrated a problem with regard to how people view the delegate and the elected/elector relationship.[9] The local delegate in that *circunscripción*, Xiomara Leiva Romero, holds many small, separate accountability meetings to encourage discussion and create a more intimate atmosphere (Interview, Leiva Romero 2008).

In the accountability session, a fierce argument broke out over excessive noise during the night near the apartment block where the neighbours held their session. The existence of a nearby grocery store that sells rum at all hours — even though this is not permitted — encourages heavy drinking to take place during the night in a small park near the liquor outlet. The result is a loud cacophony of voices and music. The neighbours were furious that this had been going on for some time, despite their previous complaints. It was impossible to have a good night's sleep under these conditions. They explained that many of them worked in the morning and their children had to get up early as well to go to school. All the anger was directed against the delegate, Leiva Romero, even though she had brought to the meeting the area's Director of Commerce and Food, who was responsible for this liquor outlet. He tried to convince the people that he would take action. However, many neighbours did not have faith. One, in fact, said that she would no longer come to any more accountability meetings if the delegate could not solve this problem. It was obvious in the accountability session that most neighbours wrongly believed that their delegate was meant to be at their

---

9. This was one of several accountability sessions that I attended.

service. This perception is opposed to the concept whereby the delegate and the people, who are sovereign, govern together. It underscores a problem in Cuba's political system, which will be dealt with in the next section.[10]

Cuban Democracy: Representative or Participatory?

This issue of "representative or participatory democracy," as if to respond to the contradiction that surfaced in the neighbourhood *rendición de cuentas* meeting discussed in the previous section, arose in another very important debate. "Representative democracy" in the Cuban context is not the same as what exists in the U.S. In Cuba, at the municipal level, people are elected, in theory, as representatives within a revolutionary state.

To take a different context, in Venezuela, Hugo Chávez is the most repeatedly elected representative in South America. However, he and other elected activists at all levels of the Bolivarian Revolution are not "representatives" in the U.S. meaning of the word, as elaborated in the Chapter 3 analysis of the October 2012 presidential elections. In contrast to the U.S. path, but similar to the Venezuelan approach, the Cuban Council of State leaders — all elected representatives — are primarily revolutionary leaders. This concept was exemplified earlier in this chapter through an examination of the life and work of ANPP deputies and their role in involving the grass roots in drafting legislation. Representative democracy and participatory democracy cannot be juxtaposed as though one (representative) were based on the liberal model and the other (participatory) belonged to another paradigm. The revolutionary concept of "representative," as it is developing in some countries of Latin America and the Caribbean, is not the same as the experience in the North. In the South, based on examples such as those in Chapter 3 (Venezuela, Bolivia and Ecuador) and in these chapters on Cuba, representation is part of a revolutionary movement whose goal is to combine representation and sovereignty vested in the people. Therefore, these systems are not hybrids, that is, part liberal and part revolutionary, at least not in theory. Is the new combination of representation and participation always fully attained? No, but these democracies in motion are striving to head in this direction. To what extent this is actually the case in Cuba is another issue. We have seen with the above example of the *rendición de cuentas,* and others raised by Cuban journalists, that the liberal manner of viewing representation exists in Cuba.

As part of this ongoing quest to advance the mutation of representation into revolutionary political power of the people, this issue of "representative or participatory democracy" arose in a January 2008 Plaza de la Revolución

---

10. Cuban citizens have at their disposal the right to revocation. Elected representatives at any level can be revoked at any time. However, I do not deal with revocation in the book, because space does not allow here to describe it fully. In addition, given the current situation in Cuba, there are other themes that take on greater importance.

Municipal Assembly.[11] The issue of electors and elected has been addressed since the time of Rousseau and is still on the agenda today in the twenty-first century. In some Indigenous nations, the issue of the relationship of leaders to others has been raised, albeit in other forms, over many centuries. In these Indigenous nations, there exists the ancient vision of people living in harmony with Mother Earth. In Bolivia, everyone is equally bound to this Mother Earth concept — the leaders and the grass roots, out of which Evo Morales himself emerged. By discarding the Eurocentric and U.S.-centric notions of elected and electors, the manner in which political cultures of the South deal with this differently can be explored with fresh insight and with a different vocabulary. In this context of rejecting a homogeneous vocabulary from the North, one should keep in mind, as quoted in Chapter 3, Noam Chomsky's warning to "sophisticated Westerners" to refrain from ridiculing the demand of Evo Morales for Mother Earth (Chomsky 2012b).

The January 2008 municipal assembly deliberation centred on a report originally issued by ANPP president Alarcón. The Alarcón report addressed provincial and municipal assemblies. The ANPP, as reflected in his paper, expressed its preoccupation with several aspects. The first was the need for flexibility in liberating the delegate from the normal workday in a fair and dignified manner. He or she carries out the function of an elected person on a voluntary basis after work hours to ensure grass-roots links. A policy of adjustability by the workplaces is necessary to allow these individuals to carry out their responsibilities as delegates. The second, related to the first, is to make sure that delegates do not get bogged down in superfluous meetings and in tasks not related to their responsibilities, such as administration. The assignment of the delegate is not to administer, but rather to control and monitor. The goal is to ensure that economic and other entities in the territory are fulfilling their tasks in the service of the people. Alarcón sees this in conjunction with the local people's power, as part of the further promotion of people's participation (Alarcón de Quesada 2006).

Two issues were dealt with in the report by the Municipal Permanent Working Commission on Local People's Power presented to the January 2008 session of the municipal assembly. Participating in this assembly along with the delegates were ANPP president Ricardo Alarcón and deputy José Luis Toledo Santander. Both Alarcón and Toledo Santander had been elected to the ANPP from the municipality of Plaza de la Revolución. Also present was Tomás Cárdenas as president of the ANPP's national Permanent Working Commission on Local Organs of People's Power. The head of the Municipal Local Organs Permanent Working Commission was frank in the reading of her report. She pointed to weaknesses, such as the relatively low attendance rate of delegates and representatives. She said that the Commission was

---

11. This was the second of the municipal assemblies that I attended.

preoccupied with the capacity of the delegates to get assistance in carrying out its work outside their working hours.

This was followed by a candid debate in which many delegates intervened. One of them raised the need to provide the delegates with sufficient time off from work in order to exercise the role of delegate.[12] He also developed the concept that a delegate governs not as an individual, but rather as part of a collective in the respective municipal assembly. Others spoke about the need to clarify concepts, such as "What is a delegate?" Thus what does representation mean as opposed to direct participation by electors? This question was confronted in the assembly.

When all delegates who wanted to have their say had deliberated, Alarcón was asked to speak. He praised the report by the Municipal Local Organs Commission president, and highlighted the fact that it did not exhibit any signs of complacency and had a good critical focus. This is the type of style, he contended, that they wanted to cultivate. Alarcón was modest, saying that his *indicaciones* (talking points) had to be modified to take into account what had been said in the assembly, thus adopting a self-critical attitude. He highlighted what a delegate had remarked about the fact that the more people are consulted and participate in working out solutions, the better the opinions and results will be.

Alarcón went on to relate that the only delegate in Cuba whose authority derives directly from the people is the elected delegate or deputy. This is the sense that José Martí gave to the term "delegate." Alarcón also maintained that it is necessary to provide more importance to the role and the function of the delegate. He stated, "In a democratic society, real sovereignty, the last word, is vested in the people. However, since the people cannot be continuously exercising their sovereignty, they must delegate their sovereignty to someone." This is the source of the delegate's condition and status. Alarcón continued by asserting that there was insufficient consciousness in society about this concept of sovereignty. It was intended to mean that sovereignty is vested in the people while only being *delegated* to those elected. For some purists, looking at this assertion dogmatically, it may appear that "delegation of sovereignty" is a contradiction in terms since sovereignty is vested in the people. However, the concept depends on the context. Is the delegation of sovereignty in this way done consciously by the sovereign delegator? Is the delegated or entrusted person taking this responsibility on for personal reasons or to be as part of the people in which sovereignty is vested? For example,

---

12. In a 2004 contributing chapter on Cuba, I wrote, "As the Cuban economy continues [on] its present path, the door for some individuals to acquire more economic clout and standing than others remains open. The political system must rise to the occasion, ensuring that the electoral process will allow elected officials to effectively prevail over the growing technocratic cadres and any other serious obstacles, while defending the people's best interests" (August 2004: 241). The present book represents a continuation of this preoccupation, shared by Cuban academics and political leaders at all levels.

as mentioned above, Martí was the Cuban historical personality who first employed the term "delegate" for Cuba. With this concept, he differentiated between the Cuban notion of representation and other terms circulating at the time. He was killed in action as the "delegate" defending the cause for which he had been delegated. This is an indication that the Cuban tradition of a representative, as being a revolutionary, fully and selflessly participating as part of the people, is different from the North's vision. In the latter case, representative democracy is mainly linked to selfish, individualistic interests over and above all other considerations. There is no space for the concept of vesting sovereignty in the hands of the people while sharing it with the delegate or representative. The Cuban heritage is different.

This issue was not settled on that day in the Plaza de la Revolución municipal assembly, nor has it been since then. In this sense, Alarcón summarized by conceding that there was a need to improve the system and the concept. Improving Cuban democracy is an ongoing process. Since 1959, Cuba has been democratizing its society based on socialist principles that allow for a political system founded on participation. Therefore, people's sovereignty and their direct participation must be the determining factors, and not the representative aspect, especially the liberal notion. To the extent that the representative feature of any kind predominates over direct participation by the people who are sovereign, the alienation and frustration of the people increase.

The debate on the relationship between elected and electors, or on representative versus participatory democracy, does not take place only in the municipal assemblies; it also surfaces among the people. This was reflected in some of the Cuban press in 2010–11. For example, outspoken *Juventud Rebelde* correspondent Luis Sexto holds that Cuba must go beyond "'government of the people, for the people and by the people'" because democracy means that "the people control and supervise governance" (Sexto 2010c). He further argues in favour of the need for a proper balance between horizontal and vertical views on democracy (Sexto 2010b). In other words, participation must be the dominant factor, while the vertical factor, including representative institutions, must take an important, but secondary, role. In another article, Sexto spells out his views by choosing the terms "participation" and its verb form "to participate" in order to dissect the concept of the people's role in the political system. The real meaning of "participation," he maintains, is to "take part [be fully involved]." Participation cannot be viewed superficially; "when we participate, we are truly part [of the solution]." Sexto contends that to participate is "to become a [proactive] factor, [a person who is] convinced and ethically committed…. The ethic of participation … has to be … the point of departure for improvement" of the political and economic system (Sexto 2010d). A second journalist from the same daily, Ricardo Ronquillo Bello, writes, "One of the challenges of the Revolution is to go further than a certain enshrined practice of 'governing for the people,' and rather beginning to do so *with* the people" (Ronquillo Bello 2011, emphasis added). Cuba has experimented widely in order to deepen the participation at the grass roots.

People's Councils:
Potential for Further Democratization

One of these important experiments can be found in the people's councils. Regarding Cuba's democracy in motion and its continual striving for democratization, an important, relatively new structure was established. The *consejos populares* (CPs — people's councils) are constituted within the municipalities. Their creation is perhaps one of the most significant steps taken since the establishment in 1976 of the OPP. Seeking ways to increase the participation of the people in the political process, the Third Congress of the PCC proposed the establishment of the CPs in 1986. These were then set up in some neighbourhoods as a pilot project. In 1991, the ANPP passed a resolution to ensure a CP presence throughout the country. In 1992, when the Constitution went through important political and economic reforms, its amendments comprised the inclusion of the CPs, which gained a prominent constitutional position (García Brigos 1998: 58–70).

The CPs are *not* another level of state. There are only three tiers: national, provincial and municipal. According to Article 104 of the Constitution, the CPs are composed of delegates elected to the municipality, who represent it in its decentralized territory (Constitution of the Republic of Cuba [1976] 2003). The CPs have their own law adopted in July 2000. Therefore, the CPs enjoy important constitutional authority, as well as their own legislation within the municipal assemblies' functions, as part of the OPP. The law indicates that they are not an intermediary within the political-administrative division of the country. However, their role is to enhance socialist democracy by increasing the active participation of the people and assistance provided to the municipal assemblies (*Ley No. 91 de los Consejos Populares* 2000).

Each municipal assembly constitutes itself into a number of small CPs. The number of CPs per municipality is determined by population density and socio-geographic characteristics. The case study is Consejo Popular No. 8 (Vedado) (CP Vedado) of the municipality of Plaza de la Revolución. This municipality contains 108 *circunscripciones*. Each of the 108 elected delegates to each *circunscripción* represents about 1,400 to 1,500 voters. The total number of electors for the municipality is approximately 125,000. Plaza de la Revolución comprises eight CPs, including CP Vedado, which is named after the part of the neighbourhood in which it is located, as are the seven other CPs in the municipality. The total number of electors in this CP is approximately 21,000. CP Vedado is composed of seventeen delegates from the total

108 delegates to Plaza de la Revolución. CP Vedado has fourteen non-elected representatives from mass organizations and economic and cultural entities in its area. Elected delegates must form the majority of all CP members.

In order to explore the CPs, the author attended two sessions of CP Vedado (in February 2008 and January 2009) and carried out several interviews with its president, Eduardo González Hernández. The latter explained that his CP is composed of seventeen delegates elected to the Plaza de la Revolución Municipal Assembly. The president, vice-president and secretary of CP Vedado are chosen by the seventeen delegates. The CP president's work is normally carried out as a full-time responsibility, the elected person being excused from his or her job while earning the same salary. The CP, under the law, has the right to include designated representatives of mass organizations and important economic, social, cultural, health service and other entities located in the CP territory. The purpose is to facilitate and enhance people's participation in governing. These representatives are *not* among those elected to the municipal assembly. The representatives of two mass organizations, the FMC and the CDR, along with those of the most important economic and social entities in the area, are present in CP Vedado. For example, among those represented are the local telecommunications enterprise and the Casa de la Amistad (Friendship House) of the Instituto Cubano de Amistad con los Pueblos (ICAP — Cuban Institute of Friendship with the Peoples). CP Vedado, with its seventeen elected delegates and fourteen non-elected representatives, is thus composed of 31 members (Interview, González Hernández 2009).

In the February 1, 2008, monthly meeting of CP Vedado,[13] several issues were on the agenda. The first one came from a report by the head of the Commercial Division who was attending the meeting. The testimony concerned the deteriorating condition of the building containing a small local grocery store (*bodega*), which presented a danger to passersby. This may seem, from the view of the North, a banal or trivial discussion topic. However, while all Cubans may have access to the basic necessities such as food (unlike millions of people in other developing nations and, increasingly, in some rich capitalist ones), every meal at home is a major effort, compared with the consumer societies of the North.[14] One of the solutions to relieving this problem in Cuba is easy access to the *bodega*. The head of the Commercial Division reported that, as complaints had been made, they were working toward a renovation. The president of CP Vedado announced that he and other delegates, as part of their regular CP work, would visit the *bodega* along with the head of the Commercial Division in an effort to deal with this issue.

In an interview held with González Hernández one year later, he said that a temporary solution had immediately been found for relocating the *bodega*. He

---

13. This was the first of two that I attended.
14. I am able to attest to this first-hand, having experienced this while living with a Cuban family in the course of carrying out my fieldwork.

added that the renovations had been started and thus the *bodega* mentioned in the assembly was repaired (Interview, González Hernández 2009).

In a CP Vedado monthly meeting held in January 2009,[15] another example came to the fore that illustrated the need for collective participation by the people in order to resolve a major ongoing problem. It has been proven in a full scientific account that the U.S. had introduced hemorrhagic dengue in Cuba (Pérez Alonso 2008: 68–112). While it has basically been controlled by meticulous prevention and treatment, it remains a potential problem if not monitored regularly. Other factors, such as heat and heavy rains — as was the case in 2012 — act as incubators for dengue carriers that are not directly related to the U.S. introduction of this deadly disease. In other countries in the South, there are hundreds of thousands of deaths every year (Fitz 2012).

The doctor who is subdirector of the Department of Hygiene and Epidemiology of the polyclinic located in CP Vedado's territory is responsible for heading the continual fumigation program of the area. In this capacity, she participates in at least two of the monthly CP sessions per year.

The doctor announced that they were reorganizing the prevention program to create continuity that would make it possible to assign the same brigade leaders to specific areas, thus allowing the population to get to know the leaders for their neighbourhood. This change and other measures, she explained, were geared to facilitating the participation of the citizens. The full involvement of the people is important because, in order to fumigate inside a house, for example, it is necessary for the inhabitants of the household to be present. If they are unable to be home at the time, they must organize with their neighbours to allow the fumigation team to enter the household. The CDR and other mass organizations play an important role in this collective endeavour. The CP is thus an active participant in these efforts, which, if not managed properly, can result in suffering and death.

While being interviewed about the work of CP Vedado, González Hernández was proud to discuss his CP's plan of action for 2008. It amounted to a full-time program for himself, the vice-president and secretary involving all the daily needs of the people. With regard to the ongoing fight against dengue, he said that he took it very seriously and thus had become a self-taught, knowledgeable person in the field (Interviews, González Hernández 2008, 2009).

Had it not been for CP Vedado, González Hernández would have simply remained one of the 108 delegates in the Municipal Assembly. His peers have elected him president of the CP for three mandates. He proudly but humbly presides over the CP, along with the vice-president and secretary and the seventeen delegates as part of his team. He is professional in the sense that he can work full-time at his post because he is retired. However, even if this

---

15. This was the second of two that I attended.

were not the case, he would be working full-time with the same salary as he received from his former employment. He also demonstrates a professional attitude toward his role as municipal delegate; he knows what it entails in relation to vesting sovereignty in the hands of the people. He takes the lead and sees himself as being part of the people, not a representative of the people he replaces.

All of these sources of input and efforts to find solutions, as illustrated by the work of CP Vedado and its officials, comprise significant substantiation for one of the book's focuses. The potential for further democratization of Cuban society at the grass roots lies in the CPs. The relatively larger municipal assembly, with its 108 delegates and the entire municipality under its authority, could not have done what is being accomplished by the CPs. The larger municipal assembly meets four or five times a year. However, CP Vedado meets regularly, every month on a fixed day. Its president, vice-president and secretary appear to be in constant contact with each other. In addition, the CP's officials have easy access to the elected delegates as well as the non-elected members and representatives, who together total 31 — still a very compact grass-roots-level dynamic.

We have briefly examined the work of the municipal assembly and the people's council in 2008–09. The goal is to provide readers with a general idea of how they function and what their responsibilities are between elections. However, today's Cuba is quite different, further highlighting the potential importance of the municipal assemblies and people's councils.

The Potential of the Local Level and Need for Enhanced Participation

The local level of people's power in 2013 can no longer be viewed in comparison to the post-1959 epoch or even be measured in relation to the 2010–11 period. The basic socio-economic landscape of Cuba is undergoing radical transformations. The new economic policies, as translated into ANPP legislation, are beginning to alter the nature of Cuban political needs. The economy is largely being decentralized, meaning more responsibilities devolved toward the municipalities. This has direct effects on municipal assemblies and, within these, the people's councils.

In the July 2012 session of the ANPP, the vice-president of the Council of Ministers, Marino Murillo Jorge, who heads the special commission for overseeing the economic and related political changes, spoke for over two hours. It was a well-structured, yet spontaneous, speech. The demeanour of this relatively new leader (born in 1961) itself represents part of the metamorphosis going on in Cuba. According to *Granma* journalists, he is reported to have announced in relation to self-employment: "By the end of June 2012, the sector had grown to include 390,598 people: 233,227 more than in September 2010, a month before regulations expanding this employment alternative went into effect." In addition, he stated, "The sector is set to grow, with prohibitions being relaxed and obsolete regulations ... eliminated." The creation of cooperatives as "the preferred non-state economic structure" was further encouraged, for the first time, in non-agricultural activities. This new urban co-op movement will even have the right to rent state-owned facilities (e.g., restaurants in Old Havana). Approximately 200 such urban cooperatives concerned with service activities (e.g., restaurants, agricultural products and transportation) and the production of goods are being favoured. More than half of these non-rural co-ops deal with agricultural marketing. Although it is billed as an experiment, if it proves to be positive, this urban co-op movement will spread across the island. As an indication of the importance attached to these types of co-ops, the government is injecting $100 million into its 2013 economic plan to encourage the movement (Fonticoba Gener, de la Osa and Leyva 2012).

However, the move to self-employment is not fulfilling one of its main goals. In Chapter 6, we saw how new 2010 legislation was designed to reduce overstaffing while vastly opening up new self-employment opportunities. Despite this, as of the first half of 2012, only 31 percent of the new self-employed come from former state employees.[16] Valdés Mesa, general secretary of the CTC, conceded in 2012 that the problem of reducing bloated payrolls is "'the most complicated'" of the economic tasks (González 2012).

With regard to leasing rent-free fallow land in usufruct, Decree-Law No. 259 was modified in 2012 to expand the area of land granted. As well, the new legislation allows the "right of family members, or those working on the land, to continue to do so in the event of the landholder's death." The right to build houses on the land is also new. A new policy allowing farmers to directly market agricultural products to the public is being done on a trial basis in several provinces. This pilot project is to be expanded to the entire country if the results are positive (Fonticoba Gener, de la Osa and Leyva 2012). These different forms of agriculture and marketing take place within the local municipalities and are being expanded in 2012–13.

Bank credit to individuals has been increased through Decree-Law No. 289, 90 percent of which provides resources for the completion of construction projects. However, Murillo criticized "the initial slow response from the [municipalities] on granting subsidies to persons lacking economic resources and in urgent need of home repairs" (Fonticoba Gener, de la Osa and Leyva 2012). (Thus the municipalities are inheriting responsibilities as well as bureaucratic obstacles.)

Murillo announced that the new 2012 tax law discussed and approved in the July 2012 ANPP session is "more modern and flexible, [and] will allow

16. Rafael Alhama Belamaric, researcher at the Ministry of Labour and Social Security, email message to author, August 18, 2012.

[the country] to advance in updating the model" (Fonticoba Gener, de la Osa and Leyva 2012). The importance of the municipal assemblies' role in the new situation concerning collecting taxes is amplified by the fact that, according to a report by the Ministry of Finances and Prices, the self-employed sector made a "notable increase" in income to the 2011 state budget from taxes and sales of basic products. This trend was expected to continue in 2012 (Rodríguez Cruz 2012). Government ministry officials explained the new tax law (Bill No. 113) in the first of four November/December 2012 special prime-time TV *Mesa Redonda* programs. It would come into effect in January 2013. It is a key instrument in further developing self-employment in urban and rural areas by applying taxes in a suppler manner to additionally stimulate this non-state sector. The new legislation is also a crucial source of tax funds for local municipal development programs. This, in turn, is geared to stimulating local self-government and economic development in the municipalities. In addition, the taxes from the self-employed and other entities located in the municipalities are collected for central state requirements to fulfill social/educational programs. Those who work are to be remunerated for their efforts (*Mesa Redonda*, November 28, 2012, notes taken by author). However, the panelists pointed out that the new tax system is geared to "opposing the concentration of property" and even "reducing social inequality," as stipulated by Guidelines 3 and 57 adopted at the 2011 Party Congress (VI Congreso del Partido Comunista de Cuba 2011a). Cuba is thus counting on the 2013 tax disposition and a new tax-related culture (formerly virtually non-existent in Cuba) in order to redistribute income as the economy develops. The new tax system, two years in the making and involving two ANPP permanent working commissions, is flexible and to be applied gradually (*Mesa Redonda*, November 28, 2012, notes taken by author). This means that the municipalities and, within them, the people's councils have increased responsibilities to ensure that the tax law and other related measures adopted in the coming years are applied in their respective territorial demarcations. Therefore, more than ever, the municipal assemblies are being severely tested.

In the July 2012 ANPP session, further decentralization was announced to the ANPP's Permanent Working Commission on Local Organs of People's Power (OLPP — Órganos Locales del Poder Popular). This is taking the form of 117 local development projects under the responsibility of 51 municipalities (there are 168 municipalities in Cuba). To this end, there is funding from the central government to foster a program that includes food production and improvement of construction materials and services to the population. The goal is for these programs to eventually become self-sufficient (*Cubadebate* 2012).

Deputy Cárdenas García, the president of the ANPP Permanent Working Commission on Local Organs, divulged in an interview that 31 of the 37 members of this commission (in 2008) over which he presides are *de base* deputies from the municipal assemblies (Interview, Cárdenas García 2008a). This provides an opportunity for the national and municipal levels to coordinate with each other in order to face the challenges in this complex situation of decentralization and further responsibilities in the application of the new tax system as part of the overall economic changes.

This decentralization is not antagonistic to the state maintaining the control of the main means of production. Murillo asserts that the "socialist state enterprise is the principal structure in Cuba's economy." He is reported to have "emphasized that the successful updating of the country's economic model is facing the none-too-easy task of making this form of management more efficient" (Fonticoba Gener, de la Osa and Leyva 2012). In the same vein, Raúl Castro, in his speech to the ANPP, said,

> Experiments with non-agricultural cooperatives … will allow the state to withdraw from the administration of a number of productive and service activities of a secondary nature, in order to concentrate on perfecting the management of the fundamental means of production, maintained as socialist state enterprises, which, as is expressed in Guideline Number 2, are the principal elements of the national economy. (Castro Ruz [Raúl] 2012b)

Thus, in addition to clearly indicating that Cuba is continuing on the socialist path, these confirmations by Murillo and Raúl Castro also increase the scope of the municipalities. They have the burden of assuring success at the local level in order to liberate the state sector to fulfill its role, which was previously hampered by the old, highly centralized state model. However, this decentralization is not the equivalent of privatization in the capitalist economies. For example, those new expanding sectors of the economy, such as self-employment, individual agricultural plots and co-ops at the local level, are part of the overall socialist goals. The new non-state sectors are linked to the centre through the new 2013 tax system that strives to maintain as much equality as possible through the involvement of the self-employed in unions and the overall Cuban ethic of socialist solidarity. Those both on the island and abroad who view the changes in Cuba through the U.S-centric neo-liberal optic are likely to be disappointed.

During the course of the 2012 municipal elections, Alarcón emphasized that the 2011–12 PCC Congress and Conference decisions focused on, among other points, decentralization and a larger role for the municipalities. He said that, therefore, the "municipal assemblies will have a greater responsibility than the previous ones" (*Mesa Redonda*, August 30, 2012, notes taken by author).

While a great deal of attention in the foreign media is focused on the economic changes, the new political restructuring directly related to the local state levels is neglected. The province of Havana was recently divided into two new provinces with specific goals in mind. The new provinces of Artemisa and Mayabeque came into being on January 1, 2011. The goal was to do so "without repeating the errors that have accompanied the work of the local bodies of People's Power" (Castro Ruz [Raúl] 2010b). One objective is the downsizing of bloated administration. Another is to establish "a clear delimitation of ... [powers] in interrelations with agencies of central state administration, national enterprises and political and mass organizations" (Castro Ruz [Raúl] 2010b). Presently, the president of the municipal assembly is also president of the administrative council of the assembly, creating a possible conflict of interest. The legislative change came about following a resolution adopted in the PCC April 2011 Congress to improve the political and electoral system and then proposed to the ANPP (Asamblea Nacional del Poder Popular 2011). These pilot projects have as "a goal to perfect leadership systems and bodies" (Fonticoba Gener, de la Osa and, Leyva 2012). Based on the results of the pilot projects, the experience can be extended to the whole island. Even though very little is known about the project, it definitely concentrates on striving to make the provincial and municipal assemblies more effective in the new conditions.

With regard to how the unprecedented transformation affects the local levels, especially the municipal assemblies and, within that, the people's councils, we recall that, according to the Constitution, "The municipality is the local society having, to all legal effects, a juridical personality." The municipal assemblies are responsible for all the economic, production and service entities in the territory, with the goal of meeting the needs of economic, health care and other such assistance, as well as the social, cultural, educational, sports and recreation services in their territory (Constitution of the Republic of Cuba [1976] 2003). Therefore, in general terms, the recent economic changes affect self-employment, usufruct farming, co-ops in both the urban and rural areas, new taxes with their related importance for the future of socialist development, housing renovation and bank credits for this and other needs, new local municipal-related development projects and downsizing of bloated payrolls. Many of these entities, transactions and adjustments (depending on the logistics and circumstances of each case) fall within the domain of the municipal assemblies and the people's councils.

In an example above, Murillo criticized the municipalities' initial slow response on granting housing renovation subsidies (Fonticoba Gener, de la Osa and Leyva 2012). Weaknesses in the control by municipalities have been divulged in the case study of the Coppelia ice cream parlour. The Coppelia case is notorious in Havana; everybody knows about it. Nevertheless, no political level or social organization is as yet able to overcome the obstacles embedded in that entity and resolve anything. It is symptomatic of a problem. (However, not all local entities are like Coppelia. For example, the author has visited several other local enterprises, in the tobacco and auto repair industries, whose standards are up to those expected in a socialist society.) The issue of improving municipal assembly domination over the entities under its jurisdiction can be traced back to a previous period. University of Havana professors and jurists Lissette Pérez Hernández and Martha Prieto Valdés made a suggestion in a 2000 book chapter appropriately entitled "Exercising Government: A Potential Capacity of the Municipal Assemblies of People's Power." They asserted that the municipalities cannot really govern if they do not fully have the "capacity of control over the entities" in their territory (Pérez Hernández and Prieto Valdés 2000a: 206). In order to enhance this potential, they proposed that a bill be worked out by the ANPP that would be dedicated to the municipal assemblies' role and rights. (Presently, there is no law for municipal assemblies, even though there are rules and other legal guidelines.) A new law would, according to these jurists, require a constitutional reform because the current Constitution does not go far enough in explicitly imposing municipal control (Pérez Hernández and Prieto Valdés 2000a: 206). It is possible that the political changes, as outlined above, that are occurring with the pilot projects in two provinces allow for this new legislation and constitutional reform. To take but one example of the increasing responsibilities for the municipalities — taxes — Pérez Hernández and Prieto Valdés were imploring in 2000 for the municipal assemblies and the people's councils to be "more aggressive in collecting taxes" (Pérez Hernández and Prieto Valdés 2000a: 207). The application of the new economic activities also invites further corruption and bureaucratic stalling tactics by those who are entrenched in their enclaves.

Based on another study on the local organs, this one in Havana, the same authors point to the successes of some people's councils in the "struggle against crimes and violations of the law." They rate the people's councils highly, compared with the municipal assemblies, which meet only several times a year. Therefore, the municipal assemblies are "lacking regularity in their work" in contrast with the more decentralized and mobile people's councils (Pérez Hernández and Prieto Valdés 2000b: 201). The authors are concerned about the "real authority of the municipality" and ask whether there is a "real correspondence between the legal basis and the [actual] exercise of municipal authority" (Pérez Hernández and Prieto Valdés 2000b: 200). If this was the concern in the year 2000, how would it translate now? It is presently far more serious. The evolving situation indicates that the challenge facing the municipal level cannot simply be reduced to "control." The entire concept of governing with people's participation and enhancing the delegate's role as part of the municipal assembly is at stake.

More recently, in August 2012, Alarcón himself asserted that in the new current conditions of updating the Cuban economic model, the battle against errors, bureaucracy and corruption can only be won by involving the people and the delegates (*Mesa Redonda*, August 30, 2012, notes taken by author).

Social scientists who place the emphasis today on the political solution of enhanced people's participation are also on the right track. For example, Olga Fernández Ríos contends,

> There is one condition in order to advance toward a more political and comprehensive conception of the socialist transition.... [Success can be obtained] only if it achieves a permanent social dialogue and interaction between the authorities that lead the various entities and the people that they are obliged to represent. (Fernández Ríos forthcoming)

In this context, she highlights "the potentialities of people's participation." For this to be achieved, Fernández Ríos is hopeful that "the means and forms of people's participation can renovate themselves according to the new needs of society" (Fernández Ríos forthcoming).

This need for enhanced and effective participation has been discussed for some time and is thus currently at a critical juncture.

It can be added that the renewal of people's participation at all levels (national and local) requires further transforming the representative aspect of Cuba's political system into its participatory feature. The principle that sovereignty resides in the people *is* an issue, as we saw in the example of the Plaza de la Revolución Municipal Assembly. Participation by the people at the grass-roots level in national decisions surrounding the PCC Congress and in some ANPP legislation is indicative of the Cuban state's potential to further develop its resilient democracy in motion.

The Future of Democratization: Facing the Tests

In this concluding comment, I highlight some of my views regarding the tests that are to be faced in the future by the democracies in motion under consideration. In countries that are neighbouring Cuba, such as Venezuela, Bolivia and Ecuador — and in Cuba itself — the thoughts and actions of both the people and the leaderships are increasingly turning toward further democratization. Despite the differences in their respective paths and contexts, these countries share a common experience: they are shielding themselves to varying degrees from the supposed inherent superiority of the U.S.-centric political and economic system. The context is different for Cuba's other neighbour analyzed in this book, the U.S. Some people at the base in that country, representing *its* democracy in motion, are looking toward democratization in the face of the U.S. elites' two-party dictatorial control of the economic and political system.

This concluding summary of the tests begins with the principal one that the U.S. is facing. The U.S.-centric political and economic model serves as a buffer to maintain the status quo. This screen, at times disguised, such as in the case of Obama, hinders many people in the U.S. from *profoundly* examining their own system, diagnosing the problem and debating real alternatives. We have seen once again in the 2012 U.S. presidential campaign how the Democratic and Republican candidates, as well as the media, orchestrate a major propaganda offensive. The planet is inundated with the U.S. elections as part of the attempt to Americanize the world. Most of the servile Western media and political leaders are fully complicit and directly contribute to these illusions about U.S. democracy. This has even infected some in Latin America and the Caribbean as well as other countries in the South. The world is told that "America" made a decision regarding Obama, while censoring the fact that only 50 percent of people 18 years and older voted. The U.S. and the world are likewise fed the image that, in the U.S. elections, the Democratic and Republican parties offer options for the left and the right, for socialism and the extreme right, or for liberals and conservatives. The goal is to make everyone believe that the "democratic two-party competitive system" is really the base for choosing among opposing paths.

One of the principal reasons for the relative success of this notion being maintained and fostered is the role played by some liberals and several on the left. Their vehicle for promoting this apparition is the lesser-of-two-evils prejudice. In the book, based on historical and contemporary facts and analysis regarding U.S. domestic and international policies, I conclude and confirm what a small number of people assert. Obama is the more *effective* of the two evils to serve the needs of important sectors of the elites, therefore the need to build an alternative now outside the two-party system paradigm.

Thus liberalism — the very origin and basis of the current U.S. system based on unlimited accumulation of private property — is providing the much-needed oxygen to a political system that would otherwise be in crisis. The alternative of rejecting the two-party system is thus forever relegated to the future, if it is to be considered at all. How can the open-minded general public in the U.S. oppose Obama (in favour of a new people-based option) when the fiction is maintained since his first mandate, and further promoted into his second, that the world is enamoured with him? Obama's image is so globally mediatized that the impression is given that he and the U.S. constitute the world's leadership. This mirage is greatly facilitated by Obama's repeated bragging, in the tradition of the "chosen people" concept ingrained in U.S. consciousness since the eighteenth century, that the "U.S. is the best nation in the world." More and more, it is becoming politically incorrect to criticize Obama from a progressive point of view. He is therefore once again the willing co-opted weapon in the hands of important sectors of the U.S. elites.

Barack and Michelle Obama act to anesthetize many African-Americans. Among the Obamas' assets is their ability — for the moment — to keep the historically rebellious and traditionally progressive African-Americans in line. Thus, under these conditions, it is no wonder that, in the U.S., a progressive movement against the two-party system illusion is experiencing difficulty in gaining momentum. The real alternative to the U.S. system is found mainly among the African-American left and progressives, as well as a cross-section of society, including intellectuals and academics, some local Occupy Movements, along with the more militant workers in areas such as Oakland, California. The eventual coalescence and spreading of these different sources of radical change pose a serious potential problem to the ruling elites. However, these embryonic spaces of profound transformations are not well supported outside the U.S. nor are their voices given much attention — if any at all — in the U.S. itself. Thus I believe that the single most important test, as far as democratization in the U.S. is concerned, is the capacity of these anti-status quo forces to unite and expand. The purpose would be to oppose the stifling "two-party system" and question those who insist on postponing forever its replacement under the guise of the "lesser of two evils."

I expect that some people will contest my view. However, others may feel emboldened that at least one other voice is daring to take a real stand against the "lesser of two evils" prejudice by looking at the people itself as a completely new substitute. Thus, with regard to the U.S. political system, I am seeking reactions from detractors and supporters — and from those who were already reflecting on their own. Thus, one of the goals of the book would be attained, as it seeks to contribute to the debate in the U.S. and in other countries on this issue that affects the U.S. and the world.

In the course of their respective democracies in motion, Venezuela, Bolivia and Ecuador are facing tests as they continue to stride toward transforming and creating new structures and approaches in opposing the U.S.-centric political structures.

First, Venezuela is achieving this to the extent that its U.S.-style political anatomy is barely recognizable, as I analyzed with the October 2012 Chávez presidential election victory. The economic and social transformations that provide people with the real feeling of empowerment — and effective tools — are bringing about changes. Chávez is taking steps, even more so since the October 12, 2012, electoral triumph, in order to deepen socialist transformations called twenty-first-century socialism. This new socialism, while purging the old dogmas, is consistent with the socialist principles outlined in this book. Based on its socio-economic programs, with citizen participation at its core, it is promoting democratization as an ongoing process. The Venezuelan Bolivarian Revolution stems from the capacity to experiment with fresh forms of people's participation as part of a new vision of democracy that, by its very nature, is in motion. Venezuela's biggest test in the future is overcoming problems of bureaucracy and corruption, acknowledged by Chávez to exist even within the Bolivarian Revolution's own ranks. Alongside this trial is the ever-present danger of further U.S. interference to destroy the Bolivarian Revolution. In this context, any illusion about Obama acts as poison that can contaminate the political consciousness of the Venezuelan people and leadership.

Second, the situations in Bolivia and Ecuador are different from that of Venezuela. Thus the trial is of another order. These two Andean countries are not yet on the road to socialism, even though this is their declared general aim. However, the new movements and leaderships are against neo-liberalism as *the* model. They stand strongly against U.S. domination and interference, not only in their respective countries, but also in all of Latin America and the Caribbean as well as globally. To a certain extent, the U.S. counts on some Indigenous leaders. While they may have legitimate grievances, they also have the tendency to turn a blind eye to the U.S. genocidal and hegemonic anti-Indigenous tradition going back to the very birth of the U.S. in the eighteenth century. In addition, in Bolivia, Washington holds the wealthy separatist elements as a card in its hand to destabilize the country.

Can the Bolivian and Ecuadorian paths prevail in the face of U.S. designs? Much of this depends on their capacity in the near future to develop further economic and social changes in order to undertake their respective routes toward twenty-first-century socialism. This can only take place while heeding the desires of the very experienced and mature grass roots for further democratization through increased participation in the political system and economic transformations. Success in this field will assist greatly in building a strong foundation to resist U.S. regime-change plans for these two countries. It remains to be seen whether Bolivia and Ecuador can sustain and develop their projects and thus resist U.S. inroads. However, the region south of the Rio Grande has changed in recent years. It is no longer Washington's backyard.

Cuba adheres to socialism in an unapologetic manner in its Constitution and in all political instances. In Cuba, the people themselves were the ones, in the first place, to have brought about the Revolution through their participation. This upheaval led toward fundamental changes from U.S.-dominated capitalism to socialism and sovereignty. In Cuba, there exists the real possibility to bring about the changes occurring now and thus improve the entire political and economic system. This depends on the more effective participation of the people at the grass-roots level as the main protagonist in their own evolution. The potential and proposals for further development of democratization through improved participation are being debated, as exhibited by Cuban social scientists, journalists and political leaders cited in the book. As Cuba undergoes yet another phase of democratization, it continues to experiment with a new socialism. It is opposing old taboos and stultified doctrines. Cuba, in my view, is still a laboratory — a moving one, at that — of a new socialism and democracy. Being innovative is second nature to the Cuban Revolution. Cuba's tradition of being a democracy in motion enhances the possibility of its further democratization.

This is not to say that there are no signs of stagnation in Cuba. They are found among those bureaucrats — and the corrupt who flourish among them — who view the citizens' empowerment, especially that of the working people, as a threat to their own privileges. This bureaucracy and corruption constitutes one of the two main trials facing Cuba in the future.

The other test that will decide the outcome is the struggle in the ranks of the youth, intellectuals and artists, who are targeted by the dissident bloggers of both the right and the "left," but especially the latter. Whether they admit it or not, they are inspired by the prejudiced outlook based on the U.S. model and its desire for regime change in Cuba. The objective dividing line is annexation to the U.S. on the one hand or sovereignty and Cuba's renovated socialism on the other. It is a life-and-death struggle. Is the outcome assured? I think that it has yet to be decided.

Cuba's enemies have not been able to defeat Cuba since 1959, nor do I think that they will, despite all the resources at their disposal.

Thus Cuba can surprise the world once again as the rejuvenated Revolution continues. It is my intention through this book to provide readers with some tools for following the future situation independently, without the blinders of preconceived notions.

Works Cited

Acta de constitución del Gobierno Revolucionario. 2004. In Luis M. Buch and Reinaldo Suárez, *Gobierno revolucionario cubano: Primeros pasos*. Havana: Editorial de Ciencias Sociales.

Agencia Púlsar. 2011. "Bolivia: Twenty Percent Increase Minimum Wage." *Argentina Independent* (March 3). <http://www.argentinaindependent.com/currentaffairs/newsfromlatinamerica/boliviatwenty-percent-increase-minimum-wage/>.

Agencia Venezolana de Noticias. 2012. "Venezuela's New Social Missions Aimed at Reducing Poverty and Unemployment." *Venezuelanalysis.com* (January 19). <http://www.venezuelanalysis.com/news/6760>.

Alarcón de Quesada, Ricardo. 2002a. "El destino nuestro lo decidimos nosotros." In Ricardo Alarcón de Quesada, *Cuba y la lucha por la democracia*. Havana: Editorial de Ciencias Sociales.

_____. 2002b. "El iniciador Grito de La Demajagua." In Ricardo Alarcón de Quesada, *Cuba y la lucha por la democracia*. Havana: Editorial de Ciencias Sociales.

_____. 2002c. "La filosofía democrática de Cuba, June 23, 1994." In Ricardo Alarcón de Quesada, *Cuba y la lucha por la democracia*. Havana: Editorial de Ciencias Sociales.

_____. 2002d. "Parlamentos Obreros, April 15, 1994." In Ricardo Alarcón de Quesada, *Cuba y la lucha por la democracia*. Havana: Editorial de Ciencias Sociales.

_____. 2003. "Entrevista exclusiva de Rebelión a Ricardo Alarcón, presidente de la Asamblea Nacional del Poder Popular de Cuba, por Pascual Serrano — 'La democracia cubana no se agota en la representación formal, sino que incorpora mecanismos y formas de la democracia directa.'" *Rebelión* (December 6). <http://www.rebelion.org/noticia.php?id=53>.

_____. 2006. "Indicaciones del presidente de la Asamblea Nacional del Poder Popular sobre el Labor de Control y Fiscalización a realizar por los Órganos Locales y las funciones y tareas de los delegados y consejos populares." (April 4). Report provided to author by the Plaza de la Revolución Municipal Assembly.

Albro, Robert. 2010. "Confounding Cultural Citizenship and Constitutional Reform in Bolivia." *Latin American Perspectives* (May), Issue 172, 37:3.

Alexander, Michelle. 2010. *The New Jim Crow: Mass Incarceration in the Age of Colorblindness*. NY: The New Press.

Alhama Belamaric, Rafael. 2012. "Trabajo congelado: Necesidad de cambios." Paper presented at the Instituto de Filosofía Workshop on "The Cuban Socialist Transition: The Current Situation, Challenges and Perspectives" (July 12–13), Havana.

_____. Forthcoming. *Breve lectura sobre algunos problemas actuales*. Havana: Editorial de Ciencias Sociales.

Allard, Jean-Guy. 2005. "Montaner, the Terrorist: Parts 1 and 2." *Granma International* (August 2). <http://www.walterlippmann.com/montaner.html>.

_____. 2010a. "CIA Agent and Coup Leader Slander Rafael Correa." Talk show on Colombian TV. *Granma International* (October 5), 279.

_____. 2010b. "CIA Agent Carlos Alberto Montaner Linked to Coup Plotter Lucio Gutiérrez." Talk show on Colombian TV. *Granma International* (October 4).

_____. 2012. "Paraguay: U.S. Intelligence Behind the Return of Stroessner's Mafia."

Granma International (July 1), Year 47, No. 27.

Álvarez Tabío, Fernando. 1985. *Comentarios a la Constitución socialista.* Havana: Editorial de Ciencias Sociales.

Álvarez Tabío, Pedro, and Guillermo Alonso Fiel. 1998. "Introduction." In Fidel Castro Ruz, *History Will Absolve Me.* Havana: Editorial José Martí.

Amin, Samir. 2004. *The Liberal Virus: Permanent War and the Americanization of the World.* NY: Monthly Review Press.

___. 2009. *Eurocentrism.* NY: Monthly Review Press.

___. 2012a. "The Center Will Not Hold: The Rise and Decline of Liberalism." *Monthly Review* (January), 63:8.

___. 2012b. "The First Round of the Presidential Elections in Egypt." *Pambazuka News* (May 31). <http://www.pambazuka.org/en/category/features/82595>.

Aquique, Dariela. 2012. "Venezuela's Excellent Electoral System." *Havana Times* (October 10). <http://www.havanatimes.org/?p=80028>.

Arreola, Gerardo. 2012. "Surge en Cuba resistencia a reformas que impulsa el presidente Raúl Castro." *La Jornada* (June 27). <http://www.jornada.unam.mx/2012/06/25/mundo/034n1mun>.

Arze Vargas, Carlos. 2008. "The Perverse Effects of Globalization." In John Crabtree and Laurence Whitehead (eds.), *Bolivia Past and Present: Unresolved Tensions.* Pittsburgh: University of Pittsburgh Press.

Asamblea Nacional del Poder Popular. 2002. "Dictamen de las comisiones para la atención a la actividad productiva y de asuntos constitucionales y jurídicos sobre el Proyecto de Ley de Cooperativas Agropecuarias." Report provided to author by the ANPP.

___. 2011. "Sobre la experiencia a desarrollar en la provincias de Artemisa y Mayabeque." Statement issued on August 1, 2011. *Granma* (August 2), Year 47, No. 183.

Asociación Civil Transparencia. 2005. *Datos Electorales* (November 21). <http://www.transparencia.org.pe/documentos/datos_electorales_no.01.pdf>.

Associated Press. 2008. "Cuban Assembly to Decide on Castro." *CBN News* (January 21). <cbn.com/cbnnews/world/2008/January/Cuban-Assembly-to-Decide-on-Castro->.

August, Arnold. 1999. *Democracy in Cuba and the 1997–98 Elections.* Havana: Editorial José Martí.

___. 2004. "Socialism and Elections." In Max Azicri and Elsie Deal (eds.), *Cuban Socialism in a New Century: Adversity, Survival, and Renewal.* Gainesville: University Press of Florida.

___. 2013. *Democracy in the U.S.* <http://www.democracyintheus.com>.

Azicri, Max. 2000. *Cuba Today and Tomorrow: Reinventing Socialism.* Gainesville: University Press of Florida.

___. 2010. "The Cuba-Venezuela Alliance: Dynamics of a Beneficial Solidarity Exchange in Hard Times." Paper presented at the International Congress of Latin American Studies Association (October 6–9). LASA, Toronto, Ontario.

Barragán, Rossana. 2008. In John Crabtree and Laurence Whitehead (eds.), *Bolivia Past and Present: Unresolved Tensions.* Pittsburgh: University of Pittsburgh Press.

Barredo Medina, Lázaro. 2012. "Respuesta a la directora de la empresa de revisión técnica automotor: La razón que nos asiste." *Granma* (March 12), Year 48, No. 60.

Barredo Medina, Lázaro, and Yaima Puig Meneses. 2011. "Sesionó el Tercero Pleno del Comité Central del Partido." *Granma* (December 23), 47:306.

Barrionuevo, Alexei. 2009. "Bolivian President Says Plot on His Life Was Tied to Coup Attempt." *The New York Times* (April 18). <http://www.nytimes. com/2009/04/19/world/americas/19bolivia.html>.

Beatón Ruiz, Betty. 2012. "Asamblea de la UPEC en Santiago de Cuba por un periodismo más creativo y ágil." *CubaPeriodistas* (February 8). <http://www. cubaperiodistas.cu/noticias/febrero12/08/01.htm>.

Becker, Marc. 2011. "Correa, Indigenous Movements, and the Writing of a New Constitution in Ecuador." *Latin American Perspectives* (January), 38:1.

___. 2012. "Social Movements and the Government of Rafael Correa: Confrontation or Cooperation?" In Gary Prevost, Carlos Oliva Campos and Harry E. Vanden (eds.), *Social Movements and Leftist Governments in Latin America: Confrontation and Co-Optation*. London: Zed Books.

Benton Foundation. 2008. "Obama in Landslide: 273–142 (in Newspaper Endorsements." (November 3). <http://benton.org/node/18497>.

Black, Conrad. 2003. *Franklin Delano Roosevelt: Champion of Freedom*. Cambridge, MA: Perseus Books Group.

Blackmon, Douglas A. 2008. *Slavery by Another Name: The Re-Enslavement of Black Americans from the Civil War to World War II*. NY: Doubleday.

Boothroyd, Rachael. 2011a. "More than 87,000 Senior Citizens Register in Government's New Mission for the Elderly." *Venezuelanalysis.com* (January 5). <http://www.venezuelanalysis.com/news/6724>.

___. 2011b. "Popular Movements March for Creation of the 'Patriotic Pole' to Deepen the Revolution." *Venezuelanalysis.com* (August 29). <http://www. venezuelanalysis.com/news/6453>.

___. 2011c. "President Chávez Requests 45 Billion Bolivars for Social Missions." *Venezuelanalysis.com* (June 2). <http://www.venezuelanalysis.com/news/6235>.

___. 2012a. "Venezuelans Begin Registering in Government's Knowledge and Work Mission." *Venezuelanalysis.com* (January 17). <http://www.venezuelanalysis.com/ news/6756>.

___. 2012b. "Venezuela's Chávez Outlines Vision for Next Presidency, "Greater Advance" Towards Socialism." *Venezuelanalysis.com* (October 11). <http:// venezuelanalysis.com/news/7350>.

Brennan Center for Justice. 2012. "2012 Summary of Voting Law Changes." New York University School of Law (August 21). <http://www.brennancenter.org/ content/resource/2012_summary_of_voting_law_changes/>.

Brice, Arthur. 2010. "Ecuador Declares Emergency as Police Protest, President Is Attacked." CNN World (September 30). <articles.cnn.com/2010-09-30/ world/ecuador.violence.archive_1_teleamazonas-gas-mask-rafael-correa?_ s=PM:WORLD>.

Bruce, Iain. 2008. *The Real Venezuela: Making Socialism in the 21st Century*. London: Pluto Press.

Brzezinski, Zbigniew. 2008. *Second Chance: Three Presidents and the Crisis of American Superpower*. NY: Basic Books.

Buch, Luis M., and Reinaldo Suárez. 2004. *Gobierno revolucionario cubano: Primeros pasos*. Havana: Editorial de Ciencias Sociales.

Buxton, Julia. 2009. "Venezuela: The Political Evolution of Bolivarianism." In Geraldine Lievesley and Steve Ludlam (eds.), *Reclaiming Latin America: Experiments in Radical Social Democracy*. London: Zed Books.

Buznego, Enrique, Oscar Loyola and Gustavo Pedroso. 1996. "La Revolución del 68: Cumbre y ocaso." In María del Carmen Barcia, Gloria García and Eduardo Torres-Cuevas (eds.), *Historia de Cuba: Las luchas por la independencia nacional y las transformaciones estructurales, 1868–1898*. Havana: Editora Política.

Calzadilla, Erasmo. 2012a. "Confirming Whether Cuba Is a Democracy." *Havana Times* (July 26). <http://www.havanatimes.org/?p=75166>.

____. 2012b. "Three Options: Which Will Be the Least Bad?" *Havana Times* (October 7). <http://www.havanatimes.org/?p=79828>.

Campos, Pedro. 2012a. "Cuba Can Learn from Chávez and Venezuela." *Havana Times* (October 9). At <http://www.havanatimes.org/?p=79946>.

____. 2012b. "In Cuba Too, Less Than 1% Decide." *Havana Times* (August 28). <http://www.havanatimes.org/?p=77332>.

Carroll, Rory. 2009. "Bolivian President Morales Links US Embassy to Alleged Assassination Attempt." *The Guardian* (April 20). <http://www.guardian.co.uk/world/2009/apr/20/evo-morales-bolivia-us-embassy>.

Castro Ruz, Fidel. 1959. "Speech on the Occasion of the First Anniversary of the April 9 Strike." La Alameda de Paula, [promenade in Old Havana]. (April 9). <http://www.cuba.cu/gobierno/discursos/1959/esp/f090459e.html>.

____. 1960. "Speech, September 28, 1960." <http://www.cuba.cu/gobierno/discursos/1960/esp/f280960e.html>.

____. 1972a. "The Cuban Revolution (July 23, 1953)." Translated and reproduced in Rolando E. Bonachea and Nelson P. Valdés, *Revolutionary Struggle 1947–1958: Volume 1 of the Selected Works of Fidel Castro*. Cambridge, MA: MIT Press.

____. 1972b. "General Strike Proclamation (January 1, 1959)." Translated and reproduced in Rolando E. Bonachea and Nelson P. Valdés, *Revolutionary Struggle 1947–1958: Volume 1 of the Selected Works of Fidel Castro*. Cambridge, MA: MIT Press.

____. 1972c. "Proclamation to the People of Santiago (January 1, 1959)." Translated and reproduced in Rolando E. Bonachea and Nelson P. Valdés, *Revolutionary Struggle 1947–1958: Volume 1 of the Selected Works of Fidel Castro*. Cambridge, MA: MIT Press.

____. 1990a. *Informe Central I, II y III Congreso del Partido Comunista de Cuba*. Havana: Editora Política.

____. 1990b. Speech delivered on February 20, 1990. <http://www.cuba.cu/gobierno/discursos/1990/esp/f200290e.html>.

____. 1998. In *History Will Absolve Me*. Havana: Editorial José Martí.

____. 2004. In Luis M. Buch and Reinaldo Suárez, *Gobierno revolucionario cubano: Primeros pasos*. Havana: Editorial de Ciencias Sociales.

____. 2005. Speech delivered on November 17, 2005. <http://www.cuba.cu/gobierno/discursos/2005/ing/f171105i.html>.

____. 2006a. "Revolución, June 15, 1959." In D.L. Raby, *Democracy and Revolution: Latin America and Socialism Today*. London: Pluto Press and Between the Lines.

____. 2006b. "Revolución, March 16, 1959." In D.L. Raby, *Democracy and Revolution: Latin America and Socialism Today*. London: Pluto Press and Between the Lines.

____. 2007. *My Life*. Edited by Ignacio Ramonet. NY: Penguin Books.

___. 2008a. In José Bell, Delia Luisa López and Tania Caram, *Documentos de la Revolución Cubana: 1959*. Havana: Editorial de Ciencias Sociales.

___. 2008b. "Message from the Commander in Chief." (February 18). <http://www.cuba.cu/gobierno/discursos/2008/ing/f180208i.html>.

___. 2010. *Por todos los caminos de la Sierra: La Victoria Estratégica*. Havana: Oficina de publicaciones del Consejo de Estado de la República de Cuba.

Castro Ruz, Raúl. 1974. "Speech by Division Commander (Lieutenant General) Raúl Castro, at the Closing Session of the Seminar for Delegates to the Organs of People's Power, Held in Matanzas." *Granma* (September 8), Havana.

___. 2007. Speech delivered on July 26, 2007. <http://www.cubaminrex.cu/english/SpeechesContributions/RCR/2007_2008/07-07-26.html>.

___. 2008. Speech delivered on July 11, 2008. International Conference Center, Havana. <http://www.groups.yahoo.com/group/CubaNews/message/88154>.

___. 2009. Speech delivered on August 1, 2009. <http://www.cuba.cu/gobierno/rauldiscursos/2009/ing/r010809i.html>.

___. 2010a. Key address delivered on April 4, 2010. <http://www.cuba.cu/gobierno/rauldiscursos/2010/ing/r030410i.html>.

___. 2010b. Speech delivered on August 1, 2010. *Granma*. <http://www.granma.cu/ingles/cuba-i/2agosto-discursoraul.html>.

___. 2010c. Speech delivered on December 18, 2010. <http://www.cuba.cu/gobierno/rauldiscursos/2010/ing/r181210i.html>.

___. 2011a. "Central Report to the 6th Congress of the Communist Party of Cuba." (April 16). <http://www.cuba.cu/gobierno/rauldiscursos/2011/ing/r160411i.html>.

___. 2011b. Speech delivered on August 1, 2011. *Granma International* (August 7), Year 56, No. 32.

___. 2012a. Speech delivered on January 29, 2012. *Granma International* (February 5), Year 47, No. 6.

___. 2012b. Speech delivered on July 23, 2012. *Granma International* (July 29), Year 47, No. 31.

Centro de Estudios Che Guevara. n.d. "Vida, obra y pensamiento." <http://www.centroche.co.cu/centroche/?q=node/165>.

Chaguaceda, Armando. 2012a. "Crucial Elections in Venezuela." *Havana Times* (October 4). <http://www.havanatimes.org/?p=79652>.

___. 2012b. "Elecciones cruciales en Venezuela." *Red Observatorio Crítico* (October 5). <http://observatoriocriticodesdecuba.wordpress.com/2012/10/05/elecciones-cruciales-en-venezuela/>.

___. 2012c. "Elections in Venezuela, Sketches the Day After." *Havana Times* (October 8). <http://www.havanatimes.org/?p=79942>.

___. 2012d. "The Possible, the Probable, and the Preferable: Crucial Elections in Venezuela." *El Yuma* (October 4). <http://elyuma.blogspot.ca/2012/10/venezuela-oct-7-possible-probable-and.html>.

___. 2012e. "Una Cuba mejor es posible." *Havana Times* (August 8). <http://www.havanatimes.org/sp/?p=69075>.

Chappi Docurro, Tania. 2012. "Diálogo y cultura cívica: Un debate de *Temas*." *Cubadebate* (July 1). <http://www.cubadebate.cu/especiales/2012/07/01/

dialogo-y-cultura-civica-un-debate-de-temas/>.

Chaveco, Onelia. 2012. "Balance del trabajo de la UPEC en Cienfuegos: Prensa cubana debe responder a demandas de momento actual." *CubaPeriodistas* (February 1). <http://www.cubaperiodistas.cu/noticias/febrero12/01/01.htm>.

Chávez, Hugo. 2011. "Chávez Campaign Prepares Nationwide Grassroots Coalition for 2012 Elections." *Correo del Orinoco* (October 7), 84.

Chávez, Juan Carlos. 2012. "Intelectuales y opositores hacen un llamado a favor de las libertades y el diálogo en Cuba." *El Nuevo Herald* (August 3). <http://www.elnuevoherald.com/2012/08/02/1266519/intelectuales-y-opositores-hacen.html>.

Chomsky, Noam. 2012a. "The Cairo-Madison Connection." In Noam Chomsky, *Making the Future: Occupations, Interventions, Empire and Resistance.* San Francisco: City Lights Books.

____. 2012b. "Tomgram: Noam Chomsky, The Great Charter, Its Fate, and Ours." *TomDispatch* (July 22). <http://www.tomdispatch.com/blog/175571/>.

Chomsky, Noam, and Edward S. Herman. 2002. *Manufacturing Consent: The Political Economy of the Mass Media.* NY: Pantheon Books.

Clement, Christopher I. 2005. "Confronting Chávez: United States Democracy Promotion in Latin America." *Latin American Perspectives* (May), Issue 142, 32:3.

Clinton, Hillary Rodham. 2011a. "Interview with Sharif Amer of Al-Hayat TV." U.S. Department of State (September 29). <http://www.state.gov/secretary/rm/2011/09/174882.htm>.

____. 2011b. "Introductory Remarks for President Obama's Speech on Events in the Middle East and North Africa, and U.S. Policy in the Region." U.S. Department of State (May 19). <http://www.state.gov/secretary/rm/2011/05/163831.htm>.

____. 2011c. "Statement Before the House Appropriations Subcommittee on State, Foreign Operations, and Related Programs." U.S. Department of State (March 10). <http://www.state.gov/secretary/rm/2011/03/158004.htm>.

CNN. 2010. "Police Discussed Killing Ecuador's President, Radio Transmissions Show." *CNN World* (October 6). <http://www.cnn.com/2010/WORLD/americas/10/06/ecuador.president.threats/index.html>.

Cocalero, DVD. Directed by Alejandro Lanes.

Cole, Ken. 2010. "The Bolivarian Alliance for the Peoples of Our America: Part 1, Knowledge Is What Counts." *International Journal of Cuban Studies*, 2 (3 and 4) (autumn–winter).

____. 2011. "Progress into the Twenty-First Century: The Bolivarian Alliance for the Peoples of Our America." *International Journal of Cuban Studies*, 3.2 and 3.3 (summer/autumn).

Congreso del Partido Comunista de Cuba. n.d. "V Congreso del Partido Comunista de Cuba: El Partido de la unidad, la democracia y los derechos humanos que defendemos." <http://www.congresopcc.cip.cu/wp-content/uploads/2011/03/Partido-Unidad-Democracia-V-Congreso.pdf>.

Consejo Nacional Electoral [Ecuador]. n.d. <http://www.cne.gob.ec>.

Consejo Nacional Electoral [Venezuela]. n.d. <http://www.cne.gov.ve/web/estadisticas/index_resultados_elecciones.php>.

Constitución de Baraguá. 1973. In Hortensia Pichardo, *Documentos para la historia de*

Cuba. Vol. I. Havana: Editorial de Ciencias Sociales.

Constitución de Guáimaro. 1973. In Hortensia Pichardo, *Documentos para la historia de Cuba.* Vol. I. Havana: Editorial de Ciencias Sociales.

Constitución de Jimaguayú. 1973. In Hortensia Pichardo, *Documentos para la historia de Cuba.* Vol. I. Havana: Editorial de Ciencias Sociales.

Constitución de la República de Cuba. [1976] 2003. Asamblea Nacional del Poder Popular, Havana.

———. 1940. Cámara de Representantes. Havana: Editorial Lex.

———. 1976. Ministerio de Justicia (February). Edición Oficial. Havana: Editorial Orbe.

Constitución de la República del Ecuador. 2008. Presidencia de la República del Ecuador. <http://www.asambleanacional.gov.ec/documentos/constitucion_de_bolsillo.pdf>.

Constitución de La Yaya. 1973. In Hortensia Pichardo, *Documentos para la historia de Cuba.* Vol. I. Havana: Editorial de Ciencias Sociales.

Constitución, *Ley Fundamental de Cuba.* 1959. Biblioteca Jurídica Virtual (February 7). <http://www.bibliojuridica.org/libros/6/2525/38.pdf>.

Constitution of the Bolivarian Republic of Venezuela. 1999. Ministerio de Comunicación e Información. Caracas.

Constitution of the Plurinational State of Bolivia. 2009. Enacted on February 7, 2009, by President Evo Morales Ayma (translated to English by Luis Francisco Valle Valesco), La Paz.

Constitution of the Republic of Cuba. [1976] 2003. Ministry of Foreign Affairs of the Republic of Cuba *(CubaMinRex).* <http://www.cubaminrex.cu/english/LookCuba/Articles/AboutCuba/Constitution/inicio.html#4>.

Constitution of the United States. 1791. Amendment 1 (December 15). <http://www.usconstitution.net/xconst_Am1.html>.

———. 1984. <http://www.usconstitution.net/const.pdf>.

Corcoran, Michael. 2010. "Ecuador Crisis, Media Bias." NACLA (November–December), 043:6.

Correa, Rafael. 2009. "Speech to the Social Forum in Belem, Brazil." Transcript by author from TeleSUR (January 29).

Council on Foreign Relations. 2008. "Transition 2008: Advising America's Next President: The Future American Leadership." (November 21). <http://www.cfr.org/us-strategy-and-politics/transition-2008-advising-americas-next-president-future-american-leadership-video/p17834>.

Crabtree, John, and Laurence Whitehead, eds. 2008. *Bolivia Past and Present: Unresolved Tensions.* Pittsburgh: University of Pittsburgh Press.

Cubadebate. 2012. "Diputados reciben información sobre 117 proyectos de desarrollo local." (July 21). <http://www.cubadebate.cu/noticias/2012/07/21/diputados-reciben-informacion-sobre-117-proyectos-de-desarrollo-local/>.

Cuba Encuentro. n.d. "Agradecimientos." <http://www.cubaencuentro.com/el-portal/agradecimientos>.

Cuba-L Direct. 2011. "Interview with Fidel Castro [January 4, 1960]. Cuba-L Analysis (Albuquerque) — NBC Today." *El Mundo of Habana* (translated to English by Nelson P. Valdés). (January 3). <http://cuba-l.unm.edu/?nid=86347>.

Cuba Money Project. n.d. <http://cubamoneyproject.org/>.

Cullen, Jim. 2003. *The American Dream: A Short History of an Idea That Shaped a Nation.*

NY: Oxford University Press.

Cullop, Floyd G. 1984. *The Constitution of the United States: An Introduction.* NY: Mentor.

Das, Veena, and Deborah Poole. 2004. "The State and Its Margins, Anthropology." In Veena Das and Deborah Poole (eds.), *The Margins of the State.* Santa Fe, NM: School of American Research Press.

Davalos, Pablo. 2009. "Reflections on *Sumak Kawsay* (Good Living) and Theories of Development." ALAI (América Latina en Movimiento) (December 10). <http://alainet.org/active/33609&lang=es>.

Davidow, Jeffrey S. 2009. "Upcoming Summit of the Americas." U.S. Department of State (April 6). <http://www.state.gov/p/wha/rls/rm/2009/121355.htm>.

Del Carmen Barcia, María, Gloria García and Eduardo Torres-Cuevas, eds. 1996. *Historia de Cuba: Las luchas por la independencia nacional y las transformaciones estructurales, 1868–1898.* Havana: Editora Política.

Dilla Alfonso, Haroldo. 2012a. "Immigration Reform and Ricardo Alarcon's Good Heart." *Havana Times* (April 17). <http://www.havanatimes.org/?p=67619>.

_____. 2012b. "La importancia de un llamamiento por una Cuba mejor: No podemos temer al diálogo si queremos un futuro mejor para Cuba." *Cuba Encuentro* (August 13). <http://www.cubaencuentro.com/opinion/articulos/la-importancia-de-un-llamamiento-por-una-cuba-mejor-279211>.

_____. 2012c. "The Importance of a Call for a Better Cuba." *Havana Times* (August 14). <http://www.havanatimes.org/?p=76468>.

Domínguez, Jorge I. 1979. *Cuba: Order and Revolution.* Cambridge: Belknap Press, Harvard University Press.

Dorschner, John, and Roberto Fabricio. 1980. *The Winds of December.* NY: Coward, McCann and Geoghegan.

Duharte Díaz, Emilio. 2008. "Reformas y probables tendencias de desarrollo del sistema político cubano." *Temas* (October–December), 56.

_____. 2010. "Cuba at the Onset of the 21st Century: Socialism, Democracy and Political Reforms." In *Socialism and Democracy* (March), 24:1.

DuRand, Cliff. 2009. Review of Robert Kagan, "Dangerous Nation: America's Place in the World from Its Earliest Days to the Dawn of the Twentieth Century." Center for Global Justice (June 11). <http://www.globaljusticecenter.org/2011/11/04/dangerous-nation/>.

_____. 2011. Book review. "Michael A. Leibowitz, *The Socialist Alternative: Real Human Development.*" *Socialism and Democracy* (July 11), 25:2.

_____. 2012. "The Possibility of Democratic Politics in a Globalized State." In Cliff DuRand and Steve Martinot (eds.), *Recreating Democracy in a Globalized State.* Atlanta: Clarity Press.

EcuRed. n.d. "Félix Varela." <http://www.ecured.cu/index.php/F%C3%A9lix_Varela>.

Electoral Law No. 72. 1992. "Ley Electoral No. 72." Ministry of Foreign Affairs of the Republic of Cuba (*CubaMinRex*). (October 29). <http://www.cubaminrex.cu/mirar_cuba/La_isla/ley_electoral.htm>.

Ellner, Steve. 2008. *Rethinking Venezuelan Politics: Class, Conflict and the Chávez Phenomenon.* London: Reinner Publishers.

_____. 2010. "Chávez Pushes the Limits: Radicalization and Discontent in Venezuela." *NACLA Report on the Americas* (July–August), 43:4.

___. 2011. "Venezuela's Social-Based Democratic Model: Innovation and Limitations." *Latin American Studies*, 43.

___. 2012. "The Distinguishing Features of Latin America's New Left in Power: The Chávez, Morales, and Correa Governments." *Latin American Perspectives* (January), Issue 182, 39:1.

El Nuevo Herald. 2012. "Fiscalía cubana pide 7 años de cárcel para Carromero por homicidio imprudente." (August 16). <http://www.elnuevoherald.com/>.

El País. 2010a. "Correa retoma el control en Ecuador y promete una depuración en la policía." (October 1). <http://internacional.elpais.com/internacional/2010/09/30/actualidad/1285797605_850215.html>.

___. 2010b. "'Maten a Correa para que se acabe ya esta protesta.'" (October 5). <http://internacional.elpais.com/internacional/2010/10/05/actualidad/1286229612_850215.html>.

Espejo, Amalia. 2010. "10 elecciones muestran vocación democrática del pueblo." Naciones Unidas: Bolivia. (August 11). <http://www.nu.org.bo/NoticiasNU/B%C3%BAsquedadenoticias/tabid/162/articleType/ArticleView/articleId/935/10-elecciones-muestran-vocacion-democratica-del-pueblo.aspx>.

Europa Press. 2012. "Desde que asumió el poder en 2006: Morales asegura que un millón de bolivianos han dejado de vivir en la pobreza." <http://www.europapress.es/latam/bolivia/noticia-bolivia-morales-asegura-millon-bolivianos-dejado-vivir-pobreza-asumio-poder-2006-20120803184333.html> (accessed August 3, 2012).

Fernández, June. 2012. "Independent Activism in Cuba." *Havana Times* (August 5). <http://www.havanatimes.org/?p=75825>.

Fernández Ríos, Olga. 1988. "Annex." *Formación y desarrollo del estado socialista en Cuba*. Havana: Editorial de Ciencias Sociales.

___. 2011a. "El enfrentamiento al burocratismo en Cuba: Raigambre popular contra mala hierba." *Rebelión* (September 23). <http://www.rebelion.org/noticia.php?id=136178>.

___. 2011b. "Institucionalidad y participación popular en la renovación de la hegemonía socialista." *Rebelión* (August 16). <http://www.rebelion.org/noticia.php?id=134084>.

___. 2011c. "La Revolución Cubana y los retos del presente." *Rebelión* (July 22). <http://www.rebelion.org/noticia.php?id=132732>.

___. Forthcoming. "La transición socialista en Cuba: Ajustes económicos y desafíos sociopolíticos." Paper presented at the June 19, 2012, Seminar on "Socialist Renewal and the Capitalist Crisis: A Cuba-North American Exchange," Havana.

Fitz, Don. 2012. "Why Cuba Cancelled Med School Classes in Havana: The Winter of Dengue Fever." *CounterPunch* (February 9). <http://www.counterpunch.org/2012/02/09/the-winter-of-dengue-fever/>.

Fonticoba Gener, O., José A. de la Osa and Anneris Ivette Leyva. 2012. "A Good Day's Work." *Granma International* (July 29), Year 47, No. 31.

Ford, Glen. 2012. "What Obama Has Wrought." *Black Agenda Report* (September 5). <http://blackagendareport.com/content/what-obama-has-wrought>.

Foreign Agricultural Service. 2008. "Cuba's Food and Agriculture Situation Report." United States Department of Agriculture (March). <http://www.fas.usda.gov/

itp/cuba/cubasituation0308.pdf>.

Foreign Relations of the United States, Document 11. 1958. "Telegram from the Embassy in Cuba to the Department of State, Havana, Cuba." United States Government Printing Office (February 7), Washington.

___, Document 47. 1958. "Memorandum from the Deputy Director of Intelligence and Research (Arneson) to the Secretary of State." United States Government Printing Office (April 2), Washington.

___, Document 52. 1958. "Memorandum of a Conversation, Department of State." United States Government Printing Office (April 22), Washington.

___, Document 54. 1958. "Memorandum of Discussion at the Department of State — Joint Chiefs of Staff Meeting, Pentagon." United States Government Printing Office (May 2), Washington.

___, Document 55. 1958 "Memorandum from the Deputy Assistant Secretary of State for Inter-American Affairs (Snow) to the Acting Secretary of State." United States Government Printing Office (May 6), Washington.

___, Document 58. 1958. "Memorandum of a Conversation Between the Assistant Secretary of State for Inter-American Affairs (Rubottom) and the Cuban Ambassador (Arroyo), Department of State." United States Government Printing Office (May 22), Washington.

___, Document 112. 1958. "Draft Memorandum Prepared in the Office of Middle American Affairs." United States Government Printing Office (July 25), Washington.

___, Document 196. 1958. "Telegram from the Embassy in Cuba to the Department of State, Havana." United States Government Printing Office (December 29 — 7 p.m.), Washington.

___, Document 197. 1958. "Memorandum from the Director of the Office of Central American and Panamanian Affairs (Stewart) to the Assistant Secretary of State for Inter-American Affairs (Rubottom)." United States Government Printing Office (December 29), Washington.

___, Document 499. 1960. "Memorandum from the Deputy Assistant Secretary of State for Inter-American Affairs (Mallory) to the Assistant Secretary of State for Inter-American Affairs (Rubottom)." United States Government Printing Office (April 6), Washington, 1991.

___, Document 607. 1960. "Memorandum from the Secretary of Defense's Deputy Assistant for Special Operations (Lansdale) to the Deputy Secretary of Defense (Douglas), Cuba." United States Government Printing Office (November 7), Vol. VI, Washington.

Foster, William Z. 1951. *Outline Political History of the Americas*. NY: International Publishers.

Franklin, Jane. 1997. *Cuba and the United States: A Chronological History*. Melbourne: Ocean Press.

Friedman-Rudovsky, Jean. 2008. "Bolivia to Expel US Ambassador." *Time* (September 11). <http://www.time.com/time/world/article/0,8599,1840469,00.html#ixzz222RT6FkL>.

Fuentes, Federico. 2012a. "Bolivia: Challenges Along Path of 'Governing by Obeying the People.'" *Bolivia Rising* (February 19). <http://www.boliviarising.blogspot.com/2012/02/bolivia-challenges-along-path-of.html>.

___. 2012b. "Ecuador: New Left or New Colonialism?" *Green Left* (June 17). <http://www.greenleft.org.au/node/51353>.

___. 2012c. "Paraguay: US Makes Gains from Coup Against Lugo." *ZSpace* (July 16). <http://www.zcommunications.org/paraguay-us-makes-gains-from-coup-against-lugo-by-federico-fuentes>.

Fung Riverón, Thalía. 1982. *En torno a las regularidades y particularidades de la Revolución Socialista en Cuba.* Havana: Editorial de Ciencias Sociales.

Gaceta Oficial de la República de Cuba. 2008. Ministerio de la Justicia, Extraordinaria, Consejo de Estado, Decreto-Ley No. 259 (July 11), Year CVI, No. 24, Havana.

___. 2009. Ministerio de la Justicia, Extraordinaria. Ley No. 105-08 (January 22), Year CVII, No. 4, Havana.

___. 2010a. Ministerio de la Justicia, Ext. Especial, Consejo de Estado, Decreto-Ley No. 276 (October 1), Year CVIII, No. 11, Havana.

___. 2010b. Ministerio de la Justicia, Ext. Especial, Consejo de Estado, Decreto-Ley No. 276 (October 8), Year CVIII, No. 12, Havana.

___. 2010c. Ministerio de la Justicia (October 1), Year CVIII, No. 11, Havana.

___. 2010d. Ministerio de la Justicia (October 8), Year CVIII, No. 12, Havana.

___. 2011a. Ministerio de la Justicia (September 27), Year CIX, No. 31, Havana.

___. 2011b. Ministerio de la Justicia (November 2), Year CIX, No. 35, Havana.

___. 2012a. Ministerio de la Justicia (January 4), Year CX, No. 001.

___. 2012b. Ministerio de la Justicia (October 16), Year CX, No. 44.

García Brigos, Jesús P. 1998. *Gobernabilidad y democracia: Los órganos del Poder Popular.* Havana: Editorial de Ciencias Sociales.

___. 2005. "Cuba: Subdesarrollo y socialismo." Unpublished personal digital archive. Havana.

García Márquez, Gabriel. 1998. "A Personal Portrait of Fidel Castro." In Fidel Castro, *Fidel: My Early Years.* Melbourne: Ocean Press.

Golinger, Eva. 2006. *The Chávez Code: Cracking U.S. Intervention in Venezuela.* Northampton, MA: Olive Branch Press.

___. 2010a. "Ecuador: What Really Happened." *Correo del Orinoco International* (October 8), 32.

___. 2010b. "A Win for U.S. Interference." *Chávez Code* (September 30). <http://www.chavezcode.com/2010/09/win-for-us-interference.html>.

González, Ana Margarita. 2012. "Fiesta por conquistas irrenunciables." *Trabajadores* (April 30), Year XLII, No. 18.

Graham, Hugh Davis, and Ted Robert Gurr. 1969. "Violence in America: Historial and Comparative Perspectives — A Report to the National Commission on the Causes and Prevention of Violence." Vol. 2. Washington, D.C.: *U.S. Government Printing Office* (June), xxii:644.

Granma. 1990. "¡Al IV Congreso del Partido! ¡El futuro de nuestra patria será un eterno Baraguá!" Comité Central del Partido Comunista de Cuba (March 16), Havana.

___. 1993. "Estadísticas finales oficiales de las elecciones y votación de los disputados." (March 11).

___. 1998. "Resultados finales de las elecciones." (February 4).

___. 2003. "Resultados finales oficiales de las elecciones." (February 1).

___. 2005. "Victoria de la democracia revolucionaria." (April 19).

___. 2007a. "Comisión Electoral Nacional: Proceso Elecciones Generales 2007–08."

(October 26).

____. 2007b. "Comisión Electoral Nacional: Results of the Elections for Delegates to Municipal Assemblies of People's Power." (October 27).

____. 2008. "Resultados finales oficiales de las elecciones." (January 30).

____. 2009. "Chávez Announces ALBA Summit for April 14–15." *Granma International* (April 6). <http://www.granma.cu/ingles/2009/april/lun6/chavez.html>.

____. 2010. "Comisión Electoral Nacional: Resultados finales de la primera vuelta de los comicios." (April 30).

____. 2012a. "Comisión Electoral Nacional: Elecciones 21 de octubre 2012." (October 27), Year 48, No. 256.

____. 2012b. "Special Declarations from the ALBA-TCP Political Council on Cuba's Participation in the 6th Summit of the Americas and in Rejection of the Blockade." (February 26), Year 47, No. 9.

Gresh, Alain. 2011. "Reorienting History." In Henry Veltmeyer (ed.), *The Development Studies Handbook: Tools for Change.* Black Point, Nova Scotia: Fernwood Publishing.

Guevara, Ernesto Che. 2000. *El Diario del Che en Bolivia.* Havana: Editora Política.

____. 2005. "Against Bureaucratism (February, 1963)." In David Deutschmann (ed.), *The Che Reader: Writings on Politics and Revolution.* Melbourne, Australia: Ocean Press.

____. 2006. "Socialism and Man in Cuba, March 12, 1965." In Ernesto Che Guevara, *Socialism and Man in Cuba.* Canada: Pathfinder Press.

Hardt, Michael. 2007. "Introduction." In Thomas Jefferson, *The Declaration of Independence (Adopted by Congress on July 4, 1776): The Unanimous Declaration of the Thirteen United States of America.* NY: Verso.

Harnecker, Marta. 1980. *Cuba: Dictatorship or Democracy?* Westport: Lawrence Hill and Company.

Havana Times. 2012. "Call to Vote 'D' in Cuban Elections." (September 13). <http://www.havanatimes.org/?p=78495>.

Hawkins, Kirk A., Guillermo Rosas and Michael E. Johnson. 2011. "The Misiones of the Chávez Government." In David Smile and Daniel C. Hellinger (eds.), *Venezuela's Bolivarian Democracy: Participation, Politics, and Culture Under Chávez.* Durham: Duke University Press.

Hellinger, Daniel C. 2005. "When 'No' Means 'Yes to Revolution': Electoral Politics in Bolivarian Venezuela." *Latin American Perspectives* (May), 32:3.

____. 2011. "Defying the Iron Law of Oligarchy I: How Does 'El Pueblo' Conceive of Democracy." In David Smile and Daniel C. Hellinger (eds.), *Venezuela's Bolivarian Democracy: Participation, Politics, and Culture Under Chávez.* Durham: Duke University Press.

____. 2012. "Caracas Connect: Mortality, Electoral Mandates, and Revolution." *Democracy in the Americas* (October 9). <http://www.democracyinamericas.org/blog-post/caracas-connect-mortality-electoral-mandates-and-revolution/>.

Hernández, Rafael. 2010. "Los recursos de la oposición." *Cubadebate* (March 27). <http://www.cubadebate.cu/opinion/2010/03/27/los-recursos-de-la-oposicion/>.

____. 2011. "En Cuba existe un gran debate público, aún cuando no se refleje en los medios de comunicación." *Cambios en Cuba* (December 21). <http://www.cambiosencuba.blogspot.com/2011/12/en-cuba-existe-un-gran-debate-

publico.html#more>.

Hernández S., José. 2012. "Segunda vuelta electoral." *Tribuna de La Habana* (October 27). <http://www.tribuna.co.cu/cuba/2012-10-27/segunda-vuelta-electoral>.

Hofmann, Deborah. 2008. "Best Sellers: A Different Type of Ranking." *The New York Times* (February 16). <http://query.nytimes.com/gst/fullpage.html?res=9 F0CE1DE153CF935A25751C0A96E9C8B63>.

Hull, Elizabeth A. 2006. *The Disenfranchisement of Ex-Felons.* Temple Philadelphia: University Press.

Ibarra, Jorge. 2008. *José Martí: dirigente, político e ideólogo.* Havana: Centro de Estudios Martíanos.

International IDEA. 2009. "Compulsory Voting: What Is Compulsory Voting?" International Institute for Democracy and Electoral Assistance (updated in March). <http://www.idea.int/vt/compulsory_voting.cfm>.

Inter-Parliamentary Union. n.d. "Women in National Parliaments." <http://www. ipu.org/wmn-e/classif.htm#1> (accessed May 31, 2012).

Izquierdo Canosa, Raúl. 1998. *Las prefecturas mambisas (1868–1898).* Havana: Ediciones Verde Olivo.

Jameson, Kenneth P. 2011. "The Indigenous Movement in Ecuador: The Struggle for a Plurinational State." *Latin American Perspectives* (January) 38:1.

Jefferson, Thomas. 1975. "Letter to John Turnbull, Paris Feb. 15, 1789." In Merrill D. Peterson (ed.), *The Portable Thomas Jefferson.* NY: Penguin Books.

Kapcia, Antoni. 2000. *Cuba: Island of Dreams.* Berg, Oxford.

____. 2008. *Cuba in Revolution: A History since the Fifties.* London: Reaktion Books.

Kennedy, John F. 1960. "Remarks of Senator John F. Kennedy at Democratic Dinner, Cincinnati, Ohio." JFK Library (October 6). <http://www.jfklibrary. org/Research/Ready-Reference/JFK-Speeches/Remarks-of-Senator-John-F-Kennedy-at-Democratic-Dinner-Cincinnati-Ohio-October-6-1960.aspx>.

Killough, Ashley. 2012. "Obama Takes on Gun Violence in New Orleans speech." *PoliticalTicker* at *CNN Politics* (July 25). <http://politicalticker.blogs.cnn. com/2012/07/25/obama-takes-on-gun-violence-in-new-orleans-speech/>.

King, Martin Luther, Jr. 1991. "Where Do We Go from Here?" Speech delivered in 1967. In James M. Washington (ed.), *The Essential Writings and Speeches of Martin Luther King, Jr.: A Testament of Hope.* NY: Collins.

Kirk, John M. 2012. *José Martí, Mentor of the Cuban Revolution.* Black Point, Nova Scotia: Fernwood Publishing.

Kohl, Benjamin. 2010. "Bolivia Under Morales: A Work in Progress." *Latin American Perspectives* (May), 37:3.

Lacey, Marc. 2008. "Memo from Havana: Low-Key Elections May Affect Castro's Role." *The New York Times* (January 21). <http://www.nytimes.com/2008/01/21/world/americas/21cuba.html>.

Lambie, George. 2010. *The Cuban Revolution in the 21st Century.* NY: Pluto Press.

Lamrani, Salim. 2010. "Conversations with Cuban Blogger Yoani Sánchez." (April 30). <http://www.normangirvan.info/wp-content/uploads/2010/04/lamrani-conversations-with-cuban-blogger-yoani-sanchez.htm>.

Latin American Network Information Center. 1960. "Castro Speaks to Throngs on May Day." (May 2). University of Texas at Austin, Castro Speech Data Base, Speeches, Interviews, Articles, 1959–66. Havana, Radio Centro. <http://www.

lanic.utexas.edu/project/castro/db/1960/19600502.html>.

____. n.d. "About." <http://www.lanic.utexas.edu/la/cb/cuba/castro.html>.

Leal Spengler, Eusebio. 2012. "Un diálogo entre cubano." Inaugural speech, *Palabra Nueva* (April 19). <http://www.palabranueva.net/newpage/index. php?option=com_content&view=article&id=164:ir-hacia-delante-esta-es-la-formula-de-salvacion&catid=56:especial&Itemid=85>.

LeoGrande, William M. 1981. "Participation in Cuban Municipal Government: From Local Power to People's Power." In Donald E. Schulz and Jan S. Adams (eds.), *Political Participation in Communist Systems*. NY: Pergamon Press.

____. 2008. "'The Cuban Nation's Single Party': The Communist Party Faces the Future." In Philip Brenner et al. (eds.), *Reinventing the Revolution: A Contemporary Cuba Reader*. NY: Rowman and Littlefield.

Ley No. 91 de los Consejos Populares. 2000. *Gaceta Oficial de la República* (July 25), Special Edition, No. 6.

Leyva, Anneris Ivette. 2012. "Women Under-Represented in Decision-Making Positions." *Granma International* (March 18), Year 47, No. 12.

LibreRed. 2012. "Embajador de EEUU colaboró en el golpe de Estado de 2009 en Honduras." (February 29). <http://www.librered.net/?p=15817>.

Lindorff, Dave. 2011. "Obama's Attack on Social Security and Medicare." *CounterPunch* (November 1–15), 18:19.

____. 2012. "Did the White House Direct the Police Crackdown on Occupy? *CounterPunch* (May 14). <http://www.counterpunch.org/2012/05/14/did-the-white-house-direct-the-police-crackdown-on-occupy/>.

López, Félix. 2011. "Participo, luego existo." *Granma* (August 24), Year 47, No. 202.

Loyola Vega, Oscar. 2002. "La Revolución de 1868." In Eduardo Torres-Cuevas and Oscar Loyola Vega, *Historia de Cuba, 1492–1898: Formación y liberación de la nación*. Havana: Editorial Pueblo y Educación.

Lutjens, Sheryl. 1992. "Democracy and Socialist Cuba." In Sandor Helebsky and John M. Kirk (eds.), *Cuba in Transition: Crisis and Transformation*. Boulder: Westview Press.

____. 2009. "Introduction: Political Transition(s), Internationalism, and Relations with the Left." *Latin American Perspectives* (May), Issue 166, 36:3.

Machado Rodríguez, Darío. 2012. "Los Lineamientos y la estructura socioclasista en Cuba. Una opinión." *Cubadebate* (June 28). <http://cubadebate.cu/especiales/2012/06/28/los-lineamientos-y-la-estructura-socioclasista-en-cuba-una-opinion/>.

Manza, Jeff, and Christopher Uggen. 2006. *Locked Out: Felon Disenfranchisement and American Democracy*. NY: Oxford University Press.

Marrero, Juan. 2006. *Congresos y periodistas cubanos*. Havana: Imprenta Alejo Carpentier.

Marten, Sven. 2011. *The Rise of Evo Morales and the MAS*. London: Zed Books.

Martí, José. 1988. "To the Editor of *La Nación*." March 15, 1885. In Philip S. Foner (ed.), *Political Parties and Elections in the United States*. Havana: José Martí Publishing House.

____. 2007a. "Our Ideas." In Deborah Shnookal and Mirta Muñiz (eds.), *José Martí Reader: Writings on the Americas*. NY: Ocean Press.

____. 2007b. "To Manuel Mercado." In Deborah Shnookal and Mirta Muñiz (eds.), *José Martí Reader: Writings on the Americas*. NY: Ocean Press.

___. 2007c. "With All, for the Good of All." In Deborah Shnookal and Mirta Muñiz (eds.), *José Martí Reader: Writings on the Americas*. NY: Ocean Press.

___. n.d. "Bases del Partido Revolucionario Cubano." In *El Partido Revolucionario Cubano*. Havana: Editorial de Ciencias Sociales.

Martínez, Alexander. 2010. "Ecuador in Turmoil Amid Uprising by Police, Troops." *Google* (September 30). <http://www.google.com/hostednews/afp/article/ALeqM5jrnvjhcqgCKRGkE7xwszbiQS-mqA>.

Martínez Hernández, Leticia, and Yaima Puig Meneses. 2011a. "Council of Ministers Meeting." *Granma International* (May 22), Year 46, No. 21, Havana.

___. 2011b. "Expanded Council of Ministers Meeting." *Granma International* (March 6), Year 46, No. 10, Havana.

Mather, Steven. 2007. "Venezuelan Government Announces $5 Billion for Communal Councils in 2007." *Venezuelanalysis.com* (January 10). <http://venezuelanalysis.com/news/2167>.

Mayoral, Maria Julia. 2008. "Votar por todos." *Granma* (January 15).

McAuliff, John. 2011. "Counterproductive Contradictions Undermine U.S. Policy on Cuba." *Huffington Post* (March 24). <http://www.huffingtonpost.com/john-mcauliff/contradictions-undermine-_b_839243.html>.

McCallum, Jack Edward. 2006. *Leonard Wood: Rough Rider, Surgeon, Architect of American Imperialism*. NY: New York University Press.

McDonald, Michael P. 2011a. "2008 General Election Turnout Rates." Last updated December 28, 2011. Elections George Mason University. <http://elections.gmu.edu/Turnout_2008G.html> (accessed January 16, 2012).

___. 2011b. "2010 General Election Turnout Rates." Last updated December 28, 2011. Elections George Mason University. <http://elections.gmu.edu/Turnout_2010G.html> (accessed January 16, 2012).

___. 2012a. "Voter Turnout." Elections George Mason University. <http://elections.gmu.edu/voter_turnout.htm> (accessed November 10, 2012).

___. 2012b. "2012 General Election Turnout Rates." Elections George Mason University. <http://elections.gmu.edu/Turnout_2012G.html> (accessed December 31, 2012).

Mesa, Enrique. 1974. *Granma* (August 23).

Morales, Gisselle. 2012. "Prensa espirituana en el vórtice del debate." *CubaPeriodistas* (February 5). <http://www.cubaperiodistas.cu/noticias/febrero12/05/01.htm>.

Morales, Waltraud Q. 2012. "Social Movements and Revolutionary Change in Bolivia." In Gary Prevost, Carlos Oliva Campos and Harry E. Vanden (eds.), *Socialist Movements and Leftist Governments in Latin America: Confrontation or Co-Optation?* London: Zed Books.

New York Journal. 1898. "Destruction of the War Ship *Maine* Was the Work of an Enemy." (February 17), 5:572.

Nieves Ayús, Concepción, and Jorge Luis Santana Pérez. 2012. "Cuba in the XXI Century: Towards a New Model of Socialist Development." Paper presented at the Society for Socialist Studies, Congress of the Humanities and Social Sciences (May 30), Wilfrid Laurier University, Waterloo, Ontario.

Nikandrov, Nil. 2010. "Ecuador Coup Attempt Engineered by the CIA." Strategic Culture Foundation (October 10). <http://www.strategic-culture.org/

news/2010/10/03/ecuador-coup-attempt-engineered-by-the-cia.html>.

Nuland, Victoria. 2012. "U.S. Support for Egypt." U.S. Department of State (March 23). U.S. Department of State <http://www.state.gov/r/pa/prs/ps/2012/03/186709.htm>.

Obama, Barack. 2004a. *Dreams from My Father: A Story of Race and Inheritance*. NY: Random House, Inc.

___. 2004b. "Keynote Address, Democratic National Convention." *The Washington Post* (July 27). <http://www.washingtonpost.com/wp-dyn/articles/A19751-2004Jul27.html>.

___. 2008. *The Audacity of Hope: Thoughts on Reclaiming the American Dream*. NY: Vintage.

___. 2009. "Remarks by President Obama at Strasbourg Town Hall." White House (April 3). <http://www.whitehouse.gov/the_press_office/Remarks-by-President-Obama-at-Strasbourg-Town-Hall/>.

___. 2011. "Remarks by the President on the American Jobs Act." White House (November 22). <http://www.whitehouse.gov/the-press-office/2011/11/22/remarks-president-american-jobs-act>.

___. 2012a. "Remarks by the President on Election Night." White House (November 7). <http://www.whitehouse.gov/the-press-office/2012/11/07/remarks-president-election-night>.

___. 2012b. "Statement by the President on Civilian Deaths in Afghanistan." White House (March 11). <http://www.whitehouse.gov/the-press-office/2012/03/11/statement-president-civilian-deaths-afghanistan>.

OccupyArrests. n.d. "A Running Total of the Number of Occupy Protesters Arrested Around the U.S. Since Occupy Wall Street Began on Sep. 17, 2011." <http://www.occupyarrests.moonfruit.com>.

Occupy Charlotte. 2012. "DNC National Call to Action." (August 10). <http://occupyclt.net/2012/08/10/dnc-national-call-action/>.

Occupy Wall Street. 2012. "Chicago: #OccupyObama." (September 4). <http://occupywallst.org/article/chicago-occupyobama/>.

Oficina Nacional de Estadísticas. 2009. "Población residente por sexos, edades y relación de masculinidad." (December 31). <http://www.one.cu/aec2009/esp/03_tabla_cuadro.htm>.

___. n.d.(a). "22.1 — Elecciones de delegados a las Asambleas Municipales del Poder Popular por provincias." <http://www.one.cu/aec2009/esp/22_tabla_cuadro.htm>.

___. n.d.(b). "Censo de población y viviendas 2002." <http://www.cubagob.cu/otras_info/censo/tablas_html/ii_3.htm>.

Oviedo Obarrio, Fernando. 2010. "Evo Morales and the Altipalno: Notes for an Electoral Geography of the Movimiento al Socialismo, 2000–2008." *Latin American Perspectives* (May), Issue 172, 37:3.

Padgett, Tim, and Dolly Mascarenas. 2008. "After Fidel: A Guide to the Players." *Time* (February 22). <http://www.time.com/time/world/article/0,8599,1715536,00.html>.

Parada, Maria Elena. 2010. "I Will Work Together with the People to Promote Development, Unity and Integration in Bolivia." *Correo del Orinoco* (January 29), Year 0, No. 00.

Parenti, Michael. 2008. *Democracy for the Few*. Thomson Wadsworth.

Partido Comunista de Cuba. 2012. *"Primera Conferencia Nacional, Partido Comunista de Cuba: Objetivos de Trabajo del PCC Aprobados por la Primera Conferencia Nacional.* (January 29). Havana: Editora Política.

___. n.d.(a). *"Primera Conferencia Nacional, Partido Comunista de Cuba: Proyecto Documento Base."* Havana: Editora Política.

___. n.d.(b). Unión de Jóvenes Comunistas. <http://www.pcc.cu/opm_ujc.php> (accessed February 1, 2012).

Pável Vidal, Alejandro. 2012. "Monetary and Exchange Rate Reform in Cuba: Lessons from Vietnam." *V.R.F. Series* (February), 473.

Pearson, Tamara. 2011. "New Mission Sons and Daughters of Venezuela to Provide Savings and Benefits to Children." *Venezuelanalysis.com* (December 13). <http://www.venezuelanalysis.com/news/6690>.

Penúltimos Días. 2012. "Acuse de recibo: Llamamiento urgente por una Cuba mejor y posible." (August 1). <http://www.penultimosdias.com/2012/08/01/acuse-de-recibo-llamamiento-urgente-por-una-cuba-mejor-y-posible/>.

Peraza Chapeau, José. 2000. "El derecho constitucional y La Constitución." In Lissette Pérez Hernández and Martha Prieto Valdés (eds.), *Temas de derecho constitucional cubano.* Havana: Editorial Félix Varela.

Pérez, Louis A., Jr. 1991. "Cuba and the United States: Origins and Antecedents of Relations, 1760s–1860s." *Cuban Studies*, 21.

___. 1995. *Cuba: Between Reform and Revolution.* NY: Oxford University Press.

Pérez Alonso, Ariel. 2008. "Biological Warfare Against Cuba." Havana: Capitán San Luis Publishing House.

Pérez Cabrera, Freddy. 2011. "¿Hasta cuándo esta indisciplina?" *Granma* (January 27), Year 15, No. 27.

Pérez Guzmán, Francisco. 1996a. "La Revolución del 95: De los alzamientos a la Campaña de Invasión." In María del Carmen Barcia, Gloria García and Eduardo Torres-Cuevas (eds.), *Historia de Cuba: Las luchas por la independencia nacional y las transformaciones estructurales, 1868–1898.* Havana: Editora Política.

___. 1996b. "La Revolución del 95: Desde la conclusión de la Campaña de Invasión hasta el fin de la dominación española." In María del Carmen Barcia, Gloria García and Eduardo Torres-Cuevas (eds.), *Historia de Cuba: Las luchas por la independencia nacional y las transformaciones estructurales, 1868–1898.* Havana: Editora Política.

Pérez Hernández, Lissette, and Martha Prieto Valdés. 2000a. "Ejercer gobierno: Una capacidad potencial de las Asambleas Municipales del Poder Popular." In Lissette Pérez Hernández and Martha Prieto Valdés (eds.), *Temas de derecho constitucional cubano.* Havana: Editorial Félix Varela.

___. 2000b. "Funcionamiento de los órganos locales del Poder Popular." In Lissette Pérez Hernández and Martha Prieto Valdés (eds.), *Temas de derecho constitucional cubano.* Havana: Editorial Félix Varela.

Pérez-Stable, Marifeli. 1993. *The Cuban Revolution: Origins, Course and Legacy.* NY: Oxford University Press.

Pernia, Jessica, and Tamara Pearson. 2012. "The Great Patriotic Pole (GPP): How Thousands of Movements Are Constructing Their Revolutionary Organisation." *Venezuelanalysis.com* (Interview on February 28). <http://www.venezuelanalysis.com/analysis/6837>.

Phillips, Kevin. 2003. *Wealth and Democracy: A Political History of the American Rich*. NY: Broadway Books.

Pilgrim, David. 2000. "What Was Jim Crow?" Ferris State University (September). <http://ferris.edu/jimcrow/what.htm>.

Piñeiro Harnecker, Camila. 2005. "The New Cooperative Movement in Venezuela's Bolivarian Process." *Venezuelanalysis.com* (December 17). <http://www.venezuelanalysis.com/analysis/1531>.

Portuondo Zúñiga, Olga. 1965. *Historia de Cuba, 1492–1898*. Havana: Editorial Nacional de Cuba.

Powell, Colin L. 2004. "Report to the President." Commission for Assistance to a Free Cuba (May). <http://pdf.usaid.gov/pdf_docs/PCAAB192.pdf>.

Powers, Rod. 2011. "Joining the Military as a Non-U.S. Citizen." *US Military* at *About.com*. (February 11). <http://www.usmilitary.about.com/od/joiningthemilitary/a/noncitizenjoin.htm>.

Presno, Xelcis. 2012. "Indigenous People Integrate Consultation Commissions in Bolivia." *Radio Havana Cuba*. (April 16). <http://www.radiohc.cu/ing/news/world/6499-indigenous-people-integrate-consultation-commissions-in-bolivia.html>.

Prieto Valdés, Martha. 2000. "Reflexiones en torno al carácter normativo de la Constitución." In Lissette Pérez Hernández and Martha Prieto Valdés (eds.), *Temas de derecho constitucional cubano*. Havana: Editorial Félix Varela.

Puig Meneses, Yaima, and Marina Menéndez Quintero. 2012. "Debates de las cuatro comisiones de la Primera Conferencia Nacional." *Granma* (January 30), Year 48, No. 24.

Quijano, Aníbal. 2000. "Coloniality of Power and Eurocentrism in Latin America." *International Sociology* (June), 15:2.

——. 2010a. "La crisis del horizonte de sentido colonial/modern/eurocentrado." *ReVista Casa de las Américas*, Nos. 259–260 (April–September).

——. 2010b. "Questioning 'Race.'" *Socialism and Democracy Online*. <http://www.sdonline.org/43/questioning-"race"/>.

Quijano, Aníbal, and Immanuel Wallerstein. n.d. "Americanity as a Concept, or the Americas in the Modern World-System." *Socialism and Democracy Online*. <http://www.jhfc.duke.edu/icuss/pdfs/QuijanoWallerstein.pdf>.

Raby, D.L. 2006. *Democracy and Revolution: Latin America and Socialism Today*. London: Pluto Press and Toronto: Between the Lines.

Radio Rebelde. n.d. "About Us." <http://www.radiorebelde.cu/english/about-us/>.

Ramonet, Ignacio. 2011. "'Pedí una pistola para defenderme.'" *Le Monde diplomatique* (January), 183.

Ravsberg, Fernando. 2009. "Las leyes que no se votaron." BBC (January 1). <http://www.bbc.co.uk/blogs/mundo/cartas_desde_cuba/2009/01/las_leyes_que_no_se_votaron.html>.

——. 2012. "Cuba's Parliament: Unanimity vs. Institutionalism." *Havana Times* (July 5). <http://www.havanatimes.org/?p=73682>.

Reardon, Juan. 2010. "Venezuela's Chávez Supported in Call for Relaunch of Patriotic Pole." *Venezuelanalysis.com* (October 13). <http://www.venezuelanalysis.com/news/5710>.

Reed, Gail. 1992. *Island in the Storm: The Cuban Communist Party's Fourth Congress*.

Melbourne: Ocean Press.

Reglamento: Asambleas Municipales del Poder Popular. 1998. República de Cuba (April), Asamblea Nacional del Poder Popular, September 1995, Havana.

Rius, Hugo. 2010. "Escurridizo tiempo." (November 23). <http://www.juventudrebelde.cu/file/pdf/impreso/2010/11/23/iopinion.pdf>.

Robertson, Ewan. 2012. "Venezuela's Great Patriotic Pole Continues to Organise, Forms Culture Council." *Venezuelanalysis.com* (May 28). <http://www.venezuelanalysis.com/news/7015>.

Robinson, Circles. 2011. "*Havana Times* Editor Quizzed on Cuba." *CirclesOnline* (December 29). <http://www.circlesonline.blogspot.ca/>.

___. 2012. "Cuba Gov. Re-Blasts Yoani Sánchez." *Havana Times* (February 26). <http://www.havanatimes.org/?p=63013>.

Roca, Blas. 1985. "Presentación." In Fernando Álvarez Tabío, *Comentarios a la Constitución socialista*. Havana: Editorial de Ciencias Sociales.

Roca, José Luis. 2008. "Regionalism Revisited." In John Crabtree and Laurence Whitehead (eds.), *Bolivia Past and Present: Unresolved Tensions*. Pittsburgh: University of Pittsburgh Press.

Rodríguez Cruz, Francisco. 2012. "Trabajo no estatal impactará positivamente en Presupuesto de 2011. Trabajadores (July 28). <http://www.trabajadores.cu/news/2011/07/28/trabajo-no-estatal-impactara-positivamente-en-presupuesto-de-2011>.

Rodríguez Gavilán, Agnerys. 2010. "Franqueza, racionalidad y transparencia en reajuste laboral." *Juventud Rebelde* (September 18). <http://www.juventudrebelde.cu/cuba/2010-09-18/franqueza-racionalidad-y-transparencia-en-reajuste-laboral/>.

___. 2012. "Aprender a gobernar con criterio económico." *Juventud Rebelde* (February), Year 47, No. 109.

Roman, Peter. 1995. "Workers' Parliaments in Cuba." *Latin American Perspectives* (Fall), Issue 87, 22:4, 43–58.

___. 2003. *People's Power: Cuba's Experience with Representative Government.* Lanham, MD: Rowman and Littlefield Publishers.

___. 2005. "The Lawmaking Process in Cuba: Debating the Bill on Agricultural Cooperatives." *Socialism and Democracy Online* (July). <http://www.sdonline.org/38/the-lawmaking-process-in-cuba-debating-the-bill-on-agricultural-cooperatives/>.

Ronquillo Bello, Ricardo. 2011. "Mágicos hilos del poder." *Juventud Rebelde* (June 18). <http://www.juventudrebelde.cu/opinion/2011-06-18/magicos-hilos-del-poder/>.

Roosevelt, Franklin D. 1940. "The Great Arsenal of Democracy." *American Rhetoric* (December 29). <http://www.americanrhetoric.com/speeches/PDFFiles/FDR%20-%20Arsenal%20of%20Democracy.pdf>.

Rosendo González, Norland. 2012. "Asamblea de la UPEC en Villa Clara: A trabajar por mensajes atractivos, frescos y que dialoguen." *CubaPeriodistas* (February 6). <http://www.cubaperiodistas.cu/noticias/febrero12/06/01.htm>.

Rousseau, Stéphanie. 2011. "Indigenous and Feminist Movements at the Constituent Assembly in Bolivia: Locating the Representation of Indigenous Women." *Latin American Research Review,* 46:2.

Saney, Isaac. 2004. *Cuba: A Revolution in Motion*. Fernwood Publishing and Zed Books.

Santana, José Alejandro. 2012. "Ministra Isis Ochoa resalta logros del Poder Popular." Gobierno Bolivariano de Venezuela (February 29). <http://www.mpcomunas. gob.ve/noticias_detalle.php?id=7608>.

Serafimov, Alex. 2012. "Social Change in Venezuela." *Venezuelanalysis.com* (March 2). <http://www.venezuelanalysis.com/analysis/6849>.

Serrano, Pascual. 2009. "Guerra fría cultural contra Cuba: Gobierno español, estadounidense y fundaciones privadas se unen para financiar el proyecto anticastrista Encuentro." (September 9). <http://www.pascualserrano.net/ noticias/guerra-fria-cultural-contra-cuba/>.

Sexto, Luis. 2009. "Libras de más o de menos." *Juventud Rebelde* (March 20). <http:// www.juventudrebelde.cu/opinion/2009-03-20/libras-de-mas-o-de-menos/>.

___. 2010a. "Al compromiso llaman, Sancho." *Juventud Rebelde* (September 30). <http://www.juventudrebelde.cu/columnas/coloquiando/2010-09-30/al-compromiso-llaman-sancho/>.

___. 2010b. "Arenas movedizas." *Juventud Rebelde* (July 15). <http://www. juventudrebelde.cu/columnas/coloquiando/2010-07-15/arenas-movedizas/>.

___. 2010c. "La geometría democrática." *Juventud Rebelde* (August 19). <http:// www.juventudrebelde.cu/columnas/coloquiando/2010-08-19/la-geometria-democratica/>.

___. 2010d. "Por uno y por todos." *Juventud Rebelde* (December 30). <http://www. juventudrebelde.cu/columnas/coloquiando/2010-12-30/por-uno-y-por-todos/>.

Sharpe, Errol. 2011. "Cloistering Criticisms or Breaking Bonds?" In Henry Veltmeyer (ed.), *21st Century Socialism: Reinventing the Project*. Black Point, Nova Scotia: Fernwood Publishing.

Stein, Daniel. 2011. "Barack Obama's *Dreams from My Father* and African American Literature." *European Journal of American Studies*, 1.

Stephen, Lynn. 2008. "Reconceptualizing Latin America." In Deborah Poole (ed.), *A Companion to Latin American Anthropology*. Malden, MA: Blackwell Publishing.

Street, Paul. 2012. "Killer-Cops and the War on Black America." *Black Agenda Report* (August 15). <http://blackagendareport.com/content/killer-cops-and-war-black-america>.

Tamayo, Juan O. 2012. "Asamblea Nacional parece obviar la reforma migratoria." (July 21). <http://www.elnuevoherald.com/2012/07/21/1255977/asamblea-nacional-parece-obviar.html>.

TeleSUR. 2012. "Inicia construcción de carretera del Tipnis con el apoyo de 45 comunidades." (October 6). < http://www.telesurtv.net/articulos/2012/10/06/con-la-aprobacion-de-45-comunidades-se-inicia-construccion-del-primer-tramo-de-la-carretera-del-tipnis-6033.html>.

Temas. 2002. (September). <www.temas.cult.cu/temas.php>.

Terra Noticias. 2011. "Hillary Clinton vuelve a pedir a Cuba que ponga en libertad a Alan Gross." (March 10). <http://www.noticias.terra.es/2011/mundo/0310/actualidad/hillary-clinton-vuelve-a-pedir-a-cuba-que-ponga-en-libertad-a-alan-gross.aspx>.

Torrado, Fabio Raimundo. 1998. "A 40 años de las leyes de la Sierra Maestra." *Granma* (May 15), 34:97.

Torres-Cuevas, Eduardo. 2001. "La ruptura de la sociedad criolla: La sociedad esclavista." In Eduardo Torres-Cuevas and Oscar Loyola Vega, *Historia de Cuba, 1492–1898: Formación y liberación de la nación.* Havana: Editorial Pueblo y Educación.

Torres-Cuevas, Eduardo, and Oscar Loyola Vega. 2002. *Historia de Cuba, 1492–1898: Formación y liberación de la nación.* Havana: Editorial Pueblo y Educación.

Torres-Cuevas, Eduardo, et al. 1996. "La Revolución del 68: Fundamentos e inicios." In María del Carmen Barcia, Gloria García and Eduardo Torres-Cuevas (eds.), *Historia de Cuba: Las luchas por la independencia nacional y las transformaciones estructurales, 1868–1898.* Havana: Editora Política.

Trabajadores. 2010. "Pronunciamiento de la Central de Trabajadores de Cuba." (September 13), XL:37.

Tribunal Supremo Electoral. n.d. <http://www.cne.org.bo>.

Urie, Rob. 2012. "Paul Krugman Learns the Facts on Health Insurance." *CounterPunch* (January 1–15), 19:1.

Van Auken, Bill. 2010. "Cuba's Raúl Castro unveils plan for massive job cuts." *World Socialist Web Site* (August 5). <http://www.wsws.org/articles/2010/aug2010/cuba-a05.shtml>.

Vega Vega, Juan. 1997. *Cuba, su historia constitucional: Comentarios a la Constitución cubana reformada en 1992.* Madrid: Ediciones Endymion.

Veltmeyer, Henry, ed. 2011. *21st Century Socialism: Reinventing the Project.* Black Point, Nova Scotia: Fernwood Publishing.

VI Congreso del Partido Comunista de Cuba. 2010. "Proyecto de lineamientos de la política económica y social." (November 1), Havana.

____. 2011a. "Información sobre el resultado del debate de los lineamientos de la política económica y social del Partido y la Revolución." (May), Havana.

____. 2011b. "Lineamientos de la Política Económica y Social del Partido y la Revolución." (April 18), Havana.

Voice of America News. 2012. "Clinton Clears $1.3 Billion in Aid to Egypt." (March 22). <http://www.voanews.com/content/clinton-to-approve-military-aid-to-egypt-143947716/179244.html>.

Wallerstein, Immanuel. 1997. "Eurocentrism and Its Avatars: The Dilemmas of Social Science." Binghamton University. <http://www.binghamton.edu/fbc/archive/iweuroc.htm>.

____. 2001. *The Limits of Nineteenth-Century Paradigms: Unthinking Social Science.* Philadelphia: Temple University Press.

____. 2006. *European Universalism: The Rhetoric of Power.* NY: The New Press.

Weatherford, Jack. 1988. *Indian Givers: How the Indians of the Americas Transformed the World.* NY: Ballantine Books.

White House. 2009a. "Briefing by Press Secretary Robert Gibbs and Dan Restrepo, Special Assistant to the President and Senior Director for Western Hemisphere Affairs (including Spanish text)." (April 13). <http://www.whitehouse.gov/the-press-office/briefing-press-secretary-robert-gibbs-and-dan-restrepo-special-assistant-president->.

____. 2009b. "Fact Sheet — Reaching Out to the Cuban People." (April 13). <http://www.whitehouse.gov/the-press-office/fact-sheet-reaching-out-cuban-people>.

____. 2012. "Statement by the Press Secretary on Egypt." (June 24). <http://www.

whitehouse.gov/the-press-office/2012/06/24/statement-press-secretary-egypt>.

Whiten, John. 2008. "Alt-Weeklies Resoundingly Say: Vote Obama." (October 31). <http://www.altweeklies.com/aan/alt-weeklies-resoundingly-say-vote-obama/Article?oid=669453>.

Whitney, Mike. 2011. "Obama and the Economy." *CounterPunch* (September 1–15), 18:15.

Wikipedia. n.d. Haroldo Dilla Alfonso. <http://es.wikipedia.org/wiki/Haroldo_Dilla_Alfonso> (accessed August 18, 2012).

Wilpert, Gregory. 2007. *Changing Venezuela by Taking Power: The History and Policies of the Chávez Government.* New York: Verso.

___. 2010. "A New Opportunity for Venezuela's Socialists." *Venezuelanalysis.com* (October 1). <http://www.venezuelanalysis.com/print/5683>.

___. 2011. "An Assessment of Venezuela's Bolivarian Revolution at Twelve Years." *Venezuelanalysis.com* (February 2). <http://www.venezuelanalysis.com/analysis/5971>.

Winthrop, John. 1630. "City Upon a Hill." Mtholyoke. <http://www.mtholyoke.edu/acad/intrel/winthrop.htm>.

Wolin, Sheldon S. 2010. *Democracy Inc.* Princeton: Princeton University Press.

Zacharia, Janine. 2007. "Brzezinski Embraces Obama Over Clinton for President." Bloomberg (August 24). <http://www.bloomberg.com/apps/news?pid=newsarchive&sid=aOqL38D5EntY&refer=home>.

Zinn, Howard. 2002. *You Can't Be Neutral on a Moving Train: A Personal History of Our Times.* Boston: Beacon Press.

___. 2005. *A People's History of the United States.* NY: Harper Perennial.

Personal Interviews with the Author

Azicri, Max. 2009. (May 9). Queen's University, Kingston, Ontario.
Professor, Political Science, Edinboro University, Pennsylvania
Balseiro Gutiérrez, Alina, and Tomás Amarón Díaz. 2008. (January 31). Havana.
Members, Comisión Electoral Nacional (CEN)
Cárdenas García, Tomás Victoriano. 2007. (September 15). Havana.
Deputy, ANPP; president, ANPP Permanent Working Commission on the Organs of Local People's Power
____. 2008a. (July 17). Havana.
____. 2008b. (December 19). Havana.
Castanedo Smith, Luis Manuel. 2008. (December 15). Havana.
Deputy, ANPP; vice-president, ANPP Permanent Working Commission on Economic Affairs; member, National Secretariat, Central de Trabajadores de Cuba (CTC)
Castell Cobol, Bernardo, et al. 2008. (December 18). Havana.
Member, Local Central de Trabajadores de Cuba (CTC); Raquel Pérez primary school; and other CTC members
Castro Espín, Mariela. 2009. (May 9). Queen's University, Kingston, Ontario.
Director, Centro Nacional de Educación Sexual (CENESEX), Havana
Chirino Gamez, Luis Alberto. 2008. (July 1). Havana.
Journalist
Comisión de Candidaturas Nacional. 2008. (January 18). Havana.
Members, Comisión de Candidaturas Nacional (CCN)
Comisión Electoral Provincial. 2008. (September 19). Havana.
Members, Comisión Electoral Provincial (CEP), former province of Ciudad de La Habana
Cristóbal, Armando. 2009. (January 11). Havana.
Professor and member, Political Science Group, University of Havana; member, Sociedad Cubana de Investigaciones Filosóficas
Duharte Díaz, Emilio. 2009. (May 1). Havana.
Professor, Philosophy and Political Theory, University of Havana
Fernández Ríos, Olga. 2008. (January 22). Havana.
Researcher, Instituto de Filosofía; Professor, Philosophical Sciences, University of Havana
Fung Riverón, Thalía. 2008. (December 29). Havana.
Professor, Political Science and Philosophy; director, Political Science Group, University of Havana; president, Sociedad Cubana de Investigaciones Filosóficas
____. 2009. (January 9). Havana.
García Brigos, Jesús P. 2007. (September 1). Havana.
Researcher, Political Philosophy, Instituto de Filosofía; supervisor, Instituto de Filosofía PhD Program
____. 2009a. (January 10). Havana.
____. 2009b. (January 11). Havana.
Gómez, Carmen. 2008. (January 16). Havana.
Professor, History, University of Havana
Gómez Barranco, Jorge Jesús. 2008a. (July 17). Havana.
Deputy, ANPP; vice-president, ANPP Permanent Working Commission on Education, Culture, Science and Technology

___. 2008b. (December 15). Havana.

Gómez Barranco, Jorge Jesús, and Maria Josefa Ruíz Mederos. 2008. (February 1). Havana.

Maria Josefa Ruíz Mederos: former deputy, ANPP; former member, ANPP Permanent Working Commission on Education, Culture, Science and Technology

González Hernández, Eduardo. 2008. (February 2). Havana.

Delegate, Plaza de la Revolución Municipal Assembly; president, Consejo Popular Vedado (CPV)

___. 2009. (January 11). Havana.

Hernández, Rafael. 2009. (May 8). Queen's University, Kingston, Ontario.

Director, Temas magazine, Havana

Leiva Romero, Xiomara. 2008. (December 15). Havana.

Delegate, Plaza de la Revolución Municipal Assembly

Lezcano, Jorge. 2007. (September 18). Havana.

Adviser to ANPP president Ricardo Alarcón de Quesada

___. 2008a. (July 17). Havana.

___. 2008b. (December 15). Havana.

___. 2009. (July 7). Havana. By email.

Liranza García, Carlos. 2008a. (July 17). Havana.

Municipal delegate; deputy, ANPP; president, ANPP Permanent Working Commission on Industry and Construction

___. 2008b. (December 16). Havana.

Lor Mogollon, Henrys. 2009. (October 19). Montreal.

Deputy, Yaracuy State, Venezuela

Martínez Canals, Elena. 2009. (January 5). Havana.

President, CDR No. 9, Zone 12, Municipality of Plaza de la Revolución

Martínez López, Leonardo Eugenio. 2008a. (January 10). Havana.

Deputy, ANPP; president, ANPP Permanent Working Commission on Food and Agriculture

___. 2008b. (January 17). Havana.

___. 2008c. (July 15). Havana.

___. 2008d. (December 26). Havana.

Martínez Martínez, Osvaldo. 2008. (July 16). Havana.

Deputy, ANPP; president, ANPP Permanent Working Commission on Economic Affairs; director, World Economy Research Center

Miranda, Olivia. 2008. (January 22). Havana.

Researcher, Instituto de Filosofía; professor, Philosophical Science, University of Havana

Municipal Electoral Commission. 2007. (September 18). Plaza de la Revolución, Havana.

Members, Municipal Electoral Commission

Nieves Ayús, Concepción. 2008. (January 24). Havana.

Director, Instituto de Filosofía

Pérez Santana, Amarilys. 2008. (December 16). Havana.

President, Comisión de Candidaturas Nacional (CCN), 2007–08; member, National Secretariat, Central de Trabajadores de Cuba (CTC)

Pérez Santana, Amarilys, Albert Marchante Fuentes and Héctor Fajardo Marin. 2008. (January 30). Havana.

Members, Comisión de Candidaturas Nacional (CCN), 2007–08

Quirot Moret, Ana Fidelia. 2008. (February 1). Havana.
    Deputy, ANPP; member, ANPP Permanent Working Commission on Health and Sport
Reus González, María Ester. 2008. (January 28). Havana.
    Minister of Justice; president, Comisión Electoral Nacional (CEN) (2007–08)
Rojas Hernández, Elsa. 2008. (July 16). Havana.
    Deputy, ANPP; president, ANPP Permanent Working Commission for the Focus on Youth, Children and the Equality of Women's Rights; member, National Secretariat, Federación de Mujeres Cubanas (FMC)
___. 2009a. (January 6). Havana. By email.
___. 2009b. (July 21). Havana. By email.
Toledo Santander, José Luis. 2008. (January 23). Havana.
    Deputy, ANPP; president, ANPP Permanent Working Commission on Constitutional and Legal Affairs; dean, University of Havana Law Faculty
Torrado, Fabio Raimundo. 2008. (January 9). Havana.
    Doctor of Law; specialist in Constitutional and Electoral History
Valdés Mesa, Salvador. 2009. (January 9). Havana.
    Deputy, ANPP; secretary general, Central de Trabajadores de Cuba (CTC); member, Council of State

Index